the canadian
genealogical hand

A Comprehensive Guide to Finding Your Ancestors in

BY ERIC JONASSON

SECOND EDITION
Revised and Enlarged

wheatfield press
winnipeg, manitoba 1978

For Elizabeth

My partner in all things

All correspondence with the author should be
addressed in care of the publisher.

WHEATFIELD PRESS
Box 205, St. James Postal Station
Winnipeg, Manitoba, Canada R3J 3R4
(catalogue available upon request)

PRINTING HISTORY

First edition published 1976

Second edition:
1st printing   May 1978
2nd printing December 1978

ISBN 0 920374 02 6

Map artwork and illustration enhancement by
carto graphics, Winnipeg, Manitoba

Printed in Canada by
Industrial Art and Printing
Winnipeg, Manitoba, Canada

TABLE OF CONTENTS

PREFACE

In 1976, after over two years of research and preparation, the first edition of THE CANADIAN GENEALOGICAL HANKBOOK was published. As it was the first publication which dealt comprehensively with the elements of Canadian genealogy, I was hopeful that it would be well received by researchers in this country. My enthusiasm was also clouded by some doubts. The question "If this book is so badly needed, why hasn't someone else written it before now?" tended to haunt me. However, any misgivings I may have had quickly disappeared with the ready acceptance of my work as a valuable tool in Canadian research. At that time, I became determined to improve on the first edition, and continued on my quest for more Canadian genealogical sources. This new edition combines my recent findings and the information contained in the first work.

Due to Canada's close proximity to the United States, researchers in this country have long relied on publications on American genealogy for guidance in searching Canadian records. Although there are many similarities between the records of the two countries, Canada has also produced a large number of sources which are unknown in the United States and on which little or no information has been written. My primary aim in compiling this work was to provide a comprehensive discussion on, and guide to, the records of Canada, and thereby fill the gaps which have plagued researchers in this country. I sincerely believe that this second edition achieves this aim.

Inexpensive general publications which discuss research essentials and proceedures for beginners are fairly abundant and although they are oriented to American readers, the advice they contain applies equally to the Canadian researcher. By concentrating my efforts on Canadian records and sources only, rather than on the "how to" of conducting genealogical research, I feel that I have increased the value of my work as a "Canadian" guide. Not wishing to leave the beginner wondering how to begin and how to continue their research, however, I have included a short chapter on research essentials which I believe is sufficient for making a start.

A reference work of this nature is valuable only as long as it is fairly up to date. With Archives constantly receiving new genealogical material and the addresses of organizations and societies continuously changing, it is impossible for all the information in this book to be perpetually correct. While it would be desirable to revise this publication every couple of years, the work involved would be enormous and the cost to the publisher prohibitive. As well, it is unfair to expect researchers to purchase a new edition every few years in order to keep up to date. As a result, I have decided to compile short supplements to this edition from time to time, which will update and revise information in this volume as well as documenting new collections and sources which become available. A third edition will be issued once there is sufficient supplementary information to warrent its publication.

I sincerely hope that this volume will prove beneficial to all who use it and will become an often-used reference book in their personal libraries.

Winnipeg, Manitoba   E.L.J.
March 1978

ACKNOWLEDGEMENTS

All reference works have many contributors in addition to their authors. This work is no exception. In the course of compiling both the first and second editions of the HANDBOOK, I have been assisted by many people from a wide range of organizations, both government and private. Without their help, this work would only be a skeleton of what it is now. For their assistance, I am truly thankful. Although it is impossible for me to list everyone who has contributed in some way to this guide, there are a number of people who were particularly generous with their time and advice.

At the Public Archives of Canada, Ottawa: Thomas A. Hillman, Patricia Kennedy, Betty Kidd, Edward W. Laine, and Auguste Vachon.

At the various provincial archives: A. D. Ridge, E. J. Holmgren, and Mrs. E. Kreisel (Alberta); Leonard C. DeLozier (British Columbia); John Bovey, Gilbert-Louis Comeault, and Barry Hyman (Manitoba); Mrs. H.H. Sewell (New Brunswick); F. Burnham Gill (Newfoundland); C. Bruce Fergusson (Nova Scotia); J. Mezaks, and David Russell (Ontario); N.J. De Jong and H.T. Holman (P.E.I.); Roland J. Auger and Raymond Gingras (Quebec); I. Wilson, D.H. Bocking, and Edwin Morgan (Saskatchewan); and their staffs.

As well, I would like to thank my father, Victor Jonasson, and friend, Peter Gould, for their advice and assistance. Also, thanks to Dexter Hawn, Ottawa, who chose many of the illustrations in this book from the collections at the Public Archives of Canada.

I would like to extend a special thank you to everyone who purchased a copy of the first edition of the HANDBOOK. Without their support, this second edition would not be possible.

Finally, I wish to thank my wife, Elizabeth, who has had to contend with me through two writings of this work. Without her encouragement, I may well have never finished.

1
UNDERSTANDING GENEALOGICAL RESEARCH

1:1 INTRODUCTION TO GENEALOGICAL RESEARCH

Genealogy is a branch of history which deals with the scientific determination of family relationships, not by copying from the work of another, but from personal research into original documents and sources. The genealogist discovers each individual's relationship to other family members, recording events in his life and relating all this to the times and society in which he lived. Above all, genealogists are concerned with real people and we must never lose sight of this fact.

Successful genealogical research is dependant on your ability to prove beyond any reasonable doubt who your ancestors were. Proof of descent may take many forms. For yourself, your parents and your grandparents it may take the form of an official birth certificate. For your great-grandparents and other earlier ancestors it may be a church baptismal record, or some other record. In all cases, it must contain a reference to the names of the parents of an ancestor and to have been recorded as close to the birth date as possible, preferably by a witness to the actual birth. It must also be an "official record" and not one which is found printed in a book or related to you by an aunt, uncle or other relative in a letter or a personal interview. Other official records must be used to tie together the life of an ancestor to that of his/her children. Marriage records must be firmly tied to the birth records so that there is no mistake of identity. Often with common names such as John Smith, you may find that two were born or married on the same day and that you must be able to accurately prove which of the two is your ancestor. Children of an ancestor can often be proven through the use of birth records or census listings.

At first, finding one's own genealogy and researching it accurately and completely may seem difficult and complicated, especially if one has never done anything like it before. The beginner is likely to ask many questions on how to get started and where he must go for the information he needs. Generally, beginners wonder _where_ rather than _how_ to find information or what to do with the information once they have found it. However, it is not the _where_ but the _how and what_ that will bring success in genealogical research.

With experience, you will discover that by knowing how you will also know where to look. By understanding the basic procedures of research, standard methods of recording information, ways of effectively organizing your time, and above all, how to write effective letters and ask questions, you will quickly find that you will be able to determine where records can be found as well as how you can use them to locate other sources.

Throughout this book, many sources are indicated which will provide the proof needed to secure the ties between generations. As well, other sources are indicated which will provide the clues necessary to locate the original records, show the path to be followed in your research or provide interesting, but not really necessary, details on your ancestors.

EVALUATING EVIDENCE

In your research it will be necessary for you to determine whether a record you have acquired can be used to prove an event or line of descent beyond any reasonable doubt or whether it can only be used to make calculations and assumptions. Information can be classified as either Direct or Circumstantial.

DIRECT INFORMATION:
Information which provides an answer directly without any assumptions or calculations. This includes all information given by a witness to an event or a participant in an event and given at or near the time of the event (for example: birth record, death record, land deed, etc.)

CIRCUMSTANTIAL INFORMATION:
Information which assumes an answer or which provides an answer after some calculations. This includes all information not given by a witness to or participant of an event and/or not given at or near the time of the event. (For example: family stories and traditions, birth information on census records or obituaries, etc.)

In all cases, direct information must be used if it is available, being the only acceptable proof. In cases where direct information is not available for one reason or another, circumstantial information may be used provided that it is clearly indicated that it is only circumstantial and the reasons why direct information is not available. Circumstantial information should never be used when direct information can be obtained.

STARTING OUT

From the very beginning of your research, you must realize that your success or failure depends largely on your ability to work from the KNOWN to the UNKNOWN. In fact, this aspect can be regarded as the single most important rule of genealogy.

The process begins when you record the material you know about yourself. Following this, list what you know about your parents, then your grandparents, and so on. After you have recorded what you know about these ancestors you will then be in the position to check other records to fill in the details which remain unknown. In turn, you will find that the records you consult to locate unknown information on your ancestors will often provide leads to other records and additional sources.

Working from known to unknown will also help to develop your skills as a genealogist. Records created during the last 50 years are quite abundant and very complete, in addition to being easily accessible. As your research takes you further into the past you will find that the records you require to prove your pedigree will become more scarce, more scattered and less complete, and you will have to search farther afield for the proof you need to link one generation with another. The experience you will have gained searching the more accessible modern records will be invaluable when the ancestral trail becomes more difficult to follow.

The steps you will follow in finding your ancestors will largely depend on the information you start with or can easily find. Every family is unique. Some left more records behind than others, and the type of records left by one will differ from those left by another. You will also find that available records will vary from one part of the country to another and from one time period to the next. All of these factors will influence the direction of your research.

In the beginning, you will need to establish a "starting point" for your research and to acquire an understanding of the sources available to extend the information you start with. In doing so, you will be wise to follow these steps:

● Gather together the records in your home and interview or write your various relatives in order to bring together as much information on your family as possible. This will establish your starting point.

● Purchase and read one or two general genealogical books to acquaint yourself with general research proceedures and the records available to you. Purchasing these books is best because they will then be available to you at all times should you encounter a problem during your research. Also, join your local genea-

logical society so that you can take advantage of the
experience of other genealogists in your area and can
keep up to date on genealogical developments in Canada.

● Develop a system of organization for the information
you find. This way you will always be able to see
exactly what you know and don't know at any time in
your research. (see chapter 1.2)

● Visit you local library and familiarize yourself with
the various genealogical guides located there. Conduct
some background reading into the history of the areas
in which your family has lived. (see chapter 1.5 & 2.1)

● Begin consulting the various official records for
references to your family. Which records you will
check first will largely depend on what information you
start with.

Genealogical Research, like any other research is very
time consuming, and answers to questions and problems may
not be discovered immediately but may require many months
or even years of searching. A great deal of patience is
required in compiling any family history and you will only
get out of it what you are willing to put into it in the
first place.

Throughout the course of your research, you should
bear in mind that your ancestors were once living people
with hopes, dreams and aspirations. Whether king or common-
er, each has played a part in your existance. A family tree
which contains only names and dates does not do justice to
the memory of those who came before you. It is only a
skeleton of what once was. Flesh out the bones by relating
your ancestors' lives to the events of the time and the
place in which they lived. Seek out those records which
will make them come alive. You will not be sorry that you
did!

The balance of Chapter 1 is devoted to briefly explaining some basic principles of research. However,
beginning researchers are advised to acquire and consult
one or two general reference books listed in the bibliography in Section 1 - 6, before proceeding too far in
their research in order to obtain a better grounding in
basic research principles.

1:2 ORGANIZING FOR RESEARCH

The basic approach to genealogical research is to gather records of an ancestor from various sources, compile them into a meaningful form and then to evaluate them to determine genealogical connections. However, this is an almost impossible task without some type of system for organizing your research efforts and your findings.

Without organization, you will never really know what you have done or what you must do. This may not seem evident when you first begin and have only a few documents gathered, but as time goes on, the sheer volume of material you are likely to gather will undoubtedly overwhelm you. The lack of a system of organizing all this material will probably lead you to duplicate information which you have already gathered because you could not remember whether you already had it or not!

The backbone of any type of research is an organization and filing system which will allow you to see what you have and what you still require. It will allow you to pursue your research in an orderly fashion and will enable information which you have gathered to be easily accessible at all times. It will eliminate your "headaches", save you time and effort, and enable you to conduct your research as you would expect a professional researcher to do.

PEDIGREE CHART

The first component of your organizational system is the PEDIGREE CHART, which, while limited in uses, can be very helpful. The Pedigree Chart is a graphical presentation of your findings and falls into two main types:

THE PROGENITOR OR LINEAL CHART:
This type shows only the ancestors of a single individual

THE POSTERITY CHART:
This type indicates all the known descendants of one ancestor.

As a rule, the Lineal Chart is the more common in individual family research. It's main strength, it's simplicity, is also it's main weakness. It is primarily useful as a limited indexing tool for the Family Research Forms or as a means of quickly identifying yourself to other researchers working on the same surnames because of the limited amount of information that can be legibly placed on it.

FAMILY RESEARCH FORM

The second component of genealogical organization is the INDIVIDUAL OR FAMILY RESEARCH FORM. This form is restricted to one individual or to a married couple and their children. On this you will record key events in the lives of the individual or married couple, and it will help you to reconstruct families and enable you to see what you have and what you still require to complete the record. Essentially, it is a worksheet only, although some researchers use similar forms for recording their completed genealogies.

As children of couples you are researching are married, separate forms for each will be started. These can be cross-referenced back to their parents' sheet by means of sheet reference numbers, as shown on the sample form or simply by arranging all forms in alphabetical order and using the names of couples plus the common birth, marriage and death information to locate correctly either children or parents listed on separate forms. Either system works quite well, although if the family (one surname) being researched is very large with many common given names, the sheet numbering system may prove to be of greater value in the long run.

It is best not to record any information on your Pedigree Charts or Family Research Forms until you have documents which substantiate the data. This can be quite awkward, as you will likely gather a lot of material in the beginning which will have to be proven later. In order to get around this problem, some researchers keep two Pedigree Charts and two Family Forms for each group or family. One of these forms is their "working" sheet on which they make notes and comments and the other form contains only the information for which they have documentary proof. Another method is to use only one form of each type for each group or family, recording unproven data in pencil and then, as you acquire the documentary proof, going over the pencilled-in information with ink. Both methods work very well, but they must be kept up to date to be really effective.

FAMILY RESEARCH FORM
INDICATE THE SOURCES OF INFORMATION ON THE REVERSE SIDE OF THIS PAGE

REFERENCE

	HUSBAND	REFERENCE	WIFE	REFERENCE
SURNAME				
GIVEN NAMES				
BORN				
PLACE				
DIED				
PLACE				
BURIED AT				
FATHER				
MOTHER				
CHURCH				
OCCUPATION				
MARRIAGE DATE PLACE				
RESIDENCES				

CHILDREN	M F REFERENCE	M F REFERENCE	M F REFERENCE	M F REFERENCE
NAME				
BORN				
PLACE				
MARRIED				
PLACE				
SPOUSE'S NAME				
DIED				
PLACE				
CHILDREN	M F REFERENCE	M F REFERENCE	M F REFERENCE	M F REFERENCE
NAME				
BORN				
PLACE				
MARRIED				
PLACE				
SPOUSE'S NAME				
DIED				
PLACE				
CHILDREN	M F REFERENCE	M F REFERENCE	M F REFERENCE	M F REFERENCE
NAME				
BORN				
PLACE				
MARRIED				
PLACE				
SPOUSE'S NAME				
DIED				
PLACE				

16

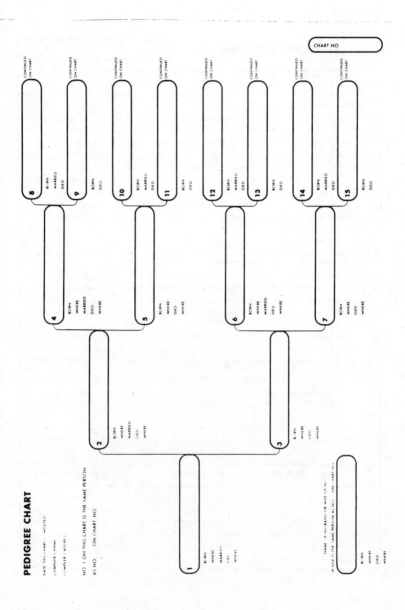

PEDIGREE CHART

DATE THIS CHART WRITTEN

COMPILER'S NAME

COMPILER'S ADDRESS

NO 1 ON THIS CHART IS THE SAME PERSON

AS NO ___ ON CHART NO

CHART NO

1
BORN
WHERE
DIED
WHERE

2
BORN
WHERE
MARRIED
DIED
WHERE

3
BORN
WHERE
DIED
WHERE

4
BORN
WHERE
MARRIED
DIED
WHERE

5
BORN
WHERE
DIED
WHERE

6
BORN
WHERE
MARRIED
DIED
WHERE

7
BORN
WHERE
DIED
WHERE

8
BORN
MARRIED
DIED
CONTINUED ON CHART

9
BORN
DIED
CONTINUED ON CHART

10
BORN
MARRIED
DIED
CONTINUED ON CHART

11
BORN
DIED
CONTINUED ON CHART

12
BORN
MARRIED
DIED
CONTINUED ON CHART

13
BORN
DIED
CONTINUED ON CHART

14
BORN
MARRIED
DIED
CONTINUED ON CHART

15
BORN
DIED
CONTINUED ON CHART

NAME IF HUSBAND OR WIFE OF NO

PERSON IS THE SAME PERSON AS NO ON CHART NO

BORN
WHERE
DIED
WHERE

The previous two components of your genealogical organizational system are useful for providing you with a synopsis of your research at any given time or as an indexing system (by individual) to the material you have gathered. It will also serve, in part, to inform you of the direction your future research should take. The "meat of your efforts", however, is contained in the documents and material you gather or will gather. Since this information comes from a variety of sources over a period of time, it is necessary that your research endeavours be carefully documented and that the information you gather be carefully indexed and filed so that all material can be quickly recovered when required.

RESEARCH CALENDAR

Just as the Family Research Form is the backbone of your genealogical research in general, the RESEARCH CAL-ENDAR holds the same relationship to your document and information files. No matter which filing system you may use, each requires that you keep a list of the sources you have searched. The Research Calendar should include all pertinent information about every source you personally check or research, and whether it proves useful in answering your questions. Your Research Calendar should keep you in touch with what you did, why you did it, when it was done, and what was found. Nothing is more wasteful than checking through a voluminous record only to find later that you had checked it before but failed to record the fact.

Research Calendars are generally arranged by family, that is, one calendar is used for each family being researched so that all the work within that group can be quickly scanned without distractions created by having other families in the same calendar. Some researchers also like to break this down even further, generating a calendar for each locality where a particular family lived. This allows them to quickly check to see which records in a given geographical location have been searched for a particular family and which records remain to be checked. Sometimes Research Calendars are combined with Correspondence Calendars (discussed in Chapter 1-4), although some researchers caution against this practise and maintain that they should be kept separately. However, combination systems work well in some cases and your own personal preference will probably determine which system will suit you best.

FILING DOCUMENTS

Until now we have been concerned with systems of
indexing and recording the chronology and extent of research, without discussing the various methods of filing
information obtained through that research in a logical
manner for easy retrieval. This can be done in several
ways:

SEPARATE DOCUMENT FILE:
A separate file folder for each ancestor holding all
documents and notes gathered and compiled during research may be kept. Correspondence is placed in separate file folders and cross-referenced back to the
document files.

ENVELOPE AND BOOK FILE:
All documents and notes for each ancestor are placed
into large envelopes and placed into a standard three-
ring binder or other similar type of book. Correspondence is kept in a separate binder.

COMBINATION FILE:
While the previous two systems require correspondence
to be kept separate from the document files, this system incorporates letter files and document files together. Manilla file folders are the most useful for
this system. Large or oversize documents may be stored
in a separate "oversize" file and cross indexed back to
the main file.

NUMBERING SYSTEM

All filing systems depend on some type of numbering
system to make the documents readily accessible and use-
able. In the first two filing methods, a separate column
on the Research Calendar is normally allocated for recording a document number. As you acquire each document,
you assign it a number, indicate the number on the Research Calendar and then file it in numerical sequence.
In the second method, the name of the ancestor or the
reference number is indicated on the front of the envelope and documents relating to the ancestor are placed
inside the envelope and cross-referenced to the Research
and Correspondence Calendar numbers. The third filing
system is generally used in conjunction with a combination Research and Correspondence Calendar. In this system every letter and document has a number and is filed
in numerical sequence using the number indicated on the
Combination Calendar.

RESEARCH CALENDAR

REFERENCE:

NO.	DESCRIPTION OF SOURCE	LIBRARY CALL NO.	REASON FOR SEARCH	COMMENTS	DATE

CORRESPONDENCE CALENDAR

REFERENCE:

NO.	DATE SENT ($ SENT)	REPLY REC'D (REFUND)	CORRESPONDENT	SUBJECT	COMMENTS	FOLLOW UP

RESEARCH AND CORRESPONDENCE CALENDAR

REFERENCE:

MAIL	RESEARCH	No.	DATE SENT/ SEARCHED ($ SENT)	REPLY RECD (REFUND)	CORRESPONDENT/ OR DESCRIPTION OF SOURCE	SUBJECT	COMMENTS	FOLLOW UP

As you gradually gather documents and notes relating to your family, always ensure that the Family Research Forms are kept up to date. Otherwise, their value is lost. You may also find it helpful to include on the Family Research Forms the numbers of the documents and letters you collect and generate on that particular family and a brief description of their contents for the day when you write a detailed history of the family. This information is generally placed on the back of the Research Form. If only the numbers of documents and letters are recorded on the back of the Research Forms, these numbers can always be checked against the Research and Correspondence Calendars and Document Files when you desire to know the extent of the information you have gathered on a particular family.

In closing this section, it will again be emphasized that the organization of your research is one of the most important tasks you will perform. It is wise to remember that your ability as a researcher will never be judged more critically than from your notes and record keeping.

1:3 FAMILY RECORDS

When beginning any genealogical research it is always best to start right in your own home with yourself. Gather all the documents, records and papers dealing with yourself. Enter the information obtained from them on your first Family Research Form and then file them according to the system you have chosen to use. Go on to your parents, your grandparents and others until you have gone over all records and documents available to you at home or at the homes of your relatives. At the same time, you can start to interview your close relatives (parents, aunts, uncles, etc.) to learn as much as possible about your family. You will find that it is not so easy as it may first appear.

RECORDS

Within your home and the homes of your relatives, is an immense store of documents and records, many of which are very useful in genealogical research. Some of the more common "home records" are: Family Bibles, journals, diaries, old letters, old and new photographs, scrapbooks wedding albums, baby books, wills, deeds, mortgage papers contracts, tax notices, certificates and announcements of births, marriages, divorces, and deaths, graduation records, baptismal and confirmation certificates, military records (discharge papers, pensions), citizenship papers, school records, employment records, newspaper clippings, membership records, health records, licenses, and tax records, to name only a few.

Some of these records may seem of little or no importance, but you can never tell when a name related in an old newspaper clipping may give you the clue to the birth place of your grandfather or whether his one-time membership in a fraternal association may lead you to someone still alive who was once his best friend and has many interesting stories about your ancestor which he would be happy to tell you. Never forget that all these documents and papers are records of the events in someone's life, and that they were saved because they had value to that person. They may seem insignificant now, but they may provide clues to your family's past as you progress in your research. They are indispensible if you wish to completely and accurately re-construct the events of an ancestor's life.

FAMILY BIBLES

Before proceeding further, a short discussion on Family Bibles and on Surnames may prove helpful to those who are not familiar with the benefits and problems of them. In the typical household before universal education, the only book to be found was likely to be the Bible. Because it was a cherished volume, it slowly became the catch-all for a variety of information. Within its' pages, old letters and documents may have been placed for safe-keeping, and on some of the blank pages, births, marriages and deaths within the family are likely to have been recorded. Of course this is not always true of all Bibles, however, if you have "the old Family Bible of Grandma's", or know the relative who has it, you would be very wise to make this one of the first places you look. It may save you a lot of work. All information in it should be thoroughly checked against official records because even Grandma was capable of getting dates and names mixed up, especially if she had 'umpteen children, cats and dogs' around the house when she decided to make an entry in the book.

SURNAMES

Surnames can be a problem for genealogical researchers especially if you have an "ethnic" background. Many people from continental Europe translated or "anglicized" their names when they came to North America or took the name of the town or area from which they came to make it easier for the immigration officials to spell. Still in other instances, there are dozens of variations in the spelling of a name, as for example, the German name Dippel, which has also been spelled Dipple, Dippl, Dippell, Dibble, Dibbel, Diffle. Spend an hour or so comparing spellings in a telephone book for more examples. Special care should always be taken to ensure that you don't overlook someone because the name was spelled slightly differently.

INTERVIEWING RELATIVES

While deriving as much information as possible from the documents and papers around the home, be sure to spend some time interviewing your various relatives. It can be said that they are the 'living documents' in genealogical research. Their experiences, stories and knowledge of deceased family members will prove invaluable as stepping-stones to further research. While individually you may find each knows only a little, collectively they may be able to supply you with the blueprint of your genealogy. When interviewing them, it is advisable to capture their experiences with a tape recorder, if possible. They may be a bit nervous to begin with, but if the tape recorder is placed in a spot where it isn't too conspicuous, they will quickly relax and will probably forget that it's there. Say little yourself. Your job is to guide them through the experiences you want to document. Let them do the talking even if they repeat themselves. You will find that the repetition is an excellent means of checking the accuracy of their memory. If possible, return often and discuss the information that you find as your research progresses. You will probably find that this will help them to remember other incidents which they couldn't recall the first time. After the interview play back the tape to yourself and extract the information that's contained on it. As always, you will have to search further for documented proof of the experiences and incidents that are related to you. Memory, unfortunately, is not infallible.

Having gathered all the paper documents and living documents available to you, you will have assembled the foundation of information on which you can build your genealogy.

1:4 CORRESPONDENCE IN GENEALOGICAL RESEARCH

Much information can be gathered through the mail. Therefore, it is very important that when you write to others you do so in a way that makes it a pleasure to answer your requests. The most important thing in correspondence is getting an answer! When you do not, you must analyze WHY not and take measures to correct yourself.

CORRESPONDENCE CALENDAR

Before writing your first letter, set up a CORRESPONDENCE CALENDAR. Very much like a Research Calendar, this enables you to keep track of the letters you have sent and the replies you have received, along with some indication of the results of your correspondence. This can be established to compliment the Research Calendar and therefore should have the same breakdown by family and locality as it's compliment; or the two can be combined into one calendar (See Chapter 1-2 for further explanation of the calendars). Either one will work quite effectively.

RULES OF GOOD CORRESPONDENCE

When writing your letters, you will be wise to follow a few proven rules of good correspondence:

- Use a typewriter if you can, or write legibly on one side of the paper only.

- Make at least two copies of every letter you write, keeping one copy for your own records.

- Don't "hoard" information on your family; be willing to exchange any information you have on the correspondent's family and let them know you are willing to exchange.

- Don't tell your life story, but be friendly. Once you get to know them better, you can tell them about yourself in more detail.

- Be specific and to the point in your request. Asking for "all the information you have on _____ family" will undoubtedly lead you to a "NO REPLY RECEIVED" entry on your correspondence calendar.

● Do not offer to pay for "all expenses" in getting some information until you have an idea of the cost involved. Ask them to quote on the cost, if any.

● When writing your first letter to someone, always enclose a stamped, self-addressed envelope for their reply.

● When writing to Government Departments, be especially brief and limit your request to one subject only. They are busy people with many other requests to fill. Make it easy for them to fill your request. Always ask for an estimate of costs from them before sending any money; they prefer it that way.

● Always use PLEASE and THANK YOU. They are used so rarely today that seeing them in a letter becomes a pleasure.

● When it is not possible to determine the exact address of an organization or institution, a general address is usually acceptable. For example:

Local Library,	Minister,
City or Town, Province	Name of Church
	Town or City, Province

IMPORTANCE OF CORRESPONDENCE

The importance of being successful in your correspondence cannot be over-emphasized. Even if you live near an extremely good reference or genealogical library, you will find that at some time or another, you must depend on the Post Office and your letter writing abilities to obtain the answer to a research problem. For those who do not have access to reference materials, success in correspondence takes on an even greater significance.

Many records and sources can be explored by mail. This is true of many of the sources which are discussed throughout this book. In some cases it is possible to compile the majority of a genealogy by using this media.

There are numerous publications available at local book stores or libraries which will assist you in writing good letters, instructing you in the proper methods of composition, punctuation, grammar, etc. It will be to your advantage to read one or two for more extensive knowledge of good correspondence.

Because there are so many records and sources which can be explored by mail, it is very important that you are able to conduct successful correspondence. Work diligently to make a success of every letter you write!

1:5 USING A LIBRARY

Libraries are the storehouses of a tremendous variety of books and material indispensable to successful genealogical research. It is here that you will find many of the reference books you will need to locate the particular records you require. Although the extent of the Reference Section will depend on the size of the community in which the library is located, most libraries now have Reference Sections which can be used to advantage.

Many libraries now have some publication explaining the procedures used in locating books or material by way of the card catalogue system. If not, Library Staff will be happy to explain the procedure to you. Therefore, this aspect will not be discussed here.

SERVICES OF THE LIBRARY

CIRCULATION OR LOAN DEPARTMENT

In this department, patrons may "check out" books from the library. If the library has "open stacks", the borrower may choose the appropriate books and check them out at the loan desk. If it has "closed stacks", the borrower presents a slip detailing the filing information for the book(s) he/she wishes to borrow and an attendant locates the book(s) in the stacks for the borrower.

REFERENCE DEPARTMENT AND READING ROOM

Books which are constantly consulted for reference purposes are often not allowed to circulate and are made available in one central location, generally called a reference room. Types of publications located here include encyclopedias, dictionaries, bibliographies, etc. Often the reference room has desks and chairs at which researchers can examine reference books, although some libraries provide a separate reading room for this purpose.

MICROFILM ROOM

Many libraries now have facilities for reading microfilm copies of books and original documents. The microfilming process (16 mm. and 35 mm. rolls are most popular) has opened new doors to the genealogist, enabling him to view photographic copies of original documents and out-of-print books which would otherwise

be unobtainable. Many libraries' microfilm readers
are located in the Reference Department and/or Reading
Room.

MAP COLLECTION

Map collections are often organized in a central
location of the library, frequently within the Reference
Department. The collections generally include single
maps, bound atlases and other geographical finding aids.

SPECIAL COLLECTIONS

Some libraries may specialize in collecting material
relating to a special interest, such as the History of
the Town or Region in which the library is located. Material of this nature is often arranged in a special
area of its' own. Most Special Collections are found in
University or larger Public Libraries as a rule.

COPYING SERVICE

Most libraries now have a photocopy service where
library materials can be copied by or for the patron.

INTER-LIBRARY LOAN

The inter-library loan allows a local public library
to borrow materials from other libraries for the use of
its' patrons. Further information on this policy can be
obtained from the Reference Librarian.

CORRESPONDENCE

Uncomplicated inquiries can often be answered by
mail by library staff. This may include information on
some specific collection at the library or a request for
the address of another organization in the same locality.
It is often not necessary to know the exact address of
the library when writing to one in another city or town.
Simply address the letter to the Public Library at the
city or town in question and in most cases it will be
received there with no trouble.

TAKING NOTES

After selecting the books you want, you are in the
position to start taking notes of the information you will
find. It is generally best to use $8\frac{1}{2}$ x 11 inch paper,
(which will fit in a looseleaf binder) to record your information, although some researchers prefer file cards.
When taking your notes, indicate the source of your information at the top of the page noting especially the title,
author and date of publication and Library catalogue number if applicable. Besides providing you with the name of
the source, the other information (i.e., author and date
of publication) will later enable you to determine how reliable your source is. Examine the material slowly so that

nothing is missed, recording pertinent information on one side of the paper only. You will find it easier in some cases to make condensed notes of the information you find, but for the sake of clarity you should copy the printed text verbatim as a rule. Some researchers insist that all information should be copied exactly as it appears in the book and no condensed notes should be made at all. All the foregoing refers to research in published books (See Chapter 3-1 for a discussion on works compiled by others).

When researching original documents, that is, records of first entry such as actual deeds, family bibles, etc., it is advisable to copy everything as you find it. It can be very easy to misinterpret a statement in an original document or pass over a piece of information which you may feel at the time has no bearing on your research, only to find that later when you find that you now require the data, you haven't the original wording to refer back to.

Most books and other compiled sources are indexed in some way and the value of these indexes should be clearly understood by all researchers. Many books have a prepared index at the end, and while it can be useful, it should always be remembered that this is only one person's idea of what is important in the book. Invariably, these indexes were compiled by people who's major concern was historical and not genealogical. When you are in doubt as to the thoroughness of an index, simply open the book at any page, select a few names which appear thereon and check if they are listed in the index. The table of contents, at the beginning of each book, however, is more indicative of what may be found within and in most cases the best place for the genealogist to look. Watch for the books where each section of the table of contents is further indexed at the beginning of that section in the text. Indexes can be helpful and can save you a great deal of time if used with a degree of caution. It should be mentioned however that many of the best genealogical sources have no index at all.

In general, libraries give access to a variety of publications such as histories, biographies, directories, bibliographies, atlases, maps, and other reference books which are out of reach to the pocketbook of the average researcher. As well, Inter-Library Loan policies now enable even the most remote local library to borrow rare books and microfilm from larger libraries for the use of their patrons. The local Reference Librarian is definately someone that every researcher should endeavor to get to know. Their knowledge of what is located in their library and other libraries will help in making any research run more smoothly.

1:6 SUMMARY

Up to now, we have been primarily concerned with information gathering and filing processes and with general
organization and recording of your research efforts.
Research analysis is simply the process of putting the
gathered information to work for you, either to help you
in locating more information or to provide you with a
logical history of the lives of your ancestors.

The most important aspect to remember in analysis is
that you must always work from the KNOWN to the UNKNOWN.
If you have information on yourself, your parents, and
your grandparents, you must realize that you can only use
the information you have to determine and prove who your
great-grandparents were. Do not try, as some people do,
to find out if you are a descendent of, say, William Lyon
Mackenzie, the rebel leader of 1837, by starting with him
and tracing all his descendents. We all should realize
that just because a surname is the same is no reason to
assume that there is any relationship between ouselves and
someone who lived 150 years ago. So, always work from the
known to the unknown, from the present generation to the
past generation.

In attempting to locate records on your family, you
must have the ability to logically determine where records
could be deposited. Since all records have been kept by
someone or by some jurisdiction authorized to keep them,
we have to think of records in relationship to this authority. Therefore, school records are compiled under School
Board Jurisdiction; assessment records under Municipal
Jurisdiction; records of business by the business jurisdiction, and so on. To locate the records after having an-
alyzed the jurisdiction, you must first discover if that
particular jurisdiction or authority is still in operation
and if it is, locate it's correct address. If it has been
disbanded or amalgamated with another jurisdiction, you
must track down the new authority responsible for the records. This may be another government department, a large
conglomerate business, or a library or archives where the
records of disbanded organizations are often located. By
the process of elimination, you will learn of the where-
abouts of virtually any record, unless of course it no
longer exists.

When you have a problem which seems insurmountable, it
may be possible to split it up into several smaller, more
easily solved problems, than to try to cope with the whole

at one time. Approach your research one step at a time, and you will find that one solution often leads to another.

In order for you to be very effective in analyzing the steps you should take, it will be important for you to have a background in the history of the area your research is being conducted in, and a knowledge of the types of information you will find in various records. The balance of this book is devoted to explaining some of the major records available and to inform you of the major repositories of records in Canada to help you in this regard.

There are numerous books and pamphlets available which discuss the fundamentals of genealogical research in much greater detail than what has been given in this chapter. Before going too far into your family research, it would be advisable to obtain one or two of the following publications to acquire a full understanding of genealogical research methods:

American Genealogical Research Institute: How to Trace Your Family Tree (New York, 1975)

American Society of Genealogists: Genealogical Research: Methods and Sources Volume 1 (Washington 1960)

* Doane, Gilbert H.: Searching for your Ancestors (Bantam Book Edition, N.Y. 1974)

Greenwood, Val D.: Researcher's Guide to American Genealogy (Baltimore 1973)

Jacobus, Donald L.: Genealogy as Pastime and Profession (2nd ed. Baltimore 1968)

* Jaussi & Chaston: Fundamentals of Genealogical Research (Salt Lake City 1972)

* Jones, Eakle and Christensen: Family History for Fun and Profit (Provo, Utah 1972)

* Nichols, Elizabeth: Genesis of Your Genealogy (Logan, Utah 1972)

* Nichols, Elizabeth: Help is Available (Logan, Utah 1972)

Parker, D. D.: Local History: How to Gather It, Write It, and Publish It (Revised ed., N.Y., 1944)

* Williams, Ethel W.: Know Your Ancestors: A Guide to Genealogical Research (Rutland, Vt. 1964)

* RECOMMENDED FOR BEGINNERS

2
INTRODUCTION TO CANADIAN GENEALOGY

2:1 HISTORY FOR GENEALOGISTS

Genealogy and history are inseparable. It is impossible to disassociate ancestors from the times and places in which they lived and still re-construct their lives so that they can be clearly understood. Without an awareness of the background of our ancestors, it is impossible to realize the full extent of the research possibilities open to us.

The types of records and their contents have actually been dictated by historical processes as well as which of these records were to be kept and which were to be destroyed. Profound effects were exerted upon genealogical records in Canada as the direct result of wars, land policies, persecutions, politics, diseases, over-population, droughts, among other factors.

Therefore, it is imperative that, along with the gathering and filing of documents and other papers dealing with our ancestors, we also thoroughly familiarize ourselves with their social, religious, political and economic backgrounds through the study of local, regional and national history.

CHRONOLOGICAL HISTORY

The following chronological history of Canada is included here to provide a working knowledge of some of the major developments in the history of Canada and can be used as a guide to organize a more thorough program of historical familiarization suited to each individual family's particular requirements.

1608   Founding of Quebec City, the first permanent settlement in Canada.
1610   Petition granted to John Guy for a "plantation" in Newfoundland and settlement followed.
1617   Louis Hebert, the first colonist, arrived at Quebec City. Only five other families follow in the next ten years.
1621   Code of Laws issued and Parish Registers opened in Quebec. Nova Scotia granted to Sir William Alexander by James I.
1623   First British settlement in Nova Scotia.
1629-32 Canada and Acadia controlled by British (returned to France 1632).

1633	First serious attempt at colonizing Canada. 100 families arrive at Quebec from France.
1642	Founding of Ville-Marie (Montreal).
1654-55	Acadia taken and held by British, later returned to French control.
1662	French colonization in Newfoundland at Placentia.
1666	First Canadian Census: Population of New France was 3,215.
1667	Acadia restored to France.
1670	Hudson's Bay Company is chartered.
1674	Further immigration to Newfoundland prohibited by the Crown; immigration ceases.
1689-97	War of the Grand Alliance.
1701	British population of Newfoundland 3,574; French population (1702) is 466.
1702-13	War of the Spanish Succession.
1713	Population of New France is 18,469; Louisbourg is founded by the French.
1744-48	War of the Austrian Succession.
1749	Founding of Halifax.
1755	Expulsion of 5000 Acadians from Nova Scotia.
1756-63	Seven Years' War.
1758	First meeting of the Legislature of Nova Scotia.
1759	Quebec City falls to the British.
1762	First British settlement in New Brunswick.
1763	Canada ceded by France to the British. Cape Breton and P.E.I. annexed to Nova Scotia.
1763-64	Pontiac Indian Rebellion.
1769	P.E.I. separated from Nova Scotia. Charlottetown founded in 1768.
1775	Quebec Act (passed in 1774) comes into force. American Revolution begins.
1775-83	American Revolution.
1783	Major influx of United Empire Loyalists from U.S.
1784	Nova Scotia divided into three provinces: Nova Scotia, New Brunswick, Cape Breton Island.
1791	The Constitutional Act divides province of Quebec into Upper and Lower Canada.
1792	First Legislatures of Upper Canada and Lower Canada convene.
1793	York (Toronto) founded. Importation of slaves into Upper Canada forbidden.
1803	Settlers sent by Lord Selkirk to P.E.I.
1806	Population: Upper Canada 70,718; Lower Canada 250,000; N.B. 35,000; N.S. 65,000; P.E.I. 9676.
1811	Founding of Red River Settlement in Manitoba by Lord Selkirk's colonists.
1812-14	War of 1812.
1820	Cape Breton re-annexed to Nova Scotia.
1821	North West Company merges with Hudson Bay Company.
1824-25	Population: U.C. 150,000; L.C. 479,000; Newfoundland 56,000.

1826   Founding of Bytown (Ottawa).

1832   Representative Government in Newfoundland.

1836   First railway in Canada opened in Quebec.

1837-38 Rebellion in Upper and Lower Canada.

1841   Union Act, uniting Upper and Lower Canadas as the Province of Canada.

1843   Victoria, B.C. founded.

1849   Signing of Rebellion Losses Act. Population of Assiniboia (Red River area) 5,000.

1851   Responsible Government to P.E.I. Population: U.C. 952,000; L.C. 890,000; N.B. 194,000; N.S. 277,000.

1854   Seigneurial tenure in Lower Canada abolished. Secularization of Clergy Reserves.

1855   Militia Act of Province of Canada passed.

1856   First meeting of Legislature of Vancouver Island.

1857   Ottawa chosen as future Capital City of Canada.

1857-58 Indian Mutiny (Canadians volunteer to serve with British forces).

1858   Gold discovered in Fraser River Valley, B.C. Colony of British Columbia established.

1861   Population: U.C. 1,396,000; L.C. 1,112,000; N.B. 252,000; N.S. 330,000; P.E.I. 81,000.

1864   Conferences on Canadian Confederation at Charlottetown and Quebec City.

1861-65 American Civil War.

1866-70 Fenian Raids on Canada in Ontario and Red River.

1866   Vancouver Island unites with British Columbia.

1867   Canadian Confederation.

1868   Federal Militia Act passed; Canadian Pontifical Zouaves formed in Quebec to fight in Rome against Garibaldi.

1869   Ruperts' Land (Prairie Provinces mainly) ceded to Canada by Hudson Bay Company.

1869-70 Red River Rebellion.

1870   Province of Manitoba created in Red River area of Assiniboia.

1871   First Dominion Census: Population: 3,689,000. British Columbia enters Confederation.

1872   Canadian Pacific Railway charter passed by Dominion Parliament.

1873   North West Mounted Police (later R.C.M.P.) established. Prince Edward Island enters Confederation.

1874   Population of Newfoundland 161,000.

1875-77 First major influx of settlers into the Prairies begins.

1882   Regina becomes Capital City of the North West Territory.

1884   Canadians serve under Wolseley in fighting in Egypt.

1885   Northwest Rebellion in Saskatchewan.

1891   Population of Canada 4,833,000.

36

1896	Gold discovered in Klondike.
1898	Yukon District established as separate Territory.
1899-1902	South African War (Boer War).
1905	Provinces of Saskatchewan and Alberta created
1911	Population of Canada: 7,207,000; Newfoundland 243,000.
1912	Boundaries of Ontario, Quebec and Manitoba extended.
1914-18	World War I.
1921	Population of Canada: 8,788,000; Newfoundland 263,000.
1929	Start of the Great Depression.
1931	Population of Canada 10,377,000.
1934	Newfoundland Constitution suspended; government by Crown Commission.
1939-45	World War II.
1949	Newfoundland joins Confederation.
1950-53	Korean War.

HISTORICAL PUBLICATIONS

History books come in all shapes and sizes and the information contained in them will vary with the size of geographical area covered by the book, the time span covered by the book, whether the book is a general interest publication or if it deals with a specific segment of history and with the date the book was written. From a genealogist's point of view, the most interesting historical book is that which deals with a small or local area. There is a greater tendancy to include short biographical sketches along with other important historical information in this type of history than with any other. These biographies, plus the more detailed local historical information allow the researcher a more intimate look into the day to day affairs of the time span in which an ancestor lived and will better serve to assist in analyzing the relationship of those ancestors to their immediate locality.

Provincial histories can supplement the local histories by relating them to the events of the region in which they are situated. As well, most of the early provincial histories also contained an impressive number of biographical sketches of the provinces' most prominent people, and can easily be described as local histories that covered a larger geographical area. National histories help to tie these regional histories to the history of the country in general and will provide an overview of the events of national consequence which may have shaped some of the decisions and policies of the local and provincial levels. As well, special historical topics (i.e., social history, religious history, economic history, military history,

etc.) written at the local, provincial and national plane
can provide greater insight into these specific areas.

The following lists detail a few of the many
national and provincial histories available. While many
of the publications which appear here are the most
current or easily accessible histories available at this
time, a number of out of print books are also included
to acquaint the researcher with the wide variety of
publications of this nature. All of these books will
provide a working knowledge of the history of Canada or
it's provinces. Numerous bibliographical publications
have appeared in the last 20 years which amply document
the various local, regional and national histories and
should be consulted before beginning any research.
Several bibliographies are listed in Chapter 3-1 and,
therefore, are not included here. Local public libraries
will usually have a reasonable selection of regional and
national histories with some local histories and the
Reference Librarian can be very helpful in locating books
relating to specific areas of the country.

CHRONOLOGICAL HISTORIES

    Audet, Francis-Joseph: Canadian Historical Dates and
        Events, 1492-1915 (Ottawa 1917)
    Canadian Chronology, 1497-1960, reprinted from Canada
        Year Books (Ottawa 1961)
    Canadian Pocket Encyclopedia (published annually by
        Quick Canadian Facts Ltd., Box 99, Terminal M,
        Toronto)

NATIONAL HISTORIES

    Brebner, John B.: Canada: A Modern History (Ann
        Arbor 1960)
    Brown, George William: Building the Canadian Nation
        (Toronto 1958)
    Careless, J.M.S.: Canada: A Story of Challenge
        (Toronto 1963)
    Cook, Ramsey: Canada: A Modern Study (Toronto 1963)
    Creighton, Donald G.: Dominion of the North. A
        History of Canada (Toronto 1944, 1958, 1962)
        _____ : The Empire of the St. Lawrence
        (Toronto 1956)
    Graham, Gerald S.: A Consise History of Canada (London
        1968)
    Lower, Arthur R.M.: Colony to Nation: A History of
        Canada (Toronto 1966)
    Lower, J.A.: Canada: An Outline History (Toronto 1966)
    Masters, Donald C.: A Short History of Canada (Toronto
        1958)

McInnis, Edgar: <u>Canada</u> (Toronto 1969)
Morton, W.L.: <u>The Kingdom of Canada</u> (Toronto 1963)

NATIONAL HISTORY SERIES

These series of books will provide a very thorough understanding of Canadian history and are written in a style which makes them easy to read and very enjoyable.

<u>The Canadian Centennial Series</u>. This series is published by McClelland and Stewart Ltd., 25 Hollinger Road, Toronto and contains 17 volumes. Each individual book is complete in itself at the same time as forming a part of the entire series. Following is a list of the various volumes in this set with the names of the author in parenthases.

1. The North to 1632 (Oleson)
2. New France 1534 - 1662 (Trudel)
3. New France 1663 - 1701 (Eccles)
4. New France 1702 - 1743 (Blain)
5. New France 1744 - 1760 (Stanley)
6. Quebec 1760 - 1791 (Neatby)
7. Upper Canada 1784 - 1841 (Craig)
8. Lower Canada 1792 - 1841 (Ouellet)
9. Atlantic Provinces 1712 - 1857 (MacNutt)
10. Canada 1841 - 1857 (Careless)
11. The North 1670 - 1857 (Rich)
12. Confederation 1857 - 1873 (Morton)
13. Canada 1874 - 1896 (Waite)
14. Canada 1897 - 1921 (Cooke)
15. Canada 1922 - 1939 (Graham)
16. The North 1870 - 1965 (Zaslow)
17. Canada 1939 - 1967 (Creighton)

<u>The Canadian History Series</u>. This series was originally published by Doubleday and Company Ltd., 105 Bond Street, Toronto in hardcover. A paperback edition was released through Popular Library, Toronto. Like the previous series, each volume is complete in itself. The publications were edited by Thomas B. Costain.

1. Costain, Thomas B.: <u>The White and the Gold</u> (Covers the period from 1497 to 1690)
2. Rutledge, Joseph Lester: <u>Century of Conflict</u> (Covers the period from 1672 to 1763)
3. Raddall, Thomas H.: <u>The Path of Destiny</u> (Covers the period from 1763 to 1850)
4. Hardy, W. G.: <u>From Sea Unto Sea</u> (Covers the period from 1850 to 1910)
5. Allen, Ralph: <u>Ordeal By Fire</u> (Covers the period from 1910 to 1945)

PROVINCIAL HISTORIES

The following provincial histories are representative of those which can be found today. Included here are a number of earlier provincial histories as well as some current publications which are more easily accessible to the general researcher. This list is not meant to be exhaustive, however, and the researcher is directed to the various Canadian bibliographies for more detailed lists of these types of histories. When using these particular publications, it should be remembered that the older editions generally contain a significant number of biographical sketches of the prominent men in the province.

ALBERTA

Blue, John: Alberta Past and Present (Chicago 1924, 3 vols.)

MacGregor, J.G.: A History of Alberta (Edmonton 1973)

McRae, Archibald O.: A History of the Province of Alberta (no place 1912, 2 vols.)

BRITISH COLUMBIA

Bancroft, Hubert Howe: History of British Columbia, 1792-1887 (San Francisco 1887, New York 1967)

Begg, Alexander: History of British Columbia from its Earliest Discovery to the Present Time (Toronto 1894)

Ormsky, M.A.: British Columbia: A History (Toronto 1961)

MANITOBA

Morton, W.L.: Manitoba: A History (Toronto 1961)

Jackson, J.A.: A Centennial History of Manitoba (Winnipeg 1971)

Ricker, John C. and Saywell, John T.: Nation and Province: The History and Government of Canada and Manitoba since Confederation (Toronto 1963)

NEW BRUNSWICK

Hannay, James: History of New Brunswick, 2 volumes, (Saint John 1909)

MacNutt, W.S.: New Brunswick, A History 1784-1867 (Toronto 1963)

NEWFOUNDLAND

Chadwick, St. John: <u>Newfoundland: Island into Province</u>
(Cambridge 1967)

Perlin, Albert B.: <u>The Story of Newfoundland</u> (St. John's
1958)

Prowse, D.W.: <u>History of Newfoundland</u> (London 1895)

NOVA SCOTIA

Blakeley, Phyllis R.: <u>The Story of Nova Scotia</u> (Toronto
1950)

Blakeley, Phyllis R.: <u>Nova Scotia: A Brief History</u>
(Toronto 1955)

Campbell, G.G.: <u>The History of Nova Scotia</u> (Toronto
1948)

Haliburton, Thomas: <u>History of Nova Scotia</u> (Halifax
1829, 2 volumes, Reprinted Belleville 1973)

ONTARIO

Canniff, William: <u>History of the Province of Ontario</u>
(Toronto 1872)

Fraser, Alexander: <u>A History of Ontario. Its Resources
and Development</u>, 2 volumes (Toronto & Montreal 1907)

Middleton, Jessie E. and Landon, Fred: <u>The Province of
Ontario: A History 1615-1927</u>, 5 volumes (Toronto
1927)

Scott, J.M.: <u>The Story of Ontario</u> (Toronto 1949)

PRINCE EDWARD ISLAND

Bolger, F.W.P.: <u>Canada's Smallest Province</u> (1973)

Callbeck, Lorne C.: <u>The Cradle of Confederation: A
Brief History of Prince Edward Island from its
Discovery in 1534 to the Present Time</u> (Fredericton
1964)

Warburton, Alexander B.: <u>History of Prince Edward Island</u>
(Saint John 1923)

QUEBEC

Garneau, Francois-Xavier: <u>Histoire du Canada</u> (Montréal
1944, 8 volumes)

Lemonnier, L.: <u>Histoire du Canada français</u> (Paris 1966)

Rumilly, Robert: <u>Histoire de la province de Québec</u>
(Montréal 1940, 34 volumes to 1963)

Sulte, Benjamin: <u>Histoire des Canadiens-Français 1608-
1880</u> (Montréal 1882-84, 8 volumes)

SASKATCHEWAN

Black, Norman F.: <u>History of Saskatchewan and the Old
   North West</u> (Regina 1913)
Hawkes, John: <u>The Story of Saskatchewan</u> (Regina 1924)
Wright, J.F.C.: <u>Saskatchewan: The History of a Province</u>
   (Toronto 1955)

NORTHWEST TERRITORIES AND YUKON TERRITORY

Berton, Pierre: <u>The Klondike Fever: The Life and Death
   of the Last Great Gold Rush</u> (New York 1958)
Hamilton, Walter: <u>The Yukon Story: A Sourdough's
   Record of Gold Rush Days from the Earliest Times to
   the Present Day</u> (Vancouver 1964)
Kitto, F.H.: <u>The North West Territories</u> (Ottawa 1930)

2:2 ARCHIVES AND LIBRARIES IN CANADA

In recent years many of the records, documents and published books of historical significance have been gathered together into large collections by various archives and libraries in Canada at an ever increasing rate. This centralization of major sources is of primary importance to genealogical researchers, eliminating a considerable amount of "hunting for records" which was necessary in the past.

Archives can be classified into four major types: National, Provincial, Regional (or Local) and Private. The Public Archives of Canada, Ottawa, Ontario, is primarily responsible for the preservation of records of national historic importance, including all federal government records. It also has sizeable collections of provincial, local and private records from all over Canada which are indispensable for good genealogical research. The various provincial archives function along much the same lines as the Public Archives of Canada, although the majority of their collections relate only to the general and local historical development of the province in which they are located. Some, however, have special collections which deal with the history of an area greater than the size of their provinces. The regional or local archives, a development of more recent times, are concerned with the records of small areas (a city, county, municipality, etc.) Because they deal with such localized areas, the extent of the records they may have may be more detailed or specialized than either the national or provincial archives and can sometimes be the most useful of all the archives. Private archives can take the form of a repository of a commercial company's history retained by that particular company, a government departments' private archives, private records of an extended family, or archives covering a specific subject (such as military history etc.) operated by a private individual or organization. Anyone conducting research will find that they will eventually contact some organization in all of the above four categories.

Library classification is virtually the same as that of the archives, with the addition of university and genealogical libraries. The national libraries (National Library of Canada and the Library of the Public Archives

of Canada) and the provincial and private libraries deal
mainly with the jurisdictions they are assigned, and the
range of their holdings is similar to that of their
archival counterparts. The local library is primarily
devoted to providing a wide range of books to the general
public, including fiction, general non-fiction and a limited degree of local historical books. Their reference
sections are generally very helpful in locating records
and providing an inter-library loan service (See section
1-5 for more details on local libraries). Since the local
library must satisfy the needs of a wide variety of people
it is unlikely that a researcher will find all the information books necessary in genealogical research in this
type of library, but will find it useful nevertheless.
The University library is a more specialized institution,
dealing mainly with books of a non-fiction or research
nature. As a rule, these libraries are significantly larger than local libraries and the reference sections are
of a much greater functional value to the genealogical
researcher. These libraries are open for the use of any
person and should one exist near the researcher should
be used in preference to the local library. The genealogical library is a special library designed for genealogical research only. They concentrate on a national, international, provincial, regional or special area, or any
combination of these.

FINDING LIBRARIES & ARCHIVES

Some of the most important sources for the genealogist are the various provincial and federal archives and
libraries. Summaries of the archival collections of each
provincial archives is given in chapter 5, and information
on the Public Archives of Canada in chapter 4.

There are over 3000 public and special libraries in
Canada, many of which will provide some assistance to researchers. To locate Canadian libraries, researchers are
directed to the following publications which are generally
found in most public libraries:

> American Library Directory (RR Bowker: New York,
> triennial). Lists over 3000 Canadian libraries.

> "Canadian Library Directory/Répertoire des biblio-
> tèques canadiennes", published annually in Jan-
> uary in Canadian Library, publication of the
> Canadian Library Association.

> Canadian Almanac and Directory (Copp Clark: Toronto
> annual) Has a·select list of libraries.

> Corpus Almanac of Canada (Corpus Publishers: Tor-
> onto, annual) Has a select list of libraries.

Further information on provincial and special libraries can also be obtained from the various library associations in Canada. Many of these organizations also publish
book and pamphlets of interest to researchers.

Archival Assn. of Atlantic Canada, c/o Public Archives
   of Nova Scotia, Halifax, N.S. B3H 1Z9
Atlantic Provinces Library Assn., c/o Dalhousie School
   of Library Science, Dalhousie University, Halifax
   Nova Scotia B3H 4H8
Assn. des Archivistes du Québec, CP 159, Haute-Ville,
   Québec, P.Q. G1R 4P3
Assn. des bibliotècaires du Québec/Quebec Library Assn,
   c/o Dawson College Library, 1001 Sherbrooke St. E,
   Montréal, P.Q. H2L 1L3
Assn. of Canadian Map Libraries, c/o Public Archives
   of Canada, 395 Wellington, Ottawa, Ont. K1A ON3.
Assn. des Libraries du Québec, 436 rue Sherbrooke E.,
   Montréal, P.Q. H2L 1J3
Bibliographical Society of Canada, 32 Lowther Ave.,
   Toronto, Ontario M5R 1C6
B.C. Library Assn., Box 46378, Stn G, Vancouver, B.C.
   V6R 4G6
Canadian Assn. of College and University Libraries,
   151 Sparks Street, Ottawa, Ont. K1P 5E3
Canadian Assn. of Public Libraries, 151 Sparks, St.,
   Ottawa, Ontario K1P 5E3
Canadian Library Assn., 151 Sparks St., Ottawa,
   Ontario K1P 5E3
Church Library Assn., c/o 10 Allanhurst Dr., Apt 302,
   Islington, Ontario M9A 4J5
Library Assn. of Alberta, Box 1000, Lacombe, Alberta
   TOC 1S0
Manitoba Library Assn., 301-190 Rupert Ave., Winnipeg,
   Manitoba R3B ON2
Newfoundland Library Assn., c/o Public Library
   Services, Arts & Culture Centre, Allandale Road,
   St. John's, Newfoundland A1R 3A3.
Ontario Library Assn., 2397-A Bloor St. West, Toronto,
   Ontario M6S 1P6
Saskatchewan Library Assn., Box 3388, Regina, Sask.
   S4P 3H1

2:3 GENEALOGICAL SOCIETIES IN CANADA

Genealogical societies and organizations can provide a considerable amount of information about available records and repositories in their provinces or regions. In the past 15 years, many new societies have been formed as genealogy has become more popular and, through them, researchers now have a better opportunity to learn of some of the previously little-known sources.

Most of the genealogical societies publish a newsletter or journal in order to inform their members of society activities and to provide members with informative articles on various aspects of genealogy. The articles contained in these journals generally contain tips for the beginner and the advanced researcher and pertinent articles on various genealogical sources available in that province or in other contries. Through the journals members can keep up to date on new records which have been made available to researchers and, if they wish, can place advertisements or queries in special sections of the publications, in which they can indicate problems they are having or request information on their ancestors.

Many of these societies (or their local Branches) also hold regular meetings generally on a once-a-month basis for members who reside close by. This allows members to meet one another in order to exchange information and assistance with problems, in addition to hearing lectures or participating in workshops designed to increase their genealogical knowledge. In addition to these regular meetings each society often holds an "annual seminar" at which time members meet from all over their province to spend several days in lecture theatres, in workshops and at social gatherings of the society, all with genealogy in mind.

As a rule, each society also maintains a genealogical library for the use of its members and may also be involved with special record gathering projects in order to make previously unknown or difficult-to-use genealogical records more accessible to researchers. Some of the societies may also provide some assistance in the personal research of members, although generally in a very limited way.

In the following list, each genealogical society in Canada is examined briefly to provide those interested with a little background information on each. Information contained here was gathered by various means and is not meant to be all inclusive however. Those interested should contact each society for more current information regarding their services or fees.

ALBERTA

ALBERTA GENEALOGICAL SOCIETY, Box 3151, Station A,
Edmonton, Alberta   T5J 2G7
    Established: 1973
    Publications: "Relatively Speaking" (quarterly
                     journal)
    Library: c 100 vols.
    Branches: Edmonton, Calgary, Lethbridge, Cardston,
                     Grande Prairie, Medicine Hat, Red Deer

NORTH AMERICAN GENEALOGICAL SOCIETY, 507-30th Ave. SW,
Calgary, Alberta
    No information available.

BRITISH COLUMBIA

BRITISH COLUMBIA GENEALOGICAL SOCIETY, Box 94371,
Richmond, B.C.   V6Y 2A8
    Established: 1972?
    Publications: "The British Columbia Genealogist"
                     (quarterly journal)
    Library: includes source files to major lib-
                     raries in B.C. and an extensive
                     card catalogue listing the names
                     and details on almost 100,000 B.C.
                     residents, from the 1850s onward.

MANITOBA

MANITOBA GENEALOGICAL SOCIETY, P.O. Box 2066, Winnipeg,
   Manitoba   R3C 3R4
    Established: 1976
    Publications: "Generations" (quarterly journal)
                     and "MGS NEWS" (occasional news-
                     letter)
    Library: c 50 vols.
    Branches: Brandon, Winnipeg

NEW BRUNSWICK

LA SOCIÉTÉ HISTORIQUE NICHOLAS DENIS, Site 19, C.P. 6,
   Bertrand, N.B.   E0B 1J0
   Devoted to local history of Acadians in N.E. New
   Brunswick although many members interested in
   genealogy.

NOTE: In late 1978, plans were underway to establish a
New Brunswick Genealogical Society. For further informa-
tion on these developments, researchers should contact
Mr. Robert Fellows, Provincial Archives of New Brunswick,
P.O. Box 6000, Fredericton, New Brunswick E3B 5H1.

NOVA SCOTIA

GENEALOGICAL COMMITTEE, NOVA SCOTIA HISTORICAL SOCIETY,
   Box 895, Armdale P.O., Halifax
     (NOTE: This is a section of the N.S. Historical
     Society devoted to genealogical pursuits)
     Established: 1971
     Publications: "Genealogical Newsletter" since
                    1972 (quarterly journal)
     Library: None

ONTARIO

GLENGARRY GENEALOGICAL SOCIETY, P.O. Box 460, Lancaster,
   Ontario KOC 1NO
     (Note: This society covers the "old Eastern District"
     of Ontario, namely Glengarry, Stormont, Dundas, and
     surrounding counties)
     Established: 1974
     Publications: "Newsletter" (6 times per year), also
                    publishes a series on tombstone tran-
                    scriptions from Glengarry County.
     Library: small, emphasis on area families

ONTARIO GENEALOGICAL SOCIETY, Box 66, Station Q, Toronto,
   Ontario M4T 2L7
     Established: 1961
     Publications: "Families" (quarterly journal) and
                    "OGS Newsleaf" (Quarterly newsletter)
     Library: c 1000 vols, of which 600 are family
                    histories, located at Canadiana
                    Collection, North York Public Library,
                    35 Fairview Mall Drive, North York.
     Branches: (Note: OGS is one of the largest
                    genealogical societies in Canada.
                    As a result, its branches are also
                    quite large often containing as
                    many or more members as some other
                    provincial societies. In view of
                    this fact, the addresses of OGS
                    branches are included below for those
                    who are interested. Those marked *
                    publish a regular newsletter)

                    *Bruce & Grey: Box 1606, Port
                       Elgin NOH 2CO
                    *Halton-Peel: Box 373, Oakville
                       L6J 5A8
                    *Hamilton: Box 904, Hamilton
                       L8N 3P6
                    *Kawartha: Box 162, Peterborough
                       K9J 6Y8

Kent: Box 964, Chatham N7M 5L3
*Kingston: Box 1394, Kingston
K7L 5O6
Leeds & Grenville: c/o Mildred
Livingstone, St. Lawrence Ct.
RR 1, Prescott KOE 1TO
London: c/o 1110 Guildwood Blvd,
London N6H 4G6
*Ottawa: Box 8346, Ottawa K1G 3H8
*Toronto: Box 74, Station U,
Toronto M8Z 5M4
*Waterloo-Wellington: Box 603,
Kitchener N2G 4A2

NOTE: Leeds & Grenville Branch was
formerly an independent genealogical
society, joining OGS in 1978.

PRINCE EDWARD ISLAND

PRINCE EDWARD ISLAND GENEALOGICAL SOCIETY, c/o PEI Heri-
tage Foundation, Box 922, Charlottetown, P.E.I.
C1A 7L9
Publications: "Newsletter" (quarterly)
(Note: the Society does not undertake research or
answer general queries - see also PEI Heritage
Foundation in Chapter 5)

QUEBEC

NORTH AMERICAN ANCESTRY RESEARCH SOCIETY, R.R. 1, Lachute,
Québec J8H 2C5
(Note: this society is primarily the individual
endeavours of W.M. Cottingham into the ancestry of
Anglo-Saxon families in the Ottawa Valley. It
publishes no newsletter)

THE QUEBEC FAMILY HISTORY SOCIETY, Box 1026, Pointe
Claire P.O., Pointe Claire, Québec H9S 4H9
Established: 1977/78
Still in general process of organization at time of
this listing.

SOCIÉTÉ D'HISTOIRE ET DE GÉNÉALOGIE DE RIVIERE-DU-LOUP,
55 rue de Rocher, Riviere-du-Loup
No information available

<u>SOCIÉTÉ DE GÉNÉALOGIE DE QUÉBEC</u>, C.P. 2234, Québec City, Québec, G1K 7N8

Established: 1961
Publications: "L'Ancêtre" (journal)
Library: c 300 vols. located at 537, boulevard Charest Est, Québec

<u>SOCIÉTÉ GÉNÉALOGIQUE CANADIENNE-FRANÇAISE</u>, C.P. 335, Place d'Armes, Montréal, Québec, H2X 3H1

(Note: this is the largest Quebec genealogical society - one of the largest in Canada)
Established: 1943
Publications: "Memoires" (quarterly journal since 1944) also "Le Mois généalogique" for 1948-60. Also publish "Complément au Dictionnaire Tanguay" (3 vols) plus many off-prints and special publications.
Library: Extensive genealogical library for members only located at 6515, rue St-Denis, Montréal, containing hundreds of family histories, parish and local histories, etc. Also maintains a 2,000,000 card index to Quebec marriages and has all published marriage "répertories" and others in manuscript form covering most regions of Quebec plus French parishes in Ontario, New England and Louisiana.

<u>SOCIÉTÉ GÉNÉALOGIQUE DES CANTONS DE L'EST</u>, C.P. 635, Sherbrooke, Québec, J1H 5K5

Established: 1968
Publications: No regular publication. However, society has published marriage repertories for counties Sherbrooke, Compton, Stanstead, Richmond, Wolfe, Mégantic, Arthabaska and south half of Frontenac, and are undertaking the collecting of marriage records to publish additional repertories for Nicolet and Drummond counties (Later intend to collect births and deaths for these areas).
Library: c 500 vols., primarily marriage repertories and local, town and parish histories

SOCIÉTÉ GÉNÉALOGIQUE TRIFLUVIENNE, 839 rue Richard,
Trois-Rivières
No information available

SASKATCHEWAN

SASKATCHEWAN GENEALOGICAL SOCIETY, Box 1894, Regina,
Saskatchewan, S4P 0A0
Established: 1969
Publications: "S.G.S. Bulletin" (quarterly
journal)
Library: c 400 vols.
Branchs: Saskatoon, Moose Jaw, Regina,
RM 3 & 33

U. S. A.

AMERICAN-CANADIAN GENEALOGICAL SOCIETY, c/o Edgar
Geoffrion, 138 Kimball St., Manchester, New Hampshire,
03103
Established: 1973
Publications: "Bulletin" (journal, twice per year)
(Note: this society serves genealogists interested
in ancestries of Canadian origin)

There are also many other societies to which genealogists may turn for assistance, including local and provincial historical societies, local and national cultural
organizations, special museums and other organizations,
etc. Many of these are listed in fairly accessible directories, a list of which is included in Chapter 3-1. Other
organizations which may be beneficial to genealogical researchers will also be found listed in Chapter 5 under the
various provincial headings.

2:4 L.D.S. RECORDS
AND LIBRARIES

The largest and most active genealogical organization in the world is the Genealogical Society of Utah (formerly the Genealogical Society Department of the Church of Jesus Christ of Latter-Day Saints) with headquarters in Salt Lake City, Utah. Through this organization, a tremendous number of original records of genealogical value have been micro-filmed in virtually every major country in the world and have been made available for examination by researchers in their large genealogical library in Salt Lake City, and in their numerous branch libraries located throughout North America and elsewhere. Due to the extensive collections of microfilmed and other compiled records, no research into an ancestry can be regarded as complete until the material con-tained in this library has been examined or checked for any reference to an ancestor or ancestors.

The Society itself was founded 13 November 1894 in Salt Lake City primarily to assist members of the Church of Jesus Christ of Latter-Day Saints, more widely known as Mormons, in researching their own particular family back-grounds. Genealogy to Mormons everywhere is far more than just a fascinating hobby, it is an integral part of their religious doctrine which holds that family relationships are not just restricted to our earthly existance but, in fact, are eternal and continue beyond the grave. In order to verify ancestral relationships so that the family may be united generation by generation in the here-after, Mormons are encouraged to - and do - actively search out their ind-ividual genealogies and then submit the names they find for processing at various LDS temples so that a record exists of all such ancestral relationships. This devotion was a prime reason for the establishment of the Genealogical Socity of Utah, which derives its operating funds largely from the Mormon Church although some funding is obtained through gifts and bequests to the Society. Everyone invo-lved in genealogy, whether Mormon or non-Mormon, however, has come to recognize and appreciate the tremendous efforts of the Genealogical Society in gathering and making access-ible to all, the records so definately needed to research an ancestry.

The Genealogical Society's activities can largely be defined as covering three main areas: their extensive mic-rofilming and information gathering programs; the operation of their large genealogical library in Salt Lake City; and the operation of their numerous branch libraries.

MICROFILMING PROGRAM

The microfilming program, designed to record and preserve important records relating to individuals and their
relationships, can be said to be the primary base on which
all other activities of the Society are built.

In 1977 the Society was actively involved in over 30
separate countries microfilming their various genealogical
records. In all, over 80 microfilm cameras were kept continuously busy photographing every conceivable record of
genealogical value including parish registers, marriage and
probate records, census returns, deeds, land grants, cemetery records and many others. Since this program began in
the late 1930s, a grand total of close to one million reels
of microfilm (each of which is 80-100' in length) have been
produced. These films are equivalent to a library containing over 4,000,000 printed volumes of 300 pages each.
Through the activities of their work crews, approximately
4000 rools of microfilm are added to this already massive
collection every month.

After each roll of film has been exposed, it is sent
to the Society in Salt Lake City, where it is processed and
the resulting microfilm negative stored in the unique
Granite Mountain Records Vault, built by the Mormon Church
in the mountains southeast of Salt Lake City to protect
this valuable collection. Located seven hundred feet ben-
eath a mountain of solid granite, these storage vaults
ensure that the microfilmed records housed there will be
fully protected from any major calamity and that the conditions they are preserved in will ensure their longevity.
Positive copies of these negative microfilms are made here
and all unrestricted film positives are made available to
the public at the genealogical library in Salt Lake City,
or at the various branch libraries. In addition to the
microfilm collection, interviewers are collecting oral
genealogies from the native peoples of the South Pacific,
where written records are of fairly recent orgin. Over
500 hours have been gathered so far and the work is still
continuing.

The chart on the following page will better illustrate
the extent of the microfilm collections for various
countries (Source: "The Genealogical Society of Utah" -
Salt Lake City, Utah 1976, p 2). Microfilming programs are
still continuing in many of the countries contained in this
chart, as well as in some countries which are not.

Countries with more than
50,000 microfilm reels. -

Denmark
France
Germany
Great Britain
Mexico
Netherlands.
Sweden
United States

20,000-50,000 reels

Belgium

10,000-20,000 reels

Canada
Finland
Poland

1,000-10,000 reels

Argentina
Australia
Austria
Chile
China
Guatamala
Hungary

1,000-10,000 reels cont.

Ireland, Republic of
Italy
Japan
Korea
Norway
Pacific Islands
Switzerland

Fewer than 1,000 reels

Bahamas
Brazil
Caribbean
Costa Rica
Czechoslovakia
Hong Kong
Iceland
Luxembourg
Macao
New Zealand
Panama
Philippines
Portugal
Singapore
South Africa
Spain
U.S.S.R.

GENEALOGICAL LIBRARY

The administrative offices and genealogical library of the Society occupy 14,200 square metres (153,000 square feet) of space in the 28 story office building of the Church of Jesus Christ of Latter-Day Saints at 50 East North Temple Street in Salt Lake City. The library itself occupies 4 complete floors and is open to the public, without charge, every day of the week except Sundays.

This library serves over 3500 patrons each day which include, in addition to family historians, scholars in the fields of history, economics, genetics, demongraphy, and medicine. To assist the researchers in fully utilizing the resources of the library, a large staff of consultants trained in the languages, history, customs, and handwriting of most countries and cultures represented in the microfilm collection is available.

Although the microfilm collection forms the real basis for the library, researchers will also find over 150,000 volumes of reference books of all descriptions, including large numbers of biographies, local and family histories,

and other aids. The library also subscribes to more than
1700 periodical publications of special interest to the
genealogist. The microfilms themselves can be viewed on
any one of more than 250 microfilm reading machines located
strategically throughout the library.

In addition to the microfilm and book collections, the
library also houses a number of indexes and other aids to
facilitate researchers, including:

FAMILY GROUP RECORDS ARCHIVES AND FOUR-GENERATION PROGRAM RECORDS

This collection contains over 8 million
separate family group records compiled by
members of the Mormon Church. The
information in this collection is
recorded on standardized forms and
filed in post binders in alphabetical
order by the husband's surname. In
addition to fairly complete information
on each person in a family, sources from
which the information was extracted is
also provided for convenience in returning
to the original records.

TEMPLE RECORDS INDEX BUREAU (TIB)

This collection of over 30 million cards
represents the names that have been processed by LDS temples from 1842 to 1969,
and contains much information on Church
members and their ancestors. Only trained
library personnel have access to this file
although anyone can request a search for
individual names on a special request slip.

COMPUTER FILE INDEX (CFI)

This is a computer index to the names submitted for processing in LDS temples since
1970, in addition to material gathered from
the library's name extraction program. This
extraction program is basically the systematic
extraction and recording of names appearing
in various parish registers in many countries
of the world. At present, more than 35,000,000
names are to be found in this special index,
which is available for examination either on
microfilm or on computer print-out.

Other special services of the library have also been
established to assist researchers in their genealogical
pursuits. Some of these include:

Research Papers: These specially-prepared
briefs provide timely and informative data
on the available genealogical records in
many foriegn countries in addition to
fairly comprehensive discussions of some
specific types of records in selected
countries. They are available from General
Church Distribution Center, 1999 West
1700 South, Salt Lake City, Utah 84104, USA.

Photocopy Facilities: Photocopy machines
for both film and books are located throughout the library.

Researchers: A list of accredited professional researchers is maintained by the
library for those wishing to contact and
hire a qualified person to conduct research
for them. A copy of this list is available
on request. State the province, state or
country in which the research is to be done
when requesting a copy.

Other pamphlets and information on the library and its
services may be obtained by writing:

> Reference
> Genealogical Department
> 50 East North Temple
> Salt Lake City, Utah 84150, U.S.A.

BRANCH LIBRARIES

To make the material contained in the Genealogical
Library at Salt Lake City even more accessible to researchers throughout the United States, Canada, and other countries, the Genealogical Society has established more than
260 (1977) branch libraries, with new ones being established every year. These libraries may be used by anyone
interested in genealogical research.

These branches are staffed and supported by local
members of the LDS Church and are usually housed in two
rooms of a local LDS Church building. Each library contains a select group of genealogical books and films,
several microfilm readers, and a microfilm copy of the
card catalogue of the library in Salt Lake City. Microfilms can then be borrowed from Salt Lake City through a
special interlibrary loan arrangement and used by the

researcher in or near his city of residence. A small handling fee to cover incidental costs is paid at the time the films are ordered.

There are a number of these branch libraries located in Canada. They are situated at: (BGL = Branch Genealogical Library):

Calgary Alberta BGL: 2021-17th Ave. SW, Calgary, Alberta T2T 0G2 (Phone: 403-244-5910) (Mailing Address: same)

Cardston Alberta BGL: 348 Third St., W, Cardston, Alberta (Phone: 403-653-3288) (Mailing Address: P.O. Box 839, Cardston, Alberta TOK OKO)

Edmonton Alberta STAKE BGL: 9010-85 St., Edmonton, Alberta (Mailing Address: 9211-82 St., Edmonton, Alberta T6C 2X4)

Lethbridge Alberta BGL: Stake Center, 2410-28th St., S, Lethbridge, Alberta (Phone: 403-328-0206) (Mailing Address: 321-27th St. S, Lethbridge, Alberta T1J 3R7

Vancouver B.C. Stake BGL: Stake Center, 5280 Kincaid, Burnaby, B.C. (Phone: 604-299-8656) (Mailing Address: P.O. Box 82081, N. Burnaby, B.C. V5C 5P2)

Vernon B.C. Stake BGL: Kelowna Ward, Glenmore and Ivans St., Kelowna, B.C. (Mailing Address: P.O. Box 1508, Kelowna, B.C. V1Y 7V8)

Hamilton Ontario Stake BGL: Stake Center, 701 Stonechurch Rd. E, Hamilton, Ontario (Phone: 416-385-5009) (Mailing Address: Box 4425, Station D, Upper Gage Avenue, Hamilton, Ont.)

Toronto Ontario BGL: 95 Melbert St., Etobicoke, Ontario (Phone: 416-621-4607) (Mailing Address: Box 247, Etobicoke, Ontario)

As well, it should also be pointed out that in 1977 branch libraries were pending in the following places:

Cranbrook, B.C.   Saskatoon, Sask.
London, Ontario   Taber, Alberta
Ottawa, Ontario

Although the Genealogical Society of Utah does not have every genealogical record in the world, they do have considerably more than any other single organization. For this reason, this tremendous resource should NEVER be overlooked when searching for your ancestors.

2:5 GENEALOGICAL PUBLISHING COMPANIES

One thing which is most evident in genealogical research is that the more you know, the more you will find that
you do not know. Although this can be rather exasperating
to any researcher, it can be particularly discouraging at
first to the "budding" genealogist. However, there are a
number of publishing companies and special interest periodicals now available which are helping to fill the large gaps
in genealogical knowledge. Several publishers particularly
devoted to publishing or re-printing genealogical or genealogically related books are:

Cumming Atlas Reprints
Box 23
Stratford, Ontario N5A 6S8
(This company is primarily involved in the
reprinting of the Ontario county atlases of
the 19th century although they do issue
other books of interest to researchers.)

Editions Elysée
P.B. 188 Station Côte St-Luc
Montréal, Québec H4V 2Y4
(This company specializes in reprints of
important French language historical and
genealogical publications.)

Mika Publishing Company
Box 536
Belleville, Ontario K8N 5B2
(This company reprints important historical
and genealogical publications mainly relating
to Ontario, Quebec and the Maritimes. It is
the largest publisher of genealogical reprints
in Canada.)

Wheatfield Press
Box 205, St. James Postal Station
Winnipeg, Manitoba R3J 3R4
(This company publishes the Canadian
Genealogical Handbook, as well as publish-
ing and distributing other books, aids and
genealogical forms)

In addition to these publishers, there are a number of individuals in the province of Quebec who publish or distribute "marriage répertoiries", which are indispensible to those researchers who are working on a Quebec ancestry. The names and addresses of these individuals including the regions of Quebec covered by their publications are listed in Chapter 3-13.

Genealogical periodicals can be of particular value to researchers, providing up-to date information about various sources through the articles contained in them and offering researchers the opportunity to have "queries" or advertisements printed in which they can outline specific problems they are having with particular ancestors in the hope that other readers may be able to assist them. Virtually all the genealogical societies in Canada publish a journal or newsletter which provides these services to their members (see Chapter 2-3). As well, there are several other privately published periodicals of this type which are of particular interest to Canadian researchers. They are:

"Acadian Genealogy Exchange"
863 Wayman Branch Road
Covington, Kentucky 41015, U.S.A.

"French Canadian and Acadian Genealogical
    Review"
J. Roland Auger, Editor
Box 845, Upper Town
Quebec City, Quebec

"The Genealogical Helper"
The Everton Publishers
P.O. Box 368
Logan, Utah 84321, U.S.A.
(This is perhaps the largest general
periodical of this type in North
America. Everton also publishes a
wide variety of genealogical books,
aids and forms.)

"Lost in Canada? Canadian-American Query
    Exchange"
Joy Reisinger, Publisher
1020 Central Avenue
Sparta, Wisconsin 54656, U.S.A.

In recent years, many out-of-print or unpublished books and family histories in addition to newspapers, journals, reports, etc have been made available to researchers on microfilm by companies specializing in this type of "publishing". A few of the companies offering these services include:

Bell & Howell, Micro Photo Division
Old Mansfield Road
Wooster, Ohio 44691, U.S.A.

Micro Media Ltd.
Box 34, Station S
Toronto, Ontario M5M 4L6

University Microfilms International
300 North Zeeb Road
Ann Arbor, Michigan 48106, U.S.A.

The United States also has a large number of publishing companies which are largely devoted to producing genealogical books. The companies in the following list are some of the better known distributors of genealogical publications in the U.S., although some of them also publish their own works:

Deseret Book Company
P.O. Box 659
Salt Lake City, Utah 84110, U.S.A.
(This company publishes and distributes numerous genealogical books and forms.)

The Genealogical Publishing Co, Inc.
111 Water Street
Baltimore, Maryland 21202, U.S.A.
(Publishers of reprints of rare out-of-print books of a genealogical nature. They are the largest reprint publishers dealing with genealogical works.)

Genealogists' Bookshelf
Box 468
New York, New York 10028, U.S.A.
(This company distributes a number of general genealogical publications of particular interest to beginners.)

General Church Distribution Center
Church of Jesus Christ of Latter Day Saints
1999 West 1700 South
Salt Lake City, Utah 84104, U.S.A.
(This is the Publications Division of the
Genealogical Department of the Mormon Church.
They publish and distribute a large number of
aids for their church members including an
extremely good series of short research
reports on the extent of available genealogical
sources in many countries of North and South
America, Europe and Asia. They are invaluable
as a quick reference and are quite inexpensive.)

Polyanthos
Drawer 51359
New Orleans, Louisiana 70151, U.S.A.
(This company publishes a number of publications
of interest to researchers in Quebec and the
Maritimes.)

Stevenson's Genealogical Center
230 West 1230 North
Provo, Utah 84601, U.S.A.
(This company distributes a wide variety of
books, forms and other aids for genealogical
research.)

Of course, there are many other companies which publish and distribute genealogical publications. The names
and addresses of these can generally be found in such periodicals as the "Genealogical Helper" or in a latest edition of Books in Print, which can be found in local libraries.

In addition to book publishers, researchers should not
overlook the possibility of locating useful publications in
used book stores, many of which operate a mail order service.

3
GENEALOGICAL RECORDS IN CANADA

3:1 COMPILED SOURCES AND NEWSPAPERS

COMPILED SOURCES

In historical and genealogical research there are two types of sources generally referred to, namely, primary and secondary sources. A primary source is one which is a record of the first entry, or the first time the information has been recorded, and is usually found in manuscript or handwritten form. Examples include: diaries, original deeds, letters, birth and death records, etc., all of which were written at the time the event happened by someone who was acquainted with the event. Secondary sources are those which have been compiled from or derived from primary sources, including: transcripts or handwritten copies of original documents, compiled histories and genealogies, etc. There is chance of error in secondary sources caused by typographical error when being printed or misrepresentation or misinterpretation by the transcriber or author. Therefore, when dealing with secondary material it is necessary to check all information with the primary records from which it was taken whenever possible to ensure absolute accuracy.

All compiled sources are secondary and those of importance to genealogists can be classified into the following types: Family histories and genealogies;Local histories; Biographical works; genealogical and historical periodicals; and compiled lists (directories, catalogues, etc.).

Family histories and compiled genealogies are most useful to researchers in providing clues to future sources, but must be thoroughly checked before any information in them can be used with any degree of certainty. This is necessitated by the fact that the number of really excellent genealogists are few. Compilers do not always use proper methods in their research thus leading to incorrect family connections. Generally, this inability to use proper procedures is a result of laziness in the researcher in following prescribed methods and proving all statements,or it may be the result of ignorance on the part of the compiler of record sources which are available and therefore, basing all conclusions on inaccurate or scanty, printed information. The expense of proper research may also be a factor in a compiled work's accuracy. As well, some people can be just plain bored with proper methods, may conduct their research sloppily, accepting a lineage which they "like" rather than properly checking it to make certain that it is correct.

When examining compiled genealogies it is important to carefully check the various sources which were used in their construction. If primary sources were used for the majority of the information there is a better chance of higher accuracy than if only secondary sources were used. Also, a higher degree of confidence can be placed in the work when the analysis of difficult problems are carefully and properly explained. However, despite how good a compiled work may seem, it is always best to check everything against the original primary source material. Just because it is "in the book" doesn't mean that it is necessarily correct.

Many local histories were compiled in the nineteenth and early twentieth centuries as much of the country became settled, or had been settled for a relatively short period of time. Most of these early histories contained extensive biographical sections which outlined the lives of the early pioneers of the area. Some of these biographies can be very accurate because the particular families involved provided the information used to compile them, while others are not so accurate for the same reason. These histories are very useful in providing a general history of the settlement of a local area although, once again, all information in the biographies should be thoroughly checked before being accepted as fact.

Biographical works contain many of the same general problems as are found in local histories. As a rule, people portrayed in them were prominent in the community which resulted in very few bad remarks being made of them. It is not often found that a biographical listing is absolutely correct.

Genealogical and historical periodicals come in many varied forms, and there are literally hundreds to choose from. Most libraries will probably subscribe to one or more of the important ones, but as a rule these publications provide only limited information. Articles cover a wide variety of topics: genealogies, local histories, bibliographies, source lists, etc. Some of these publications and articles will prove helpful, but the same cautions are extended to them as are to other compiled sources. Researchers should also be particularly careful in not spending too much time labouring over periodicals which may not yield any information of enough value to warrent the time involved.

The final category to be discussed here are the compiled lists. These primarily include lists of early settlers, pensioners, soldiers, immigrants, etc., made from original records, as a rule. These lists can be quite accurate because they are generally compiled by experienced persons but they can be subject to typographical errors generally found in all published materials.

FINDING AIDS

The various publications generally regarded as "finding aids" can prove to be the most useful of all. Their main purpose is to assist in locating the various records available. These publications can be broken down into three main areas: guides for establishing locality; guides for locating secondary data and guides for locating primary materials.

Locality identification can be a particular problem to the genealogist especially when the place being searched for has long since disappeared. This was quite a common occurance at one time when 'boom towns' could spring up anywhere and then disappear or become ghost towns within a short period of time. This is also true of places which have gone through periodic name changes in their histories, or of places which are unfamiliar to the researcher. The important thing is to find the place by using a variety of sources: atlases, gazeteers, postal directories, and other specialized locality sources. These publications will be discussed more completely in Chapter 3-6.

Also of tremendous importance are those aids which can help in locating secondary source locations which pertain to individual research problems. These mainly take the form of directories to libraries, newspapers, societies, cities, telephone users, and of bibliographies of published materials. All of these can answer the question of where a record may be located and can put the researcher in touch with a variety of potential sources.

A large number of guides to primary sources also exist for the benefit of the researcher. These are generally catalogues of archival collections and government documents and will prove very useful in locating the primary sources which are pertinent to individual research.

NEWSPAPERS

Newspapers can be a goldmine of information to researchers who are willing to take the time to search through them. Buried within their pages can be found obituaries, marriage and birth notices, probate court proceedings, notes of thanks, and numerous news items on the individuals of the community in which the paper was published.

Newspaper articles can sometimes provide the necessary information to conclude or continue research on an ancestor and should never be overlooked as a source. Many older newspapers as well as those published in smaller communities were often issued on a weekly basis and were quite 'gossipy' in their presentation. Their major concern was the people of the community.

A number of newspaper directories are available which are very helpful in locating where and when various newspapers were published and the present location of their files. When checking through these directories it is advisable to extend the search to the communities all around a known locality of an ancestor just in case the local weekly newspaper came from a nearby town rather the one in which the ancestor lived.

Once located, if the newspaper is still in operation it may be possible to find someone in the local area who will search the old files for the information desired, or the newspaper may conduct limited searches for a fee. If the newspaper no longer is published it will be necessary to write to the agency which now has it's files. Many of the older newspapers have now been microfilmed by the Canadian Library Association, who maintain a list of the completed newspapers at their Ottawa headquarters. These microfilmed copies can either be purchased from the Association or borrowed from other libraries and archives on inter-library loans.

One of the most useful newspaper articles is the obituary. It deserves the special attention of all researchers. It is frequently the obituary which can supply the information necessary to continue the research to another part of the country, or to the country where an ancestor was born. As the last piece of recorded information on an individual, an obituary quite often contains a short biographical sketch of a person's life and, as a rule, will provide much more information than can generally be found on a death certificate.

In some instances, the obituary may provide the only record of a person's death. Many archives and libraries will supply photocopies of obituaries from local newspapers for a small fee if they are provided with the name of the individual and the exact date of their death. This information can be obtained in most cases either from the appropriate death certificae or from family traditions and stories told by family members. No matter how it is done, the obituary is one record which is a must in all genealogical research.

The other articles often found in newspapers can be equally as enlightening as the obituary. Birth and marriage notices can contain the only reference to parents' names or of the event itself. Other articles can provide interesting glances into the day-to-day affairs of ancestors or into tragedies or successes which they encountered. However, unless specific dates of events and articles are known, it also involves a considerable amount of work in 'digging' through the newspapers, although it will all seem justified when the additional information shines new light onto some aspect of an ancestor's life.

BIBLIOGRAPHY

The following books are representative of the types to be found under the various categories of this section and are provided here as a guide to the researcher. Many other books of these types have been issued and will come to be known to the researcher through consulting some of the publications listed here.

BIOGRAPHIES

Biographical Society of Canada: <u>Prominent People of the Province of Quebec</u> 3 volumes (Montreal 1923-4)

<u>Biographies Canadiennes-Françaises</u> (Ottawa 1921; Montréal 1922)

<u>Biographies et portraits d'écrivains Canadiens</u> (Montréal 1913)

<u>Les biographies françaises d'Amérique</u> (Sherbrooke 1950)

British Columbia: <u>Pictorial and Biographical</u> 2 volumes (Montreal 1914)

Cameron, James J.: <u>Political Pictonians; the Men in the Legislative Council, Senate, House of Commons House of Assembly, 1767-1967</u> (Ottawa 1966)

<u>Canadian Biographical Dictionary and Portrait Gallery of Eminent and Self-Made Men. Quebec and Maritime Provinces</u> (Toronto 1881)

<u>Canadian Who's Who</u> (Toronto 1910-triennial)

Cohen, William (Ed.): <u>The Canadian Album: Men of Canada</u> 5 volumes (Brantford 1891-1896)

<u>A Cyclopedia of Canadian Biography, Being Chiefly Men of the Time</u> 2 volumes (Toronto 1866)

<u>Dictionary of Canadian Biography: Dictionnaire Biographique du Canada</u> edited by Alan Wilson and Andre Vachon (Toronto and Montréal 1966- major work on Canadian biographies)

Kerr, J.B.: <u>Biographical Dictionary of Well-Known British Columbians</u> (Vancouver 1890)

<u>Newfoundland's Who's Who</u> (St. John's 1952)

<u>Prominent People of the Maritime Provinces</u> (Saint John 1922)

<u>Prominent People of the Province of Ontario</u> (Ottawa 1925)

<u>Social Register of Canada</u> 3 volumes (Montreal 1958-61)

Tache, Louis-Joseph: <u>Men of the Day: A Canadian Portrait Gallery</u> 17 volumes (Montreal 1890)

Wallace, W. Stewart: <u>Macmillan Dictionary of Canadian Biography</u> (London and Toronto 1963; 2 volumes)

<u>Who's Who in Canada</u> (Toronto 1914; Biennial)

DIRECTORIES OF NEWSPAPERS AND PERIODICALS

Ayer Directory of Newspapers and Periodicals (Philade-
    lphia, annual publication)
Beaulieu, André and Hamelin, Jean: Les Journaux du
    Québec de 1764 a 1964 (Québec 1965)
Canadian Periodical Index (Ottawa 1928; Annual)
Graves, Eileen (Ed.): Ulrich's International Periodcals
    Directory (New York; Annual)
Gregory, Winnifred: American Newspapers 1821-1936; A
    Union List of Files Available in the United States
    and Canada (New York 1937)
Harper, J.R.: Historical Directory of New Brunswick
    Newspapers and Periodicals (Fredericton 1961)
List of Canadian Newspapers on Microfilm (Canadian
    Library Association, Ottawa)
MacDonald, Mary C.: Historical Directory of Saskatc-
    hewan Newspapers 1878-1950 (Saskatoon 1951)
Standard Periodical Directory (Lexington, New York)
Têtu, Horace: Historique des journaux de Québec
    (Québec 1875, 1889)
Titus, Eva Brown: Union List of Serials in Libraries
    of the United States and Canada (New York 1965)

DIRECTORIES OF LIBRARIES AND SOCIETIES

American Library Directory (New York; Annual)
Anderson, B.L.: Special Libraries and Information Cen-
    tres in Canada: A Directory (Canadian Library
    Association, Ottawa 1970)
Ash, Lee (Comp): Special Collections, A Guide to Special
    Book Collections and Subject Emphases as Reported
    by University, College, Public and Special Librar-
    ies in the United States and Canada (New York 1961)
Corpus Directory and Almanac of Canada (Toronto; Annual
    publication)
Directory of Historical Societies and Agencies in the
    United States and Canada (American Library Associ-
    ation, Nashville, Tennessee; Biennial publication)
Kruzas, Anthony: Directory of Special Libraries and
    Information Centres (Detroit 1963)
Land, Brian: Directory of Associations in Canada/Réper-
    toire des associations du Canada (Toronto 1974)
Markotic, V.: Ethnic Directory of Canada (Calgary)
Meyer, Mary (Ed.): Directory of Genealogical Societies
    in the United States and Canada (Baltimore 1976)

ALMANACS AND YEARBOOKS

Canadian Almanac and Directory (Toronto 1848-present;
     Annual)
Corpus Directory and Almanac of Canada (Toronto; Annual)
Statistics Canada: The Canada Year Book (Ottawa;
     Annual)
Yearbook of American and Canadian Churches (New York;
     Annual)

SELECT GUIDES TO PRIMARY SOURCES

Archives du Québec: L'État général des archives pub-
     liques et privées (Québec 1968)
New Brunswick Museum: Inventory of Manuscripts (Saint
     John 1967)
Public Archives of Canada: General Inventory: Manu-
     scripts (Ottawa, continuing series)
Public Archives of Canada: Public Records Division:
     General Inventory Series (Ottawa, continuing series)
Public Archives of Nova Scotia: Inventory of Manuscripts
     in the Public Archives of Nova Scotia (Halifax 1976)
Union List of Manuscripts in Canadian Repositories
     (Ottawa 1968), (1 volume)
Union List of Manuscripts in Canadian Repositories
     (Ottawa 1975, 2 volumes - supplement issued 1976,
     1 volume)

BIBLIOGRAPHIES

Aitkin, Barbara: Local Histories of Ontario Municipal-
     ities 1951-1977: A Bibliography (Ontario Library
     Association, Toronto 1978)
Beaulieu, André et Mosley, William: Histoires Locales
     et Regionales canadiennes des Origines á 1950: La
     Province de Québec (Toronto 1971)
Boyle, Gertrude M. (Ed.): Bibliography of Canadiana
     (Toronto 1960)
Canadiana (National Library of Canada, Ottawa 1962 -
     Periodical listing publications received by the
     National Library
Gregorovich, Andrew: Canadian Ethnic Groups Bibliog-
     raphy (Toronto 1972)
Halifax Library Association: Nova Scotia in Books,
     From the First Printing in 1752 to the Present
     Time (Halifax 1967)
Historical and Scientific Society of Manitoba: Local
     History in Manitoba (Winnipeg 1976)

Humanities Research Council of Canada: Canadian Grad-
     uate Theses in the Humanities and Social Sciences
     1921-46 (Ottawa 1951)
Kugsford, Wm.: The Early Bibliography of the Province
     of Ontario (Toronto 1892)
Lowther, Barbara J.: Bibliography of British Columbia:
     Laying the Foundations 1849-99 (Victoria 1968)
Mode, Peter G.: Source Book and Bibliographical Guide
     for American Church History (Boston 1964)
Morley, William: Canadian Local Histories to 1950: A
     Bibliography - Volume 1: The Atlantic Provinces
     (Toronto 1967)
Ontario Historical Studies Series: Ontario Since 1867:
     A Bibliography (Toronto 1973)
Peel, Bruce: A Bibliography of the Prairie Provinces to
     1953 (Toronto 1973)
Scott, Michael M.: A Bibliography of Western Canadian
     Studies Relating to Manitoba (Winnipeg 1967)
Simoneau, Gerald (Ed.): Canadian Books in Print (Tor-
     onto; Annual)
Tanghe, Raymond (Comp.): Bibliography of Canadian
     Bibliographies (Toronto 1960) (Supplements avail-
     able)
Thibault, Claude: Bibliographia Canadiana (Toronto
     1973)

GENEALOGICAL BIBLIOGRAPHIES:

Filby, P. William: American and British Genealogy and
     Heraldry (Chicago 1975, 2nd Edition)
Genealogy and Local History: An Archival and Bibliogr-
     aphical Guide (Evanston, Ill. 1959)
Roy, Antoine: "Bibliographie de généalogies et histoires
     des familles" Rapport de l'Archiviste de Québec
     1940-41 (Québec 1941)
Schreiner-Yantis, Netti: Genealogical Books in Print
     (Springfield, VA. 1975)
_____: Genealogical and Local History
     Books in Print (Springfield VA. 1976)
Varennes, Kathleen M. de: Annotated Bibliography of
     Genealogical Works in the Library of Parliament
     with Locations in other Libraries in Canada
     (Ottawa 1963)

CANADIAN GENEALOGICAL RESEARCH GUIDES

Auger, Roland-J.: "Tracing Ancestors through the Pro-
    vince of Quebec and Acadia to their place of origin
    in France" in French-Canadian and Acadian Genealog-
    ical Review (Volume 2 1969)
Baxter, Angus: In Search of Your Roots: A Guide for
    Canadians Seeking their Ancestors (Toronto 1978)
Grégoire, Jeanne: Guide du généalogist à la recherche
    de nos ancêtres (Montréal 1974) (for Quebec re-
    search)
Jonasson, Eric: The Canadian Genealogical Handbook
    (Winnipeg 1976, 1st Edition)
Keffer, Marion and Kirk, Robert and Audrey: Some Ref-
    erences and Sources for the Family Historian in
    the Province of Ontario (Ontario Genealogical
    Society, Toronto 1976)
Major Genealogical Record Sources for Canada, Genea-
    logical Department of Mormon Church, Research Paper,
    Series B, No. 3, 1972. (for French Canadian and
    Acadian research)

SELECT GENEALOGICAL PUBLICATIONS

Arsenault, Bona: L'Acadie des ancêtres; avec la généa-
    logie des premières familles acadiennes (Québec
    1955)
              : Histoire et généalogie des Acadiens
    (2 volumes) (Québec 1965)
Chadwich, Edward Marion: Ontarian Families-Genealogies
    of United Empire Loyalist and other Pioneer Families
    of Upper Canada (2 volumes), (Toronto 1894-98)
Godbout, Archange: Nos ancêtres au XVIIe Siecle, dict-
    ionnaire généalogique et bibliographique des famil-
    les canadiennes (5 volumes), (Québec 1952-60)
Institut Généalogique Drouin: Dictionnaire national des
    canadiens-français (Montréal 1958) (3 volumes)
Ontarian Genealogist and Family Historian (Toronto 1898-
    1901), (1 volume)
Tanguay, Cyprien: Dictionnaire généalogique des familles
    canadiennes (7 volumes), (Montréal 1871-90)

3:2 VITAL RECORDS

The primary concern of every researcher is to establish beyond any reasonable doubt the parentage of an ancestor or person. One of the best sources of parentage information are the records of birth, marriage and death, commonly referred to as the Vital Records. These can be broken down into two main groupings: a) Church Records, which are discussed in the following chapter, and b) Civil or Non-Church Records. As civil records are a rather recent innovation, they may not apply to every researcher's particular family, but where they do exist, they are an essential part of any research program.

The development of Civil Records throughout the world has been a very slow process, and particularly so in North America. One of the earliest systems in Europe was established in France in 1792 with the secularization of the Clergy and, through the Napoleanic conquests, spread to several countries nearby. The English system of civil registration began in July 1837, primarily the result of the cholera epidemic of 1831-32. As with many early systems, its principle function was to provide a record of deaths resulting from the various diseases prevalent at that time.

The earliest complete system of civil registration in Canada was begun in Ontario in 1869. Over the next 50 years, the remaining provinces of Canada slowly established their own procedures for recording vital records. Unlike Great Britain, which has a national repository for all vital records in the country, civil registration in Canada is a provincial responsibility with each province maintaining its own vital records department and system. Therefore, if several ancestors each died in a different province, for example, it is necessary to write to each province for the death records of the people who died there. The names and addresses of these provincial agencies are listed by province in Chapter 5.

TYPES OF RECORDS

Civil registration is basically restricted to the recording of births, marriages and deaths, although there are other records which could technically be classified under the general heading of vital records. The following desc-

riptions will provide researchers with a brief summary of
the extent of information to be found in the various civil
records.

BIRTH RECORDS: Birth records contain the
name of the child, date and place of birth,
parents' names, their ages, residences and
occupations. In some provinces, restrictions
have been placed on these records, allowing
only the persons concerned and their parents
the right to obtain copies of the original
records. This aspect should be explored by
the researcher before requesting a birth
record of a person who is a distant ancestor.

MARRIAGE RECORDS: Marriage records, as a
rule, will provide more information on one
form than the birth records although they
too have their restrictions in some provinces. Generally they contain the names of
the couple, the date and place of marriage,
sometimes their ages, witnesses, the person
conducting the ceremony, the names of
parents of each, and the residences of the
couple. Copies of these records are often
restricted to only the couple concerned,
their parents, or their children.

DEATH RECORDS: Of all vital records, perhaps the death record provides the greatest
wealth of information to the genealogist.
On one form, the entire life of the individual can be laid out for examination, and
there are no restrictions of any kind as to
who may receive copies. This allows the
death records of uncles, cousins or other
more distant relatives to be collected with
ease, possibly uncovering other previously
inaccessable or unknown information. Death
records generally include: the name of the
deceased, date and place of birth or age,
date and place of death, occupation, name
and residence of the informant, sometimes
date and place of burial, sometimes cause
of death, sometimes parents' names, sometimes parents' place of birth. Generally
speaking, this record should be obtained
first when investigating the life of an
ancestor who is deceased. Many times it
will supply the information necessary to
check other records.

OTHER RECORDS: Some of the other records which could be classified as vital records include those relating to divorce or separation, adoptions, and name changes. However, these actions are primarily the responsibilities of the courts in each province and more information regarding their extent and availability should be obtained from the respective provincial Attorney-General's Departments early in the course of research. It should be pointed out that in most provinces these records are classified as very confidential and may not be available to researchers.

As a rule, the contents of the various documents will vary according to the date of the event. Earlier records always contain less information than is now required. Some of the other problems likely to be encountered are:

- place of birth on death records listed simply as "Canada" or "Ontario" rather than a more specific location.

- illegible handwriting and misspelled names (expecially on older records).

- the fact that although, registration was compulsory in a particular province, the registration of the particular event never took place.

- some records have been destroyed or damaged due to inadequate storage.

In cases where the time of an event pre-dates civil registration in a province or where the event was not registered, it will be necessary to consult other records for proof of the event. The next-best reliable source are the records of the various churches, which are discussed in the following chapter. However, there are also a number of other types of records which can be "substituted" for civil certificates, including cemetery records (see chapter 3:3), obituaries in newspapers (chapter 3:1), and wills and probate records (chapter 3:5). Approximate birth dates can also be determined from census records (chapter 3:4), or any other source which provides the age of an ancestor at a given time. With the exception of the civil records and the church records, which tend to be quite reliable, caution should be exercised by researchers in completely accepting the information contained in other records.

LOCATING CIVIL RECORDS

As mentioned earlier, civil registration is a provincial responsibility and each province maintains its
own department responsible for compiling and recording
vital records within its area of jurisdiction. When
writing to the provincial agency it is not necessary
(or helpful) to provide a detailed long explanation of
how you are related to the person whose record you wish
to obtain. In all cases, be precise and short. This
will enable the order to be processed with a minimum of
trouble to the agency and yourself. There are many provinces which require all requests for vital records to be
made on their own special forms, which can be obtained by
writing to the agency beforehand, although some will answer written requests.

The following example is illustrative of the type of
written request appreciated by the vital records Staff:

Dear Sir:

Please send me a copy of the DEATH CERTIFICATE
of the following person:

NAME: William Jones
DIED: 22 August 1922
PLACE: Exeter, Huron County, Ontario
PARENTS' NAMES: Unknown
WIFE'S NAME: Mary Jones (nee Evens)
MY RELATIONSHIP TO PERSON NAMED: Nephew
REASON CERTIFICATE REQUIRED: For Family Records

Please find enclosed $0.00 to cover the cost of
the above. Thank you for your assistance.

Researchers should note that the Province of Quebec
did not institute civil registration until 1926 although
they have the most complete system of vital records in
Canada, dating back to 1621. Prior to 1926 (and continuing
even today) the churches in the province deposited a second
copy of their parish registers at the local court house,
which serves as a local vital statistics office. Also
located there are the registers of people who professed no
religious convictions. This system is discussed more completely in following chapters of this book.

The addresses of the provincial vital records offices
along with pertinent information on the extent of their records are included under the respective provinces in chapter
5.

OTHER CIVIL RECORDS

Before the advent of complete civil registration in
Canada there were various civil registration plans on a
local or limited basis throughout the country. In Ontario
and the Maritime Provinces, in particular, many records
of births, deaths and marriages covering various periods
of time were kept in the local town or township minutes,
and should not be overlooked when researching in these
areas. These records are presently deposited in the various provincial archives or are still retained in their
respective county, town or municipality. An enquiry to
these places will determine if such records exist for an
area where an ancestor lived, and the proper procedure
required to have them searched for a specific event can
be explained. However, this type of system was not kept
or has not survived for all areas. Nevertheless, it is
worthwhile checking on the chance that they were.

The Upper Canada and Lower Canada Marriage Bonds located at the Public Archives of Canada (see Chapter 4)
are another excellent source of pre-civil registration
records. These bonds were required to be posted prior to
the issuing of a marriage license (as security) and are,
therefore, not positive proof that the marriage took place
although in most cases this occurred within a few days or
weeks of the bond. In Upper Canada, they cover the period
1803 - 1845, and in Lower Canada, 1818 - 1867. The information shown on the bond consists of the names of the be-
trothed, the residence of the groom and possibly his occupation. Generally, the parents' names are not indicated.
These records are quite important in establishing an approximate date and place of marriage (to enable further
research to be conducted) and in finding the maiden name
of the bride. The records are indexed alphabetically by
the groom's surname on a yearly basis.

In addition to the Marriage Bonds, a considerable number of Marriage Contracts exist for Quebec and Acadian
families. These are very useful documents, constituting
an agreement to marry between two people sworn before a
Notary. Located now in the various court houses and
archives in Quebec, they are quite complete, extending
back into the 17th Century. A detailed discussion of their
contents is included in Chapter 3 - 13.

3:3 CHURCH AND CEMETERY RECORDS

Church and cemetery records constitute the largest under-used source of information in genealogical research, primarily due to the problems attached to determining the religious denomination of an ancestor and then in locating the records of the exact church to which he belonged.

In the previous chapter, we reviewed the problems of civil records, specifically their recent origin and the restrictions placed on obtaining copies of birth and marriage records. Church records, on the other hand, are quite the reverse. While there is some problem associated with 'missing' or destroyed records, they can predate civil registration in parts of Canada by hundreds of years, and there are virtually no restrictions on who may obtain copies or transcripts of the records. The major problem in their use is locating the present 'resting place' of the registers of interest to a researcher. Unlike the civil system of registration which is centralized in one location, church registers are scattered throughout each province and from one end of the country to the other. They can be found in provincial archives, local libraries, universities, religious archives, local parishes or in the hands of individuals. As a result, many people do not spend the time which they should in locating these records, and they are the losers for it! These are the only major records pre-dating civil registration which can be classified as an accurate source of vital information and should never be overlooked. In addition, they can greatly supplement civil records by providing information which was not required by the civil authorities at the time of the event. For example; parents' names on death certificates, etc. Research is not complete unless every effort has been made to examine this source.

HISTORICAL BACKGROUND

The first religious group to come to what is now Canada was the Recollet Order of the Roman Catholic Church, who established themselves at Quebec City in 1614. With them was laid the foundation of the predominance of the Roman Catholic Church in Quebec records, continuing to the present day. Their influence gradually spread to other areas of Canada as they opened for settlement, and at the

present time they constitute the largest single denomination in the country.

The Protestant Churches were later in establishing
themselves in Canada, primarily because of France's
sovereigncy over the country until 1763. The Anglican
Church, the first major protestant denomination in Canada,
was established 1701-06 in Newfoundland, 1749-50 at
Halifax in Nova Scotia, and 1744 in Prince Edward Island.
With the British conquest of Canada in 1760, a rudimentary
establishment of the Anglican Church was made in Quebec,
further strengthened by the Loyalist migrations of 1783,
although for the most part Quebec is considered as almost
the exclusive territory of the Roman Catholic Church. The
Loyalist migrations also herald the advent of Anglicanism
in Ontario, New Brunswick, and Cape Breton Island.

As a rule, the other protestant denominations followed
the Anglican Church. The Lutheran Church was established
in Nova Scotia in 1752, the Presbyterian and Baptist denominations both following circa 1761. By 1780, the Methodists
had also arrived. Literally all these groups had located
themselves in Ontario and Quebec prior to the Constitutional Act of 1791, to a greater or lesser degree. In Western
Canada, the missionary organizations of the Roman Catholic,
Anglican, Methodist, and Presbyterian Churches were operating by 1850.

There have been numerous books written on the histories of the various denominations which should be consulted
in order to ascertain whether or not a particular denomination was active in a given area of the country, before
spending much time locating its' church records there. However, the above brief synopsis will give an idea of the
general time span in Canada covered by the major churches.

TYPES OF RECORDS

Churches generated a considerable number of various
types of records, all designed to keep track of their
members' numbers and movements. Of this multitude, the
more important from the genealogist's point of view are:

GENERAL REGISTERS

These contain the lists of Baptisms, Marriages and Burials;
lists of Communicants and the Membership Lists; and the
lists of those people confirmed into the Church.

RECORDS OF REMOVAL OR ARRIVAL

These document the removal or arrival of members to or
from another congregation, although they tend to be
generally incomplete.

VESTRY MINUTES AND PROCEEDINGS

These contain some items such as Poor, Orphan and
Illegitimate Childrens' Records kept by the Church;
lists of Donors to the Church; some information which
is generally found in Civil Court Records; brief notations on particular events in the lives of Church
Members; sometimes Biographical material on Church
members, etc.

General registers will probably supply the majority
of information usually sought by the researcher. Here
are documented the vital records so important in proving
the line of descent of a family. The following list illustrates the type of information which is likely to be found
in each type of record in this category. However, the actual content of a document will vary from church to church
and from time to time, with the best and more complete information to be found in the more recent records:

BAPTISMAL RECORDS

These contain name, date of baptism, date of birth
or age, parents' names, sponsors' names (Godparents),
place of baptism, place of birth, minister's name,
and sometimes some notes.

CONFIRMATION RECORDS

These contain name, minister, date and place of
confirmation, age, father's or parents' names,
sometimes some notes.

COMMUNICANT AND MEMBERSHIP LISTS

These contain names, a date and location of the
church, sometimes the minister's name, sometimes
a note on a member or communicant. (These are
periodic lists compiled to show the membership
of the church at a given time or those who
received communion on a particular date.)

MARRIAGE RECORDS

These contain names of the couple, date and place of
marriage, ages, sometimes their places of residence,
minister's name, sometimes the names of the couples'
parents.

Record of Baptisms on the Rideau Circuit

Name of Child	Name of Parents & Where born	When Baptised	When born	By Whom Baptised
Nathaniel	Son of Nathaniel & [...] Whitehead	Wdry 8 Oct 1829	30 Nov 1829	Revd S. Waldron
Jennet	Daughter of John & Cornelia Riddell	22 Nov 1829	4 Oct 1829	by do
Almeda	Daughter of William & Rebecca Fairweather	Wedly 16 Sept 1829	9 Dec 1829	do — do
Isabella	Daughter of do	do 15 Oct 1829	9 Dec 1829	do — do
Susanna McCauley Gray	Daughter of John Wolford 26 June 1829	17 Aug 1830	do — do
Lucea	Son of John and Elizabeth [...] Montague	1829	2 Aug 1830	do — do

RECORD OF BAPTISMS ON THE RIDEAU CIRCUIT

Source: MG 9, D7-12 (Rideau Methodist Circuit)
(Courtesy of the Public Archives of Canada)

BURIAL RECORDS

These contain the name, date of death, place of death,
age or birthdate, date and place of burial, wife's or
parents' names, sometimes cause of death or other
notations, minister's name.

RECORDS OF ARRIVAL OR REMOVAL

These contain the name, date of arrival or removal,
congregation arriving from or going to; sometimes
some notations on the people.

Once it has been determined that a Church Record must
be used in order to prove a particular event in an ancestor's life, it is necessary to approach the problem in
two parts: (1) The denomination of the ancestor must be
determined. This can be accomplished by one of several
means. In some cases, the present affiliation of the researcher may be the answer. However, other sources may
assist in this search such as family traditions, the
national origin of the ancestor, a bequest in a will, or
a deed, a notation in an obituary, or a listing of religious affiliation on a census document. One aspect to remember, particularly when an ancestor was an original pioneer to an area, is that perhaps his initial affiliation
was determined by what church first located in the community. In many pioneer settlements there was only one
church which all the settlers attended irrespective of
their beliefs. As the settlement grew and more churches
of varying denominations moved into the district, the
congregation of the original pioneer church gradually
diminished, with its' communicants joining the churches
of their original persuasions. Therefore, the records of
an ancestor may be located in a church other than the one
which he may eventually have belonged to.

(2) The records of the particular church must be located.
As mentioned earlier, this is the major problem in using
church records. Once the denomination of the church and
the history of it and other churches in a locality has
been obtained from various sources (i.e., Local Histories)
the first thing to do is to contact the specific church
of that denomination in the area of interest. This can
be done by checking through the current telephone books
of the area. If that fails to produce results, the central
archives or the diocese office of that religious group
should be contacted as well as local, provincial and national archives and libraries to see what help they can
be. Advertisements placed in local newspapers may yield
records which are now in private hands. In addition to
these, it is advantageous to check old directories, lists,
maps, etc. to locate the exact positions of the churches

in an area at a given time so that a proper assessment of the most probable church an ancestor may have belonged to can be conducted. These may also help in determining if a local church was on a "circuit", that is, if it was served from another church nearby, in which case the records will probably be in the parent church. This system was used extensively by the Methodists.

Before discussing cemetery records, there is one aspect of church history in Canada which should be understood by all researchers. During the early period of the protestant churches in Canada, there was a considerable power struggle between the Anglican Church and the other Protestant denominations. Since the Anglican Church was the officially recognized church of England, it was granted special priveledges not acquired by the others. One of these priviledges was a monopoly on marriage by license. Laws to this effect were passed in Nova Scotia in 1758, New Brunswick in 1784, Ontario in 1792, and Prince Edward Island in 1803. In the Maritimes, due to the insufficient numbers of Anglican Clergy, Justices of the Peace were allowed to perform marriage ceremonies if no "recognized" clergy were available. Gradually, the right to marry was extended to the ministers of other denominations until, by 1834, all clergy in the Maritimes had this priviledge. A similar development took place in Ontario resulting in the right to solemnize marriage by all clergy in 1831. However, up until 1859 all non-Anglican clergy were required to obtain certificates of marriage from the Justices of the Peace before they could conduct the marriage ceremony. Therefore, it is quite likely that many ancestors who were married during this period may be found in the local Anglican parish register (regardless of their denomination) or a record of their marriage license found in the records of the local Justices of the Peace. Both of these sources are well worth checking.

CEMETERIES

A supplement to the death or burial records kept by the civil or church authorities are the records that can be found in cemeteries. These generally are broken down into two major types: (a) gravestone inscriptions (the information appearing on the cemetery markers) and (b) sexton's records (the information kept in book form by the cemetery officials). Both of these types of records may supply information otherwise not obtainable in any other place.

Cemeteries themselves can be classified according to their type: (a) Church yard cemeteries, where members of the church are buried on church grounds; (b) Church-owned cemeteries, which are not next to the church but are owned by and administered by the church; (c) Government owned cemeteries, which are owned by town, county or municipal governments and are open for public use; (d) Privately-owned cemeteries, which are owned by a corporation and run as a business; (e) Family cemeteries, which are small parcels of private land reserved for specific families.

Almost all of these cemeteries can be located on the N.T.S. Map (see Chapter 3-6) covering the particular area a researcher is interested in.

The most notable and best known record of the cemetery is, of course, the memorial or tombstone, and it is on those markers that some of the most interesting information can be found.

It is not uncommon for researchers to find such information as: name, dates of birth and death or age at the time of death, places of birth and death, date and place of marriage, parents' names, spouse's name, children's names, religious affiliation, military service, civic positions and occupation, to name but a few. The extent of this information, however, is entirely dependent on what the deceased's survivors considered important.

In some cases, the information contained on the tombstones of some cemeteries has been transcribed by local residents and written up in book form. These transcriptions can often be found in the local libraries, state and provincial archives, and local historical or genealogical societies. By referring to these printed sources, researchers can save a considerable amount of time in checking a cemetery for references to family members. However, these transcriptions are still "secondary sources" and are subject to human error in the transcribing stage. Therefore, whenever possible, researchers should examine the actual tombstones themselves to ensure that no errors or ommissions have been made. Many of the genealogical societies in Canada have established programs for recording cemetery inscriptions and should be contacted in the normal course of cemetery research.

The Sexton's records provide a complete listing of who is buried in a cemetery. This is helpful, especially in those cases where a gravestone was never erected on a lot or has been vandalized or has weathered to the point that it has become unreadable. Generally speaking however, these records only exist for government and privately-owned cemeteries, the church-owned sites being primarily related to the church registers. Family cemeteries, as a rule, have no records of this type at all. Sexton's records are generally arranged by lot number, related to a large map of the cemetery, and contain the name of the purchaser of the lot; names, dates and ages of those people buried in the lot; and in some cases, relationships of people,

although this is not generally recorded. Other useful records in the Sexton's care include cemetery deeds, burial
permits and grave opening orders. To obtain information
from these records write to the Sexton, c/o the particular
cemetery, or contact the town or municipal office for addresses of cemeteries in their area. Addresses can also be
obtained from local telephone directories.

A more detailed study of cemetery records is "Gone
but Not Forgotten: Genealogical Research in the Cemetery"
by Eric Jonasson, printed in Generations (Journal of the
Manitoba Genealogical Society) Volume 2 No.4 (1977) pp
75-89.

OTHER SOURCES

One greatly neglected source of information is the
records of funeral directors, which can be equally as good
as any other official record. Funeral homes have been in
existence now for many years and in some cases may pre-
date civil registration of vital records. However, these
are private records and are made available only at the
discretion of the funeral director. Because he has many
other obligations, he should not be expected to work for
nothing and it is always wise to enclose some renumeration
for his time. The addresses of funeral homes in particular
areas can be found in the local telephone directories.

Another possible source of information is insurance
companies. Many of them have a considerable amount of information of genealogical interest in the files of their
deceased clients. If it is known that an ancestor had an
insurance policy with a particular company, it would be
well worth a letter to see what they may have. Like the
funeral directors, however, they are not required to
divulge any information from their files.

CANADIAN CHURCHES

While it is very important to know the general types
of records found in various churches, this section would
not be complete without a brief discussion of the major
denominations in Canada today.

ROMAN CATHOLIC CHURCH: This is the largest denomination
in Canada today encompassing almost half the population
of the country. It is organized on a parish, diocese and
archdiocese basis, in that order, and has a national co-
ordinating agency in Ottawa. The first Roman Catholic
Church registers in the country are located in Quebec,
the oldest dating from 1621. Under the old French civil

system, two copies of each register were required, one
remaining in the local church and the other being deposited in the offices of the local Protonotaire.
This system still continues today. As a result, all of
these registers are located in central locations throughout the province. In other parts of the country, the general rule is that the second copy is deposited in the
diocesan offices although this procedure does not appear
to have been followed in all cases with the same rigidity
as in Quebec. In all provinces other than Quebec, researchers should direct their general inquiries to the appropriate diocesan office. In Quebec, all requests for copies of
church records should be sent to the appropriate Protonotaire. (see Chapter 5)

Beyond a doubt, the Roman Catholic Church maintains
some of the best church records available in Canada.
They are a tremendous achievement in meticulous record-
keeping and preserving. For instance, in order to avoid
bigamy, a marginal entry concerning a marriage is made
near the baptismal record of the people concerned, and
furthermore, at the time of marriage a certificate of
baptism is required on which these marginal entries are
noted. Therefore, it becomes very easy to accurately
trace the lineage of a person in that these marginal
notes help avoid confusion when two people have the same
name and approximate birthdate.

The following publications will help the researcher
learn of the dates parishes were founded and learn more
of the history of the Roman Catholic Church in Canada.
(1) Official Catholic Directory, 1859 - 1964 (Periodical)
    for the U.S.A., also lists Canadian Dioceses.
(2) Canadian Catholic Directory, 1895 - 1913 (annual),
    lists all the parishes in Canada at time of publica-
    tion. Also in French: Le Canada Ecclésiastique,
    was published as early as 1887.
(3) Study Sessions (called Annual Report prior to 1965)
    the official annual publication of the Canadian
    Catholic Historical Association (est. 1933).

In the following list, the names and addresses of the
diocese and archdiocese outside of the province of Quebec
are provided for researchers' references. Those marked
with an asterisk denote the address of the ecclesiastical
archives, while all other addresses are those of the diocese or archdiocese. Inquiries for Quebec records should
be directed to the appropriate judicial court house in
that province. Entries are arranged by ecclesiastical province with the name of the archdiocese first (marked AD)
followed by the diocese within each province.

HALIFAX (AD): P.O. Box 1527, Halifax, Nova Scotia
    B3J 2Y3
Charlottetown: P.O. Box 907, Charlottetown, P.E.I.
    C1A 7L9

Antigonish: P.O. Box 1330, Antigonish, Nova Scotia
   B0H 1B0
Yarmouth: P.O. Box 278, Yarmouth, Nova Scotia B5A 4B2

TORONTO (AD): 55 Gould St., Toronto, Ontario M5B 1G1
Hamilton: 700 King St. W., Hamilton, Ontario L8P 1C7
London: 1070 Waterloo St., London, Ontario N6A 3Y2
Thunder Bay: Box 113, Thunder Bay, Ontario P7C 4V5
St. Catharines: 122 Riverdale Ave., St. Catharines,
   Ontario L2R 4C2

*ST-BONIFACE (AD): 151 ave Cathedrale, St-Boniface,
   Manitoba R2H 0H6

*OTTAWA (AD): 256 ave King Edward, Ottawa, Ontario
   K1N 7M1
Pembroke: P.O. Box 7, Pembroke, Ontario K8A 6X1
Timmins: 65 ave Jubilee Est., Timmins, Ontario P4N 5W4
Hearst: P.O. 1330, Hearst, Ontario P0L 1N0

*KINGSTON (AD): 279 Johnson St., Kingston, Ontario
   K7L 4X8
Peterborough: Box 175, Peterborough, Ontario K9W 6Y8
Alexandria: P.O. Box 1388, Cornwall, Ontario K6H 5V4
Sault Ste Marie: P.O. Box 510, North Bay, Ontario
   P1B 8V1

ST. JOHN'S (AD): P.O. Box 37, St. John's, Newfoundland
   A1C 5H5
Grand Falls: P.O. Box 397, Grand Falls, Newfoundland
   A2A 2V8
St. George's: 16 Hammond Dr., Corner Brook, Newfound-
   land A2H 2W2

VANCOUVER (AD): 150 Robson St., Vancouver, British
   Columbia V6B 2A7
Victoria: 740 View St., Victoria, British Columbia
   V8W 1V8
Nelson: 813 Ward St., Nelson, British Columbia V1L 1T4
Kamloops: 635A Tranquille Rd., North Kamloops, British
   Columbia V2B 3H5

EDMONTON (AD): 10044-113 St., Edmonton, Alberta T5K 1N8
Calgary: P.O. Box 4130, Stn. C, Calgary, Alberta T2T 5M9
St-Paul: P.O. Box 339, St. Paul, Alberta T0A 3A0

WINNIPEG (AD): 50 Stafford St., Winnipeg, Manitoba
   R3M 2V7

REGINA (AD): 2522 Retallack St., Regina, Saskatchewan
   S4T 2L3
Prince Albert: 1415-4 Ave. W., Prince Albert, Saskatch-
   ewan S6V 5H1
Gravelbourg: P.O. Box 690, Gravelbourg, Saskatchewan
   S0H 1X0
Saskatoon: 1036 College St., Saskatoon, Saskatchewan

MONCTON (AD): P.O. Box 248, Moncton, New Brunswick
    E1C 8K9
Saint John: 91 Waterloo St., Saint John, New Bruns-
    wick E2L 3P9
Bathurst: P.O. 460, Bathurst, New Brunswick E2A 3Z4
Edmundston: Diocesan Centre, Edmundston, New Bruns-
    wick E3V 3K1

GROUARD-MCLENNAN (AD): P.O. Box 388, McLennan,
    Alberta T0H 2L0
Prince George: College Rd., Prince George, British
    Columbia V2N 2K6
Mackenzie-Fort Smith: P.O. Box 25, Fort Smith, North
    West Territories X0E 0P0
Whitehorse: 5119-5th Ave., Whitehorse, Yukon Y2A 2L5

KEEWATIN-LE PAS (AD): P.O. Box 270, Le Pas, Manitoba
    R9A 1K4
Churchill-Hudson Bay: P.O. Box 10, Churchill, Manitoba
    R0B 0E0
Moosonee: P.O. Box 140, Moosonee, Ontario P0L 1Y0
Labrador-Schefferville: P.O. Box 700, Schefferville,
    Quebec G0G 2T0

UKRAINIAN DIOCESE:
Winnipeg (AD): 235 Scotia St., Winnipeg, Manitoba
    R2V 1V7
Toronto: 61 Glen Edyth Dr., Toronto, Ontario M4V 2V8
Saskatoon: 866 Saskatchewan Cres. E., Saskatoon,
    Saskatchewan S7N 0L4
Edmonton: 6240 Ada Blvd., Edmonton, Alberta T5W 4P1
New Westminster: 550 W 14th Ave., Vancouver, British
    Columbia V5Z 1P6

Other information on the Roman Catholic Church can be
obtained from the Canadian Catholic Conference, 90 Parent
Avenue, Ottawa, Ontario, K1N 7B1.

UNITED CHURCH OF CANADA: The second largest denomination
in Canada, it was established by the union of the Methodist, Congregational and most of the Presbyterian Churches
in the country in 1925. The Evangelical United Bretheren
Church joined in 1968.
    The United Church maintains eight archives across
Canada for the deposit of historical material relating to
the church, with a central archives located in Toronto.
The addresses of these repositories are:

    Central Archives: United Church of Canada, Victoria
        University, Queen's Park Crescent East, Toronto,
        Ontario, M5S 1K7. (Also the repository for Bay
        of Quinte, Toronto, Hamilton and London Confer-
        ences)

Newfoundland Conference: 6 Kent Place, St. John's,
     Newfoundland
Maritime Conference: Pine Hill Divinity Hall, Franck-
     lyn St., Halifax, Nova Scotia B3H 3B5
Montreal-Ottawa Conference: Church Centre, 3480
     Decarie Blvd., Montreal, Quebec
Manitoba Conference: University of Winnipeg, Winnipeg,
     Manitoba
Saskatchewan Conference: St. Andrew's College, Univer-
     sity of Saskatchewan, Saskatoon, Saskatchewan
Alberta Conference: St. Stephen's College, 8830-112
     St., Edmonton, Alberta TOG 2V6
British Columbia Conference: Vancouver School of
     Theology, 6000 Iona Dr., Vancouver, B.C. V6T 1L4

Some of the major collections in the Central Archives
include: (1) Library, with 3,000 books, 2,000 volumes of
serial publications, plus other printed material, and a
biographical file of 12,000 people (1968); (2) Manuscript
collection with some congregational records for Ontario
and some papers of church leaders. (3) Map collection,
although small, with many atlases and maps indicating the
locations of churches and missions. Of special consideration is the collection of the 19th Century Methodist newspaper Christian Guardian, 1832 - 67, which contains numerous birth and death announcements and, from 1840 - 56,
marriage notices. As well, the four volume Weslayan Methodist Register of Baptisms covering all of Ontario and
Western Quebec for 1840 - 96 is very important. It is
arranged on a town or township basis.

     Further information can be obtained from either the
Central Archives or United Church House, 85 St. Clair
Avenue East, Toronto, Ontario, M4T 1M8.

ANGLICAN CHURCH OF CANADA: This is the oldest Protestant
church and the third largest religious group in Canada.
It is organized on the parish, diocese and ecclesiastical
province basis, in that order.
     Virtually all the records of the church remain at a
local parish level although copies are now being sent to
the respective diocesan offices. The General Synod Archives
of the Anglican Church is primarily concerned with accumu-
lating records of a historical nature only and does not
have any parish registers in its collections although they
do have a sizable collection of parish histories. In order
to check individual parish registers, it is often necessary
to contact the local church concerned. However, some registers are now deposited in local diocese offices.
     Following are the names and addresses of the various
diocese in Canada. Addresses of diocese archives are marked
with an asterisk.

*General Synod Archives, Anglican Church of Canada,
    600 Jarvis St., Toronto, Ontario M4Y 2V6 (central
    archives)

*Algoma: Box 1168, Sault Ste Marie, Ontario P6A 2N7
 The Arctic: 1055 Avenue Rd., Toronto, Ontario
 Athabasca: Box 279, Peace River, Alberta T0H 2X0
 Brandon: 341-13 St., Brandon, Manitoba R7A 4P8
*British Columbia and Yukon: 6050 Chancellor Blvd.,
    Vancouver, British Columbia V6T 1L4
 Caledonia: 204-Fourth Ave., Prince Rupert, British
    Columbia V8V 1P5
*Calgary: 218-7th Ave. S.E., Calgary, Alberta
 Cariboo: 360 Nicola St., Kamloops, British Columbia
 Edmonton: 10033-34 Ave., Edmonton, Alberta T6E 2S6
*Fredericton: 808 Brunswick St., Fredericton, New
    Brunswick E3B 1V1
*Huron: 4-220 Dundas St., London, Ontario N6A 1H3
 Keewatin: Box 118, Kenora, Ontario P9N 3X1
 Kootenay: Box 549, Kelowna, British Columbia V1Y 7P2
*Montreal: 1444 Union Ave., Montreal, Quebec H3A 2B8
 Moosonee: Box 830, Schumacher, Ontario P0N 1G0
*Newfoundland: 13A Winter Ave., St. John's, Newfound-
    land A1A 1T2
 New Westminster: 692 Burrard St., Vancouver, British
    Columbia V6C 2L1
 Niagara: 67 Victoria Ave. S., Hamilton, Ontario
    L8N 2S8
 Nova Scotia: 5730 College St., Halifax, Nova Scotia
    B3H 1X4
*Ontario: 90 Johnson St., Kingston, Ontario K7L 1X7
*Ottawa: 71 Bronson Ave., Ottawa, Ontario K1R 6S6
 Qu'Appelle: 1501 College Ave., Regina, Saskatchewan
    S4P 1B8
 Quebec: 34 rue Desjardins, Quebec City, Quebec
    G1R 4L5
 Rupert's Land: 66 St. Cross St., Winnipeg, Manitoba
    R2W 3X8
 Saskatchewan: Box 1088, Prince Albert, Saskatchewan
    S6V 5S6
 Saskatoon: Box 1965, Saskatoon, Saskatchewan S7K 3S5
*Toronto: 135 Adelaide St. E., Toronto, Ontario M5C 1L8

    In addition to the parish registers available through-
out Canada, there are two important collections in London,
England, which are excellant sources for older Canadian
registers. These are the Archives of the United Society for
the Propagation of the Gospel in Foreign Parts and the
Archives of the Church Missionary Society. Both were
missionary groups who maintained a considerable number of
missions and posts in many parts of Canada, both before and
after these areas were settled. Microfilmed copies of

90

29th May
18-2
Mountgomery
Buried

John Mountgomery a Private in Her Majesty's
Royal Engineers died on the twenty seventh day of
May one thousand eight hundred and sixty two
Aged thirty five years and was buried on the
twenty ninth day of May immediately following
by me   William Anderson
                                            Chaplain to the Forces

Witness   John Harrison Cople
              1/16th Regiment

15th July
18-3
Brown
baptized

Elizabeth daughter of John Brown a Sergeant
Major in Her Majesty's forty seventh and of
Margaret Mills his wife born on the sixteenth day
of May one thousand eight hundred and sixty two
and was baptized on the thirteenth day of July
immediately following by me
                              William Anderson
                                   Chaplain to the Forces

The Parents are

Afrer sons

PAGE FROM THE CHURCH OF SCOTLAND REGISTER,
MONTREAL GARRISON, QUEBEC

Source: MG 8, G66, page 6
(Courtesy of the Public Archives of Canada)

material in these collections are also available at the
Public Archives of Canada.

Further information can be obtained from the Anglican
Church of Canada, 600 Jarvis Street, Toronto, Ontario, M4Y
2V6.

THE PRESBYTERIAN CHURCH IN CANADA: At the formation of
the United Church of Canada approximately one-third of
the Presbyterian churches in Canada refused to join,
electing instead to form their own church body. Organized
on a parish, presbytery and Synod basis, the Presbyterian
Church is the fourth largest denomination in Canada.
   With the creation of the United Church, much of the
then Presbyterian Church's archival holdings were transfer-
ed to the new organization. Since that time, the new Presbyterian Church has managed to collect some older records
and archives although the bulk of the material of genealogical interest remains with the United Church. In some cases
collections were divided so that it is now necessary to
consult both churches' archival collections.
   Further information and the addresses of local parishes
and presbyteries can be obtained by writing the Archives of
the Presbyterian Church in Canada, 59 St. George St.,
Toronto, Ontario, M5S 2E6.

THE LUTHERAN CHURCHES: Up to this point, all the churches
which have been discussed have had the benefit of a strong,
central organization. Unfortunately, this is not true of
the Lutheran Church in Canada.
   The three main bodies which represent the majority of
Lutherans in Canada are:

   The Evangelical Lutheran Church of Canada, 247-1st
      Ave. N., Saskatoon, Saskatchewan S7K 1X2

   The Lutheran Church - Canada (Missouri Synod),
      3500 Askin Ave., Windsor, Ontario N9E 3V9

   Lutheran Church in America - Canada Section, 9901-
      107 St., Edmonton, Alberta T5K 1G4

   One of the major problems with the Lutheran Church is
that it has always been mainly a church of the rural areas.
This coupled with the lack of adequate numbers of trained
ministers in the early years of the church here and the
lack of centralization has made early records quite poor or
non-existant. The closest the Lutheran Church has come to
centralization is the Lutheran Council in Canada, an inter-
Lutheran co-ordinating agency to which all three main bod-

ies belong.   The Council can be contacted at 500-365 Harg-
rave Street, Winnipeg, Manitoba, R3B 2K3.

A number of local archives do exist for the various
Lutheran groups which are best contacted through the respective church bodies or the Lutheran Council in Canada.

THE BAPTIST CHURCHES: The sixth largest denomination and
the last to be discussed here in detail, the Baptist
Church is similar to the Lutheran in that it is quite
fragmented. However, it does maintain three excellant
archival collections which are very helpful to the genealogist.

The major Baptist conferences in Canada are organized
into an informal federation for fellowship and co-operation
which also acts as a general information agency for the
Canadian Baptist Church:

> Baptist Federation of Canada
> 91 Queen Street, Box 1298
> Brantford, Ontario   N3T 5T6

The following organizations are member bodies within
the Federation:

United Baptist Conference of the Atlantic Provinces,
    P.O. Box 7053, Saint John, New Brunswick E2L 4S5

Baptist Union of Western Canada, 4404-16 St. S.W.,
    Calgary, Alberta T2T 2H9

Baptist Convention of Ontario-Quebec, 217 St. George
    St., Toronto, Ontario M5R 2M2

Union of French Baptist Churches in Canada, 3674
    Ontario St. E., Montreal, Quebec H1W 1R9

A tremendous amount of Baptist historical material
including church registers, biographical material, books,
church periodicals and other records can be found in three
excellant church archives:

Atlantic Baptist Historical Collection, Acadia Univer-
    sity, Wolfeville, Nova Scotia B0P 1X0 (archives
    for the Atlantic provinces)

Canadian Baptist Archives, McMaster Divinity College,
    Hamilton, Ontario L8S 4K1 (archives for area west
    of the Maritimes)

Fellowship of Evangelical Baptist Churches, 74
    Sheppard Ave. W., Willowdale, Ontario (overlaps
    the area covered by the other archives)

Further information on the Baptist Church and its records can be obtained from the various archives and church
organizations as well as the Baptist Federation.

Other Denominations

The following list includes the addresses of denominational headquarters and archives of some of the larger or
more unique Canadian churches. The addresses of smaller
denominations not contained here can be found in almanacs
listed in Chapter 3.1:

*Apostolic Church in Canada, 27 Castlefield Ave.,
    Toronto, Ontario M4R 1G3
*Buddhist Churches of Canada, 918 Bathurst St.,
    Toronto, Ontario M5R 3G5
*Christian Church (Disciples of Christ), 39 Arkell Rd.,
    R.R. 2, Guelph, Ontario N1H 6H8
*Free Methodist Church, 3 Harrowby Court, Islington,
    Ontario M9B 3H3
*Mennonites, Mennonite Central Committee (co-ordinating
    body), 1483 Pembina Hwy., Winnipeg, Manitoba
    R3T 2C8 (Archives: Canadian Conference of Mennonite
    Brethren Archives, 77 Henderson Hwy., Winnipeg,
    Manitoba R2L 1L1; Mennonite Genealogy Inc., Box 1086,
    Steinbach, Manitoba; Mennonite Archives of Ontario,
    Conrad Grekel College, Waterloo, Ontario)
*Church of Jesus Christ of Latter-Day Saints, 50 East
    North Temple, Salt Lake City, Utah, U.S.A. 84150
    (see also Chapter 2-4)
*Jehovah's Witnesses, 150 Bridgeland Ave., Toronto,
    Ontario M4N 2C4
*Canadian Jewish Congress, (co-ordinating body), 1590
    McGregor Ave., Montreal, Quebec H3G 1C5
*Orthodox Churches:
    Greek Orthodox Church, 277 Teddington Park Ave.,
        Toronto, Ontario M4N 2C4
    Ukrainian Greek Orthodox, 9 St. Johns Ave.,
        Winnipeg, Manitoba R2W 0T3
    Antiochian Orthodox (Syrian), 555-575 Jean Talon
        St. E., Montreal, Quebec H2R 1T8
*Pentecostal Assemblies of Canada, (co-ordinating body)
    10 Overlea Blvd., Toronto, Ontario M4H 1A5
*Religious Society of Friends (Quakers), 60 Lowther
    Ave., Toronto, Ontario M5R 1C7 (Archives: Canadian
    Friends History Association, 60 Lowther Ave.,
    Toronto, Ontario M5R 1C7)
*Salvation Army, 20 Albert St., Toronto, Ontario M5G 1A6
*Seventh-Day Adventist Church, 1148 King St. E., Oshawa,
    Ontario L1H 1H8
*Unitarian Church, Canadian Unitarian Council, 175 St.
    Clair Ave. W., Toronto, Ontario M4V 1P7

94

BIBLIOGRAPHY

The following publications are representative of the
many volumes dealing with church archives or history:

Boucher, J.E.: French Protestantism in Canada
     (Ste Hyacinthe 1963)
Carrington, Philip: The Anglican Church in Canada: A
     History (London 1963)
Morice, A.G.: History of the Catholic Church in Western
     Canada (Toronto 1910)
Fitch, E.R.: The Baptists of Canada (Toronto 1911)
Cronmiller, Carl: A History of the Lutheran Church in
     Canada (Toronto 1961)
Eylands, V.: Lutherans in Canada (Winnipeg 1945)
Pidgeon, George C.: The United Church in Canada
     (Toronto 1950)
Farris, Markell and Smith: A Short History of the
     Presbyterian Church in Canada (Toronto 1965)
Boon, T.C.B.: The Anglican Church from the Bay to the
     Rockies: A History of the Ecclesiastical Province
     of Rupert's Land and Its Diocese from 1820 to 1950
     (Toronto 1962)
Levy, George: The Baptists of the Maritime Provinces
     1753-1956 (St. John 1946)
Carrier, Hervé, et Roy, Lucien: Evolution de L'Eglise
     (catholique) au Canada français (Montréal 1968)
Kage, Joseph: Two Hundred Years of Jewish Immigration
     to Canada (Montreal 1960)
Sanderson, V.E.: The First Century of Methodism in
     Canada (Toronto 1908-19, 2 volumes)
McNeill, John: The Presbyterian Church in Canada 1785-
     1925 (Toronto 1925)
Dorland, A.G.: The Quakers in Canada: A History
     (Toronto 1968)
Epp, Frank: Mennonites in Canada 1786-1920 (Toronto
     1974)
Langtry, J: History of the (Anglican) Church in Eastern
     Canada and Newfoundland (London 1892)
Binfield, E.L.: "Church Archives in the United States
     and Canada: A Bibliography" in American Archivist
     (Volume 21, No. 3, 1958)
Coderre, John E., and Lavoie, Paul A.: Parish Registers
     for the Province of Ontario (Ottawa Branch OGS,
     1974)
Campeau, Marielle: Checklist of Parish Registers (Public
     Archives of Canada, 1975)
Yearbook of American and Canadian Churches (New York,
     Annual) Best source of addresses for various denom-
     inations.
Union List of Manuscripts in Canadian Repositories,
     (PAC, Ottawa 1975, 2 volumes) Contains detailed
     descriptions of many church archives.

3:4 CENSUS RECORDS

There is probably no other record in existence which contains more information about people living in the 19th Century than the Census Schedule, and it is for this reason alone that census schedules are probably the most often searched of all genealogical documents. No genealogical research is complete until all pertinent census records have been examined and the information contained in them has been extracted.

The first Census taken in what is now Canada was the 1666 Census of New France. Since that time, Census information has been collected at varying intervals throughout our history, and regularly at ten-year intervals from 1851 to the present. In addition to the decennial census, special enumerations have been compiled on the fifth year after the general census since 1886.

CENSUS RECORDS IN CANADA

There are four types of Census Records in Canada:

AGGREGATE:
These Census returns record no names, merely the numbers of persons within various age groups, religious denominations, countries of origin, and locations. Aggregate returns are the most prevalent type of Census return compiled prior to 1851, along with those returns listing only the names of heads of families. Aggregate returns are of little value to the genealogist.

HEAD OF HOUSEHOLD:
To the genealogist, this is the most prevalent type of useful Census record compiled in Canada prior to 1851. The "head of household" return was usually followed by an "aggregate" return of the make-up of the family by age and sex along with a few other details on the head of the household.

AGRICULTURAL:
Agricultural Census returns are similar to those listing the "head of household" except that they concentrate instead on agricultural details such as: the lot and concession number of the farm; the acreage under cultivation; the crops being produced; and the

cash value of the machinery and livestock. Agricultural Census returns were primarily a supplement to
the Nominal Census returns taken after 1851. However,
they too are valuable to the genealogist, for they
can provide the information necessary to check the
land records of the particular area in which an ancestor lived.

NOMINAL:
Beginning in 1851, most of the Census returns are
Nominal. They list the name of each person in the
family along with a variety of personal details on
each person. To the genealogist, the Nominal Census
return is of primary importance. It provides a
complete list of everyone in a household by name
along with enough information on each person to determine approximate birthdates and to determine the
movements of the family within the province or country
from the birthplaces listed. It provides a complete
list of all children who were living at home during
the census year.

     To illustrate the type of information generally
found on Census Return sheets, the details asked on
the 1851, 1861 and 1871 Censuses taken in the Province
of and the Dominion of Canada are listed in the
following chart:

CENSUS INFORMATION ASKED	1851	1861	1871
Name	x	x	x
Occupation	x	x	x
Birthplace (Province or Country)	x	x	x
Age next birthday	x	x	x
Religion	x	x	x
Sex	x	x	x
Married or Single	x	x	x
Year of Marriage		x	
Marriages during Census Year		x	x
Number of Negroes	x		
Number of Indians	x		
Non - Whites		x	
Racial Origin			x
Are you a member of the family?	x		

CENSUS INFORMATION ASKED	1851	1861	1871
Members of the family who are absent	x		
Residence if person lived out of limits	x		
Widows or Widowers		x	x
Number of Deaf and Dumb	x	x	x
Number of Blind	x	x	x
Number of Lunatics	x	x	x
Number attending school	x	x	x
Number of people over twenty and unable to read/write		x	
Could not read			x
Could write			x
Births during Census Year	x		
Deaths during Census Year	x		
Cause of Death	x		
Details on the type of house the family lived in	x		
Remarks column	x		

While the above listing is indicative of what can be found in nominal censuses, it should be remembered that the information requested on the forms is a function of the time and place of the census. The nominal schedules prior to 1851 are not, as a rule, as detailed as the common information shown above. In the 1666 Census of New France and in most of the subsequent nominal returns of the French period for example, the information is generally restricted to Names, Ages, Occupation of head of family, Amount of land under cultivation, Number of animals owned, and the relationship of each person listed to the head of the household. The most unique feature of the early French censuses is the fact that the Maiden Names of the married women are listed - a truly invaluable piece of information. However, even this outstanding aspect is over shadowed by the Manitoba Census of 1870 which , while listing the majority of the information generally found in the 1851 - 71 censuses, also includes the name of the father of everyone listed in the Province!

VALUE OF CENSUS RECORDS

The primary value of census records lies in the fact that the entire family was enumerated and listed together on the census form. This organization by family unit provides researchers with virtually the entire make-up of the family at the time of the census and, by comparing the information acquired from one census to those which preceeded and followed it, the names of all family members can be located quite easily.

Some other important values of census returns include:

- The ability to determine approximate birthdates from the ages (or aggregate listings) on all members of the family given of the various census returns. Even Head of Household returns can be utilized in this way to provide the dates necessary for checking other records, such as baptisms.

- The ability to determine the movements of the family around the country. This information can be gleaned from the "places of birth" indicated for both parents and children.

- The ability to determine the financial well-being of the family from the agricultural returns or from the portions of the nominal and head of Household returns used to record the material possessions and occupations of those enumerated.

- The ability to determine the exact location of a farm from the information provided on the agricultural returns.

- The ability to learn of the religious affiliation of ancestors so that church records may be located and searched for more specific data on the birth, marriage, or death of these ancestors.

PROBLEMS WITH CENSUS RECORDS

While searching census records, the genealogist may experience problems which can be quite frustrating. Possibly the biggest disappointment is the lack of good returns prior to 1851. Many of the returns existing for this period are quite sporadic as to both content and location. This fact creates many problems, especially when no other records exist for the locality in which a particular family lived. In some cases it makes the proof of a lineage quite difficult. These early returns were primarily used to compile numerical statistics on the population and were often destroyed once the information which they contained was extracted. This explains the large number of aggregate returns existing today and the relatively low number of nominal and head of family returns. However, where records which indicate head of family do exist, they provide an excellent means of determining the size and make-up of individual families as well as providing an insight into the physical well-being of the family members.

Several other factors contribute to the difficulty of using any census returns. Some of the more prevalent are:

- The lack of adequate indices. The exact locality of the family must be known in all cases, otherwise it is a long tedious process finding them in the returns. Knowing that they lived in "Ontario", for example, is not enough even to consider attempting to find them in the censuses.

- The fallability of people's memories. Everyone forgets or gets dates and places confused at one time or another. For example, it is not uncommon to find that in the intervening ten years between censuses, according to the returns some people have aged only 8 years or as much as 15 years. All information in these records should therefore be treated with caution and should be proven from other records such as Church registers, etc.

- The enumerator. Some were quite 'sloppy' or had little formal education, resulting in incomplete, illegible returns or mis-spelled names. Others did not follow the instructions properly or would take "facts" from the children in the house or simply fill in the information themselves if no one was home when they called. Language difficulties also created problems in obtaining the correct information when an interpretor was not used.

- Effects of time. With the passage of time, many inks slowly faded and paper became so brittle that it tears or crumbles very easily now. Illegibility of handwriting and improper storage of the records over the years have also had their effects.

OBTAINING AND USING CENSUS RECORDS

The Public Archives of Canada has the three major nominal censuses (1851, 1861, 1871) on microfilm, in addition to a large number of censuses predating 1851. Other census schedules can also be found in the various provincial archives. The microfilmed census rolls in the Public Archives of Canada can be borrowed on inter-library loan through any local public libraries possessing a microfilm reader. Fur-

A List of the Inhabitants of the Township of Edwardsburgh April 2nd 1801

Names	Men	Women	Boys	Girls	Total	Names	Men	Women	Boys	Girls	Total
Hugh McElmoyle	1	1	2	..	4	Benjammen Barns Jur	1	..	..	..	1
John Dulmage	1	1	~	2	4	Thomas Petten	1	1	3	2	7
Alias Dulmage	1	1	1	..	3	Stephen Petten	1	..	..	..	1
Samuel Dulmage	1	..	..	..	1	John Petten	1	1	1	..	3
John Fraser	1	1	1	..	3	Samuel Cowderry	1	1	1	4	7
Donald Fraser	1	..	..	..	1	John Bubk	1	1	1	..	3
Thomas Fraser	1	1	1	3	6	Mrs Montgomery	..	1	..	..	1
Nathen Day	1	1	1	2	5	Daniel Plumley	1	..	..	..	1
Mrs Lorimier	..	1	3	1	5	Diana Johnson	..	1	..	..	1
Chavalier Lorimere	1	..	..	..	1	Amos Darlington	1	..	..	..	1
Alexander McIntosh	1	..	..	..	1	Stephen Darlington	1	..	..	..	1
John McIntosh	1	1	..	1	3	Peter Spencer	1	1	3	1	6
Donald McIntosh	1	1	..	..	2	Samuel Adams	1	1	..	..	2
Isaac Russell	1	1	1	..	3	John Scott Jun	1	..	..	..	1
Alexis Reaume	1	..	..	..	1	David Phelps	1	1	4	5	11
Mrs Campbell	..	1	2	2	5	Constant King	1	1	4	2	8
Alexander Campbell	1	..	..	..	1	Joakim Denout	1	..	..	..	1
Alexr Campbell Sen	1	1	1	..	3	Hugh Monro Jur	1	1	1	..	3
Hugh Montgomery	1	..	..	..	1	Nicholas Fullman	1	1	..	..	2
Chakim Whitney	1	1	..	2	4	John Galbreth	1	1	1	5	8
Henry Bedford	1	1	..	..	2	John Gaylord	1	1	1	..	3
Hugh Mauhon	1	1	..	..	2	Andrew Adams	1	1	2	3	7
Andrew Gibson	1	..	..	..	1	Petter Znackenbus	1	1	1	..	3
Sylvester More	1	1	3	2	7	Pattrick Robinson	1	1	..	2	4
Jacob Morris	1	1	3	3	8	David Stephenson	1	..	..	..	1
David Flyer	1	1	2	1	5	Jonathen Stephenson	1	..	..	..	1
James Kilborn	1	1	..	3	5	Mary Bogard	..	1	2	..	3
Hiram Kilborn	1	..	..	..	1	Dayke Sillick	1	1	2	3	7
Eli Kilborn	1	1	..	..	2	George Reed	1	1	2	1	5
Michel Cook	1	1	..	..	2	Ephraim Curry	1	1	3	4	9
Betsy Cook	..	1	..	..	1	Joel Curry	1	..	..	..	1
Benjaman Barns	1	1	..	1	3	Mrs Fewie	..	1	2	1	4
					96						117

Source: MG 9, 08-8
(Courtesy of the Public Archives of Canada)

ther information on this procedure can be obtained from your
local reference librarian.

The microfilmed censuses are generally arranged by
county, and are further subdivided into townships, towns
or city areas. In order to locate the microfilm reel that
you will need in your searches, it is necessary to know
the EXACT place of residence of an ancestor, either the
county or the town. All names in each area were listed as
they came and are not as a rule listed in alphabetical
order.

Census records which were compiled in 1871 or earlier
are open for public inspection and can be examined by any
researcher searching for his ancestors. Those enumerations
taken between 1881 and the present are still closed to researchers although it is hoped that they will be gradually
made available.

OTHER 'CENSUS' RECORDS

As mentioned earlier, the tremendous value of census
records lies in the fact that in one or two records a researcher can learn of the entire make-up of any one family
at a particular time. This can save a considerable amount
of time which would otherwise have been spent attempting to
learn the names, ages, etc. of all children in a family from
other, more diverse, records.

When no census return exists for the time period or
place of resident of an ancestor, it is necessary to examine other records for the "census" information. Most of
these other records will be more similar to the "Head of
Household" type of census that to the "Nominal" type.
While this is a disappointment, these records can be used
as a "stepping stone" to other more detailed records. A
few of the more common "census substitutes" are described
below, and are discussed in more detail elsewhere in this
book:

> Assessment and Tax Rolls: These are com-
> piled on a local basis (town, municipality,
> township, county) and are generally still
> in the hands of the local authorities, al-
> though some have now been deposited in local
> and provincial archives. Most of them con-
> tain the name of the person owning a piece
> of property plus some personal information
> on him, including data on livestock owned,
> land in cultivation, etc. Many of these
> rolls also contain aggregate returns on the
> make-up of each family. They were often
> compiled on an annual basis, although many
> were not.

Regional directories: These were compiled
for towns, municipalities and counties and
are most often found in local or regional
libraries and in provincial archives. Most
of them were issued sporadically although
some for larger towns and cities were
issued each year. They generally give the
name of the head of the household, occupation,
place of residence and sometimes the place of
work and the name of wife.

School registers and school censuses: These
were generally compiled annually by the local
school boards and can generally be found with
the local authorities or in regional and provincial archives. Although they are fairly
limited in actual scope, they do provide the
names of children either attending school or
eligible to attend schools, with many also
indicating the name of the father of each
student. Ages are also given on occassion.
Most of these types of records are of fairly
recent origin, most dating back not more
than 75 years.

Homestead applications and land grant petitions:
These records sometimes provide information
on the aggregate make-up of a family, in addition
to a considerable amount of information on the
head of the household. These records are now
deposited with provincial agencies.

Wills and probate records: These documents
contain the names of living children or relatives of a deceased person along with some
details on each, such as place of residence,
occupation, relationship to the deceased, etc.
These records are now found in the various
court districts in each province, although
in a few instances they have been deposited
in the provincial archives. The exact date
of death must be known to locate these records.

BIBLIOGRAPHY

Canada. Censuses of Canada 1665-1871 (Ottawa 1875).

"The Census of Vancouver Island 1855" B.C. Hist Q4:
    1 (1940) 9-50.

Check List of Census Returns; New Brunswick 1851-
    1871; Nova Scotia 1871 (Public Archives of
    Canada 1964).

Check List of Ontario Census Returns 1842-1871 (Public Archives of Canada 1963).

Check List of Quebec Census Returns 1825-1871 (Public Archives of Canada 1963).

Harvey, Arthur: "The Canadian Census of 1871" Cdn. Monthly & Nat Review 1:2 (1872).

Henripin, Jacques: Les Divisions de recensement au Canada de 1871 à 1951: méthode permettant d'en uniformiser les territoires (Montréal 1956).

Lamoureux, Yvette: "Index du recensement de 1667" Memoires SGCF 18-1-2 (1967).

Statistics Canada: Chronological List of Canadian Censuses (Ottawa 1942).

Thibodeau, Fernand-D: "Recensement de Terre-Neuve, 1687 à 1704" Memoires Soc. Gén. Can. Française 10:3-4 (1959), 11:1-2 (1960).

On the following pages is a chronological list of the census records of Canada and the areas they cover. More information on the full extent and content of the various returns can be obtained from the checklists listed in the bibliography or by consulting the repository in which the census returns are located.

MAJOR CANADIAN CENSUS RECORDS

Except where otherwise indicated, all Census Records listed here are available at the Public Archives of Canada. All have been microfilmed except those marked with an asterisk. The following codes have been used in this chart (code which is parenthasized indicates census is incomplete):

N = Nominal Census
LH = Landholders
HF = Heads of Family
LI = List of inhabitants
PS = Principle settlers
PT = Poll Tax Rolls

Microfilm copies of the censuses at PAC may also be found in other archives, and vica-versa.

DATE OF CENSUS	ACADIA	NEWFOUNDLAND	NEW BRUNSWICK	NOVA SCOTIA	CAPE BRETON IS OR ILE ROYALE	PRINCE EDWARD IS OR ILE ST JEAN	QUEBEC OR NEW FRANCE	ONTARIO	OTHER AREAS
1666							N (3)		
1667							N (4)		
1671	N	N (1)	(2)	(2)					
1673		N (1)							
1675		*HF (31)							
1677		*HF (32)							
1681							N (4)		
1686	N		(2)	(2)					
1691		N (5)							
1693	N	N (5)	(2)	(2)					
1698	N	HF (1)	(2)	(2)					
1701	N		(2)	(2)					

DATE OF CENSUS	ACADIA	NFLD.	N.B.	N.S.	CAPE BRETON	P.E.I.	QUEBEC	ONTARIO	OTHER AREAS
1703	HF	HF (5)	(2)	(2)					
1704		HF (1)							
1706									
1707	HF	HF (1)	(2)	(2)					
1711	N		(2)	(2)					
1714									
1716					PS,HF (7)		*N (6)		
1717					PS (8)				
1719									
1722					HF (9)		*HF (10)		
1730						HF			
1731									
1734	HF (11)		HF (11)	(2)		HF			
1735					HF	HF			
1739									
1741					LH (12)		*(13)		
1744					N		*N (14)		
1749-50									
1752			*PS (20)		*N (15)	*N (15)			
1753					HF				
1760-62							*HF (16)		
1761	LI (17)		LI (17)				*HF (18)		
1762							*HF (19)		
1765									

106

DATE OF CENSUS	ACADIA	NFLD.	N.B.	N.S.	CAPE BRETON	P.E.I.	QUEBEC	ONTARIO	OTHER AREAS
1770 1773 1775			*HF (20)	*HF (20) *HF (20) *HF (20)					
1787 1790s 1792			PT (20)	*HF (20) PT (20)			*HF (21)		
1795 1796 1798		*HF (33)				*HF (23)	*HF (21) *HF (21)	HF (22)	
1800-01 1805 1806		*HF (34)					*HF (21)	HF (22)	
1811 1813 1817				(HF) (20)	HF (35) (HF)			HF (22)	
1818 1823 1824					HF (35)			HF (22) HF (22)	
1825 1827 1828				(HF) (20)	HF		HF		*HF (30) *HF (30)
1829 1830 1831							HF		*HF (30) *HF (30) HF (24)

DATE OF CENSUS	ACADIA	NFLD.	N.B.	N.S.	CAPE BRETON	P.E.I.	QUEBEC	ONTARIO	OTHER AREAS
1832									HF (24)
1833									HF (24)
1834									HF (24)
1835					HF				HF (24)
1838				HF					HF (24)
1840									HF (24)
1841						HF	HF	(HF)	HF (24)
1842									
1843									
1846									HF (24)
1848						*HF (25)		(HF)	HF (24)
1849									HF (24)
1850								(HF)	
1851			N (26)	HF (27)				N	
1856							N		(*) (24)
1858			N	HF (28)					
1861			N	HF		HF	N	N	*(29)
1860s									
1870				N					N (24)
1871			N				N	N	
1874-75									*HF (36)
1881 to the PRESENT									

Censuses for this period have not yet been released for public examination.

108

NOTES

(1) For Plaisance only (French settlement)
(2) Refer to Acadian censuses for this period
(3) In print: Rapport des Archives du Quebec (RAQ) 1935-36, pp 1-54 (indexed)
(4) In print: Benjamin Sulte: Histoire des canadiens francais (1667 in Vol 4, 1681 in Vol 5). The 1667 census is also available in alphabetical order in Memoires de la Societe Genealogique Canadienne-Francaise, 1966.
(5) For the French settlements only.
(6) Quebec City only. In print: Abbe L. Beaudet: Recensement de la Ville de Quebec pour 1716 (Quebec 1887) pp·66.
(7) For Port Toulouse and the principle settlers at Port Dauphin only
(8) Principle settlers at Port Dauphin only
(9) For Port Toulouse only
(10) Montreal city only. In print: RAQ 1941-42
(11) Complete returns for Acadia for that year plus some incomplete for Riviere St. Jean area
(12) Those occupying land around Louisbourg only
(13) Unpublished census of Montreal
(14) Quebec City only. In print: RAQ 1939-40, p 1-154
(15) In print: Report of PAC 1905, Volume 2
(16) Trois-Rivieres (city & region) only. In print: RAQ 1946-47, pp 3-53
(17) Area from Gaspe to Baie Verte only
(18) Quebec (city & region) only. In print: RAQ 1925-26, pp 1-143

(19) Montreal and Trois-Rivieres (cities & regions) only. In print: RAQ 1936-37, pp 1-121
(20) All of these are located in Nova Scotia Archives. Those for 1770, 1773, 1787 printed in their Report for 1934.
(21) Church censuses, Quebec City only. In print: RAQ 1948-49, pp 3-250
(22) Augusta Twp, Grenville Co. only
(23) In print: Duncan Campbell History of Prince Edward Island (Charlottetown 1875)
(24) Red River area of Manitoba, at PAC & PAM
(25) One volume in Public Archives of P.E.I.
(26) Portions of this census are now being indexed
(27) Halifax City, Counties of Halifax & Kings only
(28) Halifax City only
(29) Gold commissioners' censuses of Lillooet, Lytton & Douglas in British Columbia
(30) Original MS in Hudson Bay Co. Archives,Winnipeg
(31) Bonavista to Trepassy Bay (English settlements) at Nfld. Archives.
(32) St. John's Harbour (English) at Nfld Archives
(33) St John's City, at Nfld Archives
(34) Trinity Bay, at Nfld Archives
(35) In print: Holland's Description of Cape Breton Island
(36) Province of British Columbia. Being compiled from voters lists by B.C. Genealogical Soc. 50% complete at beginning of 1978.

3:5 WILLS AND PROBATE RECORDS

All records and documents pertaining to the disposition of the estate of a deceased person are known as probate records. As a group, these records constitute one of
the most useful genealogical sources available in many
parts of Canada.

Probate records predate many other genealogical records in most areas of Canada. As settlers moved into new
areas acquiring land and other property, the need for the
orderly disposal of estates after a settler's death was
evident at an early date. It is in this early creation of
probate records that their strength is realized. In many
cases, the information contained in these records may very
well contain the only reference to the date of death of an
ancestor, particularly if his death occurred long before
civil registration was established in his province. In
addition to this, the probate documents may provide the
only complete or nearly-complete list of the deceased's
children or other relatives and can therefore be regarded as a type of "census". Although most researchers
will regard these as the primary uses of probate records,
other advantages can be realized from them if the researcher knows what to look for.

Generally speaking, probate record or, more correctly,
the probate process can be classified into two main types,
each of which generates its own unique records:

> TESTATE: When a person dies leaving a
> valid will, it is said he/she died
> "testate".

> INTESTATE: When a person dies without
> leaving a valid will, it is said that
> he/she died "intestate".

With the exception of the "will", which is created
by the individual, all probate records are the product
of the court system in each province. As a provincial
responsibility, the nature of these documents and their
contents do differ somewhat from province to province.
However, the general concept is the same - that is - to
administer the estate of a deceased person so that there
is a fair distribution of his property after his death,
either according to the laws of relationship and descent
or according to the deceased's last wishes as outlined in
his will, and to provide an impartial judgement of disputes between heirs (ie. those who will benefit from the
estate) should any such disputes arise.

PROCEDURES OF PROBATE

A knowledge of the court proceedures involved with "proving" a will or probating an intestate's estate is very important in determining the records that are available to researchers and the information they are likely to contain.

If there is a will, the proceedure is quite simple, its probate being primarily a formality (except in those cases where the will is contested or challenged). However, when a person died intestate, a longer proceedure takes place whereby the Province, in essence, makes a will for the deceased.

PROCEDURES IN "PROVING A WILL"

The person makes out the Will. Later the person dies.

The Will is presented before the proper court and is proved to be the last will and testament of the deceased (presented by the estate's executor, i.e., the person named in the will to distribute the estate), and an application or petition for probate (name varies) is presented. In recent years, these petitions are invaluable documents containing names of all the heirs, their addresses and their relationship to the deceased.

If valid, the will is admitted to probate, a hearing is set, and notices are published in the newspaper announcing the hearing. If the will is not contested at the hearing, the will is admitted to probate and letters probate or order of administration (legal authorization to proceed) are granted to the executor. The will is then registered and indexed by the court.

The executor then divides the estate according to the terms of the will. An Investory of the Estate is made and the property is appraised for value.

Upon discharging his duties, a decree of distribution is completed by the executor to show how the estate was divided (contains names, addresses, and relationships of the heirs).

PROCEDURES FOR "INTESTATE" PROBATES

Proof of death is submitted to the court (death certificate) and an application or petition for probate is submitted by an interested party. This application shows that the deceased died intestate and includes a list of value and relationship (an inventory of the deceased person's property plus the names, relationships, etc. of those who may share in the estate under that province's laws).

The court then arranges a hearing and contacts all interested parties to confirm their right to a portion of the estate. This done, the court appoints an administrator and the <u>orders of administration</u> are issued.

The administrator distributes the estate according to the laws of succession in that province, and upon completion of his duties, files a <u>decree of distribution</u> (see above).

All these records, irrespective of whether a person died testate or intestate, are normally registered and indexed in a local office of the Surrogate or Probate Court in the Province in which the death occurred. They are not restricted in any way and anyone may obtain copies of them.

The advantages of probate records in genealogical research are clearly illustrated in the aforementioned probate procedures by the numerous types of documents which are generated, in particular, those dealing with the relationships and lists of heirs to the estate.

The terminology used to name some of the above instruments varies from province to province, but their general content remains the same. In addition, these records become particularly useful when they predate civil registration in the province because they often contain data such as the exact date of death which would otherwise be unobtainable. However, there are limitations of the probate records of those dying intestate:

- For one reason or another, not all the people entitled to a part of the estate may be listed. There may be a number of reasons, one being the loss of contact between the various family members.

- Probate records are only required when there is property to distribute. If a person died without property, no probate was necessary.

- Some provinces have established minimum values of estates which can be probated. In cases where the deceased person's estate is valued below the minimum, the heirs are not required to have it probated.

WILLS

A will is a document by which a person decrees how his estate will be disposed of after his death. There are various types of documents used in this regard. The one which deals with the personal property of an individual is sometimes called a _testament_, and the one dealing with the real propery (land), a _devise_. When both of these are combined into one document it is sometimes called a _last will and testament_. However, all are generally regarded as _wills._

In addition to the standard forms which are available at local stationery stores, the following types of wills can also be found in Canada:

HOLOGRAPHIC WILL:
A Holographic will is written, dated and signed entirely in the testator's own hand. A _testator_ or testatrix is the person making the will. This type of will requires no witnesses to its' signing and is allowed in Alberta, Saskatchewan, Manitoba, Quebec, New Brunswick and Newfoundland.

NOTORIAL OR AUTHENTIC WILL:
This type of a will is one which is made by the testator/testatrix before a Notary. The will is then retained in the Notary's files until the testator's death. This type of will is found only in the province of Quebec.

NUNCUPATIVE WILL:
This is a will which is declared by a person who believes he/she is near death and can only be used to dispose of personal property. This will can be written and signed by a witness as a statement and does not require the testator's signature. However, if it is challenged, other witnesses might have to substantiate the statement.

In all cases, the person making out the will can make provisions to dispose of his property after death entirely as he sees fit. He is not required to provide only for his family, but may also include friends or organizations within the list of beneficiaries. He may impose certain conditions on the beneficiaries, which must be adhered to before they can receive their portion. In other words, the general content of any will can vary greatly from that of other wills depending on the charactor of the person making it out or the circumstances under which it was written. Some wills may be very short and uninformative while others may contain a wealth of genealogical information.

After a will has been made, the testator may reconsider some of the instructions it contains and wish to make some changes to the original document. Instead of making out a new will, he may add a _codicil_ to the original will outlining the changes to be made. This is then attached to the will and becomes part of the original document.

When someone named as beneficiary in a will decides
that he should have received more or suspects the will of
being fraudulent, he may contest (or disagree with) the
will. The probate process is then halted until the dis-
agreement is sorted out. A formal contest of a will generally takes the form of a lawsuit, in which case the records
pertaining to it are generally found in another court's
jurisdiction (see chapter 3 - 9).

Wills can have a great value in genealogical research, even more so than the standard probate records of
intestate estates. Some of the major benefits are:

- The relationships of people mentioned in
  the will are usually very correct because
  the testator would have had personal
  knowledge of them.

- Wills can generally be found when no
  other records are available and are
  readily accessible. (Particularly
  good for establishing date of death
  before civil registration of vital
  statistics commenced in a province.)

- Clues to previous residences are often
  included by reference to property which
  may still be owned there.

- References to other records (church,
  professional, land) can often be inter-
  preted from the information contained
  in the will.

Along with the benefits of wills, come some problems,
of which some of the more common are:

- Definite relationships of the beneficiaries of the will may not be given.

- Usually the names of living children
  only are indicated, although children
  of deceased sons or daughters may be
  indicated. As well, spouses may simply
  be referred to as "my wife" or "my
  husband" and the children may be referred
  to simply as "all my children" rather
  than by name.

- Names of the family's "black sheep" may be
  ommitted by a parent not wishing them to
  receive anything from the estate. Missing
  names may also include those children who
  already received their inheritance before
  the will was made.

- The Maiden Name of the wife is almost never included and the wife named may not be the mother of all the children included, if the person was married more than once.

- The general locale of the deceased and the date of death must be known to locate the proper office in which the will was registered.

- Except in Quebec and Prince Edward Island, wills do not have to be probated, although it is generally necessary if the heirs are to take title to any real property involved. However, in Ontario, for example, many wills are recorded in the Land Registry Books under the particular parcel of land which was bequeathed, and were never probated in Surrogate Court.

- Sometimes spelling, handwriting, and legal "jargon" make wills difficult to read/ understand.

LOCATING WILLS AND PROBATES

Wills and probate records are registered with the various Surrogate or Probate Courts in each of the provinces. All provinces are divided into numerous surrogate court districts, each of which is responsible for the administration of its' own records. In most provinces, there is a central registrar for surrogate records. Local courts submit a brief notice to the central agency regarding each application for probate being processed by their offices. These notices generally contain the name, residence, occupation, death date, some information regarding the nature of the probate, and the local surrogate court where the application for probate was made. This is done primarily to ensure that only one application for probate regarding a person is being processed in the province. These notices are indexed alphabetically by year (and sometimes locality) and are open for public examination. However, some provinces require searches in these records to be conducted in person. Once the notice of a particular person is obtained, the local court must be contacted for the complete probate file.

In some provinces, early probate records have been transferred from the jurisdiction of the central registrar to the provincial archives.

The addresses of the provincial courts of probate are included in chapter 5 under their appropriate provincial headings

3:6 MAPS, ATLASES AND DIRECTORIES

Maps, atlases, gazeteers, postal guides and other similar material are very important tools in genealogical research. Through their use it is possible to locate specific towns which may have long since disappeared, find the exact location and legal description of the lands owned by ancestors, follow the migrations of ancestors within a county or province in which they lived, or familiarize ourselves with the areas in which our ancestors resided.

These types of research materials can generally be found in most archives and libraries, although they may only relate to local areas. Many of these repositories will answer mail requests as long as the requests are reasonable and are not too demanding of time. As well, many of the early county atlases and directories (particularly in Ontario) are now being reprinted for researchers and are now available through a number of genealogical societies and publishing companies in Canada.

GAZETEERS AND POSTAL GUIDES

One of the main problems encountered by researchers is that of the "missing" town or locality in which an ancestor lived. Over the course of Canada's history, many communities have changed their names at one time or another or, due to economic changes, have disappeared. In order to conduct his research, a genealogist must first find where a particular community is or was once located. One of the best means of accomplishing this is through the use of gazeteers and postal directories.

Gazeteers generally list the name of a locality along with a description of where it is located in a province or other large geographical area. Depending on the type of gazeteer, other information such as a history of the locality, the derivation of the localities name or a list of the businesses situated there may also be included. Although postal directories are generally restricted only to listing communities with a Post Office, they can be extremely useful when no other directories or gazeteers exist. The following bibliography indicates a few of the many guides of this type:

Bullinger's Postal and Shippers Guide for the United States and Canada (New Jersey, 1897 annually to the present)

Canadian Almanac and Repository of Useful Knowledge published annually since circa 1847 at Toronto under various titles) contains a yearly listing of Post Offices in Canada.

Gazateer of Canada (prepared by Dept. of Energy, Mines and Resources, Ottawa, various years) is the most ambitious of all Canadian gazeteers. It has been prepared on a provincial basis, with each province being completely listed in one volume of the series. (For information on a particular province, write: The Queen's Printer, Ottawa, Ontario.)

Lovell's Gazeteer of British North America (published in Montreal in 1877. 1878, 1881, 1895, and 1908).

Smith's Canadian Gazeteer by William H. Smith (originally published in 1846; now reprinted by Coles Book Co., Toronto) contains a short history of the towns and townships of Ontario.

DIRECTORIES

More important to genealogical research than postal guides and gazeteers are the many directories compiled on a regional basis since the early 19th century. Among the contents are included the manes of all heads of families residing within the area covered by the directory, their addresses and sometimes their occupations. Although the amount of information they contain may seem small, these directories were published frequently enough to provide researchers with a quick and easy way to follow an ancestor's migrations within a region. However, because some of these guides included names of individuals "by subscription only" (i.e., those people appearing in the directory paid to have their names included), they should be treated strictly as a guide for searching original records and not accepted as being absolutely correct in themselves.

The regional areas covered by these directories varied significantly with time and place. For the most part, they were compiled on a city, town, county, or provincial basis, the more detailed directories concentrating on the smaller geographical area as a rule.

Also included in this classification are those publications dealing with specialized areas of interest, such as occupation. These include directories listing the names of doctors, lawyers, morticians, politicians, etc. The various editions of Who's Who also fall in this category. If the occupation of an ancestor is known or if they were prominent in local affairs, it is likely that they can be found in a professional directory. Listings of this type are often more biographical than other directories.

Don't overlook telephone directories in the search for answers to genealogical problems. These directories have been existence for many years now and can prove to be extremely helpful, providing the ancestor owned a telephone. Even the current directories have value to genealogists by supplying the names and addresses of people who have similar surname to that of the family being researched or for locating the names and addresses of businesses, churches, etc. in the community.

Many of these directories, including telephone directories, are found in provincial archives and regional libraries, and enquiries regarding the directories available for a province or a county should be made through these institutions. Some repositories will also answer mail inquiries. If a current telephone directory is needed to search a particular area and is not included in the local library's collection, they can be obtained for a small fee from your local telephone company.

To illustrate the many types of directories available, a few are documented in the following bibliography:

McAlpine's Maritime Provinces Directory (for Nova Scotia, New Brunswick, Newfoundland, and Prince Edward Island); was published in 1870, 1892, 1897, 1898, 1904 and 1911 from various locations. As well, published for Halifax and Sydney, N.S.

Hutchinson's Directories were published on a provincial basis, generally in the provincial capital. Some available editions include Newfoundland (1864-65); Prince Edward Island (1864); New Brunswick (1865-66); and Nova Scotia (1864-65).

Henderson's Directories are Western Canada's major source of directories. They were generally published on an annual or biennial basis and include the following areas:
Manitoba and N.W.T. (1878 - 1905); Manitoba (1876 - 78);
Edmonton (1904 - p); Calgary (1905 - p); Winnipeg
(1878 - p); Regina (1907 - p); Saskatoon (1907 - p);
Brandon (1908 - p); Moose Jaw (1908 - p); Lethbridge
(1910 - p); Prince Albert (1910 - p); and Medicine
Hat (1914 - p).

Other directories were published covering Ontario and
Quebec on a county and city basis and are too numerous to
list here. Inquire at the Provincial Archives or a Regional
library for a catalogue of the directories they hold.

MAPS AND ATLASES

Maps have been compiled for various parts of Canada
containing varying amounts and types of information since
the early days of the European explorers in North America.
While many of these earlier (and later) maps will be of
minor interest to the genealogist, there are many which
are indispensible for research and which provide information similar to that found in many county directories.

Virtually all the types of maps discussed here will be
found in local and provincial archives, and some will be
found reprinted in special atlases or by themselves. Of
particular importance to the genealogist in search of early
maps is the National Map Collection of the Public Archives
of Canada (see Chapter 4). This is the largest map repository in Canada containing over 750,000 maps, atlases and
charts.

Some of the major types of map sources of use to
researchers include:

GENERAL MAPS
These are provincial, regional or county
maps which have been compiled since Canada
was first settled. Included on them are
the boundaries of administration districts,
towns, townships, etc., and they are quite
useful in locating those "missing" towns or
in providing knowledge of changing boundaries. In the early periods of each province's
history, the boundaries of the counties or
municipalities were in a constant state of
change. Often a town, in the course of it's
history, may have been situated in several
counties or administration districts due to
these boundary fluctuations. These early
general maps may help to recreate the political divisions at the time of the maps' composition and may enable the genealogical
researcher to discern the political districts
in which he should concentrate his efforts.

LANDOWNER AND SURVEY MAPS
These maps are of primary importance in
locating the actual farms where the early
settlers in a province resided. Generally,
they are drawn on a local basis and show
the names of the persons who were originally

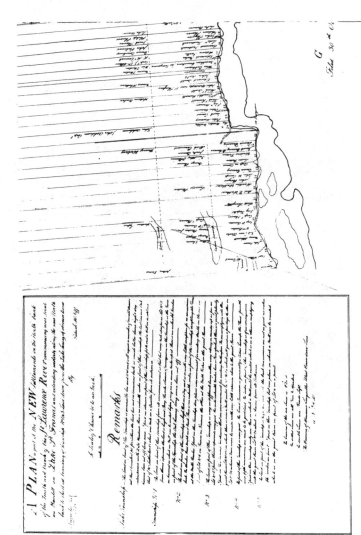

PORTION OF PATRICK McNIFF'S
MAP OF LOYALIST SETTLEMENTS
ON THE ST. LAWRENCE RIVER
1 NOVEMBER 1786

Source: National Map
Collection A1/400 1786
(Courtesy of the Public
Archives of Canada)

granted the parcel of land or were living there at the time the map was made. The oldest known map of this type is the "Catalogne or de Couragne Map of 1709" which shows the names of all the settlers along the St. Lawrence River of New France. Similar maps also were compiled for areas in Ontario and the Maritimes, indicating the sites of United Empire Loyalist farms and the owners names. Possibly the most famous of these maps is Patrick McNiff's "1786 Map of Loyalist Family Locations" which covers that part of the St. Lawrence River between Iroquois and Lake St. Francis in Ontario. In addition to these, the Crown Lands Departments of each province kept a series of maps on which they indicated the names of the original grantees of each parcel of land, as well as the reference numbers needed to locate the original grant and subsequent sales of the property in the Crown Lands files or Local Registry Offices.

For example, the maps of the Crown Lands Department of Ontario (now located in Ministry of Natural Resources, Toronto) go back to the United Empire Loyalist settlement of the province and show information on Loyalist, military and other settler grants. Similar systems developed in Western Canada for showing the name and reference number of persons homesteading on various parcels of land throughout each province. These records are generally located in the Surveys Branch of the provincial department in charge of Natural Resources and are arranged on a township basis. As a rule, no nominal indices exist for these maps (in both Eastern and Western Canada) and the map covering a specific area must be searched lot by lot for a reference to a specific person. As well, they do not include the names of subsequent owners of the property, which information must be sought in the appropriate Registry or Land Titles Office if required.

Another valuable source which generally falls into this catagory are the original "field books" compiled by the surveyors when they laid out the various survey systems. It is not uncommon to find considerable information on "squatters" included within these records in addition

to personal comments by the surveyor.
(see also Chapter 3-7). These "field
books" can often be found deposited with
provincial Surveys Branches or provincial
archives.

COUNTY MAPS AND WALL CHARTS

Most of these maps were published or
compiled during the 1860s and show the
names of some of the landholders in a
county along with the general extent or
location of their properties. As well,
many also show the early stores, churches,
roads, cemeteries, etc., which can be
useful in determining what other record
generating organizations were located in
the area at the time the map was compiled.
Although these maps do not show all the
landowners in a county, and some show only
a very small number, if they are used in
conjunction with county directories researchers will find that together they will
provide a fairly complete record of the
areas inhabitants. A list of these maps
is included in the chart at the end of
this section.

COUNTY ATLASES

The most widely used of all "landowner"
types of maps, the county atlas was
introduced into Canada in the 1870's
from the U.S.A. where they had proven
extremely popular. These atlases were
compiled primarily from the assessment
records of the counties and most show
the names of all the landowners, in
addition to providing a short county and
municipal history at the beginning of
each book. They continued to be published
into the twentieth century. Two main types
of county atlases were compiled. The first
and most useful were those which were
issued as separate publications and show
the names of all landowners within the
county. The second types were printed in
1880-81 as supplements to the Illustrated
Atlas of the Dominion of Canada and contain
only the names of "paid subscribers". As
a result, the number of landowners listed
tends to be few and makes these county
atlases not unlike the earlier county
maps. Their usefulness can be extended
by using them in conjunction with county
directories.

Most of the county atlases have now been reprinted and can be obtained from some of the Canadian publishers listed in Chapter 2-5. Copies of them may also be found in university and large public libraries. The areas covered by these atlases are included in the list at the end of this section.

DIRECTORY MAPS

Similar to the county atlases, these maps were published in the period immediately following the First World War. Most well known of this type is the Cummins Rural Directory, which was published in Toronto in the 1920's. These maps covered Ontario (3 volumes, 1924); Manitoba (1 volume, 1925); Saskatchewan (2 volumes, 1922); and Alberta (1 volume, 1923). It is believed that New Brunswick and Nova Scotia were also covered in this series although there does not appear to be any existing map sheets covering these provinces. The National Map Collection of the Public Archives of Canada, however, has a complete set for the other provinces mentioned and copies of individual map sheets can be obtained from the Public Archives of Canada. The entire set is also available on one reel of microfilm. The name of the desired town or townships should be provided when ordering copies of these maps so that the sheets covering the entire area desired can be provided, as the map sheets are not arranged by county or township. Along similar lines are the Guidal Directory or Guidal Landowners Maps produced for some Ontario townships in 1916-1917. These were arranged on a township basis (one township per map) and cover parts of the counties of Brant, Halton, Middlesex, Ontario, Oxford, Peel, Perth, Waterloo, Wellington and York. Inquiries for copies of these maps should be directed to the Public Archives of Canada.

OTHER MAPS

One type of map which may prove interesting to the genealogist is the Fire Insurance Plan. While they generally contain few if any names, they are so detailed that they show every building located within a town or city and are useful in adding a bit of flavour to any ancestor's life story. The National Map Collection presently holds the Insurance Plans of 139 cities and

PORTION OF HIBBERT TWP. FROM THE COUNTY ATLAS FOR PERTH COUNTY 1879

(Courtesy of Cumming Atlas Reprints)

special Insurance Plans of 42 cities, with
other similar types located in Provincial
and City Archives. Sometimes other maps,
old sketches, plans and diagrams will
contain a few notations of property owners.
An inquiry to the Provincial Archives will
provide an indication of what maps of a
similar nature are available for a specific
locality.

MODERN MAPS

Every researcher should obtain a modern map of the
areas in which he is researching in order to locate towns,
cemeteries, etc. that presently exist and to familiarize
himself with the general area.

One of the best sources of modern maps is the Government of Canada. The maps of the National Topographic
System are the most detailed in the country and, varying
with the scale of the map, include the location of all
roads, churches and cemeteries, etc. More information on
this valuable series can be obtained from the free publication: How to Order a Topographic Map, obtainable by
writing Map Distribution Office, 615 Booth Street, Ottawa,
Ontario, K1A OE9.

In addition to the Federal government series, many of
the provincial governments have also compiled maps of their
own province. In most cases, the maps issued by each province are restricted to showing existing administrative
boundaries, including school districts, county or municipal
districts, land registration districts, etc. Catalogues
of available map publications can be obtained from the
Surveys Division of each provincial department in charge
of Natural Resources. As well, it is possible to obtain
free provincial road maps from the Tourism Department of
each province. While rather limited in scope, the index
to towns and cities on these maps are always better than
anything found in modern atlases which are available in
local bookstores. Addresses of the provincial departments
responsible for these maps can be found in Chapter 5.

AERIAL PHOTOGRAPHS

Virtually unused by genealogists, aerial photographs can
give a printed family history a bit more sparkle. The first
photography of this type was taken in Canada in the 1920's
and, at the present time, literally no part of Canada remains
unphotographed. This resource can be helpful in providing a
picture of the family farm or house in town, particularly if

these buildings have long since disappeared and no other record of their positions exists. For more information on
aerial photography write: National Air Photo Library, 615
Booth Street, Ottawa, Ontario, K1A 0E9.

BIBLIOGRAPHY

In recent years a number of worthwhile publications
have appeared which deal with the use of maps in genealogical research. Some of these are:

Dubreuil, Lorraine (Comp.): Directory of Canadian
Map Collections (Ottawa 1977)

Canada, Department of the Interior: Catalogue of Maps,
Plans and Publications of the Topographical Survey
(Ottawa 1930)

"The Districts of Upper Canada" in Ontario History
Volume XXX1X (1947)

Kidd, Betty: Using Maps in Tracing Your Family Tree
(Ottawa Branch, Ontario Genealogical Society,
Publication 74-14)

Fire Insurance Plans in the National Map Collection
(PAC, Ottawa 1977)

Maddick, Heather: County Maps: Land Ownership Maps
of Canada in the 19th Century (PAC Ottawa 1976)

May, Betty: County Atlases of Canada: A Descriptive
Catalogue (Public Archives of Canada, 1970)

Morris, J.L.: Ontario and its' Subdivisions, 1763-
1867 (manuscript compiled by J. L. Morris with
copies in Public Archives of Canada)

Nicholson, Norman: The Boundaries of Canada, its'
Provinces and Territories (Queen's Printer, Ottawa
1964)

Poulin, Guy: Index to Township Plans of the Canadian
West (PAC, Ottawa 1964)

COUNTY MAPS AND ATLASES OF CANADA

This chart lists maps and atlases available for each county. Atlases included as supplements to the "Illustrated Atlas of Canada" are marked with asterisks. For the maps of Nova Scotia, the date in parenthasis is the date of publication.

	COUNTY NAME	MAPS	ATLASES
ONTARIO	Addington	1860 (5)	1878 (5)
	Brant	1858, 1859, 1875	1875
	Bruce		*1880
	Carleton	1863	1879
	Dufferin		*1881 (6)
	Dundas	1862 (7)	1879 (7)
	Durham	1861	1878 (8)
	Elgin	1864	1877
	Essex	1877	*1881
	Frontenac	1860 (5)	1878 (5)
	Glengarry	1862 (7)	1879 (7)
	Grenville	1861 (9)	1861 (9)
	Grey		*1880
	Haldimand	1863	1879
	Halton	1858	1877
	Hastings		1878 (10)
	Huron	1862	1879
	Kent	(1876)	*1881
	Lambton		*1880
	Lanark	1863 (11)	*1880
	Leeds	1861 (9),	1861 (9)
	Lennox	1860 (5)	1878 (5)
	Lincoln	1862 (12)	1876 (12)
	Middlesex	1862	1878
	Muskoka		1879 (13)
	Norfolk	1856	1877
	Northumberland		1878 (8)
	Ontario	1860	1877, 1895
	Oxford	1857, 1896	1876
	Parry Sound		1879 (13)
	Peel	1859	1877
	Perth	1888	1879
	Peterborough		(14)
	Prescott	1862 (15)	*1881 (15)
	Prince Edward	1863	1878 (10)
	Renfrew	1863 (11)	*1881
	Russell	1862 (15)	*1881 (15)
	Simcoe	1871	1878 (16), *1881
	Stormont	1862 (7)	1879 (7)
	Victoria	1877	*1881
	Waterloo	1861	*1881
	Wellington	1861, 1885	1877, 1906
	Wentworth	1859	1875, 1903
	York	1860	1878
	Welland	1862 (12)	1876 (12)

	COUNTY NAME	MAPS	ATLASES
QUEBEC	Deux-Montagnes	1888	
	Brome	1864 (3)	*1881 (4)
	Compton	1863 (16)	
	Huntingdon		*1881 (4)
	Iberville	1864 (3)	
	Missisquoi	1864 (3)	*1881 (4)
	Richmond	1863 (16)	
	Rouville	1864 (3)	
	Shefford	1864 (3)	
	Stanstead	1863 (16)	*1881 (4)
	Terrebonne	1886	
	Wolfe	1863 (16)	
P.E.I.	Whole province	1863	1880, 1925
NOVA SCOTIA	Annapolis	1864 (1876)	
	Antigonish	1864 (1878)	
	Cape Breton	1864 (1877)	
	Colchester	1864 (1874)	
	Cumberland	- (1873)	
	Digby	1864 (1871)	
	Guysborough	1864 (1876)	
	Halifax	1864 (1865)	
	Hants	1869 (1871)	
	Inverness	1864 (1883-87)	
	Kings	1864 (1872)	
	Lunenburg	1864 (1883-87)	
	Pictou	1864 (1867)	1879
	Queens	1864 (1888)	
	Richmond	1864 (1883-87)	
	Shelburne	1864 (1882)	
	Victoria	1864 (1883-87)	
	Yarmouth	1864 (1871)	
N. B.	Albert	1862 (1)	
	Carleton	1876	
	Kings	1862 (2)	
	Northumberland	1876	
	Saint John	1862 (2)	1875
	Westmoreland	1862 (1)	
	York		1878

NOTES
(1) Published as "Westmoreland/Albert"
(2) Published as "Saint John/Kings"
(3) Published as "Shefford, Iberville, Brome, Missisquoi and Rouville"
(4) Published as "Eastern Townships and Southwestern Quebec"
(5) Published as "Frontenac, Lennox and Addington"
(6) Found in atlases for Simcoe and Grey Counties
(7) Published as "Stormont, Dundas and Glengarry"
(8) Published as "Northumberland and Durham"
(9) Atlas compiled from 1861-62 county map by Mika
(10) Published as "Hastings and Prince Edward"
(11) Published as "Lanark/Renfrew"
(12) Published as "Lincoln and Welland"
(13) Published as "Muskoka and Parry Sound"
(14) New atlas compiled by Peterborough Historical Soc.
(15) Published as "Prescott and Russell"
(16) Published as "St. Francis"

3:7 LAND RECORDS

It is very rare to find complete basic genealogical information contained in land records. Their very nature, (i.e. to transfer property from one party to another) does not necessitate the inclusion of irrelevant names, birthdates, names of parents, etc. However, depending on the type of land record and the time period during which it was created, researchers are likely to find some basic genealogical data. Despite some shortcomings, they do comprise one of the most important early sources for genealogical research in Canada.

There are three major reasons why land records are important in genealogy. Briefly, they are:

- Early Canadians were very land-conscious. Land was inexpensive and readily available, and the majority of the population generally owned some. As a result, until well into the nineteenth century, nearly every adult male can be found somewhere in the land records.

- Land records exist from the very beginning of the first permanent settlement in Canada and are often the only records existing for early settlement periods. In such circumstances, their very existence makes them more valuable than they ordinarily would have been.

- Many of the earlier land records, such as the land petitions, contain a significant amount of basic genealogical data. This is quite different from other sources in which the older records generally contain very little genealogical data.

CANADIAN LAND SYSTEMS AND SURVEYS

Land subdivision systems have existed in Canada in one form or another since the beginning of settlement. Although the systems themselves are quite varied and their origins were directly influenced by the social, economic and political events of their time, all were primarily concerned with the orderly division of land into easily discernable small parcels which could be made available to settlers by grant or by sale. Each maintained some sort of reference system whereby an individual parcel of land could be identified as a distinct and unique unit, which enabled each to be sold or transferred to individuals without becoming confused with other parcels of land in the general vicinity or in the province.

Four major systems of subdivision have developed in Canada since the arrival of the first settlers:

RIVER LOT SYSTEM: This is the first system to appear in Canada and is characterized by long narrow lots running perpendicular to and along major rivers and water courses. Possibly the best known example of this system is the Seigeurial System of land tenure which developed in New France.

In the early period of settlement in Canada, rivers and other water courses were often the only means of transportation, and each settler required access to them in order to transport his produce and to have a direct link between his farm and the cultural and economic centres of the country. In order to guarantee accessibility, the long narrow lot was developed, each having frontage on the water course. Boundaries between lots were normally straight lines which ran perpendicular to the river and parallel to one another. Lots often varied in width.

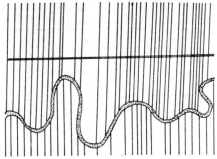

PATCHWORK SYSTEM: Also referred to as the "crazy-quilt" system of land survey, it is similar to those which developed in England and the early American colonies. Natural features such as rocks, trees, rivers, etc. were used in determining the beginning and end of boundary lines between properties. A typical description of a parcel of land within this system might read "commencing at the large birch tree west of John Miller's stable, the boundary line runs in a north easterly direction to the large granite rock about 826' from the point of commencement, then in an easterly direction to William's

Creek...." Because of this reliance on local features, few boundaries were parallel or perpendicular to one another and produced many odd-shaped lots of varying size.

As a rule, these lots are organized within a parish or township and are given numbers to set them apart from the other lots. Reference to a specific lot would read "Lot - , - Parish, - County" within a province. This system is found primarily in the Maritimes, especially in Nova Scotia and Newfoundland.

RECTANGULAR LOT SYSTEM: Like the patchwork system, this system utilizes the township or parish as its largest component. Each township was further subdivided into a series of lots, each of uniform size (about 100-200 acres) and shape (rectangular).

Possibly the best known example of this type of survey is the system which developed in Ontario (see diagram). Lots would be arranged in rows and numbered consecutively, and each row (or concession) would also be numbered. In this way a grid system was formed within each township. The lot which is asterisked in the example would be identified as "Lot 12, Concession V, - Township, - County".

This system occurs in Ontario, Quebec, and in the Maritimes. In Ontario and Quebec, provision was also made for Clergy Reserves (shown dotted in the example) and Crown Reserves (shown by dashed lines), the sale of which was to financially benefit the churches and the Crown respectively. The remaining lots were Crown Lands which were granted or sold to individuals by the government.

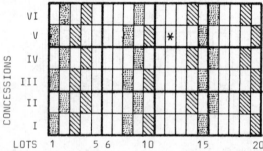

DOMINION LANDS SYSTEM: This system covers the largest area of Canada and was based on the American public lands system. It was instituted in Canada in 1870.

The base unit of this system is the township (not to be confused with the townships of eastern Canada) which contains 36 square miles. The township is divided into 36 seperate "sections", each containing one square mile (640 acres). Each section is further divided into four 160 acre parcels called "quarter-sections", which are generally the smallest unit of this system.

The townships are arranged in a grid system over the area of the survey and are numbered consecutively from south to north, beginning with Township 1 which runs along the U.S.-Canada border (49th parallel). To provide a grid index from east to west, each North-South tier of townships is designated a "range" and numbered consecutively, generally from east to west, from one of six meridians. Each of these meridians were used as the reference line for the surveys originating from it. The Principle Meridian (longtitude 97°30'W) is located in Manitoba with ranges running east and west from it. The 2nd (102°W) and 3rd (106°W) Meridians fall in Saskatchewan with the 4th Meridian (110°W) falling along the Saskatchewan-Alberta border. The 5th Meridian (114°W) falls in Alberta and the 6th Meridian (118°W) in Alberta and B.C.

Identification of individual lots is by reference to all of these components. The asterisked parcel in the example would be referred to as the "southeast quarter of Section 6, Township - , Range - , West (or East) of the - Meridian".

Certain sections within each township were set aside for particular purposes. Those lands reserved as School Lands are shown by short dashed lines in the example and those reserved for the Hudson's Bay Company are shown dotted. These two concessions generally occur in all townships. Land was also granted to the railroads to help finance the building of rail lines. Although they do not appear in all townships, they do appear in many. The general rule was to set aside all odd-numbered sections for the railroads (shown by diagonal lines) in areas affected by these grants. All the even numbered sections (except the HBC lands) were Crown Lands, which were sold or granted to individuals by the government.

The Dominion Lands System exists primarily in Manitoba, Saskatchewan, Alberta, and parts of British Columbia.

TOWNSHIP NUMBERING SYSTEM   STANDARD LAND GRANTS

31	32	33	34	35	36
30	29	28	27	26	25
19	20	21	22	23	24
18	17	16	15	14	13
7	8	9	10	11	12
6	5	4	3	2	1

Although these systems vary somewhat from place to place in order to conform to the shape of the land, their basic principles are maintained. Maps showing the num-

bering systems of each for various parts of Canada can be
obtained from the Federal and Provincial government mapping agencies, and should be consulted before attempting
to locate land records.

The types of land records which exist today are the
result of two major situations:

1.   When the government (or a land company,
     in some cases) grants or sells a parcel
     of land to an individual.

2.   When individuals deal in land, selling
     or conveying a parcel to one another.

The balance of this chapter is divided into two parts
which reflect on each of these two situations and the
records which have resulted from them.

PART 1: ORIGINAL LAND GRANTS

Originally, in theory, all land in Canada belonged
to the King, French or English, and was granted by him to
the individual settlers or land colonization companies.
The responsibility for granting the land rested with the
colonial governments who were responsible for determining
who would receive parcels or blocks of land. After the
initial granting of a parcel of land from the Crown to the
individual, the colonial government's obligation ceased.
Subsequent transfers of the property then became the
responsibility of local registrars and land titles offices.
However, the records generated by the initial granting of
the property can provice some genealogical information and
should not be overlooked in the course of research.

SEIGNEURIAL RECORDS

The Seigneurial system developed in New France and
was, in fact, a form of feudal tenure. Large grants of
land were issued to certain persons (known as Seigneurs)
who held them in feudal servitude to the King. One of
the stipulations which came with the grant was the responsibility of the Seigneur to populate his land with
tenant-farmers (known as Habitants), who held their lands
in servitude to the Seigneur. Although a French system,
it was retained after the British acquired Canada in 1763
and continued as an important system of land tenure until
it was abolished in 1854.

Many various records have developed out of this system, notably the sale of the "rights" of Habitants to
occupy specific parcels of land within a Seigneury.
Although the Habitant did not own his land, he did have

the "right of occupancy", which was often bought and sold
in much the same manner as ownership of property is today.
The feudal responsibilities of the Seigneur also resulted
in other records such as seigneurial censuses and those
of the Seigneurial courts, all of which are important in
genealogical research.

Seigneurial records and the "land sales" of the
Habitants can be found in a variety of repositories,
notably the Quebec judicial archives, the Archives
nationales de Quebec and the Public Archives of Canada
(see chapter 3:13 and chapter 5: Quebec for more
details on records and the addresses of the various
repositories).

CROWN LANDS RECORDS

Crown Grants are those records which were creáted by
the colonial (or provincial) governments primarily in
Ontario, Quebec and the Maritimes. These grants were
originally made to all Loyalists or children of Loyalists
and later to all settlers in the various provinces. Each
province maintained a system whereby a petition for a
grant had to be submitted by each settler. This petition
was reviewed by the government before the grant was
awarded. The procedures for petitioning for a land grant
varied from province to province but for the most part
were quite similar. To illustrate the various procedures
involved, the system that developed in Ontario (Upper
Canada) will be discussed below.

Land grants available in Upper Canada (and Lower
Canada or Quebec) were granted to the United Empire
Loyalists both as a reward for their loyalty to the
English Crown and as a stimulation for settlement of
the country. As a rule, the extent of the grant varied
with the rank which the Loyalist held in the various
Loyalist Regiments which fought in the American Revolution, the higher ranking officers receiving larger
grants than the privates. Loyalist grants averaged 200
acres for each head of the family, with an additional
200 acres granted to his wife if she was the daughter of
a Loyalist and a further 50 acres for each child in the
family who was under-age.

Over time, this was also extended to the Loyalist's
children, each of whom received 200 acres on reaching matur-
ity. Ordinary settlers who arrived later were entitled
to a 200 acre grant plus an additional 50 acres of family
land for each child in the family.

Beginning in 1764 in Quebec and 1795 in Ontario, any
early settler who wished to obtain a free grant of land
was required to submit a petition directly to the Governor
or Lt. Governor in which he stated his claim. These petitions went through a variety of steps before the actual

grant was made to the petitioner. Prior to 1818, the
following procedures were generally followed in Upper
Canada:

- The Petition was made to the Lt. Governor
  in Council and, if approved, a grant was
  ordered by the Council.

- A copy of the Order-in-Council with a
  Warrant to Survey was forwarded to the
  Receiver General's Office where all
  appropriate fees were paid.

- The Receiver General's receipt was sent
  back to the Council and filed.

- The Order-in-Council and the Warrant of
  Survey were then forwarded to the Attorney
  General's Office where the Order was
  replaced by a. fiat authorizing the grant
  to be made. The fiat and the Warrant
  were then taken to the Surveyor General's
  Office.

- The Surveyor General located the parcel of
  land to be granted and issued a Description
  of the Location.

- The description and the fiat were forwarded
  to the Provincial Secretary who engrossed
  the Patent or certificate which proved
  ownership of the parcel of land. A record
  of each patent was then recorded in the
  Docket Book of the Auditor General and in
  the Register of the Provincial Registrar.
  The Provincial Secretary kept the fiat
  and description and issued the patent to
  the petitioner.

In return for the grant of land, the ordinary
settler was required to perform some settlement duties,
including the building of a house, the clearing and
cultivation of a specific amount of land, etc., all to
be performed within a particular time period. Because
many settlers evaded these duties, the land granting process was later changed to require an affidavit to be
presented to the Surveyor General by the petitioner,
before the fees were paid and the Attorney-General's
fiat was issued, which attested to the fact that the
settlement duties had been performed. These settlement
duties, however, pertained to the ordinary settler only,
the Loyalists and military settlers being exempt from
them. Those grants exempt from these duties are generally
referred to as "privileged grants".

Free grants were abolished in 1827, except for those
people who were children of United Empire Loyalists and

To His Excellency Francis Gore Esquire [108]
Lieutenant Governor of the province
of Upper Canada &c &c &c

In Council

The Petition of Peter Servis of the Township of Osnabruck
Humbly Sheweth

That your Petitioner is a U.E. Loyalist and Served in
the Second Battalion as a private soldier. Command'd by
Sir John Johnson Knt and Bart and was Discharg'd from
said Regt and have been In this Province since the year
1797. and has never Reciv'd But one hundred acres of Land
from the Crown

Wherefore your Petitioner Prays that your
Excellency may be pleased to Grant your Petitioner Two hundred
acres of the waste Lands of the Crown Being the Remainder
of his Majesty Bounty to persons of his Description and
formed Allen McNabb of the Town of York yeoman to be his
agent to Locate the Same In the Township of
and Sue out the Deed when Compleated and that your
Excellency may be pleased to have his name Inserted on the U.E.
List

And your Petitioner will Ever Pray

Peter Servis

Williamsburgh 30th January 1807

THE LAND PETITION OF PETER SERVIS

Source: Upper Canada Land Petitions,
RG 1, L3, "S" Bundle, Vol. 453 (a), p. 108
(Courtesy of the Public Archives of Canada)

those who were eligible for grants for militia or military service. At that time, a commissioner of Crown Lands was appointed who became responsible for the sale of all existing Crown Lands in Ontario and to whom all petitions and applications for land purchases were then directed.

These processes produced a number of records which are potentially useful to the genealogist, as can be seen in the land grant process described earlier. In order that their value be fully recognized, these records are briefly explained below:

> PETITIONS: The petitions are potentially the most useful of all the records generated by these systems, often containing a considerable amount of information on the petitioner's family, parentage, military service, age, wife's name, the time when he settled on the land applied for, etc. This is especially true of those who applied for "priviledged grants". The petitions submitted by ordinary settlers, however, may not be as detailed.

> WARRANTS AND FIATS: These documents were created by the various government officials and were the authority on which the location and the grant were made.

> PATENTS OR CERTIFICATES: These records were the "deed" or proof of ownership which were issued to the petitioners. They generally contain the name of the grantee, a description of the land granted and the date of the grant.

> OTHER RECORDS: References to land grants and petitions can also be found in the Minutes of the Land Committees of the Executive Councils and in the Docket Books and Registers mentioned in the grant process described above. Only basic information will generally be found in these records.

Although the petitions themselves are potentially the most useful records, it is possible that not all of them have survived to the present day. Therefore, if it is known or suspected that an ancestor recieved a Crown Grant but no petition can be found, researchers may wish to check several of the other available records for references to the grant.

The early land grants of Ontario and Quebec, unlike those of other provinces, are divided between the Public Archives of Canada and the Provincial Archives This can be quite confusing and frustrating to the researcher.

The division of the records is the result of political processes and, once clearly understood, is not as ominous as may appear at first. Originally all petitions were in the custody of the Executive Councils of the two provinces. Upon the Act of Union in 1841, these records were transferred to the Executive Council of the United Province of Canada and with Confederation came under the custody of the Dominion Government. As a result, the petitions and the minutes of the Executive Councils which relate to land matters can be found in the Public Archives of Canada, while other land records are still retained by the provinces or are deposited in the provincial archives.

Those records in the Public Archives of Canada can be found in <u>Record Group 1: Executive Council Records 1764-1867</u> and are arranged as follows:

Series L1: Minute Books 1787-1867

This series contains the minute books of the Land Committees of the Executive or Legislative Councils of Quebec 1787-91, Lower Canada 1791-1835, Upper Canada 1791-1841, and the United Province of Canada 1841-67. Most volumes in this collection contain a nominal index. The complete series has been microfilmed.

Series L2: Grants, Leases and Licenses of Occupation, Upper Canada 1791-1841

This series contains a collection of surrendered grants, leases and lcenses of occupation for Upper Canada, arranged geographically by township. A nominal card index (on microfilm) is available.

Series L3: Land Petitions 1637-1867

This is the most valuable of the series, containing the original petitions for grants which were submitted to the Governor of: Quebec and Lower Canada 1637-1842, Upper Canada 1791-1841, United Canada 1841-67. In addition to the petitions, a variety of supporting documents, certificates, etc. can also be found within this series. The complete collection has been microfilmed. A nominal card index (on microfilm) is also available.

Series L7: Miscellaneous Records 1765-1867

This series contains a miscellaneous collection of warrent books, registers of Orders-in-Council, registers of land grants, Docket Book abstracts and others.

Records other than those discussed above are today located in the provincial archives or other government offices. The Ontario Archives houses the following records (RG1) which should be used in conjunction with those located at the Public Archives of Canada:

Letters, received by the Surveyor General and the Commissioner of Crown Lands, 1786-1905.

Petitions and Applications, for the period 1827-65.
Unlike the petitions found at the Public Archives of
Canada which were directed to the Lt. Governor, these
petitions were addressed to the Commissioner of Crown
Lands and, as such, constitute a seperate collection.

Fiats and Warrants, 1796-1885. These are all the fiats
and warrants which were issued in this period.

Land Files - "Township Papers", 1783-c 1880. These are
miscellaneous records relating to land and are arranged
by township, concession and lot.

In Quebec, the Archives nationales also retains a
large number of land records which supplement those in
the Public Archives:

Bureau des Roles, Grants of Land, 1788-1851 (series QB
QBC-10) contains copies of the Letters Patent and other
land records.

Bureau du Registraire, Grants and Sales of Land, 1762-
1867 (QBC-11) contains copies of land grants, indexed
alphabetically.

Bureau de l'Auditeur des Lettres Patent, 1797-1841
(QBC-12) contains Docket Books in which the Letters
Patent were registered, with a nominal index.

Terres de la Couronne, 1793-1899 (QBC-13) contains a
variety of miscellaneous records for Crown Lands.

Demandes de Terres, 1788-1900 (QBC-14) contains petitions for land and other correspondence, arranged by
township.

Demandes de Terres des Miliciens, 1812-51 (QBC-15) contains petitions for land from militiamen.

In addition to the records at the Archives
nationales, a complete list of the land grants made in
Quebec can be found in List of Lands Granted by the Crown
in the Province of Quebec from 1763 to 31 December 1890,
published in 1891 by order of the Quebec Legislature. All
the grants are arranged by township within each county with
an alphabetical index to the grantees included at the end
of the book. A copy of this can be found at the Public
Archives of Canada.

In addition to the lands which were offered by grant
or sale to individuals by the government, there were parcels of land which were put aside for special purposes and
which deserve special mention. These include: the Jesuit
Estates, the Clergy Reserves, the Crown Reserves and the
School Lands. The Jesuit Estates were the properties owned
by the Roman Catholic Society of Jesus which were confisc-
ated by the Crown following the conquest of Canada by the
British and were located entirely in Quebec. These lands

were first rented and then sold separate from the Crown
Lands in Quebec, the records of which are now located in
the Archives nationales de Quebec (series QBC-18-20). The
Clergy Reserves and the Crown Reserves were designated
parcels of land with the money obtained from their sale
going to provide financial support to the Protestant Clergy
and to the Crown. The terms here were used to describe
these reserves in Ontario and Quebec, although similar
grants under various other names were also made in the
Maritimes. These lands, along with School Lands (to provide financial support to the schools) were later sold in
much the same manner as the Crown Lands, and by the same
government agencies.

The Crown grant system was also employed throughout
the Maritime provinces, with petitions and procedures
similar to those described for Upper Canada. However,
unlike their counterparts in Ontario and Quebec, Maritime
records are more centralized and easier to find. The
Crown Land sections in Chapter 5 will direct researchers
to the appropriate agencies holding these records in each
of those provinces. As well, microfilm copies of the
records may also be found in various archives in the
Maritimes.

LAND BOARDS AND THE HEIR AND DEVISEE COMMISSIONS

In Upper Canada, the first land patents or certificates
were not issued until 1795, over ten years after the beginning of settlement. Prior to this time, a number of other
documents were used in their place to prove ownership of
property. The first of these was the "location ticket"
which was issued to the settler by the surveyor. Later
in 1789, Lord Dorchester, the Governor-General of Canada,
established four land districts in Upper Canada (later
expanded to seven) which had the authority to grant
"certificates of location" for 200 acres to each head of
family and 50 acres to each member of the family who had
settled in Upper Canada prior to February 1789. These
boards continued until 1794 when they were abolished and
individual magistrates were authorized to grant recommendations for grants of 200 acres. This system of magistrate
recommendations was dropped in 1795 with all subsequent
applications for land grants going directly to the
Governor by petition.

Although the petitions and some other records submitted to or generated by these land boards will be
found in the Public Archives of Canada, Record Group 1,
Series L1 and L3 (see above), the boards' minutes, correspondence, etc. has been preserved as a separate series
(L4) within this record group and may contain some information of value to the genealogist. There is no index
to this series, although it is arranged chronologically
by district.

The "location tickets" and the "certificates of location" were meant to be temporary proof of ownership only, and were to be exchanged for land patents at a later date. However, due to the long interval between the issuing of the first "ticket" and the first patent, many of these early certificates were used as land deeds when property was sold or were inherited by a relative when the original possesser of the certificate died. The use of these "tickets" as proof of land ownership created problems after the land grant process was assumed by the Lt. Governor and the Executive Council and in order to clarify the situation an act was passed in 1797 which provided for the appointment of commissioners in each land district to review all claims for land grants and, when valid, replace the earlier "tickets" with land patents. This was known as the Heir and Devisee Commission.

Heir and Devisee Commissions reviewed petitions from heirs (i.e., one who receives property as the legal representative of a former owner is a heir), devisees (a person who has been left property through a formal will is a devisee) and assigneees (one to whom land has been transferred, presumably through purchase, is an assignee) of the original nominees. Provided the original "ticket" holder's title to a parcel of land was valid, the commissions issued patents to the petitioners. The records generated by this review board include minutes, notices of claim, reports, certificates, location tickets, and other supporting documents for each claim and often contain a considerable amount of genealogical information.

In reality, there were two separate Commissions established, one existing for 1797-1804 and the other for the period 1805-1911. The records of the first Commission are now located at the Public Archives of Canada in Record Group 1, Series L5. They are arranged in series by district, then by type of document and chronologically or alphabetically within that. The records of the second commission are located at the Ontario Archives in Record Group 40, with the case files arranged alphabetically by claimant name on a annual basis. Although these records can be quite informative by themselves, researchers should use them in conjunction with the other crown land records.

DOMINION LANDS RECORDS

In 1869, the Canadian government concluded negotiations for the transfer of Rupert's Land from the Hudson's Bay Company to the new Dominion and with it brought most of the land in western Canada under the direct administration of the federal government. Over the next several decades, this vast territory was divided into individual parcels of land using the Dominion Lands system of subdivision, a system based on the public lands system of the United States.

According to the agreement between the Hudson's Bay Company and the Dominion, the HBC was to receive 1/20 of all the subdivided land in the territory as part-payment for the transfer. The government set aside sections 8 and 26 in each township for this purpose, transferring title to them to the HBC once the land had been surveyed. The government also set aside sections 11 and 29 in each township as School Lands, the proceeds of their sale to be used to support public education in the west. The remaining lands were retained by the government as crown lands for sale or grant to individuals or companies.

In order to help finance the building of the Canadian Pacific Railroad and other railroads, the government made large concessions of the remaining crown lands to the individual railway companies, who sold these lands through their own land departments. As a rule, the railways were granted the uncommitted odd-numbered sections in each township within a designated area or railway belt. In these areas, the remaining even-numbered sections were retained as crown lands by the government, to be sold or granted to individual settlers.

To more effectively fulfil its responsibilities in the settlement of the west and to more efficiently manage its large land holding, the federal government created the Department of the Interior in 1873 and the Dominion Lands Branch, which up until then formed part of the Department of the Secretary of State, was transferred to it to form the nucleus of the new Department.

The free grants, or homesteads, as well as other granting processes were administered by the Dominion Lands Branch from 1870 until 1930. (In 1930, the natural resources and the remaining government lands were transferred from the federal government to the provinces who then assumed all responsibility for land grants and administration.) These homesteads and the records resulting from them constitute the largest collection of records relating to government land in the west. Although the regulations for obtaining a homestead varied from time to time, the basic provision remained largely the same. The following procedure illustrates the steps each homestead went through and the settlement duties required of the homesteader:

- A prospective settler would select his land and would then file on it at the local Dominion Lands Office, where he would also pay a ten dollar homestead fee.

- The name of the settler and a description of his land would then be forwarded by the Dominion Land Agent to his head

office where it was entered in the
Homestead Application Registers.

- For three years (time period varies)
  following this, the settler was
  required to live on the land for a
  certain number of months each year
  and was also required to bring a
  specific amount of land under
  cultivation and to build a house
  and other improvements.

- At the conclusion of the three
  years residence, the settler could
  then apply for his Letters Patent
  by submitting a statement which
  detailed his period of residence
  on the land, that he was a British
  subject either born or naturalized,
  and the improvements he had made to
  the land. The information contained
  in the statement had to be approved
  by a Homestead Inspection or by two
  neighbours, who also submitted
  statements.

- If the information contained in these
  statements were verified, a Letters
  Patent would then be issued to the
  settler.

The most informative of the records created by this
process are the homestead applications and statements submitted at the end of the period of residence. These records
include the name of the applicant, his age, address, a
description of the land, and information regarding his
citzenship, occupation, the date he settled on the land,
the composition of his family, the number of acres under
cultivation, the number and kind of livestock owned, and
a description of the buildings and other structures he had
erected. These applications were transferred to the provinces in 1930 and are now deposited with provincial
agencies in Manitoba, Saskatchewan, Alberta and British
Columbia, or with the provincial archives. (see Chapter
5 for the addresses of the repositories and agencies.)
Although the applications were transferred to the provinces, the registers and indices to the land grants were
not and are located today in RG 15 of the Public Archives
of Canada, although copies of these may also be held by the
provincial agencies responsible for Dominion Lands. Some
of these registers are extremely useful in locating information on individual ancestors if the description of the
parcel of land he homesteaded is not known. They include:

Homestead Application Registers 1872-1932: 154 vols.,
contains the date of application, applicant's name, and
land description. As 41 out of every 100 homesteaders
did not get Letters Patent, the only reference to them
will likely be found in these registers.

Alphabetical Index to Patentees in Manitoba, Saskatchewan, Alberta, the Railway Belt and the Peace River
Block in British Columbia 1873-1930: contains the name
of the patentee, land description, acreage, nature of
the grant, grant number, file number, etc.

Land Description Index to Patentees of Crown Lands in
Manitoba, Saskatchewan, Alberta, the Railway Belt and
the Peace River Block in British Columbia 1873-1930:
arranged by quartersection, giving the appropriate
registration numbers to the Letter Patent for each.

The homestead is perhaps the best known of the land
grants issued in Western Canada. However, there are a
number of other grants and leases of government lands, in
addition to some pecularities within the homestead system,
whuch may contain information on ancestors. Although some
of these records were handled similar to the homesteads and
are contained within the indices and registers described
above, others were not. The brief descriptions which follow
are primarily meant to acquaint researchers with these other
processes and deviations from the homestead process rather
than to provide complete details on each:

SECOND HOMESTEADS: For a short period between 1882 and
1889, homesteaders who had filed on land and obtained
Letters patent were allowed to sell their first homestead and move to an unsettled area of the country
where they would take up a "second homestead". In this
way those settlers who were proficient at opening
virgin lands could be induced to move on once they had
established one farm, selling it to the inexperienced
homesteader. It was hoped that this would speed the
opening of the west.

PRE-EMPTION: This process developed in The United
States and was adopted in Canada in 1874. Basically, it
allowed a settler who had entered on a homestead to
obtain an "interim entry" on another quarter-section
located adjacent to his homestead. After he received
his Letters Patent for his homestead, he could then
purchase the additional "pre-emption" land at government prices. However, because of the checkerboard
pattern created by the railway grants, homesteaders
often just purchased an adjacent quarter section from
the railways instead. As a result, pre-emptions were
discontinued in 1890, but were again introduced in 1908

when both the odd and even numbered sections in some
areas were opened to homesteaders (because no more
railway grants were being made). Pre-emption was finally repealed in 1918. A variation of this was the
"purchased homestead".

HALF-BREED SCRIP: This was a method by which the Metis
or "Half Breeds" who were residents of the Hudson's Bay
Company Lands in Western Canada at the time it was
transferred to the federal government could be provided
for in light of lost or disappearing hunting rights.
The Half Breed head of family had the option of obtaining a grant of land or a specific amount in scrip (ie.
a promissory note) which was redeemable for a government land parcel of the head of family's choosing. This
scrip was originally issued to the Metis of Manitoba
in 1870 but was extended in 1885 to include the Metis
of the North West Territories. After 1876, no grant of
land was offered, only scrip. Often this scrip was sold
at a fraction of its value to various speculators who
then used it to acquire Dominion Lands.
     There are several collections of records relating
to Half Breed Scrip and grants, all of which are found
in RG 15 of the Public Archives of Canada. The first
group consists of affidavits which were made by the
Half Breed heads of families, their children, and the
Original White Settlers in support of their claims for
homestead entry in Manitoba, 1870-85. Included is
information such as name, occupation, date and place of
birth, names of parents and origin. These are listed
and filed alphabetically in 6 volumes. The second
collection consists of the Half Breed applications for
scrip, 1885 and 1900, in 36 volumes. They are arranged
in alphabetical order and contain information similar
to the first collection. The last group of records are
the alphabetical indexes and registers of North West
Half Breeds and Original White Settlers claims (74 vol
vols). These records contain an extensive amount of
personal information on each person and should not be
overlooked in the course of researching a Metis family.

VETERANS GRANTS: The first provision for grants to
veterans was made by order in Council in 1871, which
allowed a grant of one quarter-section for each soldier
who participated in the Red River Rebellion of 1870.
Grants were also made for North West Mounted Policemen
who had served 3 years continuous service from 1873 to
1879. Further legislation provided grants for veterans
of the North West Rebellion of 1885 and the South African War. Alphabetical indexes of all these grants, from
1871, are located in RG 15 at the Public Archives of
Canada. Grants provided to veterans of World War I by

the Soldier Settlement Act of 1917 are still retained
by the Department of Veterans Affairs and are not yet
available for inspection (see chapter 3:11).

SCHOOL LANDS: The sale and lease of these lands were
handled by the School Lands Branch of the Department of
the Interior. The lease records are now located in RG
15 of the Public Archives of Canada. As a rule, school
lands were not sold until the other areas of the township were settled, in order to ensure the best selling
price for them.

OTHER GRANTS AND LEASES: There are a number of other
records of sale or lease which may be of interest to
researchers. The records of leases for timber and grazing lands can be found in RG 15 of the Public Archives
of Canada. The correspondence of individuals applying
for irrigation permits, permission to build dams, etc.
can often contain an extensive amount of information
and can be found in RG 89 at the Public Archives.Other
collections include the sales records of Swamp Lands in
Manitoba (sold by the provincial government after 1889)
and the sale records of lands granted to the University
of Manitoba in 1885 (sold by the University).

The correspondence files of the Dominion Lands
Branch and other Branches of the Department of the Interior
(RG 15) located in the Public Archives of Canada can also
contain a variety of information such as progress reports,
lists of settlers, etc. on the various land and colonization companies who settled immigrants on Dominion Lands
and on the various ethnic immigrants who settled in groups
on blocks of Dominion Lands. Although the information
available is not extensive and researchers will find that
these files are more difficult to use than the registers
and applications, the correspondence files can help to show
the individual ancestor in relationship to his community,
particularly in the initial settlement period (see also
Chapter 3:10).

Records relating to "squatters" can also provide some
interesting details for the family history. A squatter
was a person who settled on a parcel of land to which he
did not hold title or on which he had not filed a homestead
entry. Because the settlement of the west advanced very
rapidly, settlers often located themselves on land which
had not been subdivided by survey. In order to protect the
squatters, many of whom had built houses and had begun the
cultivation of the land on which they had located, the
federal government allowed those squatters who had settled
in advance of the survey to have the first option of taking
up their holdings as a homestead once it had been subdivided.
If it was found that the settler had squatted on one of the
railroad sections, however, he was often required to pur-

chase it from the railroad rather than receive it as a
homestead. The registration of squatters was the responsibility of the surveyors who did the initial subdivision of
the townships. In his field books, the surveyor would
indicate the name of the squatter, the extent of his holdings as well as the positions of buildings and structures
and often remarks on the area in cultivation, etc. When
the township diagrams were drawn up from these field books,
the holdings of the squatters were often indicated as well.
The surveyor also took statutory declarations from the
squatters for the department's files. The field books and
township diagrams can be found in the various provincial
surveys departments or in the provincial archives.

OTHER LAND GRANTS

Although the majority of land in Canada was granted
directly to individuals by the government, in some cases
a third party intervened between the surrender of the land
by the government and the acquisition of the land by the
individual settler. The three best known examples of
"third party" grants are:

COLONIZATION AND LAND COMPANIES

Private land companies have been in operation in
Canada since the early part of the British regime and can
be found in almost every province at one time or another.
Under this method of land distribution, the government
would grant large blocks of land to private companies who
would agree to provide settlers for the area. For their
efforts, the companies were allowed to sell the land to the
individual settlers. By allowing these grants, the government was able to involve other agencies in the colonization
process which, it was hoped, would speed settlement. As a
result of this system, the original patent from the Crown
was held by the company which then deeded tracts of land to
individual settlers. For the records of sale between the
company and the individual, the company's land records must
be searched. Two of the better known companies of this type
are the Canada Company and the settlement company of Col.
Thomas Talbot, both of which operated in Ontario. Their
records are now deposited in the Ontario Archives.
There were many variations in these grants depending
on time and place. In the early British settlement period
in Ontario, Quebec and the Maritimes, large grants of land
were often made to individuals as payment for their service
to the Crown. It was thought that these grants would also
speed settlement by their quick sale to individual settlers.
However, many of these grants were in fact the last areas
to be settled in these provinces. Other grants, such as the

Selkirk grant in Manitoba from The Hudson's Bay Company, also resulted in some colonization.

Because there were a large number of these land companies, both large and small, researchers should contact the various provincial archives for information on those which operated in their respective provinces.

HUDSON'S BAY COMPANY LANDS

When the Hudson's Bay Company surrendered its land in Western Canada to the federal government, they were granted 5% of the lands which were to be surveyed as Dominion Lands usually section 8 and part of section 26 in each township, as partial compensation. As well, they also retained some blocks of land around their trade posts. The HBC Lands Branch later sold these parcels to settlers, the records of which are now located at Hudson' Bay House in Winnipeg or Hudson's Bay Company Archives which is housed at the Provincial Archives of Manitoba.

Prior to the transfer of Rupert's Land, the HBC had granted some lands around their trade posts to retired employees and other settlers. Records of these transactions can also be found at the HBC Archives, and at other provincial archives in western Canada.

RAILWAY GRANTS

Agreements between the Canadian government and the Canadian Pacific Railway in 1879 provided for large grants of land to the company to help finance the construction of its rail lines. These parcels were later sold through the CPR's Land Branch. Similar grants were later given to other railroads. In many ways, these grants operated in much the same way as those given to colonization companies. Railway grants were usually the odd-numbered sections in each township within the grant area, except sections 11 and 29. The land records of the CPR can now be found at the Glenbow-Alberta Institute in Calgary, Alberta, and a few records for the CNR are located in RG 30 in the Public Archives of Canada.

PART 2: LOCAL LAND RECORDS

Following the original grant to an individual, the granting body's responsibility for the land ceased. All subsequent land transfers and records will be found in the various provincial government land titles or registry offices.

LOCAL REGISTRATION SYSTEMS

In order to regulate land transactions between individuals, the provincial governments established systems at an early date which provided for the registration of all documents resulting from the transfer process. As a result, simply by visiting a registration office and examining the records there, a buyer can insure that the seller does indeed hold title to a property, as well as learning of any incumberances, before finalizing an agreement to purchase. Although this has obvious advantages to the buyer, the records which have been created as a result of these systems are also beneficial to genealogists.

The two systems in Canada regulating the registration of land transfers and sales are:

Registry System:
This is quite prevalent in Southern Ontario, Quebec and throughout the Maritimes. As well, Manitoba operated under this system from 1871 until 1885, when it adopted the Torrens System. The Registry System provides for the registration of deeds and other documents affecting the title of land, but will not guarantee the title to a parcel of land. It's Abstract Book (index book) which has one page for each parcel of land and contains a chronological list of the instruments registered with respect to that tract is the more useful genealogically of the two indexing systems.

Torrens System:
This system was developed by Sir Robert Torrens in Australia in 1858 to provide a system whereby evidence of ownership of a tract of land was by Certificate of Title guaranteed by the Government, eliminating the long procedure required in the registry system to prove the title to the land. All land transfers must be recorded under this system, the ownership of a parcel not being transferred to the purchaser until such a registration takes place. The Index Book, which has one line for each particular parcel of land, contains only the registration numbers of transfers (generally in chronological order) but no other information. As a result, it has limited use in genealogical research. This system is now in use throughout Western Canada, as well as occurring in the North and in parts of Ontario.

TYPES OF LOCAL LAND RECORDS

There is a wide variety of records and documents which have been created as a result of the land transfer process. Under the Registry System, virtually all those records listed below are registered against the particular parcel of land and a copy of each entered into the records of the registry office. The Torrens System only provides for a Certificate of Title (the document which transfers the land from one person to another) and, with the exception of abstracts of mortgages, discharges of mortgages and a few other transactions which are listed on the back of the Certificate of Title, no other documents relating to a parcel of land are preserved. Some of the major documents which are likely to be found under the Registry System are:

>DEED, CONVEYANCE, TRANSFER:
>The document which transfers the title or real estate is called the deed, conveyance, or transfer. Included in these records are the names and residences of the Buyer and the Seller, a description of the property and the name of the Seller's wife.

>MORTGAGE:
>A conditional claim against legal title to real estate given as security for a debt is called a mortgage.

>DISCHARGE OF MORTGAGE:
>This is a document releasing real estate from a mortgage.

>WILLS:
>A legal will was sometimes filed with the Registry Offices (in Ontario) when it involved the transfer of a parcel of land to an heir. As a result, these wills were never probated and only appear in the Registry Office files.

>QUIT-CLAIM DEED:
>A document used to sell or relinquish all or part interest in a parcel of land where a Transfer could not be acceptable.

These later land records provide very little basic genealogical data and should be primarily viewed as a means of confirming an ancestor's residence in a particular locality. However, most land conveyances in Canada will contain the names of the Seller's wife and a few may contain other statements of relationship as well. Other transfers may include references to the previous or later residents of the Buyer or Seller if the document was executed either before or after the person had moved. Both of these aspects

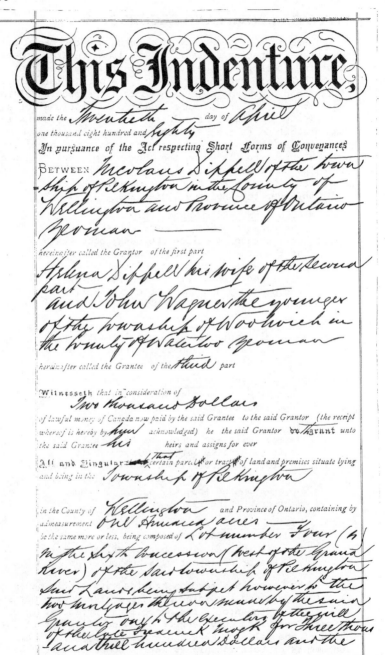

This Indenture,

made the _Twentieth_ day of _April_
one thousand eight hundred and _Eighty_

In pursuance of the Act respecting Short Forms of Conveyances

BETWEEN _Nicolaus Sippell of the Township of Pilkington in the County of Wellington and Province of Ontario Yeoman_

hereinafter called the Grantor of the first part

Athena Sippell his wife of the Second part and John Wagner the younger of the Township of Woolwich in the County of Waterloo Yeoman

hereinafter called the Grantee of the third part

Witnesseth that in consideration of _Two thousand Dollars_
of lawful money of Canada now paid by the said Grantee to the said Grantor (the receipt whereof is hereby by _him_ acknowledged) he the said Grantor do grant unto the said Grantee _his_ heirs and assigns for ever

All and Singular that certain parcel or tract of land and premises situate lying and being in the _Township of Pilkington_

in the County of _Wellington_ and Province of Ontario, containing by admeasurement _One Hundred acres_
be the same more or less, being composed of _Lot number Four (4) in the Sixth Concession (West of the Grand River) of the Said township of Pilkington said Lands being subject however to the two Mortgages thereon made by the said Grantor only to the Executors of the late Frederick Nagle for three thousand and three hundred Dollars and the_

THE FIRST PAGE OF A TYPICAL CONVEYANCE

can be quite significant if no other records exist which might provide the same information.

In other cases, a search of the records recorded under the Registry System may result in the discovery of the will of an ancestor or in a land deed which transferred a parcel from an elderly father to his son for a $1.00 consideration, provided that the son supports the father in his old age. In the latter instance, the deed may contain very detailed information on the son's obligations.

Under both the Torrens and Registry Systems an index is kept of all records in their care, arranged by the legal description of the land. Therefore, in order to obtain the records of the land owned by an ancestor, it is first necessary to know the exact legal description of the land to enable the appropriate documents to be found. These descriptions must be obtained from other sources, such as maps, directories or personal knowledge.

The index system to the Torrens System is virtually useless to the genealogist. Each parcel of land is allocated a single line in a book, and the registration numbers of the transfer documents affecting it are recorded as they are registered with the office. No names or dates appear in the index and each transfer number must be checked against the original document until the name of ancestor appears. This can be quite time-consuming.

The Index or Abstract Book of the Registry System is quite the opposite. Each page pertains to only one parcel of land and contains a short description of each document registered against the land which includes the number of the document, the type of document registered, the date the document was prepared or registered, the names of the Grantor and the Grantee, the consideration, and the quanity of land involved. By having copies made of the Abstract Index for the parcels of land on which an ancestor settled, it is possible for the researcher to have a brief history of his ancestor's land activities, as well as being able to choose the specific documents which would be of most value to his research.

All these land records, regardless of which registration system is used, are located in district offices throughout each province which must be contacted in order to obtain copies of the original documents (for addresses of local offices in a province, see Chapter 5). However, some of the indexes and documents for registration offices in Ontario and the Maritimes have been microfilmed, with copies deposited in the provincial archives for the use of reseachers.

BIBLIOGRAPHY

A thorough discussion of land records in Canada warrants a book of its' own. There are many aspects and unique types of land records which have not been discussed here. However, those which have been discussed comprise the greatest portion of the available records and the descriptions for each are sufficient to begin research in these sources. The following bibliography contains some publications which will prove helpful in more fully understanding land policies in Canada:

Coderre, John: Searching in the Public Archives, Ottawa Branch O.G.S., publication 72-1, contains a good section on Upper Canada Land Petitions.

Garson, J.E.: Historique de la colonisation dans la province de Québec de 1825 à 1940 (Québec 1940)

Gates, Lillian F.: Land Policies of Upper Canada, U. of Toronto Press, 1968.

Gentilcore, Louis, and Donkin, Kate: Land Surveys of Southern Ontario: An Introduction and Index to the field notebooks of the Ontario Land Surveyors 1784-1859 (Cartographica Monograph 8, Toronto 1973)

Harris, Richard C.: The Seigneurial System in Early Canada: A Geographical Study (Quebec 1966)

Hedges, James, B.: The Federal Railway Land Subsidy Policy of Canada (Cambridge, Mass., 1934)
_____: Building the Canadian West: The Land and Colonization Policies of the Canadian Pacific Railway (New York 1939)

Lalonde A.: "Settlement in the North West Territories by Colonization Companies (1881-1891)" unpublished doctoral dissertation, Laval University 1791.

Martin, Archer: The Hudson's Bay Company's Land Tenures (London 1898)

Martin, Chester: Dominion Lands Policy, McClelland and Stewart, Toronto, 1973.

Munro, William, B. Ed.: Documents Relating to the Seigneurial Tenure in Canada 1598-1854 (Toronto 1908)

Patterson, George C.: Land Settlement in Upper Canada 1783-1840 (Toronto 1922) - 16th report of the Ontario Public Archives

Rozovsky, L.E.: "Torrens Land Titles System" in Canadian Surveyor, Volume 23, No. 1, March, 1969.

Thomson, Don, W.: Men and Meridains: The History of Surveying and Mapping in Canada, Queen's Printer, Ottawa, 3 volumes.

Tyman, John: By Section, Township and Range: Studies in Prairie Settlement, Brandon, Manitoba, 1972.

3:8 MUNICIPAL RECORDS

Local government and administrative areas in one form
or another have existed in Canada since the time of the
French Regime. The records created by these local authorities not only allow us a closer look at the day to day
affairs of some of our ancestors but may also provide the
only documentary proof to an ancestor's duration of residence in a specific locality and sometimes will provide an
aggregate listing of the make-up of his family.

DEVELOPMENT OF LOCAL GOVERNMENT

In accordance with the policies established in France,
all government functions in New France were centralized
with the Indendent and Council. This included local administration. However, the Seigneur, the local priest and
the local Captain of Militia did exercise some local power
in community affairs, generally on an informal basis.

By 1760, all of what is now Canada had come into the
possession and control of Great Britain. However, this
area was not treated as one country but was in fact broken
down into a number of separate and distinct colonies, each
of which developed their own system of local government.
In order to fully understand the development of local
administration in the various parts of British North
America, it is best to discuss each province in turn.

With the fall of New France in 1760, Great Britain
acquired all of the area presently occupied by the provinces of Ontario and Quebec although virtually all
settlement in the area was located in present-day Quebec.
Initially, all aspects of government in Quebec were handled by the military authorities. In 1764, the British
Governor established Courts of Quarter Sessions for
various districts of the province which were composed of
the appointed Justices of the Peace in each district.
These Quarter Sessions were responsible for minor judicial matters and the general administration of local
governments, being empowered to supervise the election of
"baillis" in each parish to see to the inspection of highways and bridges and to act as local constables. Although
local affairs were handled by the "baillis" and by the
Seigneurs, priests and Captains of Militia, the real administrative authority rested with the Quarter Sessions.
This system continued in Lower Canada until 1840. In

1791, the Constitutional Act divided the Old Province of Quebec into Upper Canada (Ontario) and Lower Canada (Quebec).

In 1840, an ordinance established various Districts within Lower Canada, each having an elected council with the power to tax residents and appoint other officials. This system proved unpopular with the people and in 1845 was replaced with a parish and township system, each of which had an elected council. This lasted for two years before being replaced by a system based on the county as the municipal unit.

In 1855, the Lower Canada Municipal and Road Act provided for the incorporation of parishes, townships, towns, etc. each of which would have an elected council. The mayor of these local communities would also serve as the local representative on the county council. Both the county and the local authorities had the power to levy taxes. This is the system on which the present local administration in Quebec is based.

Local government in Quebec developed more slowly than the other provinces. This was primarily due to the general lack of popular demand for it coupled with the inexperience of the people in local government and their suspicion of the English minority who governed the province during its early history.

Initially, <u>Ontario</u> was a part of the Old Province of Quebec. The first major influx of settlers into the Ontario region was the United Empire Loyalists. In order to provide for law and order and the settlement of minor disputes, ex-officers of the Loyalists were commissioned as magistrates and by an ordinance of 1785 were given limited civil jurisdiction. In 1788, the Ontario area was divided into 4 districts, each having judges of the Court of Common Pleas, Justices of the Peace, sheriffs, clerks and coronors. These districts were named Luneburg (later Eastern), Mecklenburg (later Midland), Nassau (later Home) and Hesse (later Western). Courts of Quarter Sessions, composed of the Justices of the Peace in each district, were also established and had limited legislative and administrative powers in addition to their judicial authority. As a result, the Quarter Sessions constituted the first "local government" throughout Ontario and over the years acquired the authority to erect courthouses and gaols, lay out highways, appoint local officials, set fees for local officials, grant liquor licences, permit dissenting clergy to perform marriages, as well as other responsibilities. By 1800, the original four districts had been subdivided to provide for four additional districts, namely Johnstown, Niagara, London and Newcastle.

The Constitutional Act of 1791 separated Ontario, then called Upper Canada, from the Old Province of Quebec. The following year, the new province was divided into 19 counties for militia purposes and as the basis for electing representatives to the new parliament. Although this was the first appearance of the county in Ontario, they had no municipal significance at that time.

Despite the creation of counties, the district system with its Courts of Quarter Sessions continued as the basis of local administration and were, in fact, not responsible to the residents of the districts. Justices and magistrates were generally appointed for life by the Executive Council of the province, and many of them often had meager qualifications for their positions. These Quarter Sessions controlled all the monetary expenditures of their districts and because many of the justices were men of affluent means were generally indifferent to the needs of the average working man. These factors lead to an increasing agitation by ratepayers for a more responsible elected local government.

The "Parish and Town Officers Act" of 1793 gave the justices the power to authorize the constable of a parish or township to assemble the inhabitants of their areas at an annual meeting to choose local clerks, assessors, collectors and other officials. However, these elected officials were responsible only to the justices, and both the basis of assessment and the rates of tax were determined by the provincial parliament and not by the local officials. If these annual meetings failed to choose officers, the justices often appointed local residents to the positions.

As the population of Ontario increased and towns developed, the Quarter Sessions were given broader powers in order to deal with urban affairs. In time, however, the problems of the urban communities became so pressing that the powers of the justices in some centres were transferred in the 1830's to local representative bodies called Boards of Police. These boards were elected by the male householders and were charged with appointing town officers, making assessments, etc. Even more extensive powers than these were also granted to towns and cities incorporated under special acts of the legislature during this time.

Local government by Quarter Sessions continued until the "District Councils Act" of 1841. This act called for a council in each district elected by freeholders and householders and transferred to these councils many of the administrative powers of the justices. However, the district reasurers and executive officers continued to be appointed by the Governor, who also retained the authority to dissolve any or all of the local councils at any time. In 1846, the councils were given the right to appoint all the executive officers of the district and in 1849 the "Baldwin Act" established the county rather than the district as the division for municipal as well as judicial purposes. This basic system has continued to be the basis of local government in Ontario since that time, although recently some of the counties have been or are being con-

solidated into larger "Regional Municipalities" for more
efficient local administration.

The system of local government developed in the Atlantic provinces generally followed that which was established in other British colonies in North America.
Originally all of the Atlantic provinces, with the exception of Newfoundland, formed part of Nova Scotia, a fact
which influenced the development of local government in all
three provinces. The Executive Council in Halifax initially was responsible for all local matters although, beginning in 1749, it began to issue commissions of the peace
to the more influential settlers in order to provide more
effective local administration of justice. In 1759, the
province was divided into 5 counties. New Englanders
settling in the Annapolis Valley, however, were accustomed
to a more representative type of local government and, about
1760, began to organize township governments composed of
elected councils. These local organizations were strongly
condemmed by the Halifax government and, as a result, played
only a minor municipal role in Nova Scotia and were finally
abolished in 1859.

In 1765, the Executive Council confirmed the system
of local government by Court of General Session and grand
jury, although there is strong evidence that they were in
existance before that time. Like the Court of Quarter
Sessions in Ontario, the General Sessions were composed
of the Justices of the Peace in each county. The grand
juries consisted of local residents as jurors and had
the responsibility to make recommendations to the General
Sessions with respect to the support of the poor, payment
of officials, names of local residents recommended for
appointment as officials, and other matters. However,
the juries could only recommend, the General Sessions had
the ultimate power of decision. Although Nova Scotia is
divided into counties, these do not form the basis for
municipal government. Instead, local administration is
vested with municipalities whose boundaries often co-
incide with those of the counties. Normally there was
only one court of sessions and one grand jury in each
county. However, due to size, history, convenience, or
other reasons, some counties eventually acquired two or
more of each. This particular aspect is represented today by the fact that some counties contain two munic ip-
alities.

In 1879, the country and district government with
their elected councils that were created established the
system and boundaries existing today.

New Brunswick was created out of Nova Scotia in 1784.
From the beginning, local affairs were administered by
Courts of Quarter Sessions aided by grand juries, in conjunction with the provincial legislature. During this
early period 15 unincorporated counties were established,
the first ones in 1786. In 1851, provisions were made for

the establishment of more responsible government but due
to the disinterest of the people and the retention of financial control by the provincial legislature it proved
largely unsuccessful. The Municipalities Act of 1877,
however, established the municipal system in each county
and transferred the powers of the Quarter Sessions to
the county councils. This system continued until 1967
when the provincial government again assumed full control
of local matters.

Due to the small area occupied by <u>Prince Edward
Island</u>, local matters have always been administered by
the provincial legislature, although the province was
divided into counties and parishes two years before the
island was separated from Nova Scotia in 1769.

Municipal organization in <u>Newfoundland</u> is of recent
origin, although it was England's first established colony
in Canada. Many factors contributed to this development,
most notably the strong control exercised over the island
by fishing "admirals" and the laws forbidding residents to
own land. The majority of municipalities are towns and
communities only, although there are local government
districts.

Most of the battles in achieving local self-government had been fought and won prior to the settling of
western Canada and the development of municipal responsibility in the West is more a history of establishing a
working system than in winning self-government.

<u>Manitoba</u> municipal organization has its foundation
in the Council of Assiniboia, established in 1812 to
administer Lord Selkirk's colony. In its entire history
(1812-69) all councillors were appointed, first by
Selkirk and his heirs and later by the Hudson's Bay
Company. In 1871, Manitoba was divided into 5 counties
with local affairs administered by a Court of Sessions
based at Fort Garry (Winnipeg). However, local improvements could be decided by a meeting of the heads of
family in a parish who were then assessed the amount
needed to meet the improvements. In 1873, provision was
made for the establishment of local councils with limited
powers of taxation on petition of two-thirds of the male
freeholders in an area. In 1883 a system based on that
in Ontario was introduced and provided for 26 counties
with elected councils. Each county was composed of local
municipalities each of which had an elected council, the
mayor of which served as the representative on the county
council. This system was abandoned after 3 years and
replaced by smaller "rural municipalities". The present
system was established in 1902.

<u>Saskatchewan</u> and <u>Alberta</u> were initially part of the
North West Territories, established in 1870 from the
Hudson's Bay territories. Early local government was
administered by the territorial Department of Public
Works. In 1883, the Territorial council made provision

for the establishment of municipalities, although few
were actually created. In 1887, "statute labour and
fire districts" (later called Local Improvement Districts)
were authorized for the unorganized areas of the territories. These were made compulsory.in 1896 and provision
for elected councils was extended to them the following
year. These districts were reorganized into larger units
in 1903. Following the creation of the separate provinces
in 1905, both established provincial departments for the
regulation and control of the local municipalities. Present municipal structure is based on these original local
districts.

The mountainous terrain in <u>British Columbia</u> necessitated the early creation of local town and district government, which were originally administered by government
agents sent out by the provincial government. Most municipalities, however, are largely restricted to urban communities and the habitable areas around them.

ASSESSMENT AND TAX ROLLS

Possibly the most important municipal record from a
genealogists viewpoint is the Assessment or Tax Roll.
These records were often compiled on a yearly basis and
contain the names of landowners and ratepayers of the municipality, along with some personal information on the material possessions of each. In many respects, these records
can be regarded as a local "census" although they only list
the name of the head of the household. Some, however, do
give an aggregate summary of the make-up of the family.

These rolls can be subdivided into three major types,
each of which either contains information differing from
the others or was compiled for different purposes:

> <u>Assessment Roll</u>: Of the three major types,
> this is undoubtedly the most informative.
> In these records can be found a fairly
> complete listing of the property owned by
> the individual residents of a municipality,
> including all land, livestock, household
> possessions, etc in addition to other data.
> Of course, the extent of the information
> requested or recorded in these rolls varies
> from province to province and from time
> period to time period. In general, resea-
> rchers will find three different types of
> assessment rolls. The first contains only
> the "real property" holdings of the indiv-
> iduals, that is, only a listing of the land
> owned by each person. The second or
> "personal property" assessment only con-
> cerns itself with the possessions of an

individual other than his land holdings.
The last and most common of the three is
a combination of the first two in which
both "real" and "personal" property are
listed.

Tax Roll: These records contain the
names of the taxpayers in each municipality, followed by the total assessment for
each as taken from the assessment roll
and the amount of tax levied against his
property. Unlike the assessment roll,
the tax roll does not usually contain a
detailed listing of the property owned
by each person but merely restricts itself
to listing the total value of the property
owned. In cases where the assessment rolls
have been lost or destroyed, the tax roll
can be used as a more modest replacement.
In some provinces, the assessment roll is
also the tax roll.

Poll Tax: Also known by other names, the
Poll Tax was a special tax levied against
non-ratepayers in a community. Lodgers,
labourers, etc all come under this general
catagory. The purpose of this tax was to
insure that even thos people who had no
real or personal property would not escape
the requirement to contribute something to
the local government. This type of tax was
very prevelent in the Maritimes, although it
can also be found in other provinces.

Although all of these records were compiled for tax
purposes, they can give an excellant insight into the
financial well-being of the people of an area. As well,
they provide a reasonably good record of individuals'
residences within a municipality. Most of these records
have been quite well preserved and are fairly easy to use.

OTHER MUNICIPAL RECORDS

In addition to the assessment and tax rolls there
exists a variety of other records at the municipal level
which can assist in providing more information on ancestors. Some of these are:

MUNICIPAL MINUTES:
Records of meetings of local councils which, in addition
to regular business of councils, may contain birth, marriage and death notices, results of local elections, and
references to events in the lives of local residents.

VOTER'S LISTS:
These are self-explanatory. Many lists of voters exist
across Canada and can be found with municipal records
and in local libraries. These help to confirm a person's
residence in a given area at a given time.

POOR BOOKS:
These and other similar records were the earliest form
of welfare records. While some may still be found in
the municipalities, most have been transferred to provincial and regional archives.

OTHER RECORDS:
There is a great multitude of other records generated by
municipalities, depending on their size and the circumstances of time. Included are licenses of all types,
records of the local jail, local magistrates' records,
maps and plats, local sheriffs' reports, etc..

LOCATING MUNICIPAL RECORDS

The majority of municipal records are still in the
custody of the local municipalities, although some of the
earlier records in some provinces have been deposited with
the provincial archives or have been microfilmed and the
microfilms deposited with the provincial archives.
Researchers interested in these records should contact
the respective provincial archives first to determine the
extent of their municipal holdings. If this fails to yield
the needed material, inquiries will then have to be directed
to the appropriate municipal officials.
Further information on the municipal governments in the
various provinces and the addresses of municipal officials
can be obtained from the various provincial municipal affairs
departments. These provincial department addresses and other
information on the various municipal structure of each province can be found in Chapter 5.

BIBLIOGRAPHY

Beck, J. Murray: The Evolution of Municipal Government
    in Nova Scotia 1749-1973 (Halifax 1973)

Brittain, Horace L.: Local Government in Canada
    (Toronto 1951)

Crawford, K.G.: <u>Canadian Municipal Government</u> (Toronto 1954)

Crosbie, J.C.: "Local Government in Newfoundland" <u>Canadian Journal of Economics and Political Science</u> 22:3 (August 1956)

Dawson, George F.: <u>The Municipal System of Saskatchewan</u> (Regina 1955)

Ferguson, C. Bruce: <u>Local Government in Nova Scotia</u> (Bulletin 17 of the Public Archives of Nova Scotia, Halifax 1961)

_____: <u>The Boundaries of Nova Scotia and its Counties</u> (Bulletin 22 of the Public Archives of Nova Scotia: Halifax 1966)

Hanson, Eric J.: <u>Local Government in Alberta</u> (Toronto 1956)

Herriginton, W.S.: "The Evolution of Municipal Government in Upper Canada" <u>Transcript Royal Society of Canada</u>, 3rd Series 25 (1931)

Lanclôt, Gustave: "Le Régime municipal en Nouvelle-France" <u>Culture</u> 9:3 (1948)

Landon, Fred: "The Evolution of Local Government in Ontario" <u>Ontario History</u> 42:1 (1950)

Reid, A.N.: "Local Government in the North West Territories. The Beginnings of Rural Local Government, 1883-1905" <u>Saskatchewan History</u> 19:3 (1966)

_____: "The Rual Municipalities" <u>Saskatchewan History</u> 2:3 (1949)

Rowat, Donald C.: <u>Your Local Government</u> (Toronto 1965)

Whalen, H.J.: <u>The Development of Local Government in New Brunswick</u> (Fredericton 1963)

3:9 COURT RECORDS

Some of the records already discussed have been records generated by the Court system, such as the Probate and Land Records. However, there are a considerable number of other records created by courts which can be useful in genealogical research. As well, in order to clearly understand all of the records coming out of the Judicial System, it is ncessary to have a general background of how that system is organized.

LAW IN CANADA

Law can be classified into two major catagories - public law and private law. Public law, more commonly regarded as criminal law, deals with disputes or offences of individuals against society, with the courts responsible for bringing public offenders to justice. Included in this catagory is criminal law (offences against society), constitutional law (laws which determine our system of government), admiralty law (maritime matters such as shipwrecks, etc.), military law (regulations on the conduct of the armed services), and martial law (emergency measures which can be imposed in times of crisis) to name a few. Private law, or civil law, is generally reserved for disputes between two or more private individuals, in which case the courts responsibility is to act as an impartial arbetrator in the settling of the dispute. For the most part, there is a greater chance that ancestors were involved in a civil law case than a criminal case during the course of their lives. As a result, this chapter will concern itself primarily with public or civil law.

In civil law there exists two major types of court actions. The terms equity and chancery (which are synonymous) describe the first type of proceeding. Equity, in effect means "justice" and is used to describe actions in which one person seeks to compel the other to do something or to refrain from doing something. An example of this type of action is a suit designed to compel someone to cease trespassing on another's property. The second type of action, referred to by the term law, is one in which one party seeks to recover monetary damages for injuries to himself, his property, or his reputation. Originally these actions were handled by separate courts, although today actions in equity and law are often handled by the same civil courts.

The courts maintain an impressive variety of records including all writs, affidavits, complaints, answers, pleadings, sentences, judgements, injunctions, petitions, motions, depositions, summons, suppoenas, and all proceedings and testimony of every case, which are detailed in the courts' records and filed in a systematic order. Some of the names of these records may seem strange at first, but after becoming acquainted with them the researcher will learn of their value and will appreciate them more fully.

In civil matters, each case is carefully recorded in detail and the records are placed in a numbered file. These generally contain the <u>complaint</u> of the plaintiff or accuser, which outlines the problem existing between the individuals (or companies), the <u>plea</u> of the defendant, which is the answer to the complaint, and the <u>decree</u> or <u>final judgement</u>, which instructs the plaintiff and defendant what is to be done to rectify the matter. Of course there may be a variety of other records in the file, but these make up the basis for all the others. These files are assigned a number and are generally indexed alphabetically by plaintiff and defendant. They are stored in the local court houses for future reference and are not generally found in archives. As a rule, a court docket for each case is prepared, which is similar to an abstract index of the chronological events occurring in the case and contains the judgements, decrees, resolutions and other court actions relating to the case. Court dockets can be quite handy for providing a quick overview of each court case. Although court records rarely provide basic genealogical data, they are important in reconstructing the lives of individuals and, if a court action is known or suspected in the life of an ancestor, these records should not be overlooked.

One important aspect of civil law in Canada is the fact that there is, in reality, two basic systems in operation, one being used only in Quebec and another being used in the rest of the country. Outside of Quebec, the civil system is based on that of England which is composed of statute laws (ie. laws which are codified) supplemented by common law (ie. traditions and precedences which are not codified). In Quebec, civil law is based on old French statute law and a codified common law. This unique system of law in Canada resulted from the desire of the British to ensure the loyalty of their new French subjects after 1760 by allowing them to retain the system of law which was most familiar to them, an aspect which continues today. Because of the two systems, researchers will find that court records in Quebec differ somewhat from their counterparts in the rest of Canada.

DEVELOPMENT OF CANADIAN COURTS

Some form of administration of the law has existed in Canada since its settlement. Much like municipal government, the court system has evolved over a long period, culminating in the system we know today. Many of the earlier courts were required to rule on a wide range of offences, unlike the present system which nas been broken into smaller more specialized courts. In order to fully realize the records which may be available from these earlier courts, it is important that researchers have a basic understanding of their general development, nomenclature and responsibilities.

At the beginning of the French regime, all judicial power in New France was vested in the Governor and Council. When Royal government was established in 1663, supreme judicial responsibilities were given to the supreme council of the colony, that is the <u>Conseil Souvereign</u> (later Conseil Superieure), which became both a court of the first instance and a court of appeal. At the same time, New France was divided into 3 legal districts or <u>Prévotés</u> each responsible for civil and criminal cases. All appeals from these courts were made to the supreme council.

Although the system of Prévotés and the supreme council formed the general basis of the judicial system, a number of other courts of a lesser nature existed in the colony. <u>Seigneurial courts</u>, presided over by the Seigneur, were established in some seigneuries to handle petty crimes and disputes. The right to hold a seigneurial court was outlined in the actual grant of the seigneuries, however, and only some of the grants contained this right. Appeal from these courts could be made to the Prévotés. Another court which handled petty civil cases was the <u>Intendent's Court</u>. As a very important offical in New France, the Intendent was often asked to arbitrate in minor civil matters. Over time, as more people sought his arbitration, he found it necessary to establish a more formalized "court" in which he could adequately deal with them. Although it was not officially part of the judicial system, this court was well used and appeals from it could be made to the supreme council. Other courts of the French period included the Court of Marechal, established in 1677 and responsible for crimes committed on the highways, and the Court of Admiralty, established in 1717 and responsible for marine matters.

In 1760, New France came under the control of the British and was officially ceded to Great Britain three years later, giving that country possession of all the territories which would later make up Canada.

Although each of the British colonies in North America was administered separately, the court systems in each bear a striking resemblence to one another and, as such, their general development can be discussed without distinquishing

between them. This is not to say that regional or colonial
differences did not take place. On the contrary, it is not
uncommon to find special courts established in one province
that do not exist in others or the responsibilities of some
courts varying from province to province. The subtlties
and changes in the systems of each province, if only mod-
estly outlined, would in fact be sufficient to fill a
book in their own right.

Each province originally had a superior court of one
type of another which was responsible for both civil and
criminal actions. In Ontario and Quebec this was the <u>Court
of Kings Bench</u> (or Court of Queen's Bench). An inferior
Court of Common Pleas was also established in these provinces which dealt with the majority of civil cases, leaving the Court of Kings Bench with the major civil actions.
In the Maritimes, the tendency was to establish a Supreme
Court which largely had the responsibility of the Court of
Kings Bench in the other provinces, and to establish inferior Courts of Common Pleas for most civil matters. Originally the Courts of Kings Bench would meet several times
each year at a designated place to hear the cases which
were to come before it. In some provinces, only one superior court or Court of Kings Bench existed for the entire province while, in others, separate courts of this type
were established for the various judicial districts within
the province. As the powers of the superior courts increased, provision was often made for them to travel to various parts of the province in "circiut" to allow for more
ready access to these courts by the people. However, this
was not the case in all provinces, some preferring to
centralize the superior court at one place.

The <u>Court of Common Pleas</u> was principally a civil
court, although it often had the authority to hear minor
criminal cases. Most provinces established a court of
this type in each county or district. Like the Court of
Kings' Bench, these courts met at one place within the
district or province, although they often convened on a
more regular basis than the superior courts. In time,
many of the duties of the Courts of Common Pleas were
transferred to the superior courts in the province or
were assumed, in part, by other inferior courts, and by the
middle of the 19th century most had ceased to be a part
of their provinces judicial organization.

The Governor and Council of the various British
colonies were originally the only <u>Court of Appeal</u> for the
areas under their jurisdiction. In instances where an
action decided in the Court of Kings Bench or Common
Pleas was felt to be unfair, an appeal could be made to the
Governor and Council to re-examine the decision and make
a new ruling. In most cases, the ruling laid down by the
"court of appeal" could over-ride that of the other courts
and was considered final. In time, the appelate powers
of the Governor were gradually transferred to separate

courts for that purpose or to the superior court of the province. Similarly, <u>Courts of Chancery</u> were established fairly early in a provinces' history (in Ontario, chancery was established in 1837) to handle all matters of equity with the Governor of the province as chancellor. These too were gradually removed from the jurisdiction of the Governor.

The Courts of Kings' Bench, Common Pleas, Appeal and Chancery exist today in one form or another. As judicial affairs were centralized or restructured by the provincial governments, some of these courts were united with others to create newer courts with wider responsibilities. In Ontario, for example, all four of these courts were merged into the Ontario Supreme Court in 1881 and today administers much of the responsibilities formerly exercised by its component courts. This is true of most other provinces, although Prince Edward Island still maintains a separate Court of Chancery and Manitoba, Saskatchewan and British Columbia have Courts of Appeal separate from the superior court of the province.

The Courts of Kings' Bench and Common Pleas were responsible for administering justice for the more serious offenses and disputes within a province. There were, however, many minor cases which did not warrent a hearing or trial before these superior courts. In order to provide for justice on a local level, the early colonial administrations appointed Justices of the Peace throughout their provinces with the power not only to handle the minor crimes and disputes within their area of responsibility but also to be responsible for local government (see Chapter 3.8). The Justices for each county or district in the province would meet several times each year as Courts of Quarter Sessions or <u>Courts of the General Sessions of the Peace</u> to handle minor criminal and civil cases and regulate on local government administration. In the intervening period between Quarter Sessions, the Justices also had the power to rule on petty cases which came up in their area of the district or county. In Ontario and Quebec, provision was also made for any two Justices within a district to sit as a <u>Court of Request</u> to hear petty cases. At the Court of Quarter Sessions in those provinces, the Justices would subdivide their districts into divisions, each of which would have its own Court of Request. At first, there would only be two or three of these courts within a district but, in time, they were increased in number as circumstances warrented. When the system was abolished in 1841, Ontario had 187 such courts operating throughout the province. The Courts of Requests are important because they were the most easily accessible court for the majority of the population and were generally held twice each month on a Saturday.

Although Courts of Sessions of the Peace are still held in Ontario and Quebec, their jurisdiction is now basically limited to criminal cases. The civil responsibilities of these courts were gradually transferred to other courts in the provinces, generally in the latter half of the 19th century. In Ontario, the functions of the Courts of Requests were transferred to the Division Courts which were created in 1841 and which still exist today. With the establishment of the County Courts in that province, even more civil jurisdictions were pared from the Sessional courts, and other responsibilities previously exercised by the Courts of Common Pleas were given to the new courts. Other local, municipal or special courts which have been created since then now have responsibilities formerly enjoyed by the Courts of Sessions. Similar developments took place in other provinces.

Other courts to deal with special aspects of law were often established in the various provinces. The oldest of these is undoubtedly the Probate or Surrogate Court which appeared quite early in many provinces' histories (1793 in Ontario) to supervise the distribution of the estates of deceased persons. Courts of Admiralty or Vice-Admiralty were also established at an early date to deal with marine matters in maritime provinces. The Court of Divorce and Matrimonial Cases, which is found only in Nova Scotia and New Brunswick, dates back to the 1750s and was responsible for all matrimonial cases in those provinces. In western Canada, particularly Red River and Vancouver Island, early justice (before 1869) was administered entirely by the Hudson's Bay Company, who established courts in areas of settlement when needed.

With the creation of the Dominion of Canada in 1867, all provinces retained their own particular court systems, although the new federal government did obtain the right to appoint the judges of certain provincial courts. At the same time, provision was made for the creation of a federal Supreme Court to which appeal could be made from the provincial courts. The Federal Court of Canada (formerly the Court of Exchequer) was also provided for to determine claims against the federal government.

COURT SYSTEM TODAY

Judicial responsibility is divided between provincial and federal governments. Records generated by the provincial courts are by far the most numerous, and most are retained by the court in which the cases were reviewed. The records of the earlier courts are now deposited in the various provincial and local archives, who should be contacted for more information on their holdings (see Chapter 5).

As well, many of the earlier records of the current courts have also been deposited with the respective provincial archives.

The following describes the various types of courts generally found throughout Canada and gives a short description of their responsibilities. However, each province's system does differ slightly from the others, requiring researchers to study the court system of the province in which they are working to learn of the specific responsibilities and names of the particular courts operating in that province.

CIVIL COURT

These administer the law regarding the protection of property and are composed of the following major divisions:

DIVISION COURT:
This is also called Magistrates Civil Court, Municipal Court, Magistrates Court, Small Debts Court. It is the lowest of the Civil Courts and generally deals with small claims of less than $500.00. It is staffed by a Professional Judge and is run on a local or municipal basis.

COUNTY COURT:
This is also called District Court. It is responsible for claims greater than $500.00 but not more than $3,000.00. This court presides over a larger area than the Division Court.

PROVINCIAL SUPREME COURT:
This is also called the Court of Common Pleas or the Court of Queen's Bench. It is the highest provincial court and has civil jurisdiction in cases which involve no upper limit in amounts of money. The Judges of these courts are appointed by the Governor-General of Canada.

SURROGATE COURT:
This is also called Probate Court. It is a special provincial court, generally covering an area similar in size to the County Court, and is responsible for seeing to the legal disposition of the estates of deceased persons.

FAMILY COURT:
This is another special provincial court which deals with domestic disputes and is generally organized on a local or municipal basis.

PROVINCIAL COURT OF APPEAL:
This is a provincial court to which all judgements handed
down in all the above courts can be appealed or challenged.

FEDERAL COURT OF CANADA:
This is a federal court responsible for reviewing cases
involving patents, copyrights, taxation disputes, Crown
corporations, and the claims of individuals against the
Crown.

SUPREME COURT OF CANADA:
This is the highest court in the country, administered
by the federal government. It hears appeals from the
Provincial Courts of Appeal and the Federal Court.

CRIMINAL COURT

These administer the law regarding the bringing of public
offenders to justice and comprise the following major
divisions:

POLICE OR MAGISTRATES COURT:
This is the lowest criminal court in any province and is
responsible for relatively minor offences (misdemeanours)
such as traffic offenses, petty theft, etc.. However,
all criminal offenders first must appear before this
court, no matter how serious the crime they have been
accused of committing. In all cases, the magistrate
will hold a preliminary hearing and if sufficient evidence is submitted will 'commit the accused for trial'
before a higher court. These are operated on a local
basis.

COUNTY OR DISTRICT COURT:
(The criminal division is the Court of General Sessions)
This court is staffed by a Professional Judge appointed
by the Governor-General of Canada, before whom are tried
the more serious cases from Magistrates Court, but not
the most serious cases such as murder, manslaughter,
treason, piracy and rape.

PROVINCIAL SUPREME COURT:
This is also called the Court of Common Pleas or the
Court of Queen's Bench. It is responsible primarily
for hearing the most severe crimes which are committed.
Judges are appointed by the Governor-General of Canada.

PROVINCIAL COURT OF APPEAL:
As in civil law, the Provincial Court of Appeal hears
appeals from all the above courts.

SUPREME COURT OF CANADA:
This is the highest court in the land and hears appeals
from the Provincial Court of Appeal.

Alist of the various judicial districts in each of the provinces has been included in Chapter 5. Using these lists, researchers should be able to contact most of the courts in any particular province. For any further information on a province's judicial system, researchers should contact the respective attoney-general or justice department in the province concerned. Addresses for these government departments can also be found in Chapter 5.

BIBLIOGRAPHY

There are numerous books and publications available which describe the judicial system of Canada and the laws which govern us. Several of these which are readily available and which provide a brief description of the court systems of each province, in addition to the fundamentals of Canadian Civil Law, are:

Anger, W.H.: Summary of Canadian Commercial Law
    Pittman, Toronto, 1962
Buchanan, Arthur: The Bench and Bar of Lower Canada Down
    to 1850 (Montreal 1925)
Canada Year Book, published annually by Queen's Printer,
    Ottawa. Contains up to date information regarding each
    of the provincial judicial systems
Chapman, F.A.R.: Fundamentals of Canadian Law, McGraw-
    Hill, (Toronto 1968)
Hume, F.R. (Ed.): Anger's Digest of Canadian Law, (Canada
    Law Book Company, Toronto 1967)
Lareau, Edmond: Histoire du droit canadien depuis les
    origines de la colonie jusqu'à nos jours (Montréal
    1888, 2 volumes)
Popple, Arthur: Western Canada Law: A Concise Hand-
    book (Winnipeg 1921)
Riddell, William: The Bar and the Courts of the Province
    of Upper Canada or Ontario (Toronto 1928)
Stanley, George: A Short History of the Canadian Const-
    itution (Toronto 1969)
Townsend, Charles: "Historical Account of the Courts of
    Judicature in Nova Scotia" Canadian Law Times 19 (1899)
Vachon, André: Histoire du Notariat canadien 1621-1960
    (Québec 1962)

3:10 IMMIGRATION AND CITIZENSHIP RECORDS

One of the most significant problems a researcher in Canada can face is tracing his ancestor back to his specific place of origin in his mother country. It does no good to know that he came from "England" or "France" or "Germany" or any other country unless you also know the town or village in which he lived. This information is usually essential in continuing the research overseas. The purpose of this chapter is to familiarize the researcher with two sources which may help in solving this particular problem.

Of course, there are numerous sources other than Immigration and Citizenship records which can reveal a place of origin in Europe or other continents. Some of these include notices in the church records, birth places indicated on death certificates, family Bibles, biographical information in local histories or in the ancestor's obituary, newspaper notices announcing a visit to the old county, land records, wills, and many more. Apart from information in church or vital records, the obituary is generally the best source of this data because of the ease of obtaining copies of them and the fact that many of them are quite informative of the events of an ancestor's life. However, should all else fail, the record of the ancestor's entry into Canada or the grant of citizenship may contain the information being sought or provide the clues for further research.

PASSENGER LISTS

The passenger lists of ships bringing emigrants to Canada are perhaps the most well used source for confirming or finding the date of an ancestors arrival in Canada. These lists contain a wealth of information, including names, ages, sex, occupations, relationships, intended destination of the immigrants, and occassionally the birthplace or residence in the old country. However, as all the passenger lists are arranged chrongologically by date of the ship's arrival, it is necessary to know the date (month and year) and the port of arrival in order to locate the information on a specific ancestor. This can be frustrating, particularly if the information being sought is the date of arrival itself. When this precise information is not known, it is then necessary to search through the passenger manifests one at a time until the particular ancestor is found, or not found. This course of action can prove very

disappointing because not all of the manifests have survived
to the present and some are not in a very readable state.

The keeping of passenger lists on a regular and systematic basis began in 1855 when the British Parliment passed
"The Passenger Act" to regulate and control passenger traffic from Great Britain. The Act called for the keeping of
two lists of passengers on each ship, the first list being
given to the officer of Customs at the port of departure and
the second one given to the officer of Customs at the port
of arrival. The second list also contained a list of births
and deaths on board the ship during the voyage. Canada had
only two official ports of entry, namely Quebec City or
Halifax. The surviving records for Quebec City date from
1865 and for Halifax from 1881. The Public Archives of
Canada has the pre-1900 passenger lists on microfilm (see
chart), which are available to researchers through inter-
library loan. They also have card indexes to some of the
passenger lists (Halifax 1881-82, Quebec City 1865-69).
Post-1900 lists are still in the possession of the Department of Manpower and Immigration, although those lists for
the period 1901-10 are currently scheduled to be turned over
to the Public Archives in 1980.

MICROFILM REEL NUMBERS FOR PASSENGER LISTS OF SHIPS
ARRIVING AT:

PORT OF HALIFAX

Microfilm Reel No.	From	To
C-4511	Jan 1881	Nov 1882
C-4512	Nov 1882	Mar 1886
C-4513	Mar 1886	Apr 1888
C-4514	Apr 1888	Aug 1891
C-4515	Aug 1891	Dec 1893
C-4516	Jan 1894	Dec 1895
C-4517	Jan 1896	Apr 1897
C-4518	Apr 1897	Aug 1898
C-4519	Sep 1898	Dec 1899

PORT OF QUEBEC

Microfilm Reel No.	From	To
C-4520	May 1865	Nov 1882
C-4521	1866	1867
C-4522	1867	May 1868
C-4523	May 1868	May 1869
C-4524	May 1869	Nov 1869
C-4525	Nov 1869	Jul 1870
C-4526	Aug 1870	Aug 1871
C-4527	Aug 1871	Oct 1872
C-4528	Oct 1872	Jul 1874
C-4529	Jul 1874	Jun 1878
C-4530	Jun 1878	Nov 1880
C-4531	Apr 1881	Jun 1882
C-4532	Jun 1882	Jun 1883
C-4533	Jun 1883	Jun 1884
C-4534	Jun 1884	May 1886
C-4535	May 1886	Jul 1887
C-4536	Jul 1887	May 1889
C-4537	May 1889	Nov 1890
C-4538	Nov 1890	Aug 1892
C-4539	Sep 1892	Oct 1893
C-4540	Oct 1893	Oct 1895
C-4541	Oct 1895	May 1898
C-4542	May 1898	Apr 1900

As there were no steamship routes between Canada and Europe before this century, immigrants from countries other than Great Britain were required to transfer to British ships in order to come directly to Canada. Therefore, despite the fact that a particular ancestor may not have been British, the record of his arrival in Canada will be found on a British vessal's passenger list. Of course, foriegn ships did come to Canada and their lists will be found within this collection as well. Although Quebec and Halifax were the official ports, other ports were used to disembark immigrants to Canada. In cases such as these, no records

will likely be found to confirm an ancestor's arrival as
they were not required at the "unofficial" ports. It wasn't
until this century that other ports were made official:
St. John, N.B. in 1900; Victoria and Vancouver in 1905;
North Sydney, N.S. in 1906 and Montreal in 1919.

Although the west coast ports were not made official
until 1905, there does exist a ten volume "General Register of Chinese Immigration" which predates that time.
The Chinese Immigration Act of 1885 provided for the control of Chinese immigration through a Head Tax and for the
registration of Chinese residents in Canada. Information
was gathered by Collectors of Customs and other agents and
sent to Ottawa to be recorded in the General Register.
Each entry is recorded in chronological order by serial number and declaration number given each person, followed by
the person's name, port or place and date of registration,
identification card number and date of issue, amount of
Head Tax, sex, age, city, village and province of birth in
China, occupation, last place of residence, port and date
of arrival, name of ship and physical characteristics.
These Registers are now located at the Public Archives of
Canada and cover the period 1885-1903, although some records
go back to as early as 1860.

The Public Archives of Canada has conducted extensive
searches throughout Canada and the British Isles attempting to locate lists of immigrants arriving in Canada prior
to 1865. Unfortunately, only a few scattered registers
were located, relating primarily to subsidized British emigration schemes. Most of these records are located in the
correspondence of the British Secretary of State for the
period 1817-1831 and are available on microfilm at the
Public Archives of Canada. Generally speaking, these lists
contain names, residence, social degree or occupation and
date of entry. To make them more easily usable, and alphabetical index of the immigrants is also available.

OTHER IMMIGRATION RECORDS

A number of other records do exist which either supplement, replace or predate the passenger lists. As a rule,
these sources are either awkward and difficult to use or are
very much incomplete, but may prove useful if no records of
an ancestor's arrival can be found in the passenger lists.

Possibly the most important source of immigration information besides the passenger lists is the Correspondence
Files of the Immigration Branch (RG 17) located at the
Public Archives of Canada. Although they do not contain
extremely detailed information on family relationships,
they can provide some data on the economic state of individuals and families. As a rule, these files are often overlooked or by-passed by researchers because they are more

AN EARLY TYPE OF PASSENGER LIST

Source: RG 4, A 1, Vol. 48, p. 15874,
(Courtesy of the Public Archives of Canada)

difficult to use than other records, primarily because they have not been indexed and researchers must "dig" for any information they may contain. The following types of correspondence and information will be found scattered throughout these files:

> Quarantine Lists: Passenger ships arriving in Canada were examined by medical officers of the Immigration Branch and diseased passengers were quaranteened. However, few detailed lists of immigrants who were quaranteened were kept, the majority of records being aggregate listings of patients. The surviving lists contain only the name of the immigrant, the disease from which he was suffering, and a medical progress. There are also a few lists of immigrants receiving medical treatment or who died in the records of the Department of Agriculture (RG 17) and some other private lists of immigrants passing through quaranteen stations. All of these are in the Public Archives of Canada.

> Reports of Government Agents: These reports from overseas agents can often contain lists of immigrants being sent out by these agents, particularly in cases where the agent was given a cash bonus for each immigrant he secured.

> Railway Company Reports: The reports and correspondence of railway companies and their land companies may occassionally contain lists which detail their settlement activities or sale of lands.

> Immigration Societies: The government often undertook periodic inspection of the activities of religious and philanthropic immigration societies and their reports often contain lists of immigrants sponsored by these groups.

> Ethnic Groups: The government often encouraged ethnic groups to come to Canada en masse and the correspondence with their leaders and the individual immigrants together with the lists of settlers forms a large portion of the Immigration Branch records.

These correspondence files date from 1854 and have largely been microfilmed by the Public Archives of Canada.

A number of provincial archives have acquired microfilmed copies for their own collections.

Other records and lists of immigrants may also be found in a variety of other places. These include the private papers of individuals, such as the Peter Robinson Papers 1823-25, and the records of private land companies, such as the Canada Company who were responsible for sett- ling a large portion of Ontario, both of which will be found in the Ontario Archives. Other private papers and land company records found in other repositories may yield a wealth of information to the diligent researcher. Still other lists of immigrants have also been printed in the local histories of a few specific areas in Canada.

ONTARIO DEPARTMENT OF IMMIGRATION

For a period of time just after Confederation, the pro- vince of Ontario maintained its own department of immigrat- ion in competition with the Dominion government's immigrat- ion branch. Both of these agencies maintained agents in Europe and actively campaigned for prospective settlers. However, after a few years, the Ontario government decided that competition of this type was not really beneficial to either government and phased out it's department, leaving the Dominion government solely in charge of finding new settlers for Canada.

The result of this period of duplicated effort is a collection of immigration records covering the period 1867- 1902 now deposited with the Ontario Archives. Those records which could be of use to researchers include the Letterbooks 1869-1901 (indexed by name); the Destination Registers 1872- 74; Passage Warrants 1872-1888; Correspondence files 1873- 97 and Applications for Refunds 1872-75 (arranged alphabet- ically by applicant). Researchers whose ancestors settled in Ontario are well advised to check this important source for possible references.

DEPARTMENT OF MANPOWER AND IMMIGRATION

Records of immigrants arriving at Canadian ports since 1900 are still in the custody of the federal Department of Manpower and Immigration. Unlike most of the other records, these are quite comprehensive in their content. As well, beginning in 1905, there are also records of those immigr- ants who landed at ports in the eastern United States and who's destination was Canada. Unfortunately, these records are not open to the general public and are presently being maintained by the department only for those persons wanting confirmation of their own arrival in Canada, or as a proof

of birth if no other records exist. Inquiries and the
appropriate application forms can be obtained by writing
Entry Section, Employment and Immigration Commission, 305
Rideau St., Ottawa, Ontario, K1A 0J9.

In addition to the above information, the department
also has lists of immigrants who came through or from the
United States. These records date from 1908, but the border point of entry and the approximate date of arrival in
Canada must be provided before a search can be made.

CITIZENSHIP RECORDS

As with the passenger manifests, very few naturalization or citizenship records exist for the period prior to
1865 although some do appear in the records of the Civil
and Provincial Secretary's Office for Ontario for the years
1828 to 1850. Arranged by county for each year, they contain the name, country of birth, occupation, date of registration, and sometimes date of arrival in Canada. Applicants were required to have been a resident of Canada for 7
years before making application for citizenship although
more than a few probably applied before this time elapsed.
These naturalization records are the result of an Act
passed in 1828 which required the District or County to
keep a register of all persons naturalized within the area
each year. One copy of this register was to be sent to the
Provincial Secretary at the end of each year. However, entries in the registers do not appear to be consistent and
the registers sent to the Provincial Secretary were not properly preserved. As a result, few of these records exist,
and those which have survived can be found in a number of
repositories, mainly the Public Archives of Canada.

Before the Citizenship Act of 1949 there was no dis-
tinction made between Canadian and British subjects. As a
result, British immigrants were not required to be naturalized. Other immigrants, however, were required to become
naturalized British subjects before they could obtain title
to their homesteads or crown lands. These naturalization
records, kept by the Department of the Secretary of State,
begin in 1865.

The original records created between 1865 and 1917 have
been destroyed although the original nominal card index
has been retained. This index provides such information as
name, residence, court of certification, date of certification, occupation, nationality, and forner place of residence
(generally only the country's name). Each card shows only
the name of the head of the family and does not give any
particulars on wife or children who may have been affected
by the naturalization.

Microfilm copies have been made of those records created
after 1917. These records contain much more information than

the index cards, including birthdate and place, date and place of entry into Canada, places of former residence, names of members of the family, etc.

In order to obtain copies of the information on the index cards, it is necessary that as much information as possible be supplied for the ancestor concerned, such as his name, place of residence and approximate date of naturalization. For copies of the records subsequent to these, the name of the person naturalized and his date and place of birth should be provided. However, when not all of this key information is known, it is still possible to obtain results by supplying as much other data as possible on the person concerned.

These records are currently available through the Citizenship Registration Branch, Department of the Secretary of State, 130 Slater Street, Ottawa, Ontario, K1A OM5, or through the Public Archives of Canada.

BIBLIOGRAPHY

For more information on immigration records and procedures and on the history of immigration to Canada in general, researchers may wish to consult the following (and other) publications.

Cowan, Helen I.: British Emigration to British North America, 1783-1837 (Toronto 1961).

Godfrey, C. M. : The Cholera Epidemics in Upper Canada 1832-1866 (Toronto 1969).

Hansen, M. L. and Brekner, J. B.: The Mingling of the Canadian and American Peoples (New Haven, Conn. 1940) (on immigration to Ontario).

Harris, R. C.: "The French Background of Immigration to Canada Before 1700" Cahiers de Geographie de Quebec (Fall 1972).

Martell, U. S.: Immigration to and Emigration from Nova Scotia 1815-1838 (Halifax 1942).

McDonald, Norman: Canada 1763-1841: Immigration and Settlement; the Administration of the Imperial Land Regulations (London 1939).

Salone, E.: La colonisation de la Nouvelle-France (Paris 1906).

Smith, W. G.: A Study in Canadian Immigration (Toronto 1920).

3:11 MILITARY RECORDS

Up until the latter half of the nineteenth century, Canada depended first on the armies of France and then on those of Great Britain for it's protection, supplemented by local Militia. As a result, detailed records on Canadian personnel were not kept until this century and the records prior to this time are incomplete and sparse in content. However, where they do exist, they can be very useful to genealogical research.

HISTORICAL BACKGROUND

During the French regime in Canada. every settlement had a militia unit for its own protection, as was common with every colonial government who had to depend on all the farmers to defend their colony from the onslaughts of Indian or European invaders. This militia system was formalized about 1651 and was further strengthened under Royal government in 1663.

The basis of the defense system of New France, however, was not militia but regular troops from France. These were composed of the Regular Army (Troupes de Terre) who were the best trained and most formidable of the regular forces, and the Colonial Regulars (Troupes de la Marine) who were regular forces recruited in France but permanently stationed in Canada and who were divided into established companies which could be united to form battalions when the necessity arose. It is interesting to note that throughout the history of New France, the Regular Army was only in Canada twice, once from 1665 to 1668 and again from 1755 to 1761.

Normally, in addition to the regular army, each parish had a militia composed of all able-bodied men in the area and which was commanded by a Captain of Militia who was generally a substant (i.e. tenent farmer). As Captain of the Militia, he was second only to the seigneur in importance in the community, and in time acquired many civil functions as well, acting as local administrator and the "mouthpiece" of the central government.

However, militia units were primarily for local defense only and did not play an important part in the defense of the entire colony. When they were called out, several would be organized together for battle and would be commanded by officers of the Colonial Regulars. This system continued for a while under British rule but gradually was replaced by other systems.

All the British colonies in North America had a militia (called sedentary militia) of some form or another, requiring all able-bodied men between the ages of 16 and 60 years to serve. Musters, or training days, were required of each unit at least one day a year (or less when at peace) although these tended to be more or less social affairs, except during times of war. The sedentary militia, like the militia of New France, did not play an important roll in the defense of Canada, which was borne by the regular troops of the British Army garrisoned in Canada.

The British government, however, did establish colonial regiments or "Fencible" Regiments (five existed in 1812) who were under the jurisdiction of the regular army but who could only serve in North America. The Canadian Voltigeurs, which were raised under Lower Canada's militia laws, were in this catagory.

In the forty years following the War of 1812, Britain had been slowly withdrawing her troops from Canada in light of the increasingly peaceful Anglo-American relations. When the Crimean War broke out in 1854, the regular forces were severely reduced to 3000 from 7000 to provide troops for that event. This quick reduction in the British troops caused the government of the Province of Canada to review the defense system, and in 1855 it passed the Militia Act, which can be said to be the beginnings of the Canadian Army. The Act provided for a paid peacetime volunteer militia, to be termed the "Active Militia" to set it apart from the other militia organizations, and was limited to 5000 men. The Sedentary Militia was still retained as an emergency defense force. Similar systems were enacted in the Maritimes about the same time.

In 1861, the Civil War broke out in the United States and 11,000 British troops were immediately dispatched to Canada. At the same time, the Active Militia was increased and by 1867 numbered 33,750 men. In 1866, during the Fenian raids in eastern Canada, the Active Militia saw battle for the first time.

Shortly after Confederation, a move was underfoot to again reform the defense system of the country. This resulted in the Militia Act of 1868. This divided the country into nine military districts and modified the system slightly. The Volunteer Militia, Regular Militia, and Marine Militia were constituted collectively the "Active Militia", and all men not in the Active Militia

were constituted the "Reserve Militia". This Reserve
Militia (formerly the Sedentary Militia) was composed of
the universal service of all able-bodied men in Canada
between the ages of 18 and 60 years. Although the last
enrollment (or muster) of this force took place in 1873,
provision for this type of military service was not
dropped from Canadian defense legislation until 1950.

The Active Militia established by the Militia Act of
1868 went on to become the Canadian Army and to
distinguish themselves worldwide.

The last British troops in Canada departed in 1871
and were replaced by Canadian regulars of the Active
Militia, although they were still commanded by British
officers on loan to Canada. Their service was a relatively
peaceful one, seeing action only in 1885 during the North
West Rebellion.

Up until the turn of the century, Canada had never
supplied troops for wars occurring outside of Canada
(With the exception of some Canadians who enlisted in the
British Army to fight overseas). This changed in 1899
when Canada provided a contingent of 8300 men to serve in
the war in South Africa. Later, in 1914 - 1918, some
619,636 soldiers from Canada would serve in the First
World War, and in 1939 - 1945, more than one million
Canadians, including 761,000 in the Canadian Army, would
participate in the Second World War. Since then, with
the exception of the Korean War, Canadian troops have
been used primarily in peace-keeping operations throughout the world.

During the period when Canadians served militarily
on the world scene, a number of changes were taking place
in the armed forces of Canada. In 1910, a Canadian Navy
had it's beginnings when the country acquired several
ships from Great Britain and in 1920, a Canadian Air
Force was officially organized. As well, in 1940, the
Canadian government, feeling that the term "Active Militia"
was now out of date, renamed the force the "Canadian
Army".

LOCATING MILITARY RECORDS

Canadian military records can be found in virtually
every major archives in Canada, although the Public Archives of Canada undoubtedly holds the largest single collection in the country.

Considering the highly organized state of the Canadian
Armed Forces today, researchers may be quite surprised to
learn that military records in Canada tend to be widely
scattered and incomplete or sparse in their data content

for the earlier periods. Unlike countries such as Great
Britain or the United States which had highly centralized
military establishments at an early date, Canada's military
organization is of fairly recent origin. Military matters
prior to 1900 were generally controlled by the French and,
later, the British colonial and other government departments.
As well, it was not uncommon for individuals to raise and
finance army or militia regiments responsible only to their
benefactors. In many instances, the records of local military units were not always maintained adequately and many
have been lost through neglect and carelessness. As a
result of the lack of centralization and early concern for
the proper preservation of some military records, researchers will often find themselves compelled to conduct sometimes lengthy searches in numerous archives just to locate
the records of specific units. In this respect, the
Union List of Manuscripts in Canadian Repositories (Ottawa
1975, 2 volumes) can prove invaluable in determining the
major military collection of the various Canadian Archives.

Nor are military records of Canadians restricted
only to the archives in this country. Many valuable documents and sources are also found in French and British
archives, and some even in American archives. For the
most part, however, researchers should begin their searches
at the Public Archives of Canada.

Military records generally can be classified into
three main types. The Muster Rolls usually contain information on each soldier in the unit including his name, rank
and station. Other information such as date and place of
birth, trade, date and place of enlistment, and date of
death may also be found on some, although this additional
information is generally quite rare. Paylists are much the
same as muster rolls, although they often include the rate
of pay. Personnel files are the most valuable military
records, containing very detailed information on the soldier or officer. However, except in the case of officers,
these records are of fairly recent origin and are generally
not yet available to the public. There are also a multitude of miscellaneous records including letters, dispatches,
assignments, memorials, pensions, allowances, etc. These
are more widely scattered and more difficult to use than
the previously mentioned sources, although they should not
be ignored by researchers.

FRENCH RECORDS

The records created during the French regime in Canada
are now deposited in various archives in France, although
the Public Archives of Canada and the Archives nationales
de Québec have acquired copies of many of them. Like most
early military records, these tend to be more complete for
officers rather than individual soldiers.

The majority of the French records at the Public Archives of Canada can be found in Manuscript Group (MG) 1 and 2 (see Chapter 4 for an explanation of the Public Archives organizational system). The <u>Archives des colonies</u> (MG1) contain numerous lists of civil and military officers, rolls of companies, records of the "Troupes des colonies" and the personnel dossiers of officers and other persons in the colony. Similar lists and dossiers for the <u>Archives de la Marine</u> are located in MG2. Although not as important as the previous collections, the <u>Archives de la Guerre</u> (MG4) does contain some records which may be useful to researchers, including letterbooks order, minutes, etc., in addition to the archival collections of the various French corps.

Much of the material at the Public Archives can also be found duplicated in the Archives nationales de Québec. In addition to this, other military records will be found in the collections of private individuals, seigneuries, etc. located in both of these repositories and in smaller archives in Canada.

BRITISH AND CANADIAN RECORDS

In the period between 1760 and the close of the 19th century, military records in Canada are dominated by the British presence in this country and the division between British records and those created exclusively by Canadian departments is not as clearly defined as the division between French and British records. As a result, researchers will find that although British records concentrate on the British Army and Navy units stationed in Canada, there are also many records of Canadian militia units and corps which operated throughout the period of British pre-eminence.

Virtually all of the British records are now deposited in the Public Record Office, Chancery Lane, London WC2A 1LR, England, with the more modern documents at the Army Record Center, Hayes, Middlesex, England and other special collections located in a variety of other British institutions. However, the Public Archives of Canada has endeavoured to acquire those records which relate to Canada and have obtained copies of many of them located in these repositories. Some of the more important collections from the Public Record Office (PRO) include the records of the War Office (WO) and the Admiralty (Adm.) both located in the Public Archives MG12, and the collections of the Treasury Board (T) and Audit Office (AO) located in MG14.

There are several printed sources which can be profitably consulted by researchers. The first is the "Army List", which has been published by the British War Office under a variety of titles since the middle of the 18th century. Although listing only officers, it can provide a quick reference to their service in the British Army over a period

Pay list for duly performed at various periods by Captain Joshua Young Cozens's Company of the 1st Regt Stormont Militia between the 25th of June and 24th of November 1813.

71

Rank	Names	No. of Days	Total No. of days	amount of nete pay army Sterling Dollars at 4/8			Remarks
				£	S	D	
Captain	Joshua Young Cozens	39	9/3	18	"	9	
Lieut	Peter Eamer	38	5 3¾	10	17	8 2	
Ensign	Matthias Snetzinger	36	4/8	8	8	"	
Sergeants	Stephen Wood	35	1/4	2	0	8	
	Henry Waggoner	30	1/4	2	"	"	
	Christopher Empey	30	1/4	2	"	"	
	John McDougal	30	10	1	5	"	
Corporals	George Snetzinger	25	10	1	"	10	
	William Empey	26	10	1	1	5	
Privates	Thomas Emery	21	6	"	10	6	
	Benjamin Cottman Jur	10	6	"	5	"	
	Peter Carpenter Jur	24	6	"	12	"	
	Robert Dixon	24	6	"	12	"	
	Alin t Crosley	3	6	"	1	0	
	Philip Algune	33	6	"	10	6	
	John C. Horton	20	6	"	10	"	
	Benjamin dl Bean	2	6	"	10	"	
	John Millers	22	5	"	11	"	
	John McBean	22	5	"	11	"	
	Alexander Bruce	24	5	"	12	"	
	James Barnhart	24	5	"	12	"	
	David Watson	26	5	"	13	"	
	Donald Algune	22	5	"	11	"	
	James Baker	12	5	"	0	"	
	Horatio Brunson	12	5	"	6	"	
	John Wood	39	5	"	19	6	£55 . 19 . 7 ½

PAYLIST FOR CAPT. JOSHUA COZENS' COMPANY,
1st REGIMENT STORMONT MILITIA, 1813

Source: RG 9, IB7 Vol. 5
(Courtesy of the Public Archives of Canada)

of time. A similar list for the Royal Navy has been published since the early 19th century. As well, a "Militia
List" containing the names of officers in the Canadian
Militia has existed since the early part of the 19th century.

Although the Public Archives has a few collections
which provide information on personnel of the Royal Navy,
the bulk of the genealogically important records are only
found at the PRO in London. The Public Archives main
collections include the Returns of Officers' Services
(adm 9); the miscellaneous records of the Accounting Departments (Adm 49) which contain a variety of papers including
registers, returns of ships, etc; and the medal rolls for
Royal Navy and Royal Marines participating in Canadian ven-
tures (Adm 171). At the PRO researchers will find a more
useful collection of records including Ships' Musters
(Adm 30) which contain 10,000 volumes of ships' crew lists.
More information on Naval records can be obtained by contacting the PRO.

The British Army records at the Public Archives are
more complete than their Naval counterparts, although
researchers may still find that they must eventually contact the PRO for access to other collections, as the Public
Archives has not yet acquired all material from this institution relating to military activities in Canada. Some
of the more important collections acquired by the Public
Archives include:

MG 13, WO12 and 13: Muster Books and Paylists

These contain the muster books and paylists
of the various British units stationed in Canada
1759-1839 and of the various Canadian Militia
units 1837-1850.

MG 13, WO28: Headquarters Records

Throughout this collection can be found
numerous letters from officers in America as
well as a number of muster rolls of units in
the American Revolution, etc. Other material
includes memorials, assignments, arrears of
pay and pardons for deserters.

MG 14, T28: Treasury Board Out Letters

The Naval and Military volumes contain
communications regarding passages, pensions,
allowances, supplies to settlers, and other
documents.

MG 14, T46: Registers, Victualling Lists

These list the officers and soldiers victualled
at Halifax 1765-70, and at Quebec and Montreal
1786-88.

MG 14, T50: Miscellanea, Documents Relating to Refugees

In addition to paylists for North and South Carolina militia units, there is also material relating to the Loyalists.

MG 14, AO12 and AO13: Claims, American Loyalists

This collection contains important records relating to the United Empire Loyalists.

MG 18: Pre-Conquest Papers

The correspondence of various British generals, the Northcliffe Collection, and other smaller military and naval collections throughout this manuscript group contain numerous muster rolls, lists, journals, letters, etc. of interest to military researchers.

MG 21: British Museum

This manuscript group contains records from the British Museum which have been copied by the Public Archives. These are primarily the private papers of individuals and include, among others, the papers of Henry Bouquet and Sir Frederick Haldimand, both of which contain muster rolls and other lists.

MG 23: Late Eighteenth Century Papers

There are numerous muster rolls and other lists relating to the American Revolution found throughout this collection.

MG 24: Nineteenth Century Pre-Confederation Papers

A variety of military papers can be found here, in addition to over 75 small collections relating to the Upper Canada Militia (including muster rolls).

A particularly important source of British Army records which deserve special mention are those of The Office of the Commander of British Forces in Canada. More popularly known as the "C Series", these records were transferred to the Canadian government in 1873 and now form Record Group 8 in the Public Archives. These records relate to the units of British regulars and Canadian Militia and contain a wealth of material useful to genealogists. Once this collection was received by the Public Archives, it was arranged into various subject headings, including Appointments and Memorials 1786-1870, Claims for Losses 1812-70, Courts Martial 1790-1870, Commissariat 1788-1870, Half Pay 1787-1845, Mails 1797-1845, Militia 1794-1870, Pensioners 1787-1870, Regiments 1786-1899, Settlers 1794-1853, and United Empire Loyalists 1787-1869. Because of their value to researchers, these records should not be overlooked in the quest for a military ancestor. A card index to the names of soldiers listed in this collection is available at the Public Archives.

Another important collection of records is that of
the Canadian Department of Militia and Defense and of the
adjutants general in the pre-Confederation period (Record
Group 9). These records include paylists for some militia
units serving during the War of 1812 and from 1855 to 1914,
and the paylists of the Canadian Expeditionary Force during
the First World War. As well, this group contains the
Medal Registers, listing the names of those who received
medals for participation in various military campaigns.
An inventory of this collection is available at the Public
Archives.

Muster rolls, paylists and other records will also
be found scattered through the papers of private individuals which are located at the Public Archives and in the
various provincial archives. The Public Archives' General
Inventory of Manuscripts is especially useful in locating
military records in that repositories. Researchers should
contact the provincial archives for more information on
their military holdings.

SPECIAL RECORDS

The following records relate to specific events or to
a specific classification and have been singled out for
inclusion here to assist the researcher who is interested
only in these particular records. Most of these are located
primarily at the Public Archives of Canada.

WAR OF 1812

No fully compiled list of soldiers who fought in this war
has ever been compiled. The only lists available are the
paylists of individual militia units located in Record
Group 9 or the records of the British units in Record
Group 8. However, there is a printed list of Canadian
pensioners of this war entitled: Statement Showing the
Name and Residence of Militiamen of 1812 - 15 Who Have
Applied to Participate in the Gratuity Granted by Parliament in 1875 (Ottawa 1876). This and other lists
relating to the veterans of the War of 1812 have also be
been published in the Dominion Sessional Papers in the
following volumes: Volume 8 1875 (No 7) S.P. 25, pp 1-15;
Volume 9 1876 (No 6) S.P. 7, pp 1-95; and Volume 10 1877
(No 8) S.P. 76, pp 1-109. All these lists contain the
name, age, residence, name of corps and rank of all those
who applied.

1837 REBELLION

The Muster Rolls of Canadian Militia called out during
the troubles of 1837 - 38 are contained in the records
of the War Office 13, microfilm copies of which are at
the Public Archives. A list of Officers and Men Killed
during the rebellions is available in the Report of the
Public Archives 1904, pp 391 - 395.

RED RIVER AND NORTH WEST REBELLIONS

The paylists of the units on service are in Record Group
9. As well, there is a schedule of claims from the Red
River Rebellion in the Dominion Sessional Papers,
Volume 5 1872 (No 6) S.P. 19, pp 4-11; and a list of
troops of the Red River Rebellion applying for grants of
land in 1875 in the Dominion Sessional Papers, Volume
8 1875 (No 8) S.P. 46, pp 1-10. There are no known lists
of the rebels of either rebellions, however.

FENIAN RAIDS

There is no list of militiamen called out for these
encounters, although files relating to the militia's
prisoners are found in Record Groups 5 and 7. Record
Group 9 contains the Fenian Raids Bounty Claims of 1912-
1915, which are helpful in locating those who participated
in the skirmishes. The Fenian Raids Bounty Act of 1912
provided for land grants to those veterans who were still
living who had served in the Active Militia during the
Fenian Raids of 1866 and 1870. They contain a considerable
amount of information on each applicant, although care
should be taken when using them as they were submitted
almost 50 years after the events described in them
actually occurred. These applications have been indexed.
These records generally contain the name, unit, period
of service and address at the time the claim was made for
each applicant.

SOUTH AFRICAN WAR

Nominal rolls and paylists of the Canadian contingent are
in Record Group 9. The records of the Department of
Veterans' Affairs (Record Group 38) contain the South
African War Service Records and the applications for land
grants made under the Volunteer Bounty Act of 1908, both
of which are indexed. The service records contain enlistment papers which give a considerable amount of information including age, occupation, next of kin, and a
physical description. As well, the record of a soldiers

activities in South Africa is also included. The land applications include the veteran's address at the time he applied and some additional information on his service in South Africa.

WORLD WAR I

The paylists of the Canadian Expeditionary Force during the First World War are included in Record Group 9. As well, there are nominal rolls and paylists in many of the provincial archives relating to some of their respective provincial units. The individual service files of the men taking part in this war are not yet open for public examination.

OTHER WARS

The individual service files of the participants of all wars subsequent to the First World War are not yet open for public examination. However, many of the provincial archives contain paylists, muster rolls or other compiled lists of soldiers from their provinces who took part in World War II or the Korean War.

MEDAL REGISTERS

Medals were awarded as a mark of gratitude for the services rendered by troops in specific campaigns, in addition to those awarded solely for bravery or other exceptional service. Therefore, everyone who particpated in a campaign was entitled to receive one. Medals were awarded for service during the following campaigns: Fenian Raids (1866 and 1870), Red River Rebellion (1870), North West Rebellion (1885), and the South African War (1899 - 1902). Included in the registers is the name of the veteran, name of his unit, his specific service, his address at the time the medal was awarded, and the name of his commanding officer. All the registers are indexed.

MODERN RECORDS

Records created during and after the First World War are regarded as confidential and as such are not available for public inspection. These include the personnel files of ex-servicemen which are held by the Canadian Forces Records Centre, Public Archives of Canada, 395 Wellington Street, Ottawa, Ontario, K1A 0N3 and begin with the files of the Canadian Expeditionary Force of the First World War.

In time it is expected that these records will eventually be released to researchers.

Other personnel records and veterans land grants and applications are held by the Department of Veterans Affairs, Veterans Affairs Bldg., Ottawa, Ontario, K1A OP4. Although these records are confidential, they will be released provided the researcher obtains the consent of the person involved, or the next-of-kin in the case of a deceased veteran.

MILITARY ORGANIZATIONS

The following military and veteran's organizations may be able to assist researchers by providing pertinent information on possible sources or other information centres:

Army, Navy and Air Force Veterans in Canada, Dominion Command, 406-151 Sparkes St., Ottawa, Ont. K1P 5E3

Canadian Corps Association, 201 Niagara St., Toronto, Ontario M5V 1C9

Canadian Council of War Veterans' Association, 924A St. Clair Ave. W., Toronto, Ontario M6C 1C6

Canadian Society of Military Medals and Insignia, 14 Tamarack Pl., Guelph, Ontario N1E 3Y6

Directorate of History, National Defense H.Q., Ottawa, Ontario K1A OK2

Imperial Officers Association of Canada, 3134B Lakeshore Blvd. W., Toronto, Ontario M8V 1L4

Les Legoninaires du Québec, 6252 St. Laurent, Montréal, Québec

Naval Veterans Association, 14 Hayden St., Toronto, Ontario

Navy League of Canada, National Council; 910-85 Passage Rd., Ottawa, Ontario K1N 8V6

Royal Canadian Air Force Association, National Headquarters, 424 Metcalfe St., Ottawa, Ontario K2P 2C3

Royal Canadian Legion, Dominion Headquarters, 359 Kent St., Ottawa, Ontario K2P OR7

Royal Canadian Military Institute, 426 University, Toronto, Ontario M5G 1S9

Royal Canadian Mounted Police Veterans Association, 38 Beaurnaris Dr., Ottawa, Ontario K2H 7K3

Royal Canadian Naval Benevolent Fund, P.O. Box 505, Ottawa, Ontario K1P 5P6

BIBLIOGRAPHY

The following publications will assist researchers in understanding the history of the development of the Canadian Armed Forces and assist in locating regimental histories and developments:

Adams, H.: The War of 1812 (Washington 1944)

Chambers, E.J.: The Canadian Militia, A History of the Origin and Development of the Force (Montreal 1907)

Denison, G.T.: Soldiering in Canada (Toronto 1900)

Dornbusch, C.E. (Comp.): The Canadian Army, 1855-1965: Lineages, Regimental Histories (Cornwallisville 1966)

_____: Preliminary List of Canadian Regimental Histories (Cornwallisville 1955)

_____: Guide to the Canadian Army (Regular) and Canadian Army (Militia) Regiments (Cornwallisville 1957)

Fortescue, Sir John: A History of the British Army (London 1902-30, 13 volumes)

Goodspeed, D.J.: The Armed Forces of Canada 1867-1967/ Les Forces armées du Canada 1867-1967 (Ottawa 1967)

Hilsman, J. Mackay: Safeguarding Canada 1763-1871 (Toronto 1968)

Historical Section, General Staff, Canada: A History of the Organization; Development and Services of the Military and Naval Forces of Canada (Ottawa 1919-20, 3 volumes - covers the period up to 1784)

Jackson, H.M.: The Roll of the Regiments (The Active Militia) (no place 1960)

Jackson, H.M.: The Roll of the Regiments (The Sedentary Militia) (no place 1960)

Nicholson, G.W.L.: Canadian Expeditionary Force 1914-1919: An Official History of the Canadian Army in the First World War (Ottawa 1964)

Stacey, Colonel C.P.: Introduction to the Study of Military History for Canadian Students (available from Queen's Printer, Ottawa)

_____: The Canadian Army 1939-1945 (Ottawa 1948)

Stanley, C.F.G., and Jackson, H.M.: Canada's Soldiers: The Military History of an Unmilitary People (Toronto 1960)

Stewart, Charles H.: The Service of British Regiments in Canada and North America: A Resume (Ottawa 1962)

Sulte, Benjamin: Histoire de la milice canadienne-française 1760-1897 (Montréal 1897)

Tricoche, George-Nestler: La Vie Militaire à l'étranger. Les Milices françaises et anglaises au Canada, 1627-1900 (Paris 1902)

Tucker, Gilbert N.: The Naval Service of Canada, Its' Offical History (2 volumes) (Ottawa 1952)

Zaslow, M. (Ed.): The Defended Border: Upper Canada and the War of 1812 (Toronto 1964)

3:12 SCHOOL RECORDS

School records do not appear to be used to any large extent in genealogical research in Canada, although there is an impressive body of them. Most are still retained by the individual school districts (units, divisions) in each province ·or their respective provincial Department of Education, although some records (primarily the earliest ones) have now found their way into the provincial archives. As well, most university records are still retained by these institutions.

HISTORICAL DEVELOPMENT

In most provinces, the first schools were generally established and administered by the various religious denominations and were used primarily to provide the basic rudiments of education and religious instruction. This was often followed by a period of local schoolmasters providing instruction in their own homes for a fee paid by the children's parents and, later, local academies and boarding schools also financed by fees. Provincial acts establishing school systems often occur quite early in provincial histories, although these too often required a fee to be paid by the parents. It wasn't until the various provinces established "free schools" that the present system had its beginnings and education became universal (and later comulsory).

The first schools in what is now Canada were established in New France in the middle of the 17th century by the Roman Catholic Church. These included centralized seminars for the instruction of male students and centralized convents for the instruction of females. A few local schools were also established in some parishes in the period 1680-1760. After the British takeover the Roman Catholic institutions continued in operation, although there were a few unsuccessful attempts to establish English language schools. In 1801 an act allowed free schools to be established if the petitioners agreed to pay for their operation. This system was not very successful, however. In 1824 the Fabrique Act allowed church councils in Quebec to establish and finance schools. This right was extended further in 1841. The basis for the present educational system in that province was laid in 1875 when separate Roman Catholic

and Protestant committees were formed to administer their
respective schools.

In Ontario, education had its beginnings when Lt.
Governor Simcoe made provisions for the support of four
grammar schools and a university for the province. The
Grammar Schools Act of 1807 provided for the establishment of schools in the various districts of the province.
In 1816, the Common Schools Act allowed elementary schools to be established through subscription with rate bills
levied against the parents. Later, an act of 1843 attemp-
ted to turn the administration of these common schools
over to local authorities. In 1870 all fees and rates
were abolished in Ontario and the schools became "free"
and attendance compulsory.

In the three Maritime Provinces, the first schools
were either operated by various churches or were conducted
in the homes of local schoolmasters. By the early 19th
century, grammar schools had been established in all of
these provinces. The "free" school system was formally
enacted in Prince Edward Island in 1852, in Nova Scotia in
1864 and in New Brunswick in 1871. Unlike these provinces
who basically have public school systems, Newfoundland's
is primarily denominational. The first schools in this
province were instituted in 1726 and operated by the various churches. Attempts to make education non-denominat-
ional ended in failure. The present denominational system
was formally recognized in 1874.

Early education in Western Canada is also closely
linked with the churches. The first school in Manitoba
was established by the Roman Catholic Church at St. Boniface in 1818, who also founded the first school in Alberta at Edmonton in 1862. In B.C., the Hudson's Bay Company were largely responsible for the first church-run
school at Victoria in 1849. Education responsibilities
were also assumed by other denominations who's missionaries often provided basic education to their "parish-
ioners". Public school acts were enacted in Manitoba in
1871, in B.C. in 1872 and in Saskatchewan and Alberta in
1884, with compulsory attendance being required at an
early date. In Manitoba, a system of denominational schools existed from 1871 until 1890 when the present system
was established.

TYPES OF RECORDS

The following types of school records are often
found for various schools and school districts:

TEACHER ROLLS, TEACHER LICENSES AND AGREEMENTS

These are lists of teachers who were working within the
province or school districts in a given year and contain

names, ages and school where they taught. The licenses
are quite similar in content to the lists or rolls.

SCHOOL REGISTERS, SCHOOL CENSUSES

These list the students who were attending particular
schools in a given year and may include the age as well
as some personal remarks about each one. They will also
indicate the attendence of each student throughout the
year.

EXAMINATION RESULTS

These contain the names of each student and their examination results in a given year

SCHOOL BOARD MINUTES

These records may contain some references to teachers
and pupils which may prove interesting or helpful in
genealogical research. As well, they may also contain
references to various people who resided within the
boundaries of the school board.

Of course, records of this nature are not always
available for all school districts and early educational
records tend to be quite scarce and information contained
in them quite sparse. Many of the early records will often
be found at local and provincial archives, notably the school registers and censuses which are perhaps the most useful of the school records.

LOCATING SCHOOL RECORDS

Universities often pre-date the establishment of public schools and their records are generally more complete
and informative than those of the public schools. Many
universities have either printed or compiled student lists
which can be searched quite quickly for references to ancestors. As these institutions are self-governing, their
records are still retained by the respective universities.

In attempting to locate educational records of early
ancestors, researchers should not overlook the various
church archives (chapter 3:3) who will either have the early educational records for their denomination or will be
able to provide information on where they can be found.
Other early records in the form of the private papers of
early schoolmasters or the records of early academies can
generally be found in local or provincial archives.

Although the pertinent provincial archives should be
contacted at first regarding the extent of their school
record holdings, researchers will undoubtedly find that it

will also be necessary to contact the individual school
boards for some information lists of the various school
districts with their addresses can be obtained from the
provincial Department of Education whose addresses appear
throughout Chapter 5.

BIBLIOGRAPHY

The following publications will assist researchers
in more fully understanding the development of education
and schools in Canada and will help to identify the types
and extent of records in the respective provinces.

Adams, Howard: The Education of Canadians, 1800-1867
(Montreal 1968).

Audet, Louis-Philippe: Le système scólaire de la
province de Québec (Québec 1952, 3vols.).

Chalmers, J.W.: Schools of the Foothills Province:
The Story of Public Education in Alberta
(Toronto 1967).

Ferguson, Charles B.: The Inauguration of the Free
School System in Nova Scotia (Bulletin 21, Public
Archives of N.S., Halifax 1964).

Foght, Harold W.: A Survey of Education in the Province
of Saskatchewan (Regina 1918).

Frecker, G.A.: Education in the Atlantic Provinces
(Toronto 1957).

Gillett, Margaret: A History of Education (Toronto 1966)

Hodgins, John George (Ed): Documentary History of
Education in Upper Canada 1791 to 1876 (Toronto 1894-
1894-1910, 28 vols.).

Johnson, F. Henry: A History of Public Education in
British Columbia (Vancouver? 1964).

Johnson, F. Henry: A Brief History of Canadian Education
(Toronto 1968).

Lavergne, Armand: Les Ecoles dɈ Nord-Quest (Montréal
1907).

MacNaughton, Katherine: The Development of the Theory
and Practice of Education in New Brunswick 1784-
1900 (Fredericton 1947).

Percival, W.P.: Across the Years: A Century of Education in the Province of Quebec (Montreal 1946).

Rowe, Fred W.: The History of Education in Newfoundland
(Toronto 1952).

Smith, A.H. (Ed): A Bibliography of Canadian Education
(Toronto 1938).

3:13 FRENCH CANADA AND ACADIA

Of all the provinces of Canada, Quebec is the most advanced in the field of genealogical research. The vast resource of original and compiled records covering this unique branch of Canadian genealogy can make researching a French-Canadian ancestry much easier than other ethnic and cultural groups in the country.

Researchers will find that many of the records dealing with individuals will be found in the judicial court houses located throughout the province (see Chapter 5 for a list of these districts and their addresses), in particular the church registers and notarial records. The records created by the notaries deserve special mention because of their uniqueness in French-Canadian genealogy. In Quebec and other areas of Canada dominated by the French judicial system the Notary was a very important local official constantly consulted to witness various local transactions. As a result, the notarial records contain virtually all the transactions relating to land sales, wills, marriage contracts and many others. These particular aspects tend to make the judicial repositories more of a "local archives" than the judicial collections in other provinces.

In addition to the judicial archives, records of value to genealogists will also be found in the Archives nationales du Québec and the Public Archives of Canada, as well as in special collections of French records deposited in a variety of other organizations including the various provincial archives in Canada, the state archives in the United States and the Archives nationales and the departmental archives in France.

Because of the tremendous differences in the judicial system and customs of Quebec and those of the rest of Canada, it can be said that French-Canadian genealogy is in reality an entity unto itself and is deserving of special study by researchers. It is impossible to document all of the important records available to researchers in a general reference work such as this one. Although this chapter is meant to relate some of the more important sources and peculiarities for this area of Canada, researchers are strongly advised to acquire some of the publications exclusively devoted to French records in order to gain a full comprehension of the records available to them.

COMPILED RECORDS

Since the nineteenth century, genealogists in Quebec
have been publishing reference material in record numbers,
many of which are quite essential for anyone researching in
the province. A few of the eminent works which discuss and
document families located in a specific geographical area
are given below. These publications show the genealogies
of the families in the areas covered, indicating all known
children of couples, and are linked together by marriage
date and place. Most are arranged in alphabetical order or
with ample cross references.

Beaumont, Abbé Charles: Généalogies des familles de la
  Beauce (Report of the Public Archives of Canada 1905,
  Volume 1)

Forgues, Abbé Michel: Généalogies des familles de L'Ile
  d'Orléans (Report of the Public Archives of Canada
  1905, Volume 2)

LeBoeuf, J. Arthur: Complément au dictionnaire généalogique Tanguay (Société Généalogique Canadienne-
  Française, 1957-64; 3 volumes). This publication
  corrects the errors which appear in Mgr. Cyprien
  Tanguay's dictionary, and the two should be used in
  conjunction with one another.

Talbot, Frere Eloi-Gérard: Recueil de généalogies des
  comtés de Beauce, Dorchester et Frontenac, 1625-1946
  (11 volumes)

Talbot, Frere Eloi-Gérard: Généalogies des familles
  originaires des comtés de Montmagny, L'Islet, et
  Bellechasse (a multi-volume work now in progress)

Tanguay, Mgr. Cyprien: Dictionnaire généalogique des
  familles canadiennes (Montréal 1870-90, 7 volumes).
  This is the "bible" of French-Canadian genealogy,
  detailing the family histories of virtually every
  settler in New France, from the earliest times to
  the latter half of the eighteenth century. When
  possible, all baptismal, marriage and burial dates
  and places are given, and in the case of original
  settlers, their places of origin in France are
  indicated. No one researching in Quebec should
  neglect this set. (A reprint edition of this work
  is available from: Editions Elysée, P.B. 188,
  Station Côte St-Luc, Montréal, Québec H4V 2Y4)

Before researchers have progressed too far in their
search for their French-Canadian ancestors they will undoubtedly realize the importance of the church marriage records in establishing a pedigree. In fact, it is these
records which initially provide genealogists with the skeleton around which their entire lineage can be built.

Of all church records, those relating to marriages are
the most valuable to the genealogist, containing the name

of the father and the <u>maiden</u> name of the mother of both the
bride and the groom. Considering this aspect along with
the fact that many families continued to reside in the same
parish in Quebec for generations, it is easy to understand
their importance in linking one generation to another. It
was these records which allowed such eminent researchers as
Cyprien Tanguay to compile their monumental works.

Because of their great value, many individuals and
organizations in Quebec have seen to the publication of these
records for the convenience of researchers who do not have
direct access to the judicial archives. To date, well over
200 of these marriage "repertoiries" have been produced.
The following list contains the names and address of those
individuals who have published these records and offer them
for sale. For researchers' reference, the areas of Quebec
in which each of these publishers concentrate are given in
parenthesis.

> M.Benoit Pontbriand, 2390 rue Marie-Victorim, Sillery,
> Québec, P.Q. (Lévis, Lotbinière, Portneuf, Québec,
> Yamaska, Laprairie, Napieville, Richelieu, Hull,
> Drummond, St-Hyacinthe, Ontaouais)
>
> Rév. Dominique Campagna, Pavillon André-Coindre, Campus
> Notre-Dame-de-Foy, Cap-Rouge, Québec, P.Q.
> (Maskinongé, Nicolet, Arthabaska, Berthier,
> Sherbrooke, Frontenac, Richmond, Stanstead, Wolfe)
>
> Les Editions Bergeron Enr., 9247 24e Ave., Montréal, P.Q.
> (Laval Co., Montréal, Terrebonne, Pontiac, Lachine,
> etc.)
>
> Rév. Armand Proulx, CP 636, St-Anne-de-la-Pocatière,
> Kamouraska, P.Q. (Kamouraska, L'Islet, Montmagny)
>
> Société de Généalogie de Québec, CP 2234, Québec, P.Q.
> G1K 7N8 (Québec region, Ile d'Orléans, Québec City)
>
> Rév. Victorin Paré, 7141 Ave. Royale, Chateau-Richer,
> Montmorency, P.Q. (Beauce, Dorchester, Frontenac,
> Bellechasse, Montmagny, I'Islet, Charlevoix)

Researchers interested in these "repertoiries" should
contact the above for a catalogue and price list. As well,
the genealogical societies in Quebec should also be consulted for the names and addresses of other compilers of
marriage records.

VITAL RECORDS

Although these records fall into the two main catagories that exist in other provinces, namely civil registration
and church records, researchers will inevitably find that
the latter are the most complete and most used of the two.
Government or civil records do not begin until 1926, so

inquiries for information on persons born, married or dying before that time must be directed to the church records. Fortunately this does not pose too much of a problem.

In Chapter 3-3, the unique system of depositing second copies of the Roman Catholic Church registers at the local judicial archives was discussed in detail. This system also applies to Protestant and Jewish congregations. Therefore, the judicial archives contain virtually a complete record of all births, deaths, and marriages in Quebec since the first registers in 1621. Transcripts of these records can be obtained from the court house in the area in which an ancestor resided by supplying the name and approximate dates and places required for the specific document. This is not unlike applying for certificates at the other provincial vital records offices except that the ancestors general area of residence must be known in order to choose the appropriate judicial district.

The Régistre de la Population, of the Ministère des Affaires Sociales administers the civil registration of vital records in the province in much the same way as other vital statistics offices elsewhere in Canada. However, they do discourage enquiries, preferring researchers to contact the judicial archives instead.

With the vital records spread throughout the province in the various judicial archives it can be quite difficult to choose the correct archives if the exact place an event occurred is unknown. Fortunately, there is an index which can be used to overcome this problem or in instances when a quick pedigree is required. This source is the Loiselle Card Index to Most Marriages of the Province of Quebec compiled by Père Antonin Loiselle, Couvent des Dominicains, 5375 Avenue Nôtre Dame de Grâce, Montréal, Québec H4A 1L2. Each card contains the marriage date and place, and the names of the bride and groom and their parents, all of which enable the line to be extended backward in time to form a lineage of a particular person. All that is required to start the chain is the name of an ancestor who was married in Quebec, the husband's or wife's name and an approximate date of marriage (and place, if possible). Sometimes a lineage can be established without knowing the name of the husband or wife although in cases like these the time and place information should be more complete. When requesting a lineage from Père Loiselle, include $5.00-$7.00 for this service. (This index has also been micro-filmed by the Genealogical Society of Utah in Salt Lake City, Utah).

CENSUS RECORDS

These records have been discussed in detail in Chapter 3 - 4, which should be consulted for specific information. Many of the nominal censuses compiled in

the French Regime in Canada include names, **relationships,**
of family members, ages, occupations, residences and
maiden names of wives; all of which are extremely useful in genealogical research.

In addition to the standard censuses, there are
several other sources which can be used as census
records:

FEALTY AND HOMAGE (FOI ET HOMAGE)

These were registers of the acts of feudal recognition
of the King by the seigneur. These records contain the
names of the seigneurs and the inhabitants of his
seigneury, as well as pertinent dates, residences, occupations, and relationships. They cover the period 1637 -
1854 and are located at the Archives nationales and/or
the various judicial archives.

AVOWALS AND ENUMERATION (AVEUX ET DÉNOMBREMENTS)

At the same time as pledging fealty and homage, the
seigneur also was required to present a census of his
property. Included in these records which extend from
1677 to 1800 are names of the seigneurs and the heads of
families of those people residing on his land, plus
dates, residences and some relationships. These records
are located in either the Archives nationales or the
various judicial archives.

Some of the above records have been printed. For an
inventory of those in the Archives nationales consult P
P.G. Roy: Inventaire des concessions en fief et seigneurie,
fois et homages et dénombrements conserves aux Archives
de la province de Québec (Québec, 6 volumes). A number
of these records have also been printed in various
Rapports des Archives du Québec.

WILLS AND PROBATE RECORDS

Like their counterparts in the rest of Canada, these
records are located in the local judicial archives or at
the Archives nationales. As well, notarial wills (see
Chapter 3 - 5) are also located in the offices of
Notaries. The contents of these records are not unlike
those of the rest of Canada.

There are several other documents mainly connected
with inheritance which can be very useful for the researcher:

INVENTORIES (INVENTAIRES APRÈS DÉCÈS)

Dating from 1637 to about 1850, these records are inventories of the estates of deceased persons and include such information as the name of the deceased, spouse and children, maiden names of women, lists of important contracts with their dates and the notary before whom they were drawn up (marriages, deeds, etc.), and an inventory of the deceased's property. These records are found in the Archives nationales or at the various judicial archives. An inventory of those records in the Archives nationales is included in P.G. Roy and Antoine Roy: Inventaire des greffes des notaires du régime français (Québec 1943 - 46; 21 volumes).

INHERITANCE RECORDS (PORTAGES DE BIENS)

Located primarily in the judicial archives and dating from 1634 to the present, these records include the names and addresses of deceased persons and their heirs along with dates and relationships.

ORPHAN RECORDS (TUTELES ET CURATELLES)

Although seemingly removed from probate records, many orphan records are filed among notarial papers or with holographic wills. They date from 1637 to the present and include names and ages of orphans, names of their parents and relatives, dates and residences. They are found in the Archives nationales and the judicial archives throughout the province.

LAND RECORDS

Again a similarity exists between the land records of Quebec and those of other provinces and the information provided in this section should be used in conjuction with Chapter 3 - 7. Some of the land records of Quebec include:

LAND GRANTS (CONCESSIONS)

Covering the period 1626 - 1890, these records are available at the various judicial archives, the Archives nationales and the Public Archives of Canada. Information included on these grants is similar to that of the land records of other parts of Canada.

NOTARIAL LAND RECORDS

Located primarily at the local judicial archives and the Archives nationales, these records cover the period 1638 to the present and include names, dates, residences, relationships of people involved in land transfers. Some of the types of land records in this catagory include: baux (leases), echanges (exchanges), cessions et trans- ports (transfers), ventes (sales), deguerpissements (abandonments) and quittances (quit-claims).

PETITIONS FOR LAND

These records contain names, dates, residences, desired places of settlement, sometimes relationships and are not unlike the land petitions of Upper Canada discussed in Chapter 3 - 7. They cover the period 1680 - 1900 and are available at the Public Archives of Canada and the Archives nationales.

MISCELLANEOUS LAND RECORDS

These include sales of land, papiers terriers, declara- tions des censitaires, etc, containing names, residences, sometimes names of previous owners, neighbours, etc. They cover the period from 1626 to the present and can be found at the Public Archives of Canada, the local judicial archives and the Archives nationales.

COURT RECORDS

Virtually all records of French Canada can be classified as court records because so many of them end up in the judicial archives at some time or another. By far the greatest portion of those records described in Chapter 3 - 9 are now located in the Archives nationales, a list of which is included in the section on this repos- itory later in this chapter.

It seems opportune at this time to briefly document the types of records which are found in the judicial archives. A list of these archives can be found in Chapter 5 along with their respective addresses and a locality map. Records in the judicial archives include:

PARISH REGISTERS

These records were discussed earlier in this chapter.

NOTARIAL RECORDS (ACTES NOTAIRE)

These include land sales, marriage contracts, wills, donations, and other agreements between people. The Notary in Quebec was and is a very important person in day to day affairs in the province. It is to this person that most people turn when they wish to conclude an agreement with another, the notary's attestation guaran-

teeing the validity and legality of any document which
he draws up.

ACTS BY PRIVATE AGREEMENT

When a notary or priest was not available to draw up an
agreement, sometimes they were executed by bailliffs or
military officials. They contain much the same types of
information as notarial records.

HOLOGRAPHIC WILLS AND PROBATE RECORDS

These records were discussed earlier.

JUDICIAL DOCUMENTS

These include the records of the civil and criminal
courts within the judicial district, containing information similar to that discussed in Chapter 3 - 9.

REGISTERS OF INSINUATIONS

Now replaced by the registration of acts, these records
relate to marriage contracts (see later in this chapter)
and to property.

REGISTERS OF LEAVES OR PERMITS TO TRADE

The congés et permis de faire la traite show the names,
dates, places of residence, and destinations of explorers and fur traders from 1672 to 1752. These are particularly important in helping to identify settlers of
different localities. Some are also available at the
Archives nationales.

NOTARIAL RECORDS

In addition to the notarial records already discussed, there are several others which deserve a special
explanation. These are:

MARRIAGE CONTRACTS (CONTRATS DE MARIAGE)

Frequently, French Canadian couples signed a formal contract prior to the marriage, stipulating legal arrange-
ments surrounding the union such as bride's dowry,
responsibility of each for any debts encurred before
and after the marriage, and division of communal property should the marriage be dissolved. Each document
usually contains the names of the couple and their
parents, residences, sometimes ages, the names and occu-

pations of the contract's witnesses and their relationship to the bride and groom. These records are located
at the various judicial archives and at the Archives
nationales, and cover the period from 1636 to the present. An inventory of these contracts in the Judicial
Archives of Quebec and Charlevoix is available, entitled
P.G. Roy: <u>Inventaire des contrats de mariages du régime
français conserves aux Archives Judiciares de Québec</u>
(Québec 1937 - 38; 6 volumes) and Frere Eloi-Gérard
Talbot: <u>Inventaire des contrats de mariages au greffe
de Charlevoix</u> (Malbaie 1943). A number of the judicial
archives also maintain internal inventories of marriage
contracts in their files.

DONATIONS (DONATIONS ENTRE VIFS)

Covering the period from 1640 to the present, these
records include the names of children; their parents,
grandparents, dates and residences. These records
originate from elderly parents dividing their property
among their children before their deaths, or in other
words an early "will". One inventory of these records
is available: P.G. Roy: <u>Inventaire des testaments,
donations et inventaires du régime français conserves
au Archives Judiciares de Québec</u> (Québec 1941; 3 vols)

There are several inventories which are particularly
helpful in locating notarial records or for learning of
the available records created by each notary, including:

<u>Index des greffes des notaires décèdes (1645 - 1948)</u>,
which contains a list of the notaries of Quebec arranged
alphabetically by locality, showing the years covered by
their records and where they are presently deposited.

P.G. Roy and Antoine Roy: <u>Inventaire des greffes des
notaires du régime français</u> (Québec 1943 - 46; 21
volumes), which is an inventory of notarial records at
the Archives nationales in Quebec City.

SPECIAL RECORDS

A few special records which may be of some assistance to researchers can be found in a number of diverse
repositories. These include:

COLONIST RECORDS

These records originate in the archives of several French
ports including St. Malo, Dieppe, Rouen, La Rochelle and
Bordeaux. Some of these have been acquired by the Public
Archives of Canada. Covering the period 1634 - 1822, they

contain the names of the immigrants, dates of arrival,
ages, occupations, and sometimes places of origin or
destination. A number of lists of immigrants have also
been published by several Quebec genealogical societies.

APPRENTICE RECORDS

Located in the various judicial archives and covering
the period 1640 - 1800, these records include names, ages,
residences, occupations of the apprentices, and dates,
and the names of the fathers and masters.

FUR-TRADE EMPLOYEES

These records contain the names of fur-traders and
other employees, dates of contracts, places of origin,
and destination in western and northern Canada and the
United States. These are important records in locating
the place of origin of these people in Quebec. The
records cover 1670 - 1822 and are located at the
Judicial Archives of Montreal. They have also been
abstracted and indexed in the Rapport des Archives du
Québec for 1929 -33 and 1942 - 47. The abstracted
records cover the period 1788 - 1822.

HOSPITAL RECORDS

These records are primarily related to the three
earliest hospitals established in Quebec:

> Hôtel-Dieu, of Québec
>
> Hôpital-Ceneral, of Québec
>
> Hôtel-Dieu, of Montréal

Generally speaking, many early colonists stayed in
these hospitals at some time during their lives and they
were often used to house immigrants briefly after their
journey from France.

The records of the hospitals often contain records
of entry and release of the sick and, in some cases, a
record of death. Other information likely to be found
includes names, ages, residences and places of origin in
France or Canada.

The majority of these records are found in the
archives of the various hospitals, the addresses of which
can be obtained through the Archives nationales. Some of
the records may also be located in the various judicial
archives.

RELIGIOUS ARCHIVES

The archives of seminaries and parishes may yield an impressive amount of information for the diligent researcher. Because the church (Roman Catholic) was established in New France at an early date and exercised tremendous authority in provincial and colonial affairs, their records can be quite extensive in their scope.

Some of the documents likely to be found here are confirmation records, certificates of liberty to marry, registers of abjuration, marriage banns and dispensations, all containing a variety of information. As well, due to the Church's early responsibility in education, a large number of early school records can be found among their holdings.

Addresses of the various religious archives throughout the province can be obtained from the Archives nationales.

ARCHIVES NATIONALES DE QUÉBEC

Up to this point, the concentration of this chapter has been on discussing the types of records to be found in Quebec without regard to specific collections. Because this special section on French Canadiand genealogy has been included in this book, it seems only proper to discuss the holdings of the provincial archives at this point rather than in Chapter 5 with the other Provinces.

The Archives nationales de Québec is broken down into three main areas of interest, namely, New France (1608 - 1760), Quebec and Lower Canada (1760 - 1867), and the Province of Quebec (1867 to the present). The following brief inventory details some of the most important resources of each period. Those collections which have prepared inventories are marked with an asterisk.

NEW FRANCE PERIOD

*Judicial and Notarial Papers, 1638 - 1759 (125 vols) includes a variety of miscellaneous papers detatched from the registers.

Documents of the Jurisdiction of Trois-Rivières 1646 - 1759 (20 vols) includes registers of hearings relative to the administration of civil and criminal justice.

Seigneurial Courts, 1622 - 1760 (1 vol) includes detached documents regarding judgements, land, etc. for a few seigneuries.

Miscellaneous Registers and Detached Pieces of High
Council 1664 - 1760 (5 vols) contains petitions
to Council and other papers and a "criminal
register" for 1733 - 41.

*Registers of the Sovéreign Council 1663 - 1760
(69 vols) contains the reports of the Council
with judgements, letter of enoblement, etc.

*Insinuations of the High Council 1663 - 1760 (10 vols)
contains records of royal decrees, patents, etc.

*Ordinances of Intedents 1666 - 1760 (46 vols)
include orders of the Intendents for the administration of the colonies: re: justice, food-
stuffs, munitions, etc.

*Registers of the Provostship (La Prevote) of Quebec
1666 - 1759 (113 vols) containing reports of
Provostship hearings and cases involving marriage
promises, inquests on life and customs, special
sessions, property inventories, etc.

Fealty and Homage 1667 - 1759 (5 vols) includes all
acts of this nature.

Intendent's Registers 1672 - 1759 and Intendent's
Notebooks 1723 - 25 (8 vols) records the grants
of land and their respective titles, with some
Fealty and Homage records in the Notebooks.

Avowals and Enumerations 1723 - 58 (5 vols), see the
description earlier in this chapter.

QUEBEC OR LOWER CANADA PERIOD

Courts of Justice 1760 - 1880 (67 vols) contains a
variety of court records including militia
records, appeal court, circuit court, coroners
records, Justices of the Peace records and
Superior Court records.

Bureau of the Registrar, Grants and Sales of Land
1762 - 1867 (87 vols)

Attorney General Records 1763 - 1852 (48 vols)
includes among other judicial records, reports
of voluntary patrolmen in Quebec City and other
court proceedings for the period 1837 - 38.

Vital Statistics (Etat Civil) 1765 - 1895 (6 vols)
including a census of part of Quebec 1765, Poll
books (electors lists) by county 1814 - 36,
registers of vital records for the district of
Quebec (1854 -75; 1794 - 1844) and Montreal
(1844 - 75; 1892 - 95).

Seigneuries Records 1766 - 1862 (10 vols) includes
   Fealty and Homage records 1777 - 1854, Avowals
   and enumerations 1777 - 99, and various petitions concerning seigneuries 1766 - 1862.

Provincial Secretary 1768 - 1893 (23 vols) includes
   lists of pedlars, innkeepers, etc. 1807 - 12
   and 1815 - 40, lists of public houses and
   taverns in Quebec 1818 - 46, Seigneural records
   1830 - 57.

Army and Militia 1770 - 1871 (8 vols) includes reports
   and nominal lists of militia personnel.

Bureau of Rolls, Grants of Land 1788 - 1851 (96 vols)
   including Letters Patents by township 1788-1848,
   leases on the property of the clergy 1810 - 16,
   register of lands sold 1831 - 51, index of
   Letters Patent 1797 - 1841.

Petitions for Land Grants 1788 - 1900 (19 vols)
   arranged by township.

Lands of the King (26 vols) includes a variety of
   miscellaneous land records for 1650 - 1889.

Petitions for Land Grants by Militiamen 1812 - 51
   (85 vols)

Licenses 1818 - 67 (50 vols) for doctors, lawyers,
   notaries, surveyors, etc.

PROVINCE OF QUEBEC PERIOD

   Provincial Secretariat 1844 - 1960 includes lists of
      municipal officers, civil servants, Justices of
      the Peace, vital records for districts of
      Montreal 1873 - 96, and lists of other elected
      officials.

   Archives of the Colonies (from the French National
      Archives, Paris) includes the "General alpha-
      betical list of military and legal officers,
      etc., employed in northern and southern colo-
      nies" 1627 - 1780 (known as Laffelard Alphabet)

   War Archives (from the French National Archives,
      Paris) includes memoirs, journals, archives of
      troops in New France from the 17th to 19th
      centuries.

   Family dossiers and papers, a list of which appears
      in their inventory.

   Genealogical and biographical files.

ACADIAN RECORDS

Acadia comprises the present provinces of Nova Scotia, New Brunswick and Prince Edward Island. French settlements here began shortly after those in Quebec, continuing until this area was completely controlled by the English. In 1755, the majority of the Acadians living in Nova Scotia were deported frqm their homelands being reassigned to the British colonies to the south or ending up in Louisiana, England or France. Some, however, managed to settle in the province of Quebec or the remoter areas of New Brunswick. Those who managed to settle in France concentrated primarily in or near the French ports and on a large tract of land in the parishes of Archigny, Cenan, La Puye and St-Pierre de Maille. From here some left to go to Canada, Guiana, Santo Domingo, etc. In 1785, with the help of the King of Spain, many Acadians in France were transported to Louisiana, then a Spanish territory. With these widespread dispersions, the records kept by Acadians fell into disarray, were lost or were destroyed so that today they are not as comprehensive as those of Quebec.

There are several genealogical collections gathered by various genealogists which are of immense help to researchers. Foremost of these is the collection of Placide Gaudet, which is located at the Public Archives of Canada and is available on microfilm (Copies and other originals are also available at the Centre d'études acadiennes, Université de Moncton in New Brunswick, hereafter referred to as the Acadian Archives).

The Public Archives of Canada also has the collection of Gaudet's Notes comprising two sets of file cards on Acadian records, each card containing an individual birth, marriage, or death and shows the name of the person, date, parish, parents, and god-parents, as applicable. These entries have been compiled from a variety of official sources and cover the period before the expulsion of the Acadians in 1755. Filling over 100 file drawers, this collection is very important in assisting researchers in bridging the gap to Acadia proper. Another major collection is that of Rév. Archange Godbout, located at the Archives nationales de Quebec and containing genealogical date on Acadians in Acadia, England, France, Quebec and the United States. It is arranged alphabetically. Other collections can be found at the Acadian Archives and at the Public Archives of Canada.

The Parish Registers of Acadia have suffered the most damage of all. They were kept similarly to those in Quebec and are now located in a variety of repositories, notably the Archives nationales de Quebec, the Public Archives of Canada, and the Acadian Archives, among others. Those registers which were kept in France are now in the various departmental archives of that country and those kept in the United States are still held by the local churches or ecclesiastical archives. With the exception of the settlement

at Port Royal, registers for Acadian communities do not
exist for the period before 1700.

The __Acadian Censuses__ have been discussed earlier in Chapter
3-4 and are to be found in the Public Archives of Canada.
A few have been printed.

The __Land Grants__ for various areas of Acadia can be
found in the Archives des Colonies at the French National
Archives, Paris, France, although many of them have been
copied and deposited in the Public Archives of Canada and
other provincial archives in the Maritimes. They cover a
rough period from 1720 to the present and contain information
similar to other land grant records. The majority of these
early records pertain to Nova Scotia, in particular Ile
Royale (Cape Breton Island).

A number of __Court Records__, primarily for Île Royale,
exist for the period 1711-1758, copies of which are available at the Public Archives of Canada. Like most other
Acadian records, the __Notarial Records__ have suffered severe
dispersions and losses and the majority of the existing
documents refer only to Ile Royale and Newfoundland. Containing information similar to those in Quebec, they mainly
exist for the period 1687-1758. Copies are located at the
Public Archives of Canada. As well, there are notarial
records pertaining to the Acadians in France for 1758-1800
in the various departmental archives of France and others
of the French type are located in the Louisiana Parish
Clerk's Office for approximately 1770-1850.

Apart from these records, which are similar in nature
to many of those created in Quebec, there are several
others which are unique to the Acadians:

ALLEGIANCE LISTS

Taken in 1695, 1729 and 1730, these include the names
and residences of heads of Acadian families in Nova
Scotia who pledged allegience to the British Crown.
Copies of these are found in the Public Archives of
Canada, and the 1729 and 1730 lists have been printed in
the __Report of the Public Archives of Canada__ 1905, Vol. 2.

ACADIANS IN THE BRITISH COLONIES

There are lists of Acadians who were living in the
various British colonies in the period 1756 - 1766 and
include Pennsylvania, Maryland, Kentucky, South Carolina,
Massechusetts, Connecticut, New Brunswick, and Nova
Scotia, primarily. Names, residences, and relationships
make up the type of information found here. These records
are deposited in Manuscript Group 5 in the Public
Archives of Canada, and some have been printed.

LISTS OF DEPORTED ACADIANS

These lists record names, dates, residences, and relationships of Acadians transported to English colonies. They

are found in the Public Archives of Canada, the Archives
nationales de Quebec, and the Acadian Archives in
Moncton.

PETITIONS OF ACADIANS IN MASSACHUSETTS

Dating from 1755 - 63, these records include names, dates,
residences, relationships and places of origin in
Acadia. Copies are available at the Public Archives of
Canada.

ACADIANS IN TRANSIT

These records and registers contain a wealth of information on the Acadians who left their homeland. The
correspondence and memoirs of Acadians in France 1750 -
1797 and the lists of former inhabitants of Île
Royale, Prince Edward Island and Gaspé who landed at
Brest, France, 1758 - 84 contains names, dates, resi-
dences, ages, relationships, and places of origin in
Acadia. Copies are available at the Public Archives of
Canada. In addition to these, there are numerous other
lists of Acadians who were living in France or who
travelled to other colonies from France. These include
Censuses of Acadians in France 1762 - 84, Pension
Lists of Acadian Children in France 1763, arrivals in
Louisiana of Acadian families from New York, Santo
Domingo and Halifax 1764 - 69, records of financial
assistance paid to Acadians who lived in France 1773 -
97, passenger lists of Acadians from France to Louisiana 1785, most of which are available at the Archives
nationales, 60 rue des Francs-Gourgeois, 75 Paris III,
France; or at the Public Archives of Canada. In addition
there are innumerable local censuses in France located
in the departmental archives.

CENTRE D'ÉTUDES ACADIENNES

The Centre d'études acadiennes, Université de Moncton,
Moncton, New Brunswick E1A 3E9 can be considered as the
major repository for Acadian records in Canada, particularly
those of the Maritime provinces. Because of the close relationship between history and genealogy, the Centre has
taken a great interest in the preservation of records which
are useful to genealogical researchers. . The holdings of
this organization are best describedin a short information
leaflet which they have issued:

> "The genealogical material at the Centre
> d'Études Acadiennes consists alike of primary
> and secondary sources, of manuscript and
> printed matter. The primary sources for

Acadian genealogy are principally parish registers and census reports. The Centre d'
Études Acadiennes either has, or is in the
process of acquiring, copies of not only
the pre-dispersion registers available but
also the post-dispersion ones, for all
Acadian parishes, particularly those of the
Maritime Provinces. These registers are
greatly supplemented by the Centre's collection of copies of census reports which,
from the first Acadian census in 1671 to
the first Canadian census in 1871, is
reasonably complete. In addition to the
census reports, there are many official
lists of Acadians which provide important
information. Where primary documentation
is lacking, the Centre's collection of
secondary sources may often fill the gaps.
In addition to numberous books, periodicals,
booklets, and newspaper clippings, the
Centre d'Etudes Acadiennes possesses manuscript materials of great value. These
include all the notes of the celebrated
Placide Gaudet, plus extensive compilations
by Auguste-E. Daigle, Mgr. Louis Richard,
Rev. Archange Godbout, Rev. Arcade Goguen,
Rev. Hector Hebert, and Rev. Patrice Gallant.
A full description of the genealogical material available at the Centre d'Études
Acadiennes would, of necessity, fill many
pages. For further details the reader is
referred to the Centre's <u>Inventaire Général
des Sources Documentaires sur les Acadiens</u>,
tôme 1, (Moncton, N.B.: Editions d'Acadie,
1975), pp. 54-57, 380-469."

The Centre is currently undertaking the publication of
a definitive work on Acadian genealogy entitled <u>Dictionnaire
généalogique des familles acadiennes</u>, the first volume of
which will be released in 1978. This will be complemented
by a series of publications entitled "Sources documentaires
sur la généalogie acadienne".

Although the Centre will answer inquiries of a general
nature, the limitations of time and staff do not permit the
undertaking of extensive research projects.

FRENCH RECORDS OUTSIDE QUEBEC

Like other ethnic and cultural groups, the families of
French-Canadians settled in many other parts of Canada and
the United States as new areas of these countries opened
up. Once removed from the well organized Quebec society in

which records were carefully kept and preserved, French-
Canadian records have generally suffered the same fate as
those of other ethnic groups. In many cases, the family
ties with Quebec were completely severed, leaving no indication of the area of Quebec from which the family migrated. Researchers faced with these circumstances will
find that they may have considerable problems in linking
their families with those in Quebec.

French-Canadian records outside of Quebec can often be
found in a variety of repositories, notably the provincial
or local archives. Very few, if any, of the marriage records for Roman Catholics in Canada have been compiled into
"repertoiries" as they have in Quebec, making it necessary
for researchers to contact individual churches in order to
progress in their research (see Chapter 3:3). Other sources
may be discovered by contacting the numerous French-Canadian
Societies which have been established in recent years, some
of which are:

Alliance Française de Toronto, 62 Charles St. E.,
    Toronto, Ontario M4Y 1T1

Association Canadienne-Française de l'Alberta,
    10008-109 St., Edmonton, Alberta T5J 1M5

L'Association Canadienne-Française de Aveugles Inc.,
    6455 rue St-Andre, Montréal, Québec H2S 2K6

Association Canadienne-Française de l'Ontario,
    260 rue Dalhousie, Piece 204, Ottawa, Ont. K1N 7E4

Association Culturelle Franco-Canadienne de la
    Saskatchewan, 2800 Albert St., Regina, Sask.

Association France-Canada Inc., 400 est, rue Sherbrooke,
    Montréal, Québec H2L 1J7

L'Institute Canadien-Français d'Ottawa, 316 Dalhousie St.,
    Ottawa, Ontario K1N 7E7

Institute d'Histoire de l'Amerique Française, 261 ave
    Bloomfield, Montréal, Québec H2V 3R6

La Société Franco-Manitobaine, CP 145, St. Boniface,
    Manitoba R2H 3B4

BIBLIOGRAPHY

Because so much has been written and published on
French-Canadian genealogy, it is impossible to include all
those publications pertinent to it's study in a general reference book such as this. Therefore, researchers should
make liberal use of bibliographies, French-Canadian genealogical societies, and other finding aids in order to locate those publications most beneficial to their individual
research.

The following publications will help to compliment the
information given in this chapter and will assist in giving

researchers a better understanding of the possible sources available to them. The bibliographies in other chapters of this book should also be checked for useful publications.

GENERAL PUBLICATIONS

Archives du Québec: "Bibliographie de généalogies et histoires de familles" in Rapport de Archives du Québec 1940-41. This is a bibliography on individual family genealogies.

Auger, Roland J.: Tracing Your Ancestors Through the Province of Quebec and Acadia tô France in French Canadian and Acadian Genealogical Review, volume 2, 1969.

Grégoire, Jeanne: Guide du généalogiste à la recherche de nos ancêtres (Montréal 1974) This publication provides insight into genealogical research in Quebec. Order from Les Messageries Internationales du Livre Inc., 4550 rue Hochelaga, Montréal, Quebec.

Major Genealogical Record Sources for Canada, Genealogical Department of Mormon Church, Research Paper, Series B, No. 3, 1972 Excellant brief description of French-Canadian and Acadian records.

(Note: See also Chapter 2.1 and 3.1 for general histories of Canada and Quebec and other reference works useful in French-Canadian genealogy.)

ACADIANS

Arsenault, Bona: Histoire et généalogie des Acadiens (Québec 1965)

Arsenault, Bona: History of the Acadians (Quebec 1966)

Deville, Winston: Acadian Church Records (Mobile, Alabama 1964)

Doughty, Sir Arthur: The Acadian Exiles: A Chronicle of the Land of Evangeline (Toronto 1916,1920)

Gaudet, Placide: "Acadian Genealogy and Notes" in the Report of the Canadian Archives 1905, Volume 2.

Lauvriere, Émile: La Tragedie d'un Peuple, Histoire du Peuple Acadien de ses origines à nos jours (Paris 1924)

Poirier, Pascal: Origines des Acadiens (Montreal 1874)

Reider, Mr. and Mrs. Milton P. Jr.: The Crew and Passenger Lists of the Seven Acadian Expeditions of 1785, a listing by family groups of the refugee Acadians who migrated from France to Spanish Louisiana in 1785 (Metaire, La. 1965)
            : The Acadians in France, 1762-1776; Rolls of the Acadians distributed by towns for the years 1762 to 1776 (Metairie, La. 1967)

OUTSIDE OF QUEBEC

Beers, Henry: The French and British in the Old Northwest: A Bibliographical Guide to Archive and
Manuscript Sources (Detroit 1964)
_____ : The French in North America: A Bibliographical Guide to French Archives, Reproductions
and Research Missions (Baton Rouge 1957)

Boileau, Gilles: Les Canadiens français dans l'est de
l'Ontario (Montreal 1964)

Brunet, Godias: Alouette de Prairie; petite histoire
des Franco-Manitobains (Canadian Publishers 1967)

Canada. Department Secretary of State, Research and
Planning Branch: Select Bibliography on Franco-
phone Minorities in Canada (Ottawa 1972 Parts 1
and 2)

Chambers, H.E.: A History of Louisiana (Chicago 1925,
3 Volumes)

Dorge, Lionel: Introduction à l'étude des Franco-
Manitobians: essai historique et bibliographie

Freemont, Donatien: Les Français dans l'Ouest
Canadien (Winnipeg 1959)

Guide des sources d'archives sur la Canada français au
Canada (PAC Ottawa 1975)

Stewart, Alexander: French Pioneers in the Eastern
Great Lakes Area 1609-1791 (Rochester, New York
1970)

3:14 UNITED EMPIRE LOYALISTS

At the time of the American Revolution, a large number of inhabitants of what was to become the United States chose the side of the King in the troubles or refused to pick sides at all. These people were referred to by their neighbours and former friends as "Tories" or "Traitors" and their property and liberties were taken from them and they were generally treated as outcasts in their own country. After the end of the war, a number of them emigrated to Canada under the protection and promise of a new beginning extended to them by the British government. Here they made their homes, opening up the areas of Ontario and parts of the Maritimes and dominating the political affairs of the colonies. In time a sense of pride in being loyal to the Crown developed and with it the nomenclature United Empire Loyalist. This pride and the desire of many Canadians to be identified with this special group of immigrants has developed into a special branch of Canadian genealogy, whose unique records will be discussed in this chapter.

LOYALIST RECORDS

All United Empire Loyalists were entitled to receive land grants and other priviledges in compensation for their losses in the United States and as a reward for their loyalty to the Crown. A number of printed lists of Loyalists have been included at the end of this chapter for the researcher's reference. These lists were compiled at various times (some have been compiled only recently) to provide a record of the Loyalists who settled in various provinces and should be the first source the researcher consults when a UEL background is suspected. One of the most well known of these lists is the Upper Canada United Empire Loyalist List. This list exists in two forms, both compiled at the same time, one by theExecutive Council Office of Upper Canada and the other by the Ontario Crown Lands Office. Minor differences occur between the lists, with some names only appearing in one of them and other names having spelling differences. However, each list indicates the places of residence and often gives some reference to the man's military service in the American Revolution. They were compiled as a result of a proclamation of Lt. Governor John Graves Simcoe of Upper Canada in 1789 requesting

that a list of Loyalists be kept in order that they might
receive the benefits and priviledges due them. Subsequent
proclamations established the criteria for including or
removing new and existing names on the list, the most
important of which was the proclamation in 1798 restrict-
ing the list to those Loyalists who were residents of the
province before 18 July 1798. Because many people failed
to get on the lists in time, their usefulness is limited ·
and they should be used as a listing of "recognized"
Loyalists only. Other sources will have to be consulted
when trying to prove that an ancestor not included on
these lists was in fact a Loyalist, which can be very
difficult to say the least.

When the Loyalists left their homes in the United
States, they were guaranteed compensation for their loss
of property there by the Treaty of Paris in 1783. The
Loyalist Claims arising from this promise form a valuable
portion of the Loyalist records. In 1783, the British
government established a Claims Commission to determine
the compensation due to the Loyalists. The records of the
Audit Office 12 and 13 contain considerable records
relating to the petitions filed before the commission
including evidence of witnesses, supporting documents,and
the original memorials of the Loyalists. These records
often give names, former places of residence in the
United States, size of family, sometimes dependents' names,
details of military service, and residence at the time of
claim and an outline of the particular losses incurred
by each family. All of these records are indexed alphabetically. However, very few people submitted these
claims primarily because they had to appear before the
Commission, which only met in Halifax, Saint John, Quebec,
Montreal and London, in person and at their own expense.
Many people's claims being so small, they decided that it
wasn't worth the effort. Others who didn't appear in
person worked through the services of an agent, two of
whom were John Porteous (see PAC, Manuscript Group 23)
and Alexander Ellice (see PAC, Manuscript Group 24).
Information on Loyalists may also be found in the numerous
private papers at the Public Archives of Canada. These
Loyalist Claims are available at the Public Archives of
Canada on microfilm, and in print in the Ontario Archives
Report for 1904.

A considerable number of Loyalist Regiments were
raised during the American Revolution to serve with the
British forces and their records should not be overlooked.
In fact, these provide one of the best sources in
"proving" the loyalist tendencies of ancestors, particularly in areas other than Ontario. Many of these units
later came to Canada and settled together by regiment on
large blocks of land set aside for them. Over 50 provincial Loyalist Corps were formed during the war although

fully two-thirds of all Loyalists under arms served with the following units:

Allen McLean's Royal Highland Emigrant Regiment

Joseph Gorman's Royal Fencible Americans

Francis Legge's Nova Scotia Volunteers

Sir John Johnson's King's Royal Regiment of New York

John Butler's Loyal Rangers

Colonel John Peter's Queen's Loyal Rangers

Ebenezar and Edward Jessup's Royal Americans or
    King's Loyal Americans

Roger's King's Rangers

Major McAlpine's Royal Americans

Holland's Loyal Yorkers

MacKay's Loyal Volunteers

Captain Robert Leake's Independent Company
Oliver Delancey's New York Loyalists

Cortlandt Skinner's New Jersey Loyalists

Robert Roger's Queen's Rangers

Edward Fanning's King's American Regiment

John Bayard's King's Orange Rangers

Beverley Robinson's Loyal American Regiment

Monteforte Browne's Prince of Wales American Regiment

William Allan's Corps of Pennsylvania Loyalists

James Chalmer's Corps of Maryland Loyalists

The muster rolls, paylists and other <u>military records</u> relating to these and other Loyalist units can be found in the papers of the British Military Establishment (Record Group 8), formerly known as the "C" Series. This series includes some eight feet of muster rolls of provincial corps of Loyalist militia as well as a number of volumes relating to the settlement of Loyalists at Sorel, Quebec, and to the payment of pensions. These are located at the Public Archives of Canada and an extensive nominal card index of them is available in the Manuscript Division Reading Room.

Other sources of military records of Loyalist regiments at the Public Archives of Canada are the War Office Series, especially for those settling in the Maritimes. These records include disbandment papers, records of active service, lists of officers and monthly returns of troops, to name a few. Muster rolls are also available in a variety of private collections in Manuscript Group 23, notably the Chipman Papers and the papers of Edward Winslow. Winslow's papers refer particularly to Nova Scotia and New Brunswick.

The British Headquarters Papers (Manuscript Group 23) of the Public Archives of Canada complement and supplement the "C" Series discussed above. A printed calendar of these papers with an index is available at the Public Archives. While rather awkward to use, these papers can be very fruitful, containing petitions of people seeking pensions, compensation or assistance, and muster and provisions lists of refugees transported from New York to Nova Scotia. Further information on transportation, provisioning and pensions will also be found in the Admiralty and Treasury papers (Manuscript Group 12)

One of the most significant military collections, however, is the Haldimand Papers (Manuscript Group 21). These provide such information as military service, transportation, provisioning, compensation, land settlement, memorials and claims, records of prisoners of war, and muster rolls, all pertaining to the Loyalists. A bound index to the "Loyalist Lists" is included with this collection in the Public Archives of Canada.

Land Grants were one means of providing compensation to Loyalist subjects, and these records can be found in the Public Archives of Canada (Record Group 1) and are discussed in detail in Chapter 4. As well, it is advisable to search the oaths of allegience (Record Group 1), which was required of those persons taking up land grants, as they contain occupation, current residence and place of origin. Unfortunately, these oaths are not yet indexed. The other land records and petitions discussed in Chapter 3 - 7 should also be checked for possible references to Loyalist activities. It is important to note that the land records in Record Group 1 pertain only to Upper and Lower Canada and that for records of other provinces it is necessary to contact the respective provincial archives for more information. As well, it should be pointed out that the Public Archives of Canada have only the petitions for grants in Upper and Lower Canada and that the actual land grants or letters patent are still retained by each province. Those researching in Ontario should bear in mind that this province was part of Lower Canada (then Quebec) until 1791 and direct their searches accordingly. These land records in the Public Archives of Canada have been indexed.

There are numerous other references to Loyalists in many private papers throughout the national and provincial archives which may provide needed information. However, these require a considerable amount of work to locate and examine. Sometimes, as well, it can be quite beneficial to check the petitions or papers of other major Loyalists who resided in the same vicinity as an ancestor for some record regarding the particular family being researched.

PUBLICATIONS AND ORGANIZATIONS

Like French Canadian genealogy, Loyalist research has generated a profusion of publications, any one of which may be helpful in solving individual problems. It is essential that in order to realize the full possibilities of the known records and to assist in locating lesser known records which have not been discussed in this chapter the researcher should conduct an extensive reading program regarding Loyalist history and record sources. For the best assistance in this regard, the following should be contacted:

> The United Empire Loyalist Association of
>   Canada
> Dominion Headquarters
> 23 Prince Arthur Avenue
> Toronto, Ontario M5R 1B2

This association was established in 1914 to provide a unifying organization for descendents of United Empire Loyalists and to preserve and perpetuate the memory of the Loyalist's sacrifices. They publish a historical and genealogical journal and provide much assistance in helping members prove their Loyalist descent. Anyone who suspects that he/she is a descendent of a Loyalist should contact this association for more information.

A few publications are listed below which will assist in beginning any research on a Loyalist lineage. These constitute only a few of the major or important publications and, as acquired, they will undoubtedly guide the researcher to other sources. Those marked with an asterisk are particularly useful to the beginner in search of a Loyalist heritage.

Campbell, Wilfred: Report on the Manuscript Lists in the Archives Relating to the United Empire Loyalists (Ottawa 1909) See also the Finding Aid in PAC which supplements this list.

Coke, Daniel: Notes on the Royal Commission on the Losses and Services of American Loyalists 1783-85 (Oxford 1915)   •

Chadwick, Edward: Ontarian Families: Genealogies of United Empire Loyalists and Other Pioneer Families of Upper Canada (1894-98, 2 volumes - reprint Lambertsville, N.V. 1970)

Criuckshank, E.A.: The Settlement of United Empire Loyalists on the Upper St. Lawrence and the Bay of Quinte in 1784 (Toronto 1934)

Cumberland, R.W.: The United Empire Loyalist. Settlements Between Kingston and Adolphstown (Kingston 1923)

Evans, G.N.D.: The Loyalists (Toronto 1968)

Flowers, A.D.: The Loyalists in Bay Chaleur (Gaspe) (Victoria, B.C. 1973)

*Flowers, Jo-Ann, and Calder, K.: "A Bibliography of Loyalist Source Material in Canada" in American Antiquarian Society Proceedings, Volume 82, pt. 1, pp 67-270.

*Genealogical Publishing Company, Baltimore: "Old United Empire Loyalist List" (Ontario only) (reprint in 1969)

*Gilroy, Marion: Loyalists and Land Settlement in Nova Scotia (Halifax 1937)

*Kennedy, Patricia: How to Trace Your Loyalist Ancestors: Use of Loyalist Sources in PAC (Ottawa Branch, OGS, publn. 1973-15)

Kirk, Robert F.: "Loyalist Migrations" in OGS Bulletin Volume 8, No. 3. Contains excellent bibliography.

Ontario Archives Report 1904-05: "United Empire Loyalists: Enquiry into the Losses and Services in Consequence of their Loyalty" (2 volumes)

Paterson, Gilbert: "Loyalists in Upper Canada 1783-1840" in Report of the Department of Archives for the Province of Canada 1921

Pringle, J.F.: Lunenburgh or the Old Eastern District (Cornwall 1890)

Raymond, W.D.: Loyalists in Arms. An account of the Loyalist corps.

*Reid, W.D.: The Loyalists in Ontario (Lambertville,NJ, 1973). A listing of Loyalists and children.

Report of the Canadian Archives 1891: "Return of Disbanded Troops and Loyalists settled in the Eastern and Midland Districts"

Ryerson, E.: The Loyalists of America and Their Times: From 1620 to 1816 (Toronto 1880, 2 volumes)

Sabine, Lorenzo: Biographical Sketches of Loyalists in the American Revolution (2 volumes, Port Washington New York, reprint 1966)

Siebert, Wilber H.: "The Temporary Settlement of Loyalists at Machiche, P.Q." Trans. Royal Society of Canada, 1916

_____: The Loyalist Settlement on the Gaspe Peninsula (1916)

_____: "The Loyalists in the Eastern Seigniories and Townships of the Province of Quebec" Trans. Royal Society of Canada, 1913

Wallace, W. Stewart: The United Empire Loyalists: A Chronicle of the Great Migration (Toronto 1914)

*Wright, Esther: The Loyalists of New Brunswick (Fredericton 1955)

3:15 ETHNIC RECORDS IN CANADA

Possibly the most ignored group of Canadians genealog-ically are those whose ancestral roots are in neither the British Isles nor France. Many genealogical publications deal primarily with the general records of Canada or with those particularly useful to Canadians of British or French backgrounds yet make little or no reference to the many records which are unique to the other various "ethnic" and "cultural" groups in Canada. This is quite unfortunate as these unique records can often provide the answers to resea-rch problems where general Canadian records fail.

Upon their arrival in this country, an ethnic group had a tendency to be drawn together by their common language and customs and their desire to perpetuate them. The fear or uncertainty of the English or French Canadian cultures also tended to amplify the need for cultural co-operation and unity within the group. The result of this is a wealth of mater-ial compiled in a variety of languages and located in virt-ually every part of Canada. Many of these records are of value to the genealogical researcher.

ETHNIC SOURCES

Each ethnic group has had a tendency to create records and documents unique only to itself. Considering the large number of various ethnic and cultural communities which settled in Canada, it would be impossible to discuss all the special records of all these groups in a general reference work such as this. However, there are several major types of records and sources common to all the groups which should be explored by the researcher interested in an ethnic ances-try.

● RELIGIOUS RECORDS
Many ethnic groups brought with them their own particular religious organizations. This is especially evident for the Slavic groups, the Scandinavians and the Germans, in particular, who each established their own particular churches in Canada and the United States. This resulted in such organizations as the Danish Lutheran, German Lutheran, Ukrainian Orthodox or Rumanian Orthodox Churches which adminis-

tered to the cultural group they represented. Knowing the ethnic background and
religious persuation of a family and the
general area in Canada in which they lived,
it is possible to located church records
quite quickly, provided a church of a
similar ethnic background and denomination
existed in that area.

● ETHNIC LANGUAGE NEWSPAPERS
Containing a wealth of information, some
ethnic groups have been publishing newspapers since the first half of the nineteenth century. They are very similar in
content to their English and French counterparts which were discussed earlier in this
book. Their primary importance lies in the
fact that they provided a cultural life line,
tying families to their common language and
customs no matter where they lived in the
country. This need to use the language of
their birth and to associate somehow with
their old country roots made every family
in Canada of a particular ethnic background
a likely subscriber. News articles, obituaries, etc. in these newspapers stand a far
better chance of containing references to
places of origin than do the English language
newspapers. Current foreign language newspapers in Canada can be found listed in the
national directories of a general nature, such
as the Canadian Almanac and Directory or
the Corpus Almanac of Canada.

● HISTORIES OF ETHNIC GROUPS IN CANADA
In order to understand the thinking of ethnic
forebearers and to trace their likely movements in Canada, it is necessary to have some
idea of their history in this country. Fortunately, Canada's ethnic groups have displayed
an immense pride in being what they are and
have produced countless volumes discussing
and documenting their history in this country.
These valuable works should not be ignored.
Many leads to other records will develop from
them.

● SPECIAL COLLECTIONS
Many university libraries and provincial
archives have established special collections
of books and original documents relating to
one or more ethnic or cultural group. Under
one roof the researcher can find a multitude
of sources which can assist in the compilation

of a genealogy. One such collection is the Ethnic Archives of the Public Archives of Canada (see Chapter 4). Other collections can be located either by inquiring of your local librarian or by writing to the various libraries and archives in your province. As well, some ethnic groups have now established special libraries of their own to document their history in Canada.

ETHNIC ORGANIZATIONS

The desire for people of a similar background to associate with one another and to preserve their cultural heritage were strong factors which resulted in the early establishment of special societies and organizations to meet these ends.

The majority of these associations are organized to serve local groups, generally on a city or provincial basis. Although some are purely social organizations, many are also concerned with the retention of their cultural heritage and are very active in publishing books, periodicals and newspapers either in English or in their own particular languages.

Researchers will generally find these organizations helpful in recommending histories of their ethnic groups and providing information on ethnic churches and the addresses of special ethnic archives and libraries. As well, some may publish periodicals or maintain libraries themselves.

Although the names and addresses of most ethnic and cultural societies in Canada will be found in the Ethnic Directory of Canada published by Western Publishers (P.O. Box 30193, Station B, Calgary, Alberta), a select list of societies is provided here for general reference purposes. These societies are arranged by ethnic group and are generally national or long-established organizations.

GENERAL ORGANIZATIONS:

Canadian Ethnic Studies Association, Department of Sociology, University of Toronto, 563 Spadina Avenue, Toronto, Ontario M5S 1A1

Ethnic Referral Centre, P.O. Box 2334, Thunder Bay, Ontario P7S 5E9

Federation of Ethnic Groups of Quebec, Box 543, Stn. Snowden, Montreal, Quebec H3X 2H0

ALBANIAN: Canadian Albanian Association, 81 Edinborough Court, Toronto, Ontario

ARMENIAN: Tekeyan Armenian Cultural Association, 401-931 Yonge Street, Toronto, Ontario M4W 2H8

AUSTRIAN: Canadian-Austrian Society, 33 Elmthorte Road, Toronto, Ontario

BELGIAN: Association Belgique-Canada, 3312 Place Victoria, Montreal, Quebec H4Z 1B7

BLACK: National Black Coalition, Box 516 Station P,
Toronto, Ontario M5S 2T1

BYELORUSSIAN: Byelorussian Canadian Alliance, 524 St.
Clarens Avenue, Toronto, Ontario M6H 3W7

CHINESE: Chinese Benevolent Association, 108E Pender,
Vancouver, British Columbia

CROATIAN: Croatian Peasant Society, 2839-11 Avenue S.E.,
Calgary, Alberta

CZECHS: Czechoslavak National Association of Canada,
740 Spadina Avenue, Toronto, Ontario M5S 2V2

DANISH: Local organizations only

DUTCH: Netherlands Association, Box 2229, Vancouver,
British Columbia

ESTONIAN: Estonian Central Council, 958 Broadview
Avenue, Toronto, Ontario

FINNISH: Finnish Organization of Canada, 957 Broadview
Avenue, Toronto, Ontario M4K 2R5

GERMAN: German-Canadian Association, P.O. Box 551,
Thunder Bay, Ontario P7C 1V4

   Canadian-German Society, 386 McGregor, Winnipeg,
   Manitoba

GREEK: Hellenic-Canadian Cultural Society, P.O. Box 243,
Don Mills, Ontario M3C 252

HUNGARIAN: Hungarian-Canadian Federation, 840 St. Clair
Avenue W., Toronto, Ontario M6C 1C1

ICELANDIC: Canada-Iceland Foundation, 294 Portage Ave.,
Winnipeg, Manitoba R3C 0B9

ITALIAN: Federation of Italian-Canadian Associations
and Clubs, 756 Ossington Avenue, Toronto, Ontario

JAPANESE: Japanese Canadian Citizens Association, P.O.
Box 383, Station K, Toronto, Ontario M4P 2G7

JEWISH: Canadian Jewish Congress, 1590 McGregor Ave.,
Montreal, Quebec H3G 1C5

LATVIAN: Latvian National Federation, 491 College,
Toronto, Ontario M6G 1A2

LITHUANIAN: Lithuanian-Canadian Community, 1011 College
Street W., Toronto, Ontario

MACEDONIAN: Pan-Macedonian Association, 440 Danforth,
Toronto, Ontario M4J 1P4

MALTESE: Maltese Unity Association, Box 248, Station D,
Toronto, Ontario M6P 2A3

NORWAY: Sons of Norway, 1910 Centennial Bldg., Edmonton,
Alberta

POLISH: Canadian Polish Congress, 288 Roncesvalles Ave.,
Toronto, Ontario M6R 2M4

PORTUGESE: Portugese Association of Canada, 4170 St
Urbain, Montreal, Quebec

RUMANIAN: Rumanian Canadian Association, 1862 Eglinton
W., Toronto, Ontario

RUSSIAN: Federation of Russian Canadians, 6 Denison Ave.,
Toronto, Ontario M5T 2M4

SERBIAN: Serbian League of Canada, 212 Delaware Ave.,
    Toronto, Ontario
SLOVAKIAN: Slovak National Society, 301-91 Spencer
    Avenue, Toronto, Ontario
SLOVENIAN: Slovenian National Federation, 646 Euclid
    Avenue, Toronto, Ontario
SPANISH: Association Espagnole, 485 Sherbrooke W.,
    Montreal, Quebec
SWEDISH: Canada Svensken, 91 Hazelton Avenue, Toronto,
    Ontario
SWISS: Local organizations only
SYRO-LEBANESE: Syro-Lebanese Association of Canada,
    834 St. Matthews, Winnipeg, Manitoba
TURKISH: Turkish Cultural Association, 2985 Goyer,
    Montreal, Quebec
UKRAINIAN: Ukrainian Canadian Committee, 456 Main St.,
    Winnipeg, Manitoba R3B 1B6
WEST INDIAN: Caribbean Cultural Committee (Caribana),
    632-B Yonge Street, Toronto, Ontario

BIBLIOGRAPHY

The following bibliography contains a select list of
general reference publications on ethnic groups in Canada:

Burnet, Jean: Ethnic Groups in Upper Canada (Ontario
    Historical Society, Toronto 1972)
Canadian Ethnic Studies, Bulletin of the Research Centre
    for Canadian Ethnic Studies, University of Calgary,
    Alberta, 1969
Citizen, publication of the Citizenship Branch of Depart-
    ment of Secretary of State, Ottawa 1954
Foster, Kate: Our Canadian Mosaic (Toronto 1926)
Gibbon, John: Canadian Mosaic: The Making of a Northern
    Nation (Toronto 1938)
Gregorovich, Andrew: Canadian Ethnic Groups Bibliography
    (Toronto 1972). Available from the Government of
    Ontario Bookstore, 880 Bay Street, Toronto, Ontario.
Kinton, Jack: American Ethnic Groups: A Source Book
    (Aurora, Ill. 1973)
Markotic, J. (Ed.): Ethnic Directory of Canada (Calgary
    1976)
McLaren, Duncan: Ontario Ethno-Cultural Newspapers
    1835-1972 (University of Toronto Press 1973)
Queen's Printer: The Canadian Family Tree (Ottawa 1967)

3:16 NATIVE PEOPLES

The term Native Peoples is a comprehensive phrase generally used to describe those people of Canada who are more
commonly known as Indians and Eskimos. In fact the terms
"Indian" and "Eskimo" are in themselves misnomers, being
applied to these people by early white explorers. However,
it is not the purpose of this chapter to discuss the names
by which Canada's native peoples are known, or would prefer
to be known, but to provide some idea on the background of
the native peoples and the genealogical records which are
available on them.

THE INDIANS

The Indian Act, a piece of Federal legislation, defines
an Indian as "A person who pursuant to this Act is registered as an Indian or is entitled to be registered as an
Indian" (Section 2.1g.). This basic legal description divides all Indians into two major groups - the status group
and the non-status and Metis group.

Status Indians are also refered to as being treaty,
registered, reserve or band Indians. As a general rule,
they are members of one of 558 bands living on 2279 reserves (1973). For the sake of clarity, status Indians are
divided into two main sections:

> Treaty Indians: These are Indians who at
> some time or another have signed a treaty
> either with the British government or the
> Canadian government whereby they exchanged
> their rights to the land they occupied
> for smaller "reserves" and other concess-
> ions and assistance guaranteed them and
> their descendants by the government. As
> treaty Indians, they are duly registered
> as such and careful records are kept of
> their descendants. These treaties cover
> only the provinces of Ontario, Manitoba,
> Saskatchewan, Alberta and parts of the
> Northwest Territories and British Columbia.

> Registered Indians: These are Indians who
> have not signed a treaty ceding their lands
> but who are still none-the-less regarded
> as Indians by the federal government and

are registered accordingly. This covers
the areas of Canada not covered by treaties,
namely the Atlantic provinces, Quebec, most
of British Columbia, the Yukon, and parts
of the Northwest Territories.

In all, there are approximately 250,000 persons in
Canada (1971) who are regarded as "status Indians", the
majority of whom reside on the various reserves put aside
for their use.

The non-status Indians and the Metis are generally
described as people of an Indian ancestry, many of whom
still identify themselves with their native culture and
relatives. The Metis (also called half-breed) are people
of mixed blood whose parents were Indian and other (generally white). Historically these people lived on the
Prairies or in northwestern Ontario. Non-status Indians
are those who have lost their "federal Indian" status
either because they failed to register as status Indians,
or their registration was refused or through marriage (an
Indian woman who marries a "non-Indian" ceases to be an
Indian herself, as do her children). It is estimated
that there are about 500,000 Metis and non-status Indians
presently (1971) living in Canada, many near white towns
and villages.

THE INUIT

The Inuit (or Eskimo) live primarily in the Northwest
Territories and presently (1971) number about 16,000 persons. Although no treaties have been signed with the Inuit
and they are not regarded as "Indians" and the Indian Act
excludes them, the Supreme Court of Canada has decreed
that they are "Indians" within the meaning of the BNA Act.
As a result, all Inuit are listed and recorded with a special registry number not unlike those given to status
Indians.

NATIVE RECORDS

There are two primary repositories for records relating
to Native peoples. The first is, naturally, the Public
Archives of Canada and the second is the federal Department
of Indian Affairs and Northern Development.

Records relating to native peoples in the Public Archives of Canada are primarily located in Record Group 10
(The Department of Indian Affairs). The Public Archives
has prepared a short publication which is a basic guide to
this particular collection and is available from PAC upon
request:

Public Records Division. General Inventory
Series. <u>No 1 Records Relating to Indian
Affairs (RG10)</u> (PAC: Ottawa 1975).

The guide itself is broken down into several main sections to facilitate its use:

- Administration records of the Imperial
    government 1677-1864
- Ministerial administration records 1786-
    1970
- Field office records: Superintendency records
                                        1809-1970
                                    Agency records 1857-
                                        1971
- Indian land records 1680-1956

Following each main heading are brief explanations of
the type of records which are available and the areas of
Canada which they cover, and include treaty paylists, annuity
paylists, census records, land records, school records,
band council minutes, elections of band councils, war service pensions, etc. As this guide is quite easily obtainable and will undoubtedly remain in print for some time to
come, no effort will be made to extract the more genealogically valuable references for inclusion here. Researchers
interested in a native ancestry should be sure to acquire
a copy of it before continuing with any major research.

The records now deposited with the Public Archives
originated with the Department of Indian Affairs and
Northern Development, or its predecessors, which still retains other records of value to researchers. One particularly useful source is the Indian Register by which a record is kept of all the individuals in Canada who are or
have been registered as Indians within the meaning of the
Indian Act. This Register was first compiled in 1951 from
information received from the Department's field offices
and is continously being updated. Births, deaths, marriages,
enfranchisements and other pertinent information will be
found in the Register. Any researcher who wishes to establish whether or not his ancestors were ever registered as
Indians can direct his enquiry, together with any available
identifying information to:

Registrar, Indian Register
Department of Indian and Northern Affairs
400 Laurier Avenue West
Ottawa, Ontario K1A 0H4

The Department is also in possession of the Treaty Paylists for all Treaty Bands as well as some Interest Paylists
for a few Non-Treaty Bands. When a child was born to an
Indian who was entitled to membership in a band, he or she
was registered under the family band number. In the early
years it was very common to record births, deaths and marr-

iages on the paylists under the family band number at the
time of the treaty or interest payments, although specific
months were seldom recorded for births or deaths. However,
these records are regarded as classified documents and in
order to have a search of them conducted, an "Application
for a Search of Treaty or Interest Paylists" (form IAN-
1075) must be completed. These forms and further information on the Treaty and Interest Paylists may be obtained
from:

> Genealogical and Archival Research Unit
> Special and Administrative Services Division
> Indian and Eskimo Affairs Program
> Department of Indian Affairs and Northern
>   Development
> 400 Laurier Avenue West
> Ottawa, Ontario K1A 0H4

Genealogical records relating to native peoples will
also be found in virtually all the provincial archives
across Canada. They may be records relating specifically
to Indians or may be "buried away" in the private papers of
individuals, fur traders or clergymen. The Union List of
Manuscripts in Canadian Repositories (Ottawa 1975) published by the Public Archives and containing a general inventory of records in a variety of repositories and achives
across Canada will provide many clues regarding possible
sources. Churches located on or near present day Indian
Reserves should also be contacted for more precise references to births, marriages and deaths.

NATIVE ORGANIZATIONS

The following native organizations may also be able to provide additional information on possible sources:

> National: National Indian Brotherhood, 102 Bank St.,
>   1st Floor, Ottawa, Ontario K1P 5G4
>   Native Council of Canada, Ste. 200, 77 Metcalfe
>   St., Ottawa, Ontario K1P 5L6

> Eskimos (Inuit): Uniut Taperisat of Canada, 222
>   Somerset St. W., Ottawa, Ontario K2P 2G3
>   Labrador Inuit Association, Nain, Labrador A0P 1L0
>   Northern Que. Inuit Association, P.O. Box 76,
>   Fort Chimo, Quebec

> Indian: Indian Association of Alberta, 203-11710
>   Kinsway Ave., Edmonton, Alberta T5G 0X5
>   Native Brotherhood of B.C., 193 E Hastings,
>   Vancouver, B.C.
>   Manitoba Indian Brotherhood, 600-191 Lombard Ave.,
>   Winnipeg, Manitoba R3B 0X1
>   Union of N.B. Indians, 181 Westmorland St.,
>   Fredericton, N.B. E3B 3L6

Union of N.S. Indians, 117 Membertou St., Box
961, Sydney, N.S. B1P 6J4
Union of Ontario Indians, 3028 Danforth Ave.,
2nd Floor, Toronto, Ontario M4C 1N2
Association des Indiens du Québec, Village des
Hurons, P.Q. GOA 4VO
Federation of Saskatchewan Indians, 114 Central
Ave., Box 1644, Prince Albert, Sask. S6V 5T2
Indian Brotherhood of the N.W.T., Box 2338,
Yellowknife, N.W.T., Y1A 3TA
Yukon Native Brotherhood, Box 4252, Whitehorse,
Yukon, Y1A 3Ta
Native Association of Newfoundland/Labrador,
Box 1195, St. John's,Newfoundland A1C 5M9

Non-Status and Metis: Metis Association of Alberta,
Rm. 303, 10826-124 St., Edmonton, Alba. T4M OH3
B.C. Association of Non-Status Indians, 144 W
Hastings St., Vancouver, B.C.
Manitoba Metis Federation, 301-374 Donald St.,
Winnipeg, Manitoba
N.B. Association of Metis and Non-Status Indians,
390 King St., Fredericton, N.B.
Newfoundland/labrador Provisional Council, Box
34, North West River, Labrador
Ontario Metis and Non-Status Indian Association,
5300 Yonge St., Ste. 208, Willowdale, Ont. M2N 5R2
Association des Metis et Indiens "Lois reserves"
due Québec, 1023 boul de 1' Anse, Roberval
Metis Society of Saskatchewan, 1846 Scarth St.,
Regina, Saskatchewan
Metis Association of N.W.T., Box 1375, Yellowknife,
N.W.T. XOE 1HO
Yukon Assoication of Non-Status Indians, 22 Nisutlin
Drive, Whitehorse, Yukon Y1A 3S5

BIBLIOGRAPHY

The following bibliography is representative of the
many publications which are available on native peoples in
Canada. The researcher involved with a native ancestry is
well advised to consult one or more of these books, or
others, to better understand the history and development of
the specific group to which his ancestors belonged and to
possibly provide some additional clues as to available records:

GENERAL:
Hodge, Frederich W.: Handbook of Indians of Canada
(Ottawa 1913)
Jenness, Diamond: The Indians of Canada (6th Edition,
Ottawa 1963)

Jenness, Eileen: _The Indian Tribes of Canada_
(Toronto 1933)

Leechman, Douglas: _Native Tribes of Canada_ (Toronto,
1956)

TRIBES AND AREAS:

Barnett, H.G.: _The Coast Salish of British Columbia_
(Eugene 1955)

Canada National Museum: _The Algonkians_ (New York
1866)

Drucker, Philip: _Indians of the Northwest Coast_
(New York 1963)

Drucker, Philip: _The Northern and Central Nootkan
Tribes_ (Washington 1951)

Ewers, V.C.: _The Blackfeet_ (Norman 1958)

Harrison, Charles: _Ancient Warriors of the North
Pacific: The Haidas_ (no place 1925)

Hathaway, E.V.: _The Story of the Hurons_ (Toronto 1915)

Jenness, Diamond: _The Sarcee Indian of Alberta_
(Ottawa rd)

Jones, Peter: _History of the Ojibway Indians_ (London
1861)

Kennedy, M.S.: _The Assiniboines: From the Accounts
of the Old Ones Told to First Boy_ (Norman 1961)

Laviolette, Gontram: _The Sioux Indians in Canada_
(Regina 1944)

Speck, Frank G.: _The Iroquois_ (Bloomfield Hills 1955)

Vetromile, E.: _The Abenakis and Their History_ (New
York 1866)

Wallis, W.D. and Sawtell R.: _The Malecite Indians of
New Brunswick_ (Ottawa 1957)

Wallis, W.D. and Wilson, R.S.: _The Micmac Indians of
Eastern Canada_ (Minneapolis 1955)

Wright, Gordon K.: _The Neutral Indians: A Source
Book_ (Rochester 1963)

ESKIMOS:

Birket-Smith, Kay: _The Eskimos_ (New York 1936-1959)

Boas, Franz: _The Central Eskimo_ (New York 1888-1964)

MÉTIS:

Morice, A.G.: _Dictionnaire historique des Canadiens
et des Métis français a l'Ouest_ (Québec 1912)

Prud'homme, Louis A. _L'Element français au Nord-ouest:
Voyageurs canadiens-français et métis 1763-1870_
(Montréal 1904)

Tassé, Joseph: _Les Canadiens de l'Ouest_ (Montréal
1878, 2 volumes)

Trémaudan, Auguste-Henri de: _Histoire de la nation
métisse dans l'Ouest canadien_ (Montréal 1936)

3:17 HERALDRY

Most modern writers try to avoid defining heraldry because a dictionary definition cannot adequately give us a clear idea of what it really is. People today generally equate heraldry with a "coat of arms" which, in part, is correct. However, the science and art of heraldry goes much deeper than this and is an entire field of study in its own right, despite the fact that heraldry and genealogy are quite closely interrelated.

Heraldry had its beginnings in Europe sometime before the twelfth century. Medieval knights whose faces were entirely covered by helmets and armour needed some means of personal identification in battle to enable them to be recognized as friend or foe by other knights. In order to achieve this "personal identification" these knights began to paint brightly coloured designs on their shields, each of them differing from the designs of other knights.

Originally, these "personal identifications" belonged primarily to those persons who occuppied high offices. During the first half of the twelfth century knights began to use symbols on their shields and members of the higher nobility began to use a certain regularity in the display of changes in their "coats of arms". By the second half of the twelfth century the use of armorial devices had spread to all levels of the noble class and the main aspects of the science of heraldry had been developed. The rules and terminology of heraldry were gradually established during the 13th century and form the basis for the science's present laws and language. Towards the end of the 13th century, heraldic devices became hereditary and marks of difference began to appear on shields to denote different branches of the same family. In 1484 a College of Arms was established in England to govern the granting and confirmation of the right to a "coat of arms" in that country. This College continues in operation today.

The grant of a "coat of arms" is made to an individual, and his descendants are allowed to use the arms provided that they can prove their descent from the grantee. In this way, someone wishing to acquire the rights to a "coat of arms" must begin by tracing his family tree back to someone who was granted the original arms. Merely having the same surname as someone who was granted arms does not entitle a person to use those arms. Many "coat of arms companies" have sprung up in recent years who are prepared to sell people a "personal coat of arms" merely on the basis of their surnames.

At best, these are very dubious enterprises and researchers should avoid them altogether. Researchers wishing to acquire a "coat of arms" should contact the Heraldry Society of Canada to learn of the steps and procedures they will need to follow to prove their rights to arms.

Heraldry in Canada dates back to the French Regime. Many of the notable families of New France were granted arms by the King of France. This system continued under British rule as well, with the College of Arms in England replacing the King of France as grantor. Many ordinary individuals sought and obtained coats of arms.

For the most part, heraldry can be regarded primarily as an interesting sideline to Canadian genealogy. Most Canadians who find an ancestor who was granted arms will also find that the arms were granted prior to the family leaving the country of origin. Therefore any genealogical information on the family will generally be restricted to the country of origin only and researchers must trace their families through Canada to their country of origin before this information will be of use to them. However, some genealogical information on the family in Canada will be available for those persons who were granted arms after they arrived in this country. Any number of heraldic publications containing a drawing or description of the arms along with short genealogies of the persons to whom they were granted can be found in most local libraries. It may be possible to find references to ancestors in these although, like any other compiled source, any information obtained from them must be verified by resorting to the original records.

There is one society in Canada devoted to the study of heraldry, and anyone interested in learning more about this facinating area should contact:

The Heraldry Society of Canada
125 Lakeway Drive
Ottawa, Ontario, K1L 5A9

This Society was incoporated in 1966 to encourage an interest in heraldry, armory, chivalry, family history and kindred subjects as they relate to Canada. They publish a quarterly journal "Heraldry in Canada" which contains informative articles on heraldry and the Society's endeavours.

The following list contains a few publications of general interest as well as some relating strictly to Canada. The list is intended to provide a general idea of the types of heraldric books which are presently available.

236

<u>Almanach de Gotha</u> (1763-1944, various places of public-
    ation) This is the "Burke's Pearage" of continental
    Europe.

Brassard, Gérald: <u>Armorial des évéques du Canada</u>
    (Montréal 1940)

Burke, Sir John Bernard: <u>Burke's General Armory</u> (1884
    Reprint Baltimore 1967)

Chadwick, E.M.: <u>Ontarian Families</u> (Toronto 1894-98,
    2 volumes)

Fox-Davies, Arthur C.: "<u>Armorial Families: A Directory
    of Some Gentlemen of Coat-Armour</u>" (London 1929)

Koller, F. and Shillings, A.: <u>Armorial universel</u>
    (Bruxelles 1951)

Massicotte, Edouard and Regis, Roy: <u>Armorial du Canada
    Français</u> (Montréal 1915-18, 2 volumes - Reprint
    Baltimore 1970)

Todd, Herbert G.: <u>Armory and Lineages of Canada</u> (Yonkers,
    New York, 1913-19, 2 volumes)

4
THE PUBLIC ARCHIVES OF CANADA

Provision for the creation of the Public Archives of Canada was first made in 1872 when an officer of the Department of Agriculture was appointed to take charge of historical archives. Shortly after, a Records Branch was organized within the Department of the Secretary of State with a "Keeper of Records" in charge. While the Archivist was responsible for the accumulation of private papers and copies of French and British records, the Keeper of Records was responsible for the preservation of Canadian State Papers. In 1903, these two functions were combined under the auspices of the Department of Agriculture and the head of the archives became the Dominion Archivist and Keeper of Records. In 1912, the Archives became a seperate department and were renamed the Public Archives of Canada.

As a research institution, the Public Archives is responsible for acquiring all documents that are related to the development and history of Canada and for providing adequate research facilities to make this material available to the public. As a result, it is the largest repository of historical, governmental and genealogical records in Canada and anyone researching family history will at some time or another visit or correspond with them.

Throughout this book, numerous references have been made to specific collections located at the Public Archives. This chapter will not attempt to duplicate the material previously mentioned but rather will supplement it with a discussion of some of the other material of genealogical interest located here and the services that this organization can offer researchers.

ARCHIVES BRANCH

The Public Archives is divided into several divisions, each responsible for a specific function. The most important of these for genealogical purposes is the Historical Branch, which itself is comprised of eight sections: the Manuscript Division, Public Records Division, the National Map Collection, the Picture Division, the National Photography Collection, the Library, the Machine Readable Archives and the National Film Archives.

- MANUSCRIPT DIVISION
  The majority of the genealogical holdings of the Historical Branch are found in the various sections of the Manuscript Division. The Pre-Confederation Section and the Post-Confederation Section include such materials as private papers of statesmen and individuals, records of cultural and commercial organizations, and copies of

records in France, England and other countries
relating to Canada. In total, these collections
occupy over 10,200 metres (over 6 miles) of
shelving.

● PUBLIC RECORDS DIVISION
The Public Records Division consists of the
various records of Canadian government departments and their predecessors and occupy over
18,300 metres (over 11 miles) of shelving.

● NATIONAL MAP COLLECTION
The National Map Collection is the largest of
its kind in Canada, containing over 750,000
separate atlases, maps and charts. Included
are large collections of county atlases,
county maps, charts, general atlases and general maps relating to the discovery, explora-
tion, settlement, topography and geology of
Canada. As well, there is a large collection
of current maps, primarily topographical,
relating to numerous foriegn countries.
Photostatic or photographic copies of many of
these maps can be obtained.

● PICTURE DIVISION
The Picture Division is responsible for all
paintings, engravings, and printed images
acquired by the Public Archives. The Paintings,
Drawings and Prints Section has over 75,000
paintings, drawings and watercolours. The
Medal, Heraldry and Costume Section is responsible for arms, flags and seals and maintains
files on official heraldic devices relating   .
to Canadian history, as well as an Ethnic
Heraldic Roll of Arms which includes the
coats of arms of several hundred families,
with documentation.

● NATIONAL PHOTOGRAPHY COLLECTION
The National Photography Collection, responsible
for the acquisition and preservation of historical
photographs, now has over 3 million separate items.
These photographs are primarily of a documentary
nature, obtained from government agencies and
private sources dating from the 1850's, and
relate to people, historical events, places
and objects of Canadian interest. This collection is indexed and copies may be obtained.

● PUBLIC ARCHIVES LIBRARY
The Public Archives Library, containing well
over 80,000 volumes on Canada and its history,
was established in 1872 at the same time as
the Public Archives itself. Included in its

collection are books and pamphlets such as
journals and diaries of explorers, narratives
of early travellers, records of soldiers and
administrators, and fundamental works dealing
with history, geography, economics, genealogy,
emigrations, transportation, land, religious
groups, and institutions. Anyone visiting the
Public Archives should also check the Library's
Reference Room for the more important printed
sources.

● <u>MACHINE READABLE ARCHIVES</u>
This section contains the machine readable
records (i.e. punched cards, magnetic tape,
paper tape, and other computer oriented
materials) of the Federal government as well
as those of national importance produced by
the private sector.

● <u>NATIONAL FILM ARCHIVES</u>
This division holds an extensive collection
of Canadian film made by the public and
private sectors. As well, the Sound Archives
Section contains over 30,000 hours of recorded
speeches and interviews of national significance.

MANUSCRIPT AND PUBLIC RECORDS DIVISIONS

Researchers will find that the majority of their
searches will take place in the collections of the Manuscript Division and the Public Records Division. On visiting the Public Archives, researchers should go to the
Reference Room of the Manuscript Division at first to
register and to avail themselves of the material to be
found there.

The Reference Room contains many card indices, inventories, and finding aids to assist the researcher in locating material in the Manuscript Division. Many of the
collections mentioned in other chapters of this book have
their card indices located here, such as the Upper and
Lower Canada Land Petitions and Marriage Bonds, Gaudet's
Acadian Notes, the Military "C" Series, Medal Registers.
Haldimand Papers, and South African War Service Records.
As well, there is a complete collection of prepared inventories and finding aids to the various Manuscript Groups
and Records Groups and collections, in addition to a complete index to the material in the Manuscripts Division.
John Coderre's <u>Searching in the Public Archives</u> (see Bibliography) is an excellant guide to the resources and
proceedures of the Reference Room and other sections of
the Archives and should be consulted before visiting the
Public Archives.

The records of the Manuscript and Public Records Divisions are arranged into seperate groupings for filing and cataloguings purposes:

MANUSCRIPT GROUP (MG)
This group includes all records and documents which were not generated or created by departments of the government of Canada or their predecessors, and is administered by the Manuscript Division.

RECORD GROUP (RG)
This group includes all those records which were created by various Canadian government departments both before and after Confederation, and is administered primarily by the Public Records Division although several collections are under the custody of the Manuscript Division.

Over the years, the Public Archives has published or compiled inventories to many of the collections within these divisions. The published inventories may be obtained by purchase from the Public Archives, while the unpublished lists must be examined in person. Both, however, contain detailed listings of the material available in each Manuscript Group or Records Group and are indispensible in locating material in what may seem to be unlikely places.

MANUSCRIPT GROUPS

Following is a list of the Manuscript Groups in the Public Archives. Virtually all of these will have some material of genealogical interest, although some more than others. The records in each of these groups have been well detailed in the General Inventory Manuscripts series which is indispensible when searching for specific documents or records in this collection. Because these inventories are readily available (by purchase or at local libraries) and because names of the various collections are self-explanitory regarding the collection's origin or contents, no effort has been made here to detail the type of material to be found in each.

MG 1:   Archives des Colonies (Paris)

MG 2:   Archives de la Marine (Paris)

MG 3:   Archives Nationales (Paris)

MG 4:   Archives de la Guerre (Paris)

MG 5:   Ministère des Affaires étrangères (Paris)

MG 6:   Archives départementales, municipales,
         maritimes et de bibliothèques (France)

MG 7:   Bibliothèques de Paris

MG 8:   Documents relating to New France and
         Québec (17th to 20th Centuries)

MG 9:   Provincial, Local and Territorial Records

MG 10:   Records of Foreign Governments

MG 11:   Colonial Office Papers (London)

MG 12:   Admiralty and War Office (London)

MG 13:   Foreign Office (London)

MG 14:   Audit Office and Treasury (London)

MG 15:   Post Office (London)

MG 16:   Customs and Plantations and Other Offices
         (London)

MG 17:   Religious Archives

MG 18:   Pre-Conquest Papers

MG 19:   Fur Trade and Indians

MG 20:   Hudson's Bay Company

MG 21:   British Museum

MG 22:   Autographs

MG 23:   Late 18th Century Papers

MG 24:   19th Century Pre-Confederation Papers

MG 25:   Genealogy

MG 26:   Prime Ministers' Papers

MG 27:   Political Figures 1867 - 1950

MG 28:   Post-Confederation Corporate Bodies

MG 29:   19th Century Post-Confederation Manuscripts

MG 30:   Manuscripts of the First Half of the
         20th Century

RECORD GROUPS

The following Record Groups have a particular interest
to genealogists. Unlike the Manuscript Groups, which are well
documented in their inventory series, most Record Groups
have no published inventories although the Public Records
Division has been issuing a series of preliminary indexes
for some of these groups. When applicable,   short descriptions of the important sources in these groups have been included to enable researchers to identify records of importance
to them. Those groups marked with an asterisk are in the
custody of the Manuscript Division.

*RG 1: Executive Council, Canada 1764-1867
(Minutes, state papers, orders in Council of the
Executive Councils 1764-1867 contains petitions,
correspondence, etc; Oaths of Allegience for
government officials 1764-1862; Upper and Lower
Canada Land Petitions and papers; miscellaneous
records relating to land)

RG 2: Privy Council Office
(Printed guide available)

RG 3: Post Office Department
(Records of individual post offices and the app
appointment of postmasters)

*RG 4: Civil and Provincial Secretary's Office -
Canada East 1760 - 1867
(petitions, correspondence, marriage bonds,
licences, etc.)

*RG 5: Civil and Provincial Secretary's Office -
Canada West 1788 - 1767
(records similar to RG 4 - has been microfilmed)

RG 6: Secretary of State 1857-1973

*RG 8: British Military and Naval Records 1760-1872
(includes "C" Serices - see chapter 3.11)

RG 9: Militia and Defense 1776-1960
(various records including those of the Canadian
Expeditionary Force 1914-20)

RG 10: Indian Affairs
(Printed guide available)

RG 13: Justice 1838-1967
(records on the North West Rebellion, Seigneurial Indemnities, Penitentiary Branch, and other
court registers)

RG 15: Interior 1821-1947
(records for Dominion Lands Branch 1871-1946,
Timber Mines and Grazing Branch 1874-1947,
School Lands Branch 1904-34, Homestead and soldier grant registers 1872-1936)

RG 17: Agriculture 1842-1968
(records on quarantine and immigration 1854-1920
see also chapter 3.10)°

RG 18: Royal Canadian Mounted Police 1868-1965
(Printed guide available)

RG 26: Citizenship and Immigration 1880-1970
(see chapter 3.10 for details)

RG 31: Statistics Canada 1825-1971
(Census records - see chapter 3.4)

RG 32:   Public Service Commission 1868-1970
          (civil service personnel files, competitions,
          etc. - restrictions on access)

RG 38:   Veterans Affairs 1899-1972
          (records of veterans of South African War plus
          other veterans' records, including those of the
          Veterans Land Administration - see chapter 3.11)

RG 45:   Geological Survey 1842-1953
          (has 5000 surveyors notebooks)

RG 76:   Immigration Branch 1865-1969
          (see chapter 3.10)

RG 85:   Northern Administration Branch 1890-1971
          (has records relating to the Yukon and North-
          west Territories)

RG 91:   Yukon Territorial Records
          (includes land records 1898-1905, with indices)

NATIONAL ETHNIC ARCHIVES

     The National Ethnic Archives was established in 1972 as
a section within the Manuscript Division for the collection
and preservation of records relating to the heritage of
Canada's diverse ethno-cultural communities which are neither
French, British nor Native (Indian and Inuit) in origin.
Since that time, it has been actively gathering documentation
relating to many cultural groups.

     The kinds of archival papers and records obtained have
included correspondence, notebooks, diaries, family bibles,
scrapbooks, photographs, heraldic documentation and printed
materials. In addition to personal and family papers, the
collected records of various fraternal, benevolent, cultural
and religious organizations are also a useful source of
genealogical information.

     Since the National Ethnic Archives is actively acquir-
ing material a listing of its holdings is quickly outdated.
Therefore, persons wishing to use such material should write
for specific collections which will be of value to their
family research. Perhaps the National Ethnic Archives staff
can direct them to other ethnic collections in Canada.

SERVICES OF THE PUBLIC ARCHIVES

     In addition to providing the means to research in
their collections in person, the Public Archives has
always been willing to provide limited research assistance by mail. In matters involving the checking of card
indices for individual references or for providing addi-

tional information on a particular collection or type of
material, they have always endeavoured to provide
researchers with functional answers. However, this
service should not be abused by unreasonable requests
such as asking them to compile your particular genealogy
for you or by requesting information which may be readily
available in printed form elsewhere. Always bear in mind
that there are many others requesting information from
them and that everyone deserves only as much service as
exists for all.

The Public Archives system of inter-library loan of
microfilm is possibly the greatest help of all. Virtually
any local library which has an agreement with the
Archives may borrow microfilmed material from them on
behalf of local researchers. This opens up the immense
resources of the Public Archives to anyone, anywhere. To
take full advantage of this service, consult your local
librarian.

In addition to their library loan policy, it is also
possible to purchase microfilms from the Public Archives.
Specific "call numbers" for microfilm reels covering the
material desired can be obtained by writing the Archives,
who will also explain the proceedure for ordering microfilms. These call numbers can also be found in the
various inventories. As well, xerox or photographic
copies of material not on microfilm can be obtained. A
price list is available on request.

WRITING TO THE PUBLIC ARCHIVES

When writing to the Public Archives, address all
correspondence to the particular division or section
which holds the material of interest, i.e. Manuscript
Division, National Map Collection, National Ethnic
Archives, etc. Use the format as follows:

```
            -              Division
        Public Archives of Canada
        395 Wellington Street
        Ottawa, Ontario
        K1A ON3
```

PUBLICATIONS AND BIBLIOGRAPHY

Over the last 100 years, the Public Archives has issued numerous publications, many of which are useful in genealogical research. Some of these publications are available on request and others may be obtained by purchase. In the list that follows, all those not indicated as FREE are available by purchase. To obtain a current list of available publications or to purchase a publication, contact:

> Public Archives of Canada
> Information Services Division
> 395 Wellington Street
> Ottawa, Ontario K1A ON3

Free publications are also available from the particular division of the Public Archives which issues them. Several other publications produced by other sources are also included here if they relate to the Public Archives.

The Archivist/L'Archiviste (PAC, 6 x year, FREE)
     Periodical detailing events at PAC.
Campbell, Wilfred: Report on Manuscript Lists
     Relating to the United Empire Loyalists with
     Reference to Other Sources (PAC 1909)
Campeau, Marielle: Check List of Parish Registers (at
     the Public Archives) (PAC 1975, 69pp)
Caron-Houle, Francoise: Guide to the Reports of the
     Public Archives of Canada 1872-1972 (PAC 1975)
Check List of Census Return, New Brunswick 1851-1871, Nova
     Scoita 1871 (PAC 1964)
Check List of Ontario Census Returns 1842-1871 (PAC 1963)
Check List of Quebec Census Returns 1825-1871 (PAC 1963)
Coderre, John: Searching in the Public Archives (Ottawa
     Branch OGS, 1972, 24pp)
Collections of the Brome County Historical Society Pre-
     liminary Inventory (PAC 1954)
Collections of the Lennox and Addington Historical Society:
     Preliminary Inventory (PAC 1959)
Collections of the Norfolk Historical Society: Prelimin-
     ary Inventory (PAC 1958)
Cruikshank, Lt. Col.: Inventory of Military Documents in
     the Canadian Archives (PAC 1910)
Fire Insurance Plans in the National Map Collection (PAC
     1977 FREE)

General Inventory: Manuscripts (PAC, multi-volume, various years). This series is presently being issued and documents the material located in each Manuscript Group. It is similar in content to the Union List (see below), only much more detailed and relating only to PAC.

Guide des sources d'archives sur le Canada français au Canada (PAC 1975)

Hoogenraad, Mrs. Maureen: Genealogical Sources at the Public Archives of Canada (Ottawa Branch OGS, 1971, 10pp)

Kennedy, Patricia: How to Trace Your Loyalist Ancestors: Use of the Loyalist Sources in the Public Archives of Canada (Ottawa Branch OGS, 1973, 14pp)

Maddick, Heather: County Maps: Land Ownership Maps of Canada in the 19th Century (PAC 1976 FREE)

Martin, Chester: Red River Settlement: Papers in the Canadian Archives Relating to the Pioneers (PAC 1910)

May, Betty: County Atlases of Canada: A Descriptive Catalogue (PAC 1970, FREE)

Poulin, Guy: Index to Township Plans of the Canadian West (PAC 1974, FREE)

5
PROVINCIAL RECORDS AND SOURCES

The following section discusses the various records and sources in each of the ten provinces and two territories of Canada. Each province and territory is listed alphabetically and begins with a brief historical sketch. The balance of the information provided for each province is arranged, in order, under the following headings:

MUNICIPAL ORGANIZATION

This section begins with a brief description of the municipal organization in the province and concludes with a list of each Rural Municipality and County, along with the town or city which houses it's administrative offices. In provinces with a large number of municipalities, this section has been relocated to the end of the provincial listing. Cities and towns which do not form part of the municipalities are not listed due to space limitations. If ancestors once lived in a town or city which is not listed, correspondence regarding municipal records should be directed to the City Hall or Town Hall at the particular community.

PROVINCIAL ARCHIVES

The Archives Summary is the largest single item discussed under each provincial division. In addition to address of the provincial or territorial archives, this section details briefly the general holdings of the institution under the following catagories: Census Records; Church Records; Maps and Atlases showing Landowners; Directories; Land Records; Municipal Records; Court Records; School Records; Military Records; Immigration Records; Newspaper Collections; Special Collections; Biographical Files; Photograph Collections; and Catalogues of the Archives. The information shown in this section is based on a questionnaire which was sent to each Provincial Archives, supplemented from the Union List of Manuscripts 1975 and specific archives catalogues where available. The extent of information is subject to the detail in which the questionnaires were answered and/or the availability of printed catalogues. Current or more complete information can be obtained from the catalogues listed for each archives, or from the provincial archives themselves.

VITAL RECORDS

The summary of vital records in each province is also based on a questionnaire sent to each provincial vital statistics office. In some cases, the information has been supplemented from other published and unpublished sources. Current information on the costs of obtaining certificates or other services that may be offered can be obtained from the respective vital statistics offices.

CROWN GRANTS/HOMESTEAD RECORDS

Where Crown Grants or Homestead Records are located in an agency other than the provincial archives, the holding agency is named along with a brief discussion of the extent of the records in their possession.

LAND REGISTRATION / JUDICIAL DISTRICTS

All land transfers after the original Crown grant are deposited in provincial land registration offices, which have been listed in the Land Registration Section. The Judicial Districts section, lists the major judicial districts in the province and the addresses of their court houses.

EDUCATION / MAP SOURCES

These sections provide the addresses of the Department of Education and the provincial map agency, respectively.

SPECIAL COLLECTIONS

In a few provinces, there are some institutions other than the provincial archives which have important archival collections relating to the entire province. This section lists those institutions along with a short summary of their collections.

OTHER SOURCES OF INTEREST TO RESEARCHERS

This section contains the names and addresses of a number of other organizations in each province which may provide some additional information to researchers. It is generally divided into two sections, GENERAL (general or provincial organizations) and ASSOCIATIONS (historical or local societies), although a third catagory ARCHIVES (major archives in the province) is also included for some provinces. In order to conserve space, a number of abbreviations have been used: HS = Historical Society, HM = Historical Museum, SH = Societe historique, Sd'H = Societe de'Histoire, HSM = Historical Society Museum, or other combinations of these. Those organizations whose name is preceeded by an asterisk have their collections listed in the Union List of Manuscripts 1975.

The information in this chapter is current as of the end of 1977. The addresses of historical societies and museums, however, have been taken from a variety of sources which have been published over the past few years. Although none of the society addresses are more than 4-5 years old, some will undoubtedly have changed during that period. Further information on local historical societies may also be obtainable from the provincial historical association.

THE PROVINCES OF CANADA

NEWFOUNDLAND

P.E.I.
N.B.
N.S.

QUEBEC

ONTARIO

UNITED STATES

MANITOBA

SASKATCH-
EWAN

ALBERTA

NORTHWEST TERRITORIES

BRITISH
COLUMBIA

YUKON
TERRITORY

ALBERTA

Alberta was originally part of the territory granted to the Hudson's Bay Company in 1670, and was acquired by the Canadian government in 1870. Until 1905, when it became a province, Alberta was part of the North West Territories. The capital and largest city in the province is Edmonton, with Calgary as the second largest urban centre. Alberta's population in 1970 was 1,600,000 (Major ethnic groups: 49% British Isles, 12% German, 9% Ukrainian, 8% Scandinavian, 6% French).

PROVINCIAL ARCHIVES

ADDRESS: PROVINCIAL ARCHIVES OF ALBERTA (est. 1963), 12845 - 102 Avenue, Edmonton, T5N 0M6

CENSUS RECORDS: none.

CHURCH RECORDS: The Archives has the collections of the Anglican Dioceses of Edmonton (from 1893) and Athabaska (from 1875) in Northern Alberta, and of Mackenzie River (from 1859) in the Northwest Territories; administrative records of the Alberta Conference of the United Church and its predecessors (from c 1875); and those of the Roman Catholic Order of Mary Immaculate in Alberta and western Saskatchewan (from early 1800s). These contain records of baptisms, marriages, burials, schools, etc. As well, the Oblate collection also has records of Scrip granted to the Metis (1876-1885). (Note: a knowledge of French is essential in using the Oblate collection.) Another Roman Catholic Order's records (Sisters of the Assumption, B.V.M.) contain records of that Order's schools in the western half of the Prairie Provinces. There are also a number of ethno-cultural sources (inventory available).

DIRECTORIES: The Archives has directories of Manitoba and the Northwest Territories (later Saskatchewan and Alberta) from 1881 to 1908 (on microfilm). Edmonton-Stratcona and Calgary are covered from before World War I to the present, and there are also a few province-wide and city directories other than these. They also have a wide selection of telephone directories and the Cummins Rural Directory for 1923 and 1927.

HOMESTEAD RECORDS: The Archives has homestead records for Alberta on microfilm for the period prior to 1930. These are arranged in 4 sections: a) Alphabetical lists of applicants, b) Township registers which show who settled on a particular township, c) Microfilms of applications for homestead, and d) Index to the microfilm reels containing files. Another group of land records with an alphabetical index is Register of Water Rights. Other land records, indexed by land description, are: School Land Registers, Timber Registers, Parish and Townsite Registers and several others. Contact the Archives for more information.

MUNICIPAL RECORDS: County and Municipal records of the Archives cover the period 1895 - 1968, although the collection is not complete. These records include Assessment Records, Land Registers, Voter's Lists, School Attendance Records, School Censuses, Maps of Districts often showing landowners, Soldier's Records, Municipal Cemetery Records etc. School records generally date from the 1930's. Counties and Municipalities should also be contacted for additional information which has not been acquired by the Archives.

COURT RECORDS: These records include Inquest Files 1884-1905 and 1910-1928; Coroners' Files 1910-1927; Criminal Files 1915-1928; Justices of the Peace Records 1898-1927; most of which are alphabetically indexed. (J.P. records are indexed by name of J.P. only). These records cover the entire province.

MILITARY RECORDS: The Archives has the Department of Labour files dealing with Albertans who took part in the First World War effort. This is a small collection and is arrnaged by Units and Regiments. There is no alphabetical index.

IMMIGRATION RECORDS: There is a series of files of Applications made to the Alberta Government by British citizens for immigration to Alberta in 1950 and 1952. As well, there are microfilm copies of the Immigration records from the Public Archives of Canada

NEWSPAPERS: The Archives has microfilm copies of the newspapers of larger centres in Alberta and of those which were early publications. The most extensive collection however is in the Alberta Legislative Library, which should be consulted.

BIOGRAPHICAL FILES: Newspaper clippings, photographs, etc. of well-known Albertans are located in a special information file. As well, there are also files of clippings from Alberta newspapers on Oldtimers and their memoirs.

PHOTOGRAPH COLLECTIONS: The three major photograph collections in the Archives are: the Ernest Brown Collection
from Edmonton (1885-1947); alphabetical index of Studio
Portraits from 1898; 50,000 negatives); the Harry Pollard
Collection (1900-1955; 25,000 negatives from Calgary) and
the Alfred Blyth Collection from Edmonton (1928-1970;
25,000 negatives). There are also other smaller collections.

OTHER SOURCES: A collection of Oral Tape Recordings document the lives of many Oldtimers, businessmen, etc. in
Alberta and the areas in which they lived. These are
indexed. A collection of 5000 documents submitted to the
Department of Public Welfare as proof of age include Birth
Certificates, Immigration Records, and the like, arranged
in alphabetical order by name of applicant. These date
as early as the 1860's. The indexes to Changes in Name
in Alberta from 1916-1950 is also valuable in establishing
former or new names of ancestors.

CATALOGUES: There is no specific catalogue to the holdings
of the Archives. A short brochure which will outline the
genealogical sources in the Archives is to be published in
1978. Other information on collections can be obtained
from the Union List of Manuscripts 1975 or by writing to
the Archives.

VITAL RECORDS

All civil vital records in Alberta are available from
Director, Division of Vital Statistics, 10405-100 Avenue,
Edmonton, T5J 0A6. If only the approximate date of the
event is known, the division will conduct limited searches.
The registration of births began in 1887, and the registration of marriages and deaths began in 1898. They are
fairly complete from these dates. Birth certificates are
only issued to the person registered, their immediate
family, their spouse, or their authorized agent and marriage certificates are only issued to the husband, wife,
their parents, or their authorized agent. Death certificates may be obtained by any person. Contact this office
for further information on their fees. For divorce records
contact the Attorney General's Department (see under
JUDICIAL DISTRICTS, below).

HOMESTEAD RECORDS

All homestead records are now deposited with the
Provincial Archives. Subsequent land transfers will be
found in one of the two land registration districts in
the province:

North Alberta Land Registration District, Land Titles
    Building, 100 Street and 102 A Avenue, Edmonton
South Alberta Land Registration District, Box 7575,
    Calgary

JUDICIAL DISTRICTS

There are 12 Judicial District in Alberta (see map).
Address a correspondence to the Court House in each of
the communities listed below, except Edmonton, where
mail should be directed to the Law Courts Building.
Officials in each district include Clerk of Court, Sheriff, and Surrogate Registrar (for wills). District Court
Houses (also the name of the Judicial District) are
located in:

Calgary	Grande Prairie	Peace River
Drumheller	Hanna	Red Deer
Edmonton	Lethbridge	Vegreville
Fort MacLeod	Medicine Hat	Wetaskiwin

For further information on Alberta's courts contact the
Attorney General's Department, 9919-105 St., Edmonton,
T5K 2E8

EDUCATION

The Department of Education, Executive Building,
10105 - 109 Street, Edmonton T5J 2V2 should be contacted
for more information about student and teacher records
in their files, as well as for other school information.

MAP SOURCES

The Provincial highway map can be obtained without
charge on request from Travel Alberta, 12th Floor, 10065
Jasper Avenue, Edmonton, T5J 0H4. A catalogue of map
publications of the Alberta and Canadian governments is
available from Technical Division, Alberta Energy and
National Resources, 2nd Floor, North Tower, Petroleum
Plaza, 9945-108 Street, Edmonton, T5K 2C9.

SPECIAL COLLECTIONS

GLENBOW-ALBERTA INSTITUTE, 902 Eleventh Ave. S.W., Calgary
T2R 0E7. This organization and its predecessor have been
collecting records on the history of Western Canada
(primarily the prairies) since 1955, including government
records, church records, coporate records and the private

papers of individuals. They also have a considerable
number of records for the Calgary and southern Alberta
areas. The land records of the C.P.R. are deposited here
and include the land sales records for western Canada
(1884-1928) and the land examination files (1910-63).
Their collection is listed in the <u>Union List of Manuscripts 1975</u>.

OTHER SOURCES OF INTEREST TO RESEARCHERS

<u>GENERAL</u>

City of Edmonton Archives, 10105-112 Ave., Edmonton,
    T5G OH1
HS of Alberta, Box 4035, Station C, Calgary, T2T 5M9
*Legislative Library of Alberta, 216 Legislative Bldg.,
    Edmonton, T5K 2B6
Oblate Archives of Alberta-Saskatchewan, 9916-110 St.,
    Edmonton, T5K 1J3
Public Affairs Bureau, 9945-108 St., Edmonton, T5K 2G6
Red Deer and District Archives, 4818-49 St., Red Deer,
    T4N 1T8
Ukrainian-Canadian Archives, 9543-110 Ave., Edmonton,
    T5H 1H3
Universities: *U of Alberta (Edmonton, T6G 2E1), *U of
    Calgary (Calgary, T2N 1N4), U of Lethbridge (Lethbridge
    T1K 3M4)

<u>ASSOCIATIONS</u>

Andrew and District Local HM, Andrew TOB OCO
Barrhead and District HS, Box 546, Barrhead TOG OEO
Battle River HS, Box 99, Wainwright
Camrose and District Museum Society, 6214-48B Ave.,
    Camrose T4V OM3
Chinook Country HS, c/o 3817-7th St. S.W., Calgary
Drumheller and District MS, c/o Dinosaur and Fossil
    Museum, Box 2135, Drumheller TOJ OYO
Fort Macleod HA, P.O. Box 776, Fort Macleod TOL OZO
Fort Saskatchewan HS, P.O. Box 518, Fort Saskatchewan
    TOB 1PO
Heritage Park Society, 1900 Heritage Drive S.W., Calgary
    T2V 2X3
High Prairie and District M and HS, Box 629, High Prairie
    TOG 1EO
Kinnoull HM, Box 61, Colinton TOG ORO
Lac Ste Anne and District HS, c/o Mrs. W. Walker, Box
    186, Sangudo TOE 2AO
Medicine Hat H and M Foundation, 1302 Bomford Cres.,
    Medicine Hat T1A 5E6
Northern Alberta Pioneers' and Old Timers' Association,
    9306-89 St., Edmonton T6C 3L2

Pincher Creek and District HS, Box 1226, Pincher Creek
    TOK 1W0
Rainy Hills HS, Iddesleigh
St. Albert HS, c/o Mrs. Eileen Borgstede, 31 Glenmore
    Cres., St. Albert
Southern Alberta Old Timers and Pioneers Association,
    36 Ave. and 4 St. S.W., Calgary
Tofield HS, Tofield TOB 4V0
Viking HS Museum, Box 232, Viking
Westlock and District HS, Westlock
Willow Creek HA, P.O. Box 985, Claresholm TOL OTO

MUNICIPAL GOVERNMENT

In 1970 there were nine Cities, one hundred and one
Towns, one hundred and sixty-eight Villages, eighteen
Municipal Districts, and thirty Counties in Alberta.
The following list indicates Counties and Municipal Dis-
tricts in Alberta. Address all correspondence to the
County/Municipal Secretary of the appropriate County/
Municipality. Mailing addresses are shown in paren-
theses unless the name of the Town which houses the re-
cords is the same as the name of the County/Municipality.
A complete list of local administrative areas can be
obtained from: the Department of Municipal Affairs, Room
9925 - 107 St., Edmonton T5K 2H9

COUNTIES:

Grande Prairie
Vulcan
Ponoka
Newell (Brooks)
Warner
Stettler
Thorhild
Forty Mile (Foremost)
Beaver (Ryley)
Wetaskiwin
Barrhead
Athabaska
Smoky Lake
Lacombe
Wheatland (Strathmore)
Mountain View (Didsbury)
Paintearth (Castor)
St. Paul
Strathcona (Box 4010,
    Edmonton)
Two Hills
Camrose
Red Deer
Vermillion River (Kitscoty)
Leduc
Lethbridge
Minburn (Vegreville)
Lac Ste. Anne (Sangudo)
Flagstaff (Sedgewick)
Lamont
Parkland (Stony Plain)

MUNICIPAL DISTRICTS:

Cardston
Pincher Creek
Taber
Willow Creek (Claresholm)
Foothills (High River)
Acadia (Acadia Valley)
Rocky View (207-16 Ave
    NE, Calgary)
Starland (Morrin)
Kneehill (Three Hills)
Provost
Wainwright
Bonnyville
Sturgeon (Morinville)
Westlock
Smoky River (Falher)
Spirit River
Peace (Berwyn)
Fairview

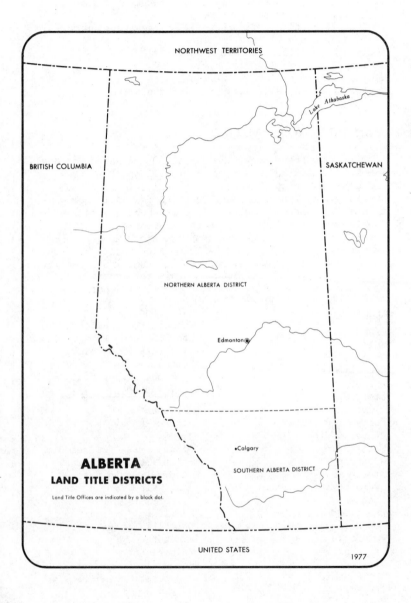

NORTHWEST TERRITORIES

BRITISH COLUMBIA

SASKATCHEWAN

Lake Athabaska

NORTHERN ALBERTA DISTRICT

Edmonton

ALBERTA
LAND TITLE DISTRICTS

Land Title Offices are indicated by a black dot.

•Calgary

SOUTHERN ALBERTA DISTRICT

UNITED STATES

1977

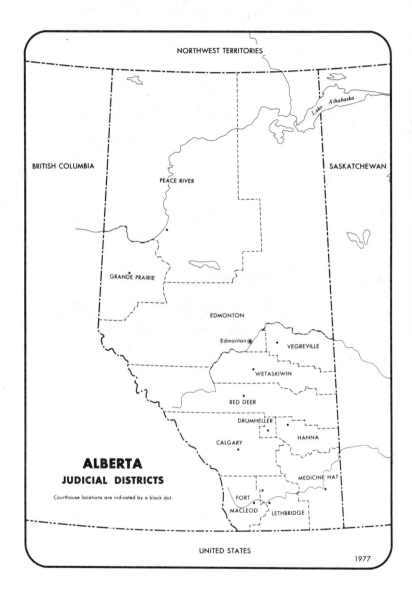

NORTHWEST TERRITORIES

Lake *Athabaska*

BRITISH COLUMBIA

SASKATCHEWAN

PEACE RIVER

GRANDE PRAIRIE

EDMONTON

Edmonton

VEGREVILLE

WETASKIWIN

RED DEER

DRUMHELLER

CALGARY

HANNA

MEDICINE HAT

ALBERTA
JUDICIAL DISTRICTS

Courthouse locations are indicated by a black dot.

FORT
MACLEOD

LETHBRIDGE

UNITED STATES

1977

BRITISH COLUMBIA

The British settlement of British Columbia began
in 1843 when Fort Victoria was established by the Hudson
Bay Company. In 1849, the Colony of Vancouver Island was
established, and in 1858 the Colony of British Columbia
was formed over much of the mainland portion of the present province. The Colony of Vancouver Island was joined
to the Colony of British Columbia in 1866, and the united
colony under its present name entered the Dominion of
Canada in 1871. The capital city is Victoria, and the
largest city in the province is Vancouver. British Columbia's population in 1970 was 2,146,000 (Major ethnic
groups: 67% British Isles, 6% Scandinavian, 5% German,
4% French).

MUNICIPAL GOVERNMENT

Unlike most other Provinces, until recently British
Columbia was almost completely unorganized municipally.
A county system was established although these areas only
covered about five per cent of the land area of the
Province and generally centered around the urban areas.
In 1967 provision was made to organize the entire Province
into Regional Districts which are assuming the responsibilities for certain services from Municipalities within
their borders. For more information on the Municipal
organization of British Columbia, contact the Ministry
of Municipal Affairs, Parliament Building, Victoria, B.C..
V8V 1X4

PROVINCIAL ARCHIVES

ADDRESS: PROVINCIAL ARCHIVES OF BRITISH COLUMBIA,
Parliament Buildings, Victoria V8V 1X4 (located at
655 Belleville Street)

CENSUS RECORDS: Census records of Lillooet, Lytton
and Douglas made by gold commissioners in the colonial
period.

CHURCH RECORDS: Registers of approximately 20 Churches
and some records kept by Registrars of birth, death and
marriage. In a few cases, the depositing churches have
imposed some access restrictions.

MAPS AND ATLASES SHOWING LANDOWNERS: A few miscellaneous
manuscript maps.

DIRECTORIES: British Columbia Rural Directories 1860-
1905, 1910, 1918-1926; Vancouver Directories 1888, 1890,
1896, 1899; Victoria Directories 1890, 1905, 1909, 1910,
1914.

PRE-EMPTION RECORDS: The Archives holds several hundred
volumes of bound pre-exemption records, most but not all
of which are indexed. As well, the Federal Department of
the Interior applications for homestead entry 1880-1930
are also deposited here along with applications for patent for the B.C. Railway Belt. Names are listed but not
indexed in these collections.

TAX RECORDS: Approximately 200 feet of Assessment Records
for the general period 1888-1924 for Alberni, Barkerville,
Comox, Cowichan, Fort Steele, Gulf Islands, Kamloops,
Kettle River, Lillooet, New Westminster, Nelson, Prince
George, Princeton, Quesnel, Revelstoke, Rossland, Slocan,
Vancouver, Vernon and Victoria Assessment Districts.
Some of these records pre-date the time span cited above,
and inquiries should be made to the Archives as to the
actual extent of records in each District.

COURT RECORDS: Attorney General's Records consisting of
inquests held 1858-1937. Registers are available for
1884-1937 and indexes for 1879-1922.

MILITARY RECORDS: Records of Vancouver Island Pioneer
Rifle Corps, 1860's.

NEWSPAPERS: Principal holdings are indexed in the Archives. Major newspapers include: Victoria Colonist 1858-
1899; Victoria Daily Standard 1870-1889; Cariboo Sentinel
1865-1875; B.C. Tribune 1866, Mainland Guardian 1869-
1889, and Vancouver Daily World 1897-1900.

BIOGRAPHICAL FILES: In addition to the newspaper index,
there are approximately 500 feet of subject files consisting of newspaper clippings and memos. Roughly half
of these files are listed under personal names.

PHOTOGRAPH COLLECTIONS: Approximately 100 fee of photographs by various photographers filed under personal
names.

OTHER SOURCES: Various Jury Lists 1876-1915. Colonial
correspondence records 1848-1871 of various departments
and public offices covering 200 feet. Forms completed by
B.C. residents who were living in Canada prior to 1892
(1967 Centennial) or 1897 (1971 Centennial) completed
for the B.C. Centennial Committee in 1967 and 1971.

CATALOGUES: G. K. Hall: <u>Dictionary Catalogue of the Library of the Provincial Archives of British Columbia</u>, (8 volumes), Boston, 1971, contains 170,000 listings. See also: <u>Provincial Archives of British Columbia: Manuscript Inventory</u> (on continuing series, begun in 1976 to detail holdings) and the <u>Union List of Manuscripts 1975</u>.

VITAL RECORDS

All civil vital records can be obtained from: Division of Vital Statistics, Ministry of Health, Parliament Buildings, Victoria, V8V 1X4. Records of birth, marriage and death begin in 1872. Divorce records begin in 1935. Birth certificates are only issued to the person registered, parents of the person registered, or their authorized agent. Marriage records are issued only to the husband or wife, their parents, or their authorized agent. Death certificates may be obtained by any person. Divorce records are only issued to parties of the divorce or their authorized agent. Contact this office for current information on its fees and services. Please note: B.C. records (all types) do <u>not</u> indicate parental information. Information on divorce records can be obtained from Department of the Attorney General, Parliament Buildings, Victoria V8V 4S6.

CROWN GRANTS

The applications for homesteads and crown grants in the Railway Belt are located in the Provincial Archives, although the original Crown Grants are with the Lands Branch, Ministry of the Environment, Parliament Buildings, Victoria V8V 1X5. These Grants are indexed by legal description of the land, which must be given when requesting information. The Lands Branch, however, does not provide copies of these Crown Grants except for court or legal purposes. Copies of all Crown Grants are on file in the local Land Registry Offices, who should be consulted when copies are required.

LAND REGISTRATION

Land Registry Offices are located in the following cities and all correspondence should be directed to The Registrar, Courthouse, at the addresses below. (see map for district boundaries.)

Kamloops District, Kamloops
Nelson District, Box 290, Nelson
New Westminster District, New Westminster

Prince George District, Box 1840, Prince George
Prince Rupert District, Market St., Prince Rupert
Vancouver District, 6th Floor, 777 Hornby St., Vancouver
Victoria District, 850 Burdett Ave., Victoria

JUDICIAL DISTRICTS

Court houses are located throughout the province and
correspondence should be addressed to the County Court
Registrar or the District Registrar of Supreme Court at
the appropriate town or city as indicated below. For
Probate records, write to the Surrogate Registrar, Law
Courts Building, Victoria V8W 1B4.

Ashcroft	Golden	Princeton
Atlin	Grand Forks	Quesnel
Burns Lake	Kamloops	Revelstoke
Campbell River	Kelowna	Richmond
Chilliwack	Kitimat	Rossland
Clinton	Lillooet	Salmon Arm
Courtenay	Merritt	Smithers
Cranbrook	Nanaimo	Surrey
Creston	Nelson	Terrace
Dawson Creek	New Westminster	Vancouver
Delta	Penticton	Vanderhoof
Duncan	Port Alberni	Vernon
Fernie	Powell River	Victoria
Fort Nelson	Prince George	Williams Lake
Fort St. John	Prince Rupert	

For further information on British Columbia courts, contact
Ministry of the Attorney General, Parliament Buildings,
Victoria V8V 4S6

For information on wills and probates, contact the
Surrogate Registrar, Law Courts Building, Victoria V8W 1B4

EDUCATION

The Ministry of Education, Educational Data
Services, Division of Communications, Victoria, B.C.,
maintains some information on Public School graduates
dating back to 1900. For more information on Public
School records and for a list of the School Divisions
in British Columbia, this department should be contacted.

MAP SOURCES

Provincial road maps can be obtained without charge
on request from the Department of Recreation and Travel
Industry, 1019 Wharf Street, Victoria V8W 2Z2. Catalogues
and lists of other provincial and Federal government produced maps are available from Map Production Division,
B.C. Lands Service, Victoria V8V 1X5.

OTHER SOURCES OF INTEREST TO RESEARCHERS

GENERAL

B.C. HA, c/o 3450 W20 Ave., Vancouver
Greater Victoria Public Library, 794 Yates St., Victoria
    V8W 1L4
Queen's Printer, Parliament Bldgs., Victoria V8V 4R6
Surveyor of Taxes, Ministry of Finance, Parliament Bldgs.,
    Victoria V8V 1X4 (has assessment records)
*Vancouver City Archives, 1150 Chestnut St., Vancouver
Vancouver Public Library, 750 Burrard St., Vancouver
    V6Z 1X5
Victoria City Archives, 613 Pandora Ave., Victoria V8W 1P6
Universities: *Simon Fraser U (Burnaby V5A 1S6), Notre
    Dame U (Nelson V1L 3CT), *U of B.C. (Vancouver V6T 1W5)
    *U of Victoria (Victoria V8W 2Y3)

ASSOCIATIONS

Alberni District M and HS, 845 River Rd., Port Alberni
Ashcroft Museum, Railway Ave., Ashcroft V0K 1A0
B.C. Railway HA, P.O. Box 114, Victoria
Bulkley Valley HS, Box 460, Smithers
Burnaby HS, c/o 6176 Walker Ave., Burnaby
Chilliwack Valley HS, 209 Corbould St. S., Chilliwack
Courtney and District HS, P.O. Box 3128, Courtney
Creston and District H and MS, Box 1123, Creston
Dawson Creek Museum, 13 St. and Alaska Ave., Dawson Creek
Delta HMS, 4858 Delta St., Delta
Fernie District HS, Box 931, Fernie
Fort St. James HS, Columbia
Fort Steele Library of Regional History, Fort Steele
    Historic Park, Fort Steele V0B 1N0
Golden and District HS, Box 992, Golden
HA of East Kootenay, c/o David Kau, 921 Fourth St. S.,
    Cranbrook
Irving House Historic Centre and New Westminster Museum,
    302 Royal Ave., New Westminster V3L 1H7
Juan de Fuca HS, 2859 Prior St., Victoria
*Kamloops Museum, 207 Seymour St., Kamloops V2C 2E7
Kootenay Lake HS, Box 537, Kaslo

Lillooet and District HS, Box 85, Lillooet
Maritime Museum of B.C., 28-30 Bastion Sq., Victoria
    V8W 1H9
Mission District HS, Box 47, Mission City
North Peach HS, Box 485, Fort S. John
North Shore M and Archives, c/o WHV Baker, 617 W 23 St.,
    North Vancouver
Okanagan HS, P.O. Box 313, Vernon
*Penticton M and Archives, Penticton
Powell River HM Association, Box 42, Powell River
Queen Charlotte Islands, MS, Box 159, Port Clements
Quesnel HS, Box 1481, Quesnel
*Rosaland HM, P.O. Box 26, Rossland
Saanich Pioneer S., P.O. Box 72, Saanichton
South Cariboo HM, Box 182, Clinton
South Peace HS, Dawson Creek
Stewart HS, Box 55, Stewart
Surrey Museum and HS, 17363-64 Ave., Surrey
Sydney HS, 2370 Lovell Ave., Sidney
Vancouver HS, P.O. Box 3071, General P.O., Vancouver
*Vernon M and Archives, 3009-32nd Ave., Vernon
Wells HS, Box 101, Wells
Windemere District HS, Box 354, Invermore

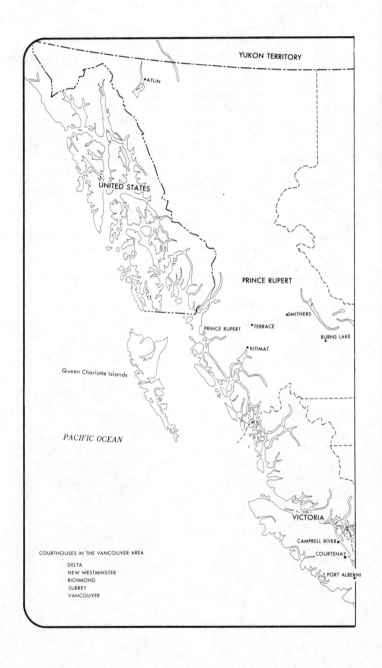

YUKON TERRITORY

•ATLIN

UNITED STATES

PRINCE RUPERT

•SMITHERS

•PRINCE RUPERT   •TERRACE

BURNS LAKE

•KITIMAT

Queen Charlotte Islands

PACIFIC OCEAN

VICTORIA

CAMPBELL RIVER•

•COURTENAY

•PORT ALBERNI

COURTHOUSES IN THE VANCOUVER AREA

   DELTA
   NEW WESTMINSTER
   RICHMOND
   SURREY
   VANCOUVER

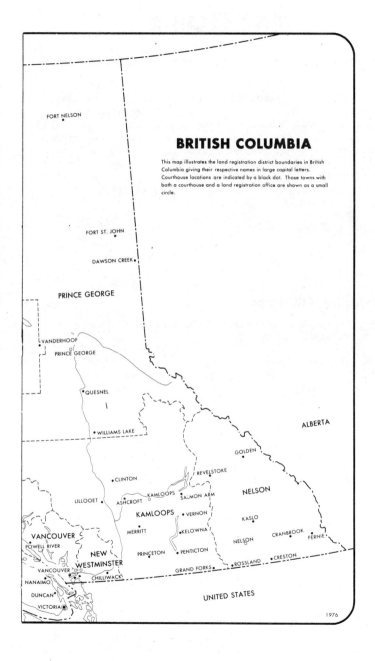

BRITISH COLUMBIA

This map illustrates the land registration district boundaries in British Columbia giving their respective names in large capital letters. Courthouse locations are indicated by a black dot. Those towns with both a courthouse and a land registration office are shown as a small circle.

FORT NELSON

FORT ST. JOHN

DAWSON CREEK

PRINCE GEORGE

VANDERHOOF

PRINCE GEORGE

QUESNEL

WILLIAMS LAKE

ALBERTA

GOLDEN

REVELSTOKE

CLINTON

KAMLOOPS

SALMON ARM

NELSON

LILLOOET

ASHCROFT

KAMLOOPS

VERNON

KASLO

MERRITT

KELOWNA

CRANBROOK

FERNIE

VANCOUVER

NELSON

POWELL RIVER

NEW

PRINCETON

PENTICTON

WESTMINSTER

ROSSLAND

CRESTON

VANCOUVER

GRAND FORKS

CHILLIWACK

NANAIMO

DUNCAN

UNITED STATES

VICTORIA

1976

MANITOBA

The first settlers in Manitoba arrived in very small groups from Quebec in the early years of the 19th century, and were primarily connected with the fur trade. In 1812 the first of the Selkirk Settlers arrived from the British Isles. Manitoba was created a province in 1870, in the midst of the Riel Rebellion of 1869-70. Her boundaries were extended in 1881 and then again in 1912. The capital city is Winnipeg, which is also the largest city in the province. Manitoba's population in 1970 was 978,000. (Major ethnic groups: 47% British Isles; 13% Ukrainian; 9% French; 7% German; 5% Netherlands; 5% Polish; 4% Scandinavian)

PROVINCIAL ARCHIVES

ADDRESS: PROVINCIAL ARCHIVES OF MANITOBA, 200 Vaughan Street, Winnipeg R3C OP8.

CENSUS RECORDS: Red River Censuses for 1831, 1832, 1833, 1834, 1835, 1838, 1840, 1843, 1846, 1847, 1849, and 1856 (incomplete). Manitoba Census of 1870 (Nominal).

CHURCH RECORDS: Numerous Church records are on deposit, the earliest of which include the following: Church of England: Headingly 1857-1928; High Bluff 1872-84; St. Andrew's 1838-84; St. Clements 1862-1928; St. James 1853-1908; St. Peter's 1839-90; St. Paul's (Middlechurch) 1850-1903; St. John's 1813-82; St. Mary's (Portage la Prairie) 1885-83. Presbyterian: Kildonan 1851-1932; Little Britain 1863-1965. Roman Catholic: St. Boniface 1825-1974; St. Norbert 1857-1934; St. Francois Xavier 1834-1900; St. Eustache 1874-1903. Lutheran: Interlake 1912-72; Arborg-Riverton 1876-1967. Contact the Archives for more information on these and other Church Records. Some of the earliest registers have been indexed.

ATLASES AND MAPS SHOWING LANDOWNERS: Early records of landowners are indicated on various parish maps and in the Hudson Bay Company Register B. There is also an alphabetical index to land script claimants 1875 and other miscellaneous records.

DIRECTORIES: Those covering Rural Manitoba include the
years 1876-1900, 1904 and 1908. A complete set of Winnipeg Directories (Henderson's) from 1876-1974 is also
deposited here. These directories are held in the Provincial Library (address is the same as Archives).

MUNICIPAL RECORDS: There are council minute books for
some Municipalities in the Province. In addition to
these are various voter's lists for some areas 1875-
1959, and the minutes of the Council of Assiniboia
1832-69.

COURT RECORDS: Records of the Court of Queen's Bench
1871-73, Sheriff's Book 1863-71, and other miscellaneous
records.

SCHOOL RECORDS: School district ledgers, school census
returns, attendance registers, etc. for many Manitoba
School Districts covering 1886-1957. Also, half-yearly
attendance returns 1915-65 on 168 reels of microfilm.

MILITARY RECORDS: Various military records are on
deposit in the Public Archives of Manitoba, including
pay lists of Des Meurons Regiment 1815-16, records of
Military District No. 10, 1871-1919 (court martials,
enlistment book, muster rolls), Red River records
1845-70, and others.

IMMIGRATION RECORDS: Records of the Immigration Branch
of the Dominion Government 1873-1953 on microfilm from
the Public Archives of Canada.

NEWSPAPERS: A large collection of local newspapers both
in their original state and on microfilm are found in the
Provincial Library, including all the major cities of the
Province.

BIOGRAPHICAL FILES: The Archives has the Manitoba Settlement Papers which cover 1875-1953 (10 feet of records)
including collections of notes, journals, scrapbooks,
land deeds, etc. of late 19th century settlers in various
parts of the Province. Biographical Files are also found
in the Provincial Library.

PHOTOGRAPHIC COLLECTIONS: Over 65,000 items relating to
Manitoba personalities, events and places are stored in
the Archives.

SPECIAL COLLECTIONS: The Provincial Archives of Manitoba
is the official repository for the Hudson's Bay Company
Archives, which cover the Company's affairs over most of
what is now Western Canada. They are being indexed.

CATALOGUES: A catalogue of some of the Provincial Library holdings is available by: Marjorie Morley, entitled:
A Bibliography of Manitoba from Holdings in the Legislative Library of Manitoba (Queen's Printer, Winnipeg,
1970). Major holdings of the Archives are listed in Eric
Jonasson: "Provincial Archives of Manitoba" generations
(Manitoba Genealogical Society Journal) Volume 1 No. 2
1976, and in the Union List of Manuscripts 1975.

VITAL RECORDS

All civil vital records are available from: Office
of Vital Statistics, Department of Health and Social Development, 104 Norquay Building, 401 York Avenue, Winnipeg,
R3C OV8. All their records begin complete coverage in
1882 with some incomplete Church records prior to that
time. All requests for copies must be submitted on a
special form available from the address given above.
Birth certificates are issued only to the person registered, their parents, or their authorized agent. Marriage Certificates are issued only to the husband or wife,
parents of the couple, children of the couple or their
authorized agent. Death Certificates may be obtained by
any person. Contact this office for current information
on their fees and services.

HOMESTEAD RECORDS

Homestead records and applications are presently held
by the Crown Lands, 1495 St. James Street, Winnipeg
R3H OW9. These records date back to 1872. The Map Office
(see map sources below) has copies of the township plans
which indicate the original homesteaders in each township
along with their respective homestead application numbers.
If the specific township that an ancestor settled in is
known, the appropriate map can be ordered through this
office (address above).

LAND REGISTRATION

After a parcel of land was homesteaded, all subsequent land transfers are recorded in the Land Titles
Offices throughout the province. Address all correspondence to: The Registrar, at the Lands Titles Offices at
the addresses below. In Winnipeg, the Land Titles office
address is the Woodsworth Bldg., 405 Broadway Ave,
Winnipeg R3C 3L6.

Boissevain	Dauphin	Neepawa	Winnipeg
Brandon	Morden	Portage la Prairie	

JUDICIAL DISTRICTS

There are five County Court Districts and six Court Houses in Manitoba. All correspondence should be addressed to the various Officials at the Court Houses in the appropriate locations as indicated below. County Court Officials include: County Court Clerk, Surrogate Registrar and Sheriff.

Central Judicial District - Portage la Prairie, Man.
Dauphin Judicial District - Dauphin, Manitoba.
Eastern Judicial District:
  (Northern Division - Woodsworth Bldg., Winnipeg)
  (Central Division - St. Boniface, Manitoba)
Northern Judicial District - The Pas, Manitoba.
Northern Judicial District - Thompson, Manitoba.
Western Judicial District - Brandon, Manitoba.

Further information on Manitoba's Courts can be obtained from the Attorney General's Department, Woodsworth Building, 405 Broadway Avenue, Winnipeg, R3C 3L6.

EDUCATION

The Dept. of Education, Robert Fletcher Bldg., 1181 Portage Ave., Winnipeg, R3G 0T3 should be consulted for further information regarding School Records and School District boundaries and addresses.

MAP SOURCES

Provincial road maps are available without charge from: Manitoba Government Travel, 408 Norquay Building, 401 York Avenue, Winnipeg, R3C 0P8. A catalogue of Provincial and Federal Government produced maps is also available from the Map Office, 1007 Century Street, Winnipeg, R3H 0W9.

OTHER SOURCES OF INTEREST TO RESEARCHERS

Historical and Scientific Society of Manitoba, M211-
   190 Rupert Avenue, Winnipeg, R3B 0N2
Hudson's Bay House, 77 Main St., Winnipeg, R3C 2R1
Jewish HS of Western Canada, 403-322 Donald Street,
   Winnipeg, R3B 2H3
Legislative Library of Manitoba, 200 Vaughan Street,
   Winnipeg, R3C 0P8
Mennonite Genealogy Inc., Box 1086, Steinbach
Mountain City HS, P.O. Box 161, Morden, R0G 1V0
Queen's Printer, 200 Vaughan St., Winnipeg, R3C 0P8

Red River Valley,HS, 55½ N. Broadway, Ste. 6, Fargo,
   North Dakota, 58102
Reveille Museum, Institute of Military and Pioneer
   Families, 443 Horton Avenue W., Winnipeg, R2C 2G5
*La Sd'H de St-Boniface, GP 125, St. Boniface, R2H 3B4
Ukrainian Cultural and Educational Centre Archives,
   184 Alexander Ave. E., Winnipeg, R3B 1C7
Universities: U of Manitoba (Winnipeg, R3T 2N2);
   U of Winnipeg (Winnipeg, R3B 2E9); Brandon U
   (Brandon, R7A 6A9)
Winnipeg Centennial Library, 251 Donald, Winnipeg

MUNICIPAL GOVERNMENT

      Manitoba has one hundred and nine Rural Municipalities
and eighteen Local Government Districts which administer
to the rural residents of the province. In addition, there
are a number of incorporated towns and cities. In the
following list, the rural organizations are listed, along
with their administrative towns. Address all correspondence to the Secretary-Treasurer of the Rural Municipalities, and the Resident Administrator of the Local Government Districts. Unless indicated otherwise, the following
are all Rural Municipalities. Further municipal information can be obtained from: the Department of Municipal
Affairs, 405 Broadway Avenue, Winnipeg, R3C 3L6.

Albert (Tilston)
Alexander L.G.D. (St. George)
Alonsa L.G.D. (Alonsa)
Archie (McAuley)
Argyle (Baldur)
Armstrong L.G.D. (Inwood)
Arthur (Melita)
Bifrost (Arborg)
Birtle (Birtle)
Blanshard (Oak River)
Boulton (Inglis)
Brenda (Waskada)
Brokenhead (Beausejour)
Cameron (Hartney)
Cartier (Elie)
Churchill L.G.D. (Churchill)
Clanwilliam (Erickson)
Coldwell (Lundar)
Consol L.G.D. (The Pas)
Cornwallis (Box 338, Brandon)
Daly (Rivers)
Dauphin (Dauphin)
De Salaberry (St. Pierre)
Dufferin (Carman)
East St. Paul (Birds Hill)

Edward (Pierson)
Ellice (St. Lazare)
Elton (Forrest)
Eriksdale (Eriksdale)
Ethelbert (Ethelbert)
Fisher L.G.D. (Fisher Branch)
Franklin (Dominion City)
Gilbert Plains (Gilbert Plains)
Gillam (Gillam)
Gimli (Gimli)
Glenella (Glenella)
Glenwood (Souris)
Grahamdale L.G.D. (Moosehorn)
Grandview (Grandview)
Grand Rapids L.G.D.
   (Grand Rapids)
Grey (Elm Creek)
Hamiota (Hamiota)
Hanover (Steinbach)
Harrison (Newdale)
Hillsburg (Roblin
La Broquerie (La Broquerie)
Lac du Bonnet (Lac du Bonnet)
Lakeview (Langruth)
Langford (Box 280, Neepawa)

Lansdowne (Arden)
Lawrence (Rorketon)
Leaf Rapids L.G.D.
    (Leaf Rapids)
Lorne (Somerset)
Louise (Crystal City)
Lynn Lake L.G.D. (Lynn Lake)
Macdonald (Sanford)
McCreary (McCreary)
Miniota (Miniota)
Minitonas (Minitonas)
Minto (Minnedosa)
Montcalm (Letellier)
Morris (Morris)
Morton (Boissevain)
Mossey River (Fork River)
Mountain L.G.D. (Swan River)
Mystery Lake L.G.D. (Thompson)
North Cypress (Carberry)
North Norfolk (MacGregor)
Oakland (Nesbitt)
Ochre River (Ochre River)
Odanah (Box 1197, Minnedosa)
Park L.G.D. (Russell)
Pembina (Manitou)
Pinawa L.G.D. (Pinawa)
Piney L.G.D. (Sprague)
Pipestone (Reston)
Portage la Prairie (Portage la
    Prairie)
Reynolds L.G.D. (Hadashville)
Rhineland (Altona)
Richot (Ste. Adolphe)
Riverside (Dunrea)
Roblin (Cartwright)
Rockwood (Stonewall)
Roland (Roland)
Rosedale (Box 100, Neepawa)
Rossburn (Rossburn)
Rosser (Rosser)

Russell (Binscarth)
St. Andrews (Clandeboye)
Ste. Anne (Ste. Anne)
St. Clements (East Selkirk)
St. Francois Xavier (Headingly)
St. Laurent (St. Laurent)
Ste. Rose (Ste. Rose du Lac)
Saskatchewan (Rapid City)
Shellmouth (Inglis)
Shell River (Roblin)
Shoal Lake (Shoal Lake)
Sifton (Oak Lake)
Siglunes (Ashern)
Silver Creek (Angusville)
Snow Lake L.G.D. (Snow Lake)
South Cypress (Glenboro)
South Norfolk (Treherne)
Springfield (Oakbank)
Stanley (Morden)
Strathclair (Strathclair)
Strathcona (Belmont)
Stuartburn L.G.D. (Vita)
Swan River (Swan River)
Tache (Lorette)
Thompson (Miami)
Turtle Mountain (Killarney)
Victoria (Holland)
Victoria Beach (304 - 283
    Portage Ave., Winnipeg)
Wallace (Virden)
Westbourne (Gladstone)
West St. Paul (3550 Main St.
    RR1, Winnipeg)
Whitehead (Alexander)
Whitemouth (Whitemouth)
Whitewater (Minto)
Winchester (Deloraine)
Woodlands (Woodlands)
Woodworth (Kenton)

276

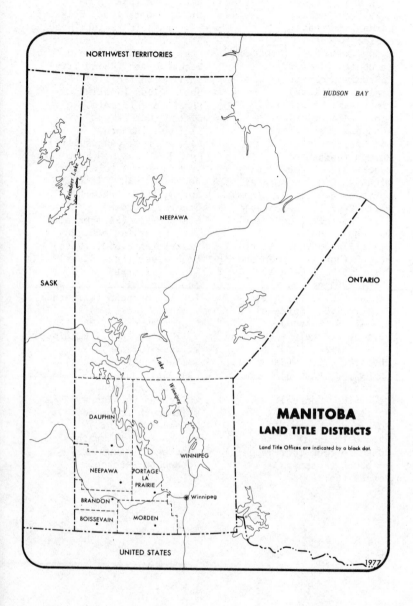

NORTHWEST TERRITORIES

HUDSON BAY

NEEPAWA

SASK

ONTARIO

DAUPHIN

WINNIPEG

NEEPAWA

PORTAGE LA PRAIRIE

BRANDON

BOISSEVAIN

MORDEN

Winnipeg

MANITOBA
LAND TITLE DISTRICTS

Land Title Offices are indicated by a black dot.

UNITED STATES

1977

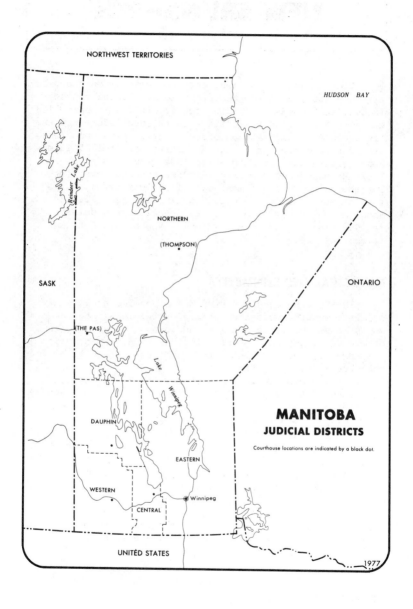

NORTHWEST TERRITORIES

HUDSON BAY

Reindeer Lake

NORTHERN

(THOMPSON)

SASK

ONTARIO

(THE PAS)

Lake Winnipeg

DAUPHIN

MANITOBA
JUDICIAL DISTRICTS

Courthouse locations are indicated by a black dot.

EASTERN

WESTERN

CENTRAL

Winnipeg

UNITED STATES

1977

NEW BRUNSWICK

New Brunswick was first settled in the French period although these settlements were sparse. It later passed into British hands in 1763. However, it wasn't until 1783 with the arrival of the United Empire Loyalists that the first major settlements occurred. Until then, New Brunswick had formed a part of Nova Scotia, but in 1783 it was separated and established as an independent colony. In 1867 it was one of the original Provinces to enter into Confederation. The Capital city is Frederickton, while the largest city in the province is Saint John, with Moncton the second largest. New Brunswick's population in 1970 was 624,000 (Major ethnic groups: 57% British Isles; 38% French).

MUNICIPAL GOVERNMENT

In 1967 the government of New Brunswick assumed complete control over the affairs of the local governments, leaving only the cities and towns with any degree of municipal autonomy. Prior to this time, the counties played an important role in the municipal structure of the Province, and continue to do so in a Judicial capacity. Following are the Counties of New Brunswick with the names of the town within each where the Court House is located (see map). Further information can be obtained from: Department of Municipal Affairs, Centennial Building, Fredericton, E3B 5H1.

Albert (Hopewell Cape)
Carleton (Woodstock)
Charlotte (St. Andrews)
Gloucester (Bathurst)
Kent (Richibucto)
Kings (Hampton)
Madawaska (Edmundston)
Northumberland (Newcastle)

Queen's (Gagetown)
Restigouche (Dalhousie)
Saint John (Saint John)
Sunbury (Burton)
Victoria (Andover)
Westmorland (Dorchester)
York (Frederickton)

PROVINCIAL ARCHIVES

ADDRESS: PROVINCIAL ARCHIVES OF NEW BRUNSWICK, P.O..Box 6000, Fredericton, New Brunswick E3B 5H1.

CENSUS RECORDS: The 1851, 1861 and 1871 Census records for most counties are available in the Archives. At present, the 1851 Census is being indexed and printed.

CHURCH RECORDS: Numerous Church records are on deposit in the Archives, which should be consulted as to their extent. The records of Civil Marriages for the period 1790 - 1889, arranged by counties are available on microfilm. Many of these records have now been indexed by male name. Marriage registers are available for the following counties: Albert Co. 1846-88; Carleton Co. 1832-88; Charlotte Co. 1806-80, and 1882-84; Gloucester Co. 1832 - 1860 and 1873-87; Kent Co. 1844-87; Kings Co. 1812-89; Northumberland Co. 1792-1887; Queens Co. 1812-87; Saint John Co. 1810-87; Westmorland Co. 1790-1887; York Co. 1812-88. The Provincial Hospital records from Saint John 1862-1957, and a list of gravestone inscriptions in Charlotte County are also available.

MAPS AND ATLASES SHOWING LANDOWNERS: The Archives have the Atlas of York County, 1878.

DIRECTORIES: The Directories covering Charlotte County 1886-87, and Saint John 1857-1931 can be found here.

CROWN GRANTS: The Archives has the original Petitions for Crown Lands for the period 1784-1850. These are contained in two series, both of which are indexed for easy consultation. Photocopies of the original Petitions can be obtained. As well, the Land Grant Index indicates all persons who received a grant of land subsequent to their petitions. Various indexes, deeds, mortgages, etc., for Charlotte, Queens, Westmorland and York Counties are also found here in addition to the Land Sales records 1829-72; Timber Petitions 1820-1913; and Surveyors' records from the Department of Natural Resources.

MUNICIPAL RECORDS: Assessment records are available for some counties: Albert Co. 1874-78; Charlotte Co. 1822-1866; Northumberland Co. 1816-65; Queens Co. 1839-69; Saint John Co. 1856-79; City of Frederickton 1835-36 and 1846-47. Other miscellaneous Municipal records such as Voters' Lists, Poll Books, Minutes, Private Papers, and General County Records are also available for many counties for the period 1785-1966. Assessment records are also found in the New Brunswick Museum for the following: Albert Co. 1830-67; Gloucester Co. 1830-65; Kent Co. 1830-66; Kings Co. 1830-65; Queens Co. 1842-66; Restigouche Co. 1838-66; Saint John Co. 1830-65; Sunbury Co. 1831-67; Victoria Co. 1850-65; Westmorland Co. 1830-65; York 1830-66; Madawaska Co. 1849; and Northumberland Co. 1826-65.

COURT RECORDS: Court papers, registers, jury lists, and other documents of the various county courts for the period 1780-1966 are deposited with the Archives. They also have the records of the New Brunswick Superior Court 1783-1928 and the Supreme Court in Equity 1845-1911. However, their most notable collection is that of Probate records which cover: Albert Co. 1846-85; Carleton Co. 1833-85; Charlotte Co. 1785-1935; Gloucester Co. 1806-1885; Kings Co. 1788-1886; Madawaska Co. 1909-49; Northumberland Co. 1872-1950; Queens Co. 1785-1940; Restigouche Co. 1839-85; Saint John Co. 1785-1887; Sunbury Co. 1786-1885; Victoria Co. 1850-85; Westmorland Co. 1787-1885; York Co. 1794-1887, most of which have been indexed.

SCHOOL RECORDS: The Archives has Teachers' records 1816-1924 and Monthly Reports from the inspection of schools 1879-1953 from the Department of Education. These are supplemented by Pupils' Lists, Examinations, Registers, Teachers' Lists from various School Boards throughout the Province 1847-1966.

MILITARY RECORDS: There are various Muster Rolls and Paylists for some units of militia in both the Provincial Archives and the New Brunswick Museum.

NEWSPAPERS AND BIOGRAPHICAL FILES: These records can be found in both the Archives and the New Brunswick Museum.

CATALOGUES: An excellent short list of the holdings of the Archives can be obtained by requesting the "Open Letter to Genealogists" (Archives address above). Hugh A. Taylor's New Brunswick History: A Checklist of Secondary Sources is an excellent supplement to the list and can be purchased through the Archives. The major collections of the Archives can be found in the Union List of Manuscripts 1975. (see also New Brunswick Museum, below).

VITAL RECORDS

All civil vital records are deposited with the Registrar General of Vital Statistics, P.O. Box 6000, Fredericton, E3B 5H1. Records of Birth, Death, and Marriage officially begin in 1888, but are incomplete until 1920. There are no restrictions on the issuance of any certificate, as long as it is for Genealogical research purposes. There are no prescribed forms required when requesting any certificate. As a rule, all documents issued by this department contain the names of the parents, the birthplace and the birthdate or age of the person(s) being registered. For Divorce decrees, it is necessary to contact the Registrar of the Divorce Court, New Justice Building, Queen Street, Fredericton. Contact the Vital Statistics Office for current information on their fees and services. Civil Marriage records for 1790-1889 can be found at the Provincial Archives.

CROWN GRANTS

The Lands Branch, Department of Natural Resources, Box 6000, Fredericton, E3B 5H1 has the original Crown grants, Surveys and Cadastral maps for New Brunswick. The Surveys on file in this department contain only survey information, and no names of landowners. The Cadastral maps show all the original grants of land regardless of the year in which they were granted. Copies of these can be obtained at a small cost. Indices to the cadastral map series are available upon request. The original Crown grants include the following information: a map of the granted property, a written description, the number and the date and the Grantee's name. These are available for a small fee. Land Petitions are located in the Provincial Archives.

LAND REGISTRATION

All transfers of land subsequent to the original crown grant are located in the County Record offices. All correspondence should be addressed to The Registrar of Deeds, at the Record Office in the appropriate county. (see addresses under "Counties")

JUDICIAL DISTRICTS

County Court officials can be contacted at the various Court Houses in each County, as listed under "Municipal Government". Court officials include: Registrar of Probate, Clerk of Circuit, Clerk of the Peace and Sheriff.

Further information on New Brunswick Courts can be obtained from the Department of Justice, Centennial Bldg., Fredericton E3B 5H1.

EDUCATION

The Department of Education, Box 6000, Fredericton, E3B 5H1 has the returns of Public Schools since 1880, containing names and ages of pupils enrolled. Records of Teachers' Licenses and Certificates issued since 1880 are also available. The Department can also be contacted for the names and addresses of current School Boards.

MAP SOURCES

A Provincial road map showing the county boundaries is available on request from Tourism New Brunswick, P.O. Box 11030, Fredericton, E3B 5C3. A catalogue of Provincial and Federal government produced maps can be obtained from Lands Branch, Department of Natural Resources, Room 575, Centennial Building, Fredericton, E3B 5H1.

SPECIAL COLLECTIONS

*CENTRE D'ÉTUDES ACADIENNES, Université de Moncton, Moncton, E1A 3E9. This important centre for Acadian research is discussed in more detail in Chapter 3:13.

*NEW BRUNSWICK MUSEUM, 277 Douglas Avenue, Saint John, E2K 1E5. This organization parallels the Provincial Archives and researchers pursuing a New Brunswick ancestry should use the resources of both. The Museum has a wide range of material covering all portions of New Brunswick and includes census records, church records, land grants, assessment rolls, court records, municipal minutes, school records, British Army and militia records, and many others. Their collection of records from Saint John and the area around it is particularly strong. Some of their collections were listed earlier in the section on the Provincial Archives. A complete list of their holdings is available in their Inventory of Manuscripts (Saint John 1967).

OTHER SOURCES OF INTEREST TO RESEARCHERS

Church of England Institute Library, 116 Princess
    Street, Saint John, E2L 1K4
Legislative Library, Box 6000, Fredericton, E3B 5H1
Moncton Museum, 20 Mountain Road, Moncton, E1C 2V8
New Brunswick HS, Box 575, Saint John
Queen's Printer, Box 6000, Fredericton, E3B 5H1
Universities: U de Moncton (Moncton, E1A 3E9), Mount
    Allison U (Sackville, E0A 3C0), *U of New Brunswick
    (Fredericton, E3B 5H5 and Saint John, E2L 4L5)
Albert County Museum, Box 505, Moncton, E1C 8L9
Carleton County HS, Woodstock, E0J 2B0
Charlotte County HS, P.O. Box 207, St. Andrews
Grand Manan HS, Castalia, Grand Manan, E0G 1L0
Kings County HS, Hampton, E0G 1Z0, c/o Kings County
    Museum
*Miramichi HS, The Old Manse Library, 225 Mary Street,
    Newcastle, E1V 1Z3
Queens County Museum, Gagetown, E0G 1V0
La SH acadienne, Box 2363, Station A, Moncton
Westmorland HS, Keillor House, Dorchester
York-Sunbury HS, P.O. Box 1312, Fredericton

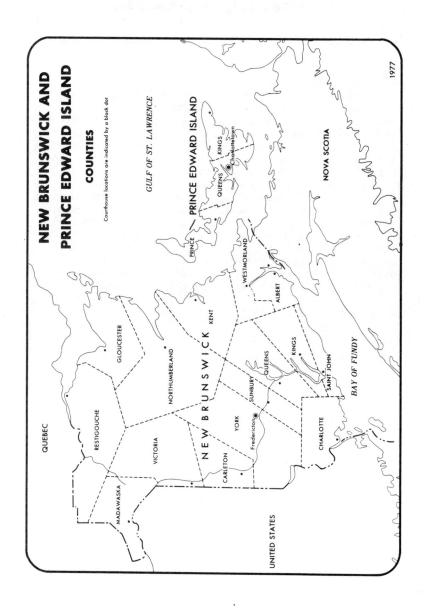

NEW BRUNSWICK AND
PRINCE EDWARD ISLAND
COUNTIES

Courthouse locations are indicated by a black dot

GULF OF ST. LAWRENCE

PRINCE EDWARD ISLAND

PRINCE

QUEENS

KINGS

Charlottetown

NOVA SCOTIA

QUEBEC

RESTIGOUCHE

GLOUCESTER

NORTHUMBERLAND

VICTORIA

MADAWASKA

CARLETON

N E W   B R U N S W I C K

KENT

WESTMORLAND

ALBERT

YORK

SUNBURY

QUEENS

KINGS

SAINT JOHN

Fredericton

CHARLOTTE

BAY OF FUNDY

UNITED STATES

1977

NEWFOUNDLAND

Newfoundland was discovered by John Cabot in 1497. Seven years later, St. John's had been established as a shore base by English fishermen, although it wasn't until 1527 that the first permanent residence is believed to have been built there. In 1583 Sir Humphrey Gilbert proclaimed British Sovereignty over the island, despite the fact that fishermen from many European countries were using it for a shore base. In the conflicts between the fishermen and settler, the fishermen prevailed, which resulted in the settlement of the island being discouraged for over 200 years. Newfoundland became a self-governing colony in 1855 and continued in this form until 1934 when financial problems resulted in the suspension of elected government. A Commission of Government appointed by the British Crown governed the island until it entered Confederation with Canada in 1949. The capital and largest city is St. John's, and the province's population in 1970 was 519,000 (Major ethnic groups: 93% British Isles, 3% French).

MUNICIPAL GOVERNMENT

Newfoundland has no rural municipalities in the usual sense, although there are many towns, rural districts, local improvement districts and other incorporated areas within the province. However, these municipalities are of relatively recent origin and represent less than 1% of Newfoundland's land area. A Municipal Directory is available from Local Government Division, Department of Municipal Affairs and Housing, Confederation Building, St. John's. They will also answer inquiries regarding Newfoundland's municipal structure.

PROVINCIAL ARCHIVES

ADDRESS: PROVINCIAL ARCHIVES OF NEWFOUNDLAND AND LABRADOR, Colonial Building, Military Road, St. John's, A1C 5E2.

CENSUS RECORDS: Most of the census records are aggragate totals only, although there are several which indicate head of the household such as those for 1796-97 and 1800-

01. The census records held by the Archives covers the period 1836-1951.

CHURCH RECORDS: The Archives has 117 various volumes of transcripts of parish registers for the period prior to 1892 and has photocopies of some parish registers for the period 1753-1973. Contact them for more information.

MAPS AND ATLASES SHOWING LANDOWNERS: There are several collections which are useful to genealogists, including Noad's Maps of St. John's 1849 (has an index); Bell Island collection; and Reid Newfoundland Atlases of Lots which show references to people settling on Reid Lands (use in conjunction with Reid Settlers Conveyances Book). The Archives also has numerous other general maps.

DIRECTORIES: In Newfoundland, almost all directories are city directories (St. John's) with various sections of the province added in. The Archives' holdings cover the period from 1845 to 1959.

LAND RECORDS: The Archives has registers of Crown Grants, but not copies of the grants themselves. The Register of Grants covers the period 1831-1931 of which the entries for 1831-80 are indexed. They also have a Register of Deeds for 1845-72, although there are many gaps in the coverage. Other land records include a record book of Crown rents 1821-64 and various Plantation Papers 1809-54.

MUNICIPAL RECORDS: There are virtually no municipal records (assessment rolls, etc.) at the Archives, although there are some miscellaneous voters lists for the period 1834-1966. The 19th century lists are quite complete for Conception Bay, especially for the Harbour Grace area. The Archives also has the voters lists for all of Newfoundland 1932-66 and the Enumerator's Books for St. John's, c. 1900.

COURT RECORDS: There are numerous court records deposited in the Archives, including the Surrogate Court 1787-1863; Supreme Court 1790-1950; Sessions Court 1753-1971; and Magistrates Court 1788-1949. There are also some miscellaneous court records found throughout other collection.

SCHOOL RECORDS: Copies of the minutes of the school board of Catalina, Conception Bay and Ferryland have been deposited with the Archives.

MILITARY RECORDS: There are some records of British troops in Newfoundland prior to 1870, especially the Royal Engineers, as well as some records of Newfoundlanders who participated in the First World War. There are no militia records (ie. muster rolls, etc.).

NEWSPAPERS: The Archives' newspaper collection covers the period from 1810 to the present.

BIOGRAPHICAL FILES: Some select files on persons, families, places and occupations are maintained.

PHOTOGRAPH COLLECTION: About 2000 photographs and negatives have been organized, although the total collection exceeds 5000.

CATALOGUES: There have been two inventories published of the Archives' holdings: Preliminary Inventory No. 1 (1970), now out of print, and a supplement to it, Preliminary Inventory No. 2 (1972). The Union List of Manuscripts 1975 should also be consulted for its major holdings.

VITAL RECORDS

Civil records of birth, marriage and death are available from the Registrar, Vital Statistics Division, Department of Public Health, Confederation Building, St. John's, A1C 5T7. Complete coverage of all records begins in 1892. The restrictions on the issuance of certificates was summarized by the Registrar as follows: "All information pertaining to copies of records is confidential. It is only given to individuals who have the need to know". A special application form is required when requesting certificates. Contact this office for current information on their fees and services. For information on divorces records, contact the Registrar, Supreme Court, St. John's.

CROWN GRANTS

Original Crown Grants and Leases are deposited with Crown Lands Administration, Department of Forestry and Agriculture, P.O. Box 4750, St. John's A1C 5T7. Each grant contains a description of the land, terms and conditions, name of grantee, and a plan of the land. All records are crossed indexed under both location and name of grantee.

LAND REGISTRATION

All subsequent transfers of land after the original grant from the Crown are registered with the Registrar of Deeds, Confederation Building , St. John's. This office holds the records for the entire province. The provincial Archives should also be contacted concerning their land record holdings.

JUDICIAL DISTRICTS

All Supreme Court officials are also Probate Court officials. Like the Registrar of Deeds, there is only one registrar in the province: the Registrar, Supreme Court, St. John's. Any inquiries of the District Court should be addressed to the Sheriff of Newfoundland, St. John's.

EDUCATION

Information on the School Boards and other educational records can be obtained from the Department of Education, Information Division, P.O. Box 2017, St. John's A1C 5R9, and from the Denominational Education Committee, Royal Trust Building, St. John's.

MAP SOURCES

A road map of Newfoundland and Labrador is available on request from Tourist Services Division, Department of Tourism, Confederation Building,. St. John's. All other map requests should be directed to the Canada Map Office, Surveys and Mapping Branch, Department of Energy Mines and Resources, Ottawa, Ontario K1A 0E9.

SPECIAL COLLECTIONS

MARITIME HISTORY GROUP, Memorial University, St. John's, A1C 5S7. This organization was established in 1971 to collect material relating to the study of fisheries and shipping, but much of its work and collection is also connected with Newfoundland history. The Group maintains a series of Name Files, including 20,000 files concerning individuals who were involved with Newfoundland, in either its fisheries, trade or settlement in the period 1660-1840. This comprises information on approximately 12,000 families and about 200,000 individuals. The collection also include parish registers or transcripts from the west of England 1600-1840 and for Newfoundland 1750-1840, as well as numerous historical records. The Group will conduct research for a fee for those interested.

OTHER SOURCES OF INTEREST TO RESEARCHERS

*Centre for Newfoundland Studies, Memorial U of Newfound-
    land, St. John's, A1C 5S7
Gosling Memorial Library, City Hall, St. John's, A1C 5M2
Legislative Library, Confederation Building, St. John's,
    A1C 5T7
Newfoundland HS, Colonial Building, Room 15, St. John's,
    A1C 2O9. (Newfoundland has no genealogical society.
    The historical society, however, will attempt to
    assist researchers desiring help. The society has
    material on all settlements on the Island as well as
    a "Who's Who" of families who settled in Newfoundland
    1660-1840.)
*Provincial Reference Library, Newfoundland Public Library
    Services, Allandale Road, St. John's, A1B 3A3
Queen's College Library, Prince Phillip Drive, St. John's
Queen's Printer, Box 967, St. John's, A1C 5M3
St. John's City Archives, City Hall, New Gower St., St.
    John's, A1C 5M2
*Trinity HS, Trinity, A0C 2S0

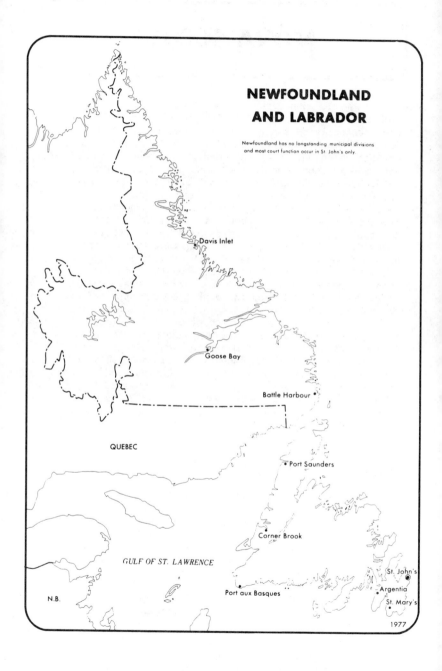

NEWFOUNDLAND AND LABRADOR

Newfoundland has no longstanding municipal divisions
and most court function occur in St. John's only.

Davis Inlet

Goose Bay

Battle Harbour

QUEBEC

Port Saunders

Corner Brook

GULF OF ST. LAWRENCE

St. John's

Argentia

St. Mary's

Port aux Basques

N.B.

1977

NOVA SCOTIA

In 1497, John Cabot was the first person to sight what is now Nova Scotia. In 1604-5 de Monts and Champlain established their short-lived colony near what is now Annapolis Royal. In 1621, the first attempts at British colonization were made. These ended in failure and it wasn't until 1749 that any major British settlement was established in the province. Meanwhile, the French established many settlements throughout the area which they referred to as Acadia. Throughout this period, intense English-French rivalry in Nova Scotia eventually led to its' being secured by the British. In 1755, many French Acadians were expelled from the province and moved to other French or British colonies. The large influx of United Empire Loyalists in 1784 greatly added to the British population there. Originally, Nova Scotia was composed of the present provinces of Nova Scotia, New Brunswick and Prince Edward Island. The latter two, however, formed separate colonies by 1784. Cape Breton Island also enjoyed separate colonial status from 1784-1820 but was later rejoined with Nova Scotia. Nova Scotia was one of the original provinces entering Confederation in 1867. The Capital and largest city is Halifax, with Dartmouth the second largest city. Nova Scotia's population in 1970 was 766,000 (Major ethnic groups: 75% British Isles; 11% French; 5% German and 3% Netherlands).

MUNICIPAL GOVERNMENT

Nova Scotia is divided geographically into eighteen Counties, twelve of which constitute separate municipalities while the remaining six Counties are each divided into two Municipal Districts. The map illustrates the County Boundaries only and the names in parentheses on the map refer to Court Districts not Municipalities. In the list below the Municipal Districts are marked with an asterisk (*). Further information on the addresses of Municipalities can be obtained from the Department of Municipal Affairs, P.O. Box 216, Halifax, N.S. B3J 2M4.

Annapolis Co. (Annapolis Royal)
Antigonish Co. (Antigonish)
*Argyle (Tusket, Yarmouth Co.)
*Barrington (Barrington, Shelburne Co.)

Cape Breton Co. (Sydney)
*Chester (Chester, Lunenburg Co.)
*Clare (Little Brook, Digby Co.)
Colchester Co. (Truro)
Cumberland Co. (Amherst)
*Digby (Digby, Digby Co.)
*Guysborough (Guysborough, Guysborough Co.)
Halifax Co. (Armdale)
*Hants East (Shubenacadie, Hants Co.)
*Hants West (Windsor, Hants Co.)
Inverness Co. (Port Hood)
Kings Co. (Kentville)
*Lunenburg (Bridgewater, Lunenburg Co.)
Pictou Co. (Pictou)
Queens Co. (Liverpool)
Richmond Co. (Arichat)
*Shelburne (Shelburne, Shelburne Co.)
*St. Mary's (Sherbrook, Guysborough Co.)
Victoria Co. (Baddeck)
*Yarmouth (Yarmouth, Yarmouth Co.)

PROVINCIAL ARCHIVES

ADDRESS: PUBLIC ARCHIVES OF NOVA SCOTIA, Coburg Road,
Halifax, B3H 1Z9

CENSUS RECORDS: The 1871 Canadian Census covering Nova
Scotia is available on microfilm and is complete except
for Shelburne County. In addition to this, there are
also a number of earlier censuses, generally showing only
the head of the household with a statistical breakdown of
the rest of the family. Dates included: 1671, 1686, 1693,
1714, 1752, 1770, 1773, 1775, 1787, 1827, 1838, 1851 and
1861 as well as Cape Breton censuses for 1811 and 1818.
All censuses prior to 1861 are incomplete. A content
report on the Archives' census holdings is available.

CHURCH RECORDS: Approximately 180 volumes of originals
and typescripts and 300 reels of microfilm of church
records covering the period since 1749 are found here.
There is no master index of names available and the
Archives is unable to provide copies from the church registers. For Anglican records, it is necessary to obtain
permission of the rector of the parish before they can
be used.

VITAL RECORDS: A number of records of birth, marriage and
death have been deposited with the Archives. These include
Marriage Bonds 1763-1854 and 1858-71 (no index); copies of
marriage licenses arranged by county 1864-1900 (indexed
by county); and a list of deaths arranged chronologically
by county 1864-77 (no index). The proceedings (1869-1921)
and papers (1901-26) of the Court of Divorce are also here.
In 1976, the marriage records of the Registrar General for
the approximate period 1850-1910 were turned over to the
Archives.

MAPS AND ATLASES SHOWING LANDOWNERS: The Archives has
Pictou County Atlas for 1879; Hopkin's Halifax City
Atlas for 1878; Dartmouth Fire Insurance Atlas for 1914;
Lunenburg Fire Insurance Atlas for 1894; and A. F. Church
County Atlases which were maps for each county showing
home owners. (see chart in Chapter 3:6).

DIRECTORIES: Provincial directories deposited here include
those for 1864-65; 1866-67; 1870-71; 1871; 1880-81; 1890-
97; 1896; 1902; 1904; 1907-08; 1911; 1914-15. There is
almost a complete set of Halifax City Directories covering
1863, 1869-1974.

CROWN GRANTS: The Archives have 330 volumes of original
petitions, grants and correspondence, 240 reels of microfilmed records, and 140 crown land maps, all concerning
crown grants. There is an alphabetical index by surname
showing all pertinent reference material necessary to locate the records for each grant. The Archives also has
1872 reels of 1749-1910. This collection is arranged
alphabetically by county. Records after 1910 are only
found in local Registry of Deeds offices.

MUNICIPAL RECORDS: There are a number of scattered and
incomplete assessment records for various parts of the
province. A Content Report is available to locate pertinent rolls. In addition to these, there are fair
sized collections of township records covering the broad
period 1720-1970, although most are restricted to the
late 18th century and early 19th century. Inquiries
for more information on the townships represented should
be directed to the Archives. A number of scattered
voters' lists also exist for 1840-1971 and there is a
good collection of Poll Tax records for the 1790s for
various areas of the province.

COURT RECORDS: There are a large number of court records
in the Archives, including Bankruptcy Court papers 1870-
1930, Coroners' Inquest papers 1791-1928; County Court
records 1876-1914; Court of Chancery Dockets, Minute
Books and other papers 1751-1855; Sheriff's papers 1808-
57; Jury Lists 1803-95; records of the Inferior Court of
Common Pleas 1749-53; 1815-31; and records of the Court
of Quarter Sessions for various counties 1785-1879.
Many of these do not cover the entire province and are
restricted to varying time periods within the dates
given. The Archives also has 1319 microfilm reels of the
records of the Probate Court arranged by county.

SCHOOL RECORDS: There are some school records for the
1820's and 1830's showing pupils' and parents' names. In
addition, there are approximately 100 volumes plus microfilms dealing mainly with the administration of various

School Boards. A number of Teachers' licenses 1811-66,
School censuses 1937, 1946 and 1961, and examinations and
Registers 1813-61 are also available. There is a content
report available for these collections.

MILITARY RECORDS: There are about 350 volumes plus microfilms of military records in the Archives, although most
deal with Headquarters and Administrative papers and some
Commission books for the British Army stationed in Halifax.

IMMIGRATION RECORDS: A few Passenger Lists other than
those kept by the Immigration Branch for Ports of Halifax
and Quebec 1865-1900 (available on microfilm) can be
found in the Archives. A Content Report is available.
There are also records relating to the Naturalization of
Aliens for the period 1849-1917.

NEWSPAPERS: The Archives maintains a comprehensive collection of Nova Scotian Newspapers. However, most obituaries and other vital record notices in those prior to the
middle of the 19th century relate only to prominent members of society.

BIOGRAPHICAL FILES: Over 1200 volumes of Family Papers are
available, with a Content Report covering a large part of
the collection.

SPECIAL COLLECTIONS: Special collections of the Archives
include Cemetery listings and 1319 microfilm reels of
Probate Court records, arranged by County. The Probate
records are not indexed and, for many counties, are very
unorganized.

CATALOGUES: There are several publications available which
will be of interest to genealogists. The best reference
source is the Inventory of Manuscripts in the Public
Archives of Nova Scotia (Halifax 1976). Two short guides
on genealogical research in Nova Scotia are Tracing Your
Ancestors in Nova Scotia (Halifax 1976) published by the
Public Archives, and Find Your Family in Nova Scotia,
published by the Nova Scotia Museum. Both of these are
only short booklets, however. Another, more comprehensive
guide to Nova Scotia genealogy by Terrence Punch is
scheduled to be printed in 1978. Researchers might also
like to check the first 14 issues of the newsletter of the
Genealogical Committee of the Nova Scotia Historical Sov
Society which contained checklists of sources for research
in each county. The Union List of Manuscripts 1975 also
contains listings of the holdings of other archives in
Nova Scotia.

VITAL RECORDS

Records of Birth, Marriage and Death are available from the Deputy Registrar General, Department of Public Health, Box 157, Halifax, B3J 2M9. Registration of Births, Marriages and Deaths dates from 1864, although Births and Deaths were not recorded for the period 1876-1908. Divorces have been recorded since 1952, but these records are not disclosed under any circumstances. Records of Divorce may be obtained only through the County Court Clerk from the Court where the divorce was granted. Each certificate issued shows only the name of the individual(s) and the date and place of the event. Contact this office for current information on their fees and services. NOTE: some records have now been turned over to the Public Archives of Nova Scotia.

CROWN GRANTS

Crown Grants and Petition Papers are available from the Registrar, Crown Lands, Department of Lands and Forests, Dennis Building, Halifax, B3J 2T9. These records cover the period 1731-1972. A Consolidated Index Book lists all the names of the Grantees of Crown Lands. In addition to the Grants and Petitions, this department also has correspondence from about 1840 dealing with petitions for grants. Correspondence prior to this may be at the Public Archives of Nova Scotia. Inquire of the Crown Lands Branch for their prices of photocopies of the various papers.

LAND REGISTRATION

All subsequent transfers of land after the original Crown Grant are recorded with the Registrar of Deeds at the County or District Court House in the districts as listed under County Court Officials (below). Microfilmed copies of records for 1749-1910 are also found in the Nova Scotia Archives.

JUDICIAL DISTRICTS

There are twenty-one Court Districts in Nova Scotia and these correspond in part to the old County boundaries. The map of the province illustrates the Counties of the Province. In some Counties, a second name appears in parenthesis, which indicates an additional County Court District which falls within the boundaries of the original County. Court Officials and codes used below are:
(C) = Clerk of the County Court and Prothonotary of the

Supreme Court; (P) = Registrar of Probate; (D) = Registrar
of Deeds; and (S) = Sheriff. In the list below, the
County Court District is named first, followed by the town
or towns in which the various officials are located.
Address all correspondence to the Court House. Not every
District has a full complement of Officials.

Annapolis (C,P,S: Annapolis Royal; D: Bridgetown)
Antigonish (C,P,D,S: Antigonish)
Barrington (P,D: Barrington)
Cape Breton (C,P,D,S: Sydney)
Chester (D: Chester)
Colchester (C,P,S: Truro; D: Colchester)
Cumberland (C,P,D,S: Amherst)
Digby (C,P,D,S: Digby)
Guysborough (C,P,D,S: Guysborough)
Halifax (C,P,D,S: Halifax)
Hants (C,P,D,S: Windsor)
Inverness (C,P,D,S: Port Hood)
Kings (C,P,D,S: Kentville)
Lunenburg (C,P,D,S: Lunenburg)
Pictou (C,P,D,S: Pictou)
Queens (C,P,D,S: Liverpool)
Richmond (C,P,D,S: Arichat)
St. Mary's (P,D: Sherbrooke)
Shelburne (C,P,D,S: Shelburne)
Victoria (C,P,D,S: Baddeck)
Yarmouth (C,P,D,S: Yarmouth)

Further information on Nova Scotia's courts can be
obtained from Department of the Attorney General, Box 7,
Halifax, B3J 2L6.

EDUCATION

A Directory of Schools listing all School Boards in
Nova Scotia is available from the Department of Education,
Publication and Reference, P.O.Box 578, Halifax, N.S.
B3J 2S9.

MAP SOURCES

A road map of Nova Scotia is available from Travel
Division, Department of Tourism, P.O. Box 456, Halifax,
B3J 2T9. A list of Provincial and Federal Government
produced maps is also available from Surveys and Mapping
Division, Department of Lands and Forests, P.O. Box 698,
Halifax, B3J 2T9.

296

OTHER SOURCES OF INTEREST TO RESEARCHERS

GENERAL

*Beaton Institute of Cape Breton Studies, College of
   Cape Breton, Box 760, Sydney, B1P 6J1. (This
   organization has a growing collection of census
   records, parish records and files on many Cape Breton
   families. They are also in the process of transcrib-
   ing all the cemeteries on Cape Breton. They will con-
   duct limited genealogical research.)
Centre Acadien, College St-Anne, Church Pointe, B0W 1M0
*Legislative Library, Province House, Halifax, B3J 2P8
Louisbourg Archives, Fortress of Louisbourg National
   Park, Louisbourg, B0A 1M0
Nova Scotia Communications and Information Centre Book
   Store, Box 637, Halifax, B3J 2T3 (for Nova Scotia
   government publications)
Nova Scotia HS, PO Box 895, Armdale PO, Halifax
Universities: *Acadia U (Wolfeville, B0P 1X0) *Dalhousie
   U (Halifax, B3H 3J5), U of King's College (Halifax,
   B3H 2A1), St. Francois Xavier U (Antigonish, B0H 1C0),
   St. Mary's U (Halifax, B3H 3C3), Mount Vincent U
   (Halifax. B3M 2J6)

ASSOCIATIONS

Cape Sable HS, Barrington B0W 1E0
Colchester Co. HS, Box 412, Truro B2N 5C5
East Hants HS, c/o 62 Mormandy Ave, Truro
Federation of Museums, Heritage and Historical Societies
   of Nova Scotia, 5516 Spring Garden Rd., Ste 305,
   Halifax B3J 1G6
Nova Scotia Museum,
Old Sydney Society, Box 912, Sydney
Pictou County HS, 86 Temperance Street, Glasgow
Queen's County HS, Liverpool
Shelburne HS, Shelburne B0T 1W0
West Hants HS, Box 177, Windsor B0N 2T0
Yarmouth County HSM, 22 Collins St, Yarmouth B5A 3C8
Hector Centre Trust & Museum, Box 1210, Pictou

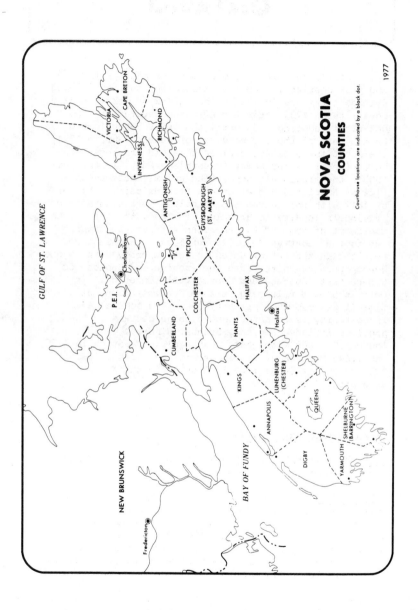

NOVA SCOTIA

COUNTIES

Courthouse locations are indicated by a black dot.

1977

GULF OF ST. LAWRENCE

NEW BRUNSWICK

Fredericton

BAY OF FUNDY

P.E.I.

Charlottetown

CAPE BRETON

VICTORIA

RICHMOND

INVERNESS

ANTIGONISH

GUYSBOROUGH
(ST. MARY'S)

PICTOU

COLCHESTER

CUMBERLAND

HANTS

HALIFAX

Halifax

KINGS

LUNENBURG
(CHESTER)

ANNAPOLIS

QUEENS

SHELBURNE
(BARRINGTON)

DIGBY

YARMOUTH

ONTARIO

Ontario was widely explored by French fur traders
and missionaries in the 150 years prior to its becoming
British territory in 1763. The influx of United Empire
Loyalists in 1784 after the American Revolution led to
Ontario's founding. Up until that time, Ontario had
been a part of the old Province of Canada but, in 1791,
the Constitutional Act divided this old Province into
Upper (Ontario) and Lower (Quebec) Canada. In the early
1800's the province's population quickly grew by an influx of Americans and emigrants from Britain. The War
of 1812 with the United States helped to strengthen the
province's loyalty to Britain. In 1837, the republican
sentiment of some of the American settlers in Ontario
led to the abortive Rebellion of 1837. This in turn
resulted in the Act of Union in 1841 whereby Ontario and
Quebec were re-united into the Province of Canada as
Canada East (Quebec) and Canada West (Ontario). In 1867
Ontario played a leading part in Confederation, at which
time it assumed its' present name. The capital and
largest city is Toronto. Other large centers in the
province include Hamilton, Ottawa, Windsor, Oshawa,
Thunder Bay and Kitchener. Ontario's population in 1970
was 7,642,000 (major ethnic groups: 67% British Isles;
10% French; 5% German; 4% Italian; 2% Netherlands; 2%
Ukrainian; 2% Polish).

PROVINCIAL ARCHIVES

ADDRESS: ARCHIVES OF ONTARIO, 77 Grenville Street,
Queen's Park, Toronto, M7A 2K9

CENSUS RECORDS: The Archives has microfilm copies of
the decennial census for the years 1851, 1861 and 1871.
Various other early census records are available for
certain areas of the Province for the period 1796-1850.
These early census records provide significantly less
information on individual members of households than is
available from the post 1850 census.

CHURCH RECORDS: The records of a number of Ontario
Churches of varying denominations are deposited here.
They include Baptism Records, Marriage Registers,
Burial Records, Congregation Lists, etc.

MAPS AND ATLASES SHOWING LANDOWNERS: There are 3 main
categories:

        1.   maps and plans c. 1784 to c. 1820
        2.   county maps c. 1860
        3.   county atlases, c. 1880

There are many additional instances where we have items
showing landowners, however, and these can be found by
consulting the card catalogue or the map archivist.

DIRECTORIES: There are a number of county and city directories for various localities throughout the province
and for varying time periods.

LAND RECORDS: The Archives has records of the Department
of Lands and Forests and its predecessors: Office of the
Surveyor-General (1763-1845) and Crown Lands Department
(1827-1905).   They are comprised of: petitions, 1827-
1860; fiats and warrants, 1796-1873; general correspondence, 1786-1905; inspection reports, 1822-1913; registers
of leases and sales, 1801-1924; land files: (a) the so-
called Township Papers, arranged by township, concession
and lot, 1784-1860, and (b) numeric files, 1853-1915.
In addition, there are survey records - field notes,
diaries and plans, 1783-1905; records of the Land and
Timber agencies, 1839-1901; and numerous departmental
land rolls and schedules, 1790-1922.   From the Department
of the Provincial Secretary the Archives has acquired
copies of all Letters Patent (free grants, leases and
sales), 1794-1970.

     The records of the Heir and Devisee Commission,
determining property rights of heirs, devisees and
assignees of the original nominees of the Crown, include
case files, reports and minutes, 1797-1895, although the
bulk of the files are for the period after 1805.   These
records are alphabetically indexed.

     The records of the numerous local Land Registry
Offices - basically Abstract Indexes to Deeds, 1794-
1958 and Deeds, 1794-1876 - have been microfilmed by the
Church of Jesus Christ of the Latter Day Saints.   Copies
of this microfilm are available to researchers at the
Archives.

MUNICIPAL RECORDS: The Archives has substantial holdings of records (originals and microfilm copies)from
municipalities throughout the Province.   The major series
include Minutes, By-Laws, Assessment Rolls, Collectors
Rolls and Poll Books as well as a number of printed
Voters' Lists.

COURT RECORDS: (Record Group 22).   The Archives of
Ontario is the official depository for all non-operational
records of the province's courts - from Provincial Criminal

and Family levels through to Court of Appeal. Only those records of enduring research importance are however preserved in the agency and much has been destroyed prior to the present system of archival control. Of those currently in custody which might be of assistance genealogically, the most significant series is that of the Surrogate Clerk of Ontario, 1859- , supported by the County Surrogate Court records from 1791- . Southern Ontario Surrogate estate files are microfilmed from their origin to about 1900 and all original files are being gradually brought into the Archives when they date earlier than 100 years ago. The records of the Court of Probate, 1791-1858, are virtually complete for estates worth more than £5 value current. Indexes are available for all the above series.

Minute books of the Courts of General Quarter Sessions for most of the early Upper Canadian judicial and administrative districts to about 1849 do exist as do certain court record pleadings and registers for District and County Courts from about 1820-1930. Further series include record books and some case files for the District and County Assizes from 1798-, for the Court of King's Bench from 1791-1881, for the Court of Chancery from 1837-1881, for the High Court of Ontario from 1881-1914 and Supreme Court of Ontario from 1914-. Court of Appeal records commence in 1836. Certain correspondence records of local officials, particularly Clerk of the Peace and Sheriff, and bench notebooks of county judges are also retained in this record group.

EDUCATION RECORDS: The education records which are of genealogical interest provide names of teachers and in some instances names of pupils. These records fall into three general catagories: statistical and inspection reports prepared by trustees, local superintendents, and inspectors at the elementary and secondary school level; teacher training records of normal schools and of provincial and county model schools; and teacher uperannuation records. The records include District and Local Superintendents' Reports, 1842-1870; Roman Catholic Separate School Records, 1852-1933; Miscellaneous Inspectors' Reports and Correspondence, 1870-1908; Records of Local Inspectorates, 1850-1851; Grammar School Trustees' Reports, 1854-1871; High School Inspectors Annual Reports, 1872-1932; Continuation School Reports, 1906-1913; Normal and Model School Records, 1847-1913; County Boards of Education Records, 1850-1910; and Superannuation Records in the form of Subscription Books, 1854-1885; Paylists, 1856-1945, and Applications, 1852-1912.

MILITARY RECORDS: A number of Muster Rolls, Order Books, Paylists, and other Military documents relating to the Militia and Regular Forces can be found here.

IMMIGRATION RECORDS: (R.G. 11). The records of the Ontario Department of Immigration cover the period 1867-1902. Included are series which could be of some use to genealogists. These are: Letterbooks: 1869-1901 (indexed by name); Destination Registers: 1972-1874; Passage Warrants: 1872-1888; Correspondence: 1873-1897; and Applications for Refunds: 1872-1875 (arranged alphabetically by applicant).

NEWSPAPERS: The Archives of Ontario has the most extensive collection of newspapers of Upper Canada, Canada West and Ontario maintained anywhere. This applies to varieties of masthead, localities represented and totality of runs. The emphasis is on the period prior to 1930. The material variously consists of originals, microfilm runs and photostats. A small collection of non Ontario newspapers is maintained. All of the above material is inventoried with newspaper "biographies" and detailed tables of contents provided for microfilm runs filmed by the Archives of Ontario.

BIOGRAPHICAL FILES: There are a large number of family histories and files on deposit.

VITAL RECORDS: There are a number of Marriage Registers from the Department of the Provincial Secretary and Citizenship for the period of 1816-69 located in the Archives, arranged by counties. Most of the collection covers the period 1850-69. As well, a large number of Tombstone Inscriptions from Ontario Cemeteries have been deposited here. See also Hiram Walker Museum below.

SPECIAL COLLECTIONS: There are a number of Special Collections in the Archives of Ontario, some of the most important of which are: Perkins Bull Collection, which is a private collection dealing with most aspects of Peel County history and including interviews with oldtimers, cemetery transcriptions, land records and files on Peel County families. Peter Robinson Papers, which include names of emigrants by ship, notes on farm equipment and supplies issued, and records of Clergy on the Character of Intending Emigrants. Peter Robinson was responsible for bringing a number of settlers to the Peterborough area 1823-25, and these records relate to those families. Canada Company Records include all the business and land papers of this company, which was responsible for settlement in a large area of southern Ontario. The most important aspect of the collection is the Land Records, in which are recorded all the settlers purchasing land from the Company. These records are indexed by the names of the settlers.

CATALOGUES: There is no single catalogue of the holdings
of the Archives of Ontario. Major material is listed in
the Union List of Manuscripts 1975.

OTHER ONTARIO PUBLICATIONS: Keffer, Marion and Kirk,
Robert and Audrey: Some References and Sources for the
Family Historian in the Province of Ontario (Ontario
Genealogical Society, 1976).

VITAL RECORDS

The Records of Birth, Marriage and Death for Ontario
are available from the Office of the Registrar General,
Macdonald Block, Parliament Buildings, Queen's Park,
Toronto, M7A 1Y5. All records begin 1 July, 1869 and
there are no restrictions on issuance provided the information is for genealogical information purposes only.
Each type of certificate contains, in addition to the
nominal information, the names of the parents, although
death records prior to 1907 do not. Divorces have been
registered here since 1931, however, copies of the documents are not issued. For copies of Divorce papers in
the period prior to and after 1931, contact the Clerk of
Court in the County where the Divorce was granted.
Contact the Registrar General's office for current information on their fees and services.

CROWN GRANTS

The Letters Patent (Titles) of Crown Lands are held
by the Ministry of Natural Resources, Lands Administration
Branch, Queen's Park, Toronto, M7A 1W3. The details of
Free Grants and sales of Crown lands are recorded in the
Land Rolls and the details of Issuance of Letters Patent
to a Grantee or purchases are recorded in the Domesday
Books. All details are indexed by Township, Concession
Number, Lot Number and Name of Person, in that order.
There is no relevant surname index. These records date
from about 1796. All requests for details on any of the
above should be sent to the Supervisor, Titles Section,
at the aforementioned address. Requests for copies of
Letters Patent must be sent to the Recording Officer,
Ministry of Government Services, Hearst Block, Queen's
Park. Toronto, Ontario, who should also be contacted
to learn of the current fees for copies. All specific
location details (Patent Numbers, etc.) must be obtained from the Ministry of Natural Resources before a
copy of the Patent can be supplied.

LAND REGISTRATION

There are sixty-six (66) Land Registry Offices in Ontario which are responsible for recording all land transactions after the initial Crown Grant. The Districts covered by a majority of these offices correspond to County Boundaries, although a few Counties have more than one Office. Address all correspondence to the Registrar of Deeds, at the appropriate Land Registry Office as indicated below:

Algoma (Sault Ste. Marie)
Brant (Brantford)
Bruce (Walkerton)
Carleton (Ottawa)
Cochrane (Cochrane)
Dufferin (Orangeville)
Dundas (Morrisburg)
Durham (Whitby)
Elgin (St. Thomas)
Essex (Windsor)
Frontenac (Kingston)
Glengarry (Alexandria)
Grenville (Prescott)
Grey North (Owen Sound)
Grey South (Durham)
Haldimand (Cayuga)
Haliburton (Minden)
Halton (Milton)
Hastings (Belleville)
Huron (Goderich)
Kenora (Kenora)
Kent (Chatham)
Lambton (Sarnia)
Lanark North (Almonte)
Lanark South (Perth)
Leeds (Brockville)
Lennox & Addington
    (Napanee)
London (London)
Manitoulin (Gore Bay)
Middlesex East & North
    (London)
Middlesex West (Glencoe)
Muskoka (Bracebridge)
Newcastle (Bowmanville)
Niagara North
    (St. Catherines)

Niagara South (Welland)
Nipissing (North Bay)
Norfolk (Simcoe)
Northumberland East
    (Colbourne)
Northumberland West
    (Cobourg)
Ottawa (Ottawa)
Oxford (Woodstock)
Parry Sound (Parry Sound)
Peel (Brampton)
Perth (Stratford)
Peterborough (Peterborough)
Prescott (L'Orignal)
Port Hope (Port Hope)
Prince Edward (Picton)
Rainy River (Fort Frances)
Renfrew (Pembroke)
Russell (Russell)
Simcoe (Barrie)
Stormont (Cornwall)
Sudbury (Sudbury)
Thunder Bay (Thunder Bay)
Timiskaming (Haileybury)
Toronto (Toronto)
Victoria (Lindsay)
Waterloo North (Kitchener)
Waterloo South (Cambridge)
Wellington North (Arthur)
Wellington South & Central
    (Guelph)
Wentworth (Hamilton)
York (Toronto)
York North (Newmarket)
York South (Toronto)

JUDICIAL DISTRICTS

There are forty-eight County or District Courts in
Ontario. Following are the names of each of these Court
Districts along with their mailing address. In most cases
the Court District boundaries correspond to those of the
Counties of Ontario. Court Officials include: Sheriff,
Local Registrar, Surrogate Registrar, County Court Clerk,
and the Clerk of the Peace. All correspondence should be
addressed to the appropriate official at the Court House
of the appropriate District as listed below:

Algoma (Sault Ste. Marie)
Brant (Brantford)
Bruce (Walkerton)
Cochrane (Cochrane)
Dufferin (Orangeville)
Durham & Ontario (Whitby)
Elgin (St. Thomas)
Essex (Windsor)
Frontenac (Kingston)
Grey (Owen Sound)
Haldimand (Cayuga)
Halton (Milton)
Hamilton-Wentworth
    (Hamilton)
Hastings (Belleville)
Huron (Goderich)
Kenora (Kenora)
Kent (Chatham)
Lambton (Sarnia)
Lanark (Perth)
Leeds & Grenville
    (Brockville)
Lennox & Addington
    (Napanee)
Manitoulin (Gore Bay)
Middlesex (London)
Muskoka (Bracebridge)
Niagara North
    (St. Catherines)

Niagara South (Welland)
Nipissing (North Bay)
Norfolk (Simcoe)
Northumberland
    (Cobourg)
Ottawa-Carlton (Ottawa)
Oxford (Woodstock)
Parry Sound (Parry Sound)
Peel (Brampton)
Perth (Stratford)
Peterborough (Peterborough)
Prescott & Russell
    (L'Orignal)
Prince Edward (Picton)
Rainy River (Fort Frances)
Renfrew (Pembroke)
Simcoe (Barrie)
Stormont, Dundas &
    Glengarry (Cornwall)
Sudbury (Sudbury)
Timiskaming (Haileybury)
Thunder Bay (Thunder Bay)
Victoria & Haliburton
    (Lindsay)
Waterloo (Kitchener)
Wellington (Guelph)
York (Toronto)

Further information on Ontario's courts can be
obtained from Ministry of Attorney General, 18 King
Street E., Toronto, M5C 1C5.

EDUCATION

Information on School Records and addresses of
local School Boards can be obtained from the Public
Information Services Branch, Ministry of Education,
Mowat Block, Queen's Park, Toronto, M7A 1L2.

MAP SOURCES

A Provincial road map showing County and Regional
Municipality boundaries is available on request from Map
Office, Ministry of Transportation and Communications,
1201 Wilson Avenue, Downsview, M3M 1J8; or Ontario
Travel, Queen's Park, Toronto, M7A 2E5. County and
District maps are also available from the Map Office,
Ministry of Transportation and Communications for a
small charge. Request their "Index Map of Southern
Ontario County and District Maps" (free of charge) which
also shows all the names and locations of the Townships
in Southern Ontario. Topographic maps, survey plans,
aerial photos and some excellant maps of the entire province (which show all geographic townships) can be purchased from Ministry of Natural Resources, Public Service
Centre, Room 6404, Whitney Block, Queen's Park, Toronto,
M7A 1W3.

OTHER SOURCES OF INTEREST TO RESEARCHERS

GENERAL

Huguenot Socity of Canada, c/o 202-136 Tollgate Road,
    Brantford, N3R 4Z7
*Legislative Library of Ontario, Parliament Buildings,
    Queen's Park, Toronto, M7A 1A2
*Mennonite Archives of Ontario, Conrad Grebel College,
    Waterloo
*Metro Toronto Central Library, 789 Yonge St., Toronto
Ontario HS, 1466 Bathurst St., Toronto, M5R 3J3
Publications Centre, 3B7 Macdonald Block, Queen's Park,
    Toronto, M78 1N8
Royal Canadian Military Institute, 426 University Ave.,
    Toronto
Universities: *Brock U. (St. Catherines); Carleton U.
    (Ottawa); U. of Guelph (Guelph); *Lakehead U. (Thunder
    Bay); Laurentian U. (Sudbury); *McMaster U. (Hamilton);
    U. of Ottawa (Ottawa); *Queen's U. (Kingston); Royal
    Military College (Kingston); *U. of Toronto (Toronto);
    *Trent U. (Peterborough); *U. of Waterloo (Waterloo);
    Waterloo Lutheran U. (Waterloo); *U. of Western
    Ontario (London); *Victoria U. (Toronto); U. of
    Windsor (Windsor); *York U. (Downsview).

ARCHIVES

Borough of Scarborough Central Records, Scarborough Civic
    Centre, 150 Borough Drive, Scarborough, M1P 4N7
Borough of York Archives, 2700 Eglinton Ave. W, Toronto,
    M6W 1C1
*Brant County Museum, 57 Charlotte Street, Brantford,
    N3T 2W6

*Bruce County HM, Southampton, N9H 2L0
*Centre de Recherche en civilisation Canadienne-française,
    University of Ottawa, 65 Hastey St., Ottawa, K1N 6N5
*Chatham-Kent Museum, 59 William St. N., Chatham, N7M 4L4
*City of Ottawa Archives, 111 Sussex Drive, Ottawa, K1N 5A1
*City of Toronto Archives, City Hall, Toronto, M5H 2N2
Clarke Museum and Archives, Clarke Twp. Library, Orono,
    LOB 1M0
Eaton's of Canada Ltd. Archives, 277 Victoria Street, 5th
    Floor, Toronto, M5B 1W1
*Henry House, 225 Mary Street, Oshawa, L1H 7K6
*Hiram Walker HM, 254 Pitt St. W., Windsor, N9A 5L5
*Joseph Brant Museum, 1240 North Shore Blvd., Burlington,
    L7S 1C5'
Kingston City Archives, c/o Queens University, Kingston,
    K7L 5C4
*Lennox and Addington County Museum, P.O. Box 160, Napanee
*Niagara HS, 43 Castlereagh St, Niagara-on-the-Lake,
    LOS 1J0
*Norfolk HS, Eva Brook Donly Museum, 109 Norfolk St. S.,
    Simcoe, N3Y 2W3
Perth County Archives, Court House, Stratford, N5A 5S4
*Peterborough Centennial Museum, P.O. Box 143, Peterborough,
    K9J 6Y5
Simcoe County Archives, R.R. No. 2, Minesing
*Thunder Bay HMS, Thunder Bay Museum, 219 S. May St.,
    Thunder Bay, P7E 1B5
Upper Canada Village, Box 740, Morrisburg, K0C 1X0
Whitby HS Archives, Whitby Centennial Bldg., 416 Centre
St. S., Whitby, L1N 4W2

ASSOCIATIONS

Ancaster HS, 28 Sulpher Springs Road, Ancaster
Aurora and District HS, c/o 128 Hillview Rd., Aurora
Bancroft HMS, Box 239, Bancroft, K0L 1C0
Bayfield HS, c/o Mrs. Robert Blair, Bayfield
Bruce County HS, c/o Mrs. Geo. Downey, Eskadale Farm,
    R.R. 1, Tiverton
Burlington HS, c/o Mrs. A. W. Ray, 1009-1249 North
    Shore East, Burlington
Chatham and Kent HS, c/o Bert Wees, R.R. 1, Chatham
Costume Society of Ontario, P.O. Box 882, Brant Street,
    Burlington
Dufferin HS, c/o.Mrs. Clifford Shields, R.R. 2, Shelburne
Dundas HS, c/o R. A. Quinn, 30 Alma Street, Dundas
East Durham HS, c/o Dr. O. B. Dickinson, 28 Inniswood
    Crescent, Scarborough
East Parry Sound HS, Box 10, Powassan
Elgin HS, 32 Talbot Street, St. Thomas
Essex County HA, 451 Park St. W., Windsor
Etobicoke HS, c/o F.R. Longstaff, 70 Riverwood Parkway,
    Toronto, M8Y 4E6

Fenelon Falls and District HS, c/o Mrs. J. M. MacKay,
  P.O. Box 388, Fenelon Falls
*Fort Erie HS, 224 Jarvis St., Fort Erie, L2A 2S7
Gananoque HS, Gananoque
Glengarry HS, Dunvegan
Grenville County HS, P.O. Box 982, Prescott
*Grey County HS, 513-21 St. W., Owen Sound, N4K 4E7
Grimsby HS, P. O. Box 294, Grimsby
*Haldimand County HS, Munsee St., Cayuga, NOA 1E0
Hastings County HS, 257 Bridge St. E., Belleville
Head-of-the-Lake HS, c/o Colin Cummings, 28 Crestwood
  Drive, Hamilton
HS of Mecklenburg Upper Canada, 34 Beattie Avenue,
  Rexdale, M9W 2M3
HS of Ottawa, P.O. Box 523, Elgin and Sparks St. P.O.,
  Ottawa
HS of Prescott County, Box 213, L'Original
Kapuskasing and District HS, SE 15th St. and Lawrence,
  Kapuskasing
Kent HS, c/o Bert Wees, R.R. 1, Chatham
Kingston HS, P.O. Box 54, Kingston
Ritley HSM, c/o Ray Gibbs, R.R. 1, Frankville
Lake Scugog HS, Box 670, Fort Perry
Lake Simcoe South Shore HS, Box 495, Sutton
Lambton County HS, c/o Mrs. Eric Steward, 728 Grove St.,
  Sarnia
Lennox and Addington HS, Dundas St.W., Napanee
*London and Middlesex HS, c/o Mrs. J.V. Bowden, 453
  Lawson Rd., London
*Lundy's Lane HS, c/o 5736 Woodland Blvd., Niagara Falls
The Macnab HA, P.O. Box 208, Orons
Manitoulin HS, c/o Mrs. H. E. Cook, P.O. Box 145, Gore
  Bay, POP 1H0
Meldrum Bay HS, c/o Mrs. Norma Townsend, Meldrum Bay
Merrickville and District HS, Box 294, Merrickville,
  K0G 1N0
Mississauga HS, c/o Walker Archer, Reliance Insurance
  Company, 100 University Avenue, Toronto
Niagara HS, 43 Castlereagh St., Box 208, Niagara-on-the-
  Lake, L0S 1J0
Norfolk HS, 109 Norfolk St. S., Simcoe
North Lanark HS, Box 91, Carleton Place
North York HS, 5172 Yonge Street, Willowdale ·
Norwich and District HS, c/o Hilton Hilliker, 26 Washin-
  gton Ave., Norwich, N0J 1P0
*Oakville HS, 291 Balsam Dr., Oakville, L6J 3X7
Oshawa and District HS, P.O. Box 17, R.R. 4, Oshawa
*Ottawa HS, 465 Tweedsmuir Ave., Ottawa, K1Z 5P1
Ottawa Valley HS, R.R. 2, Pembrooke, K8A 6W3
Oxford HS, c/o Mrs. George Chisholm, 836 Grosvenor St.,
  Woodstock
Peel County HS, 7 Wellington St.E.,,Brampton, L6W 1Y1

Pennsylvania-German Folklore Society of Ontario, c/o
    Mrs. Dorothy Sander, 732 Elizabeth St., Kitchener
Perth County History Foundation, c/o 35 William Street,
    Straftford
Pickering Township HS, Brougham
Prince Edward HS, P.O. Box 1078, Picton
Renfrew and District HS, 241 Stewart St. N., Renfrew
Rideau District HS, Box 250, Westport
St. Catherines and Lincoln HS, P.O. Box 1101, St.
    Catharines, L2R 7A3
*Sault Ste Marie HS Museum, Public Library, Sault Ste
    Marie
Scarborough Township HS, c/o Charles Tilston, 117 Church
    St. S., Pickering
Seventh Town of Ameliasburgh HS, c/o Mrs. Susan Bevor,
    R.R. 1, Carring Place
Simcoe County HS, P. O. Box 144, Barrie
La Société Historique du Nouvel-Ontario, Université de
    Sudbury, Sudbury
Sombra Township HS, P.O. Box 72, Sombra
Stormont, Dundas and Glengarry HS, P.O. Box 773, Cornwall
Thunder Bay HMS, 219 May St. S., Thunder Bay
Toronto Historical Board, Exhibition Park, Toronto M6K 3C3
Victoria County HS, c/o Mrs. B. Coulter, 66 Colborne St.
    W., Lindsay, K9V 3S9
Waterloo HS, c/o Henry Bowman, 1630 Queen St., Preston
Welland County HS, c/o Mrs. D. Sourwine, 16 Springhead
    Gardens, Welland
Wellington County H Research Society, c/o Mrs. Enoch
    Kraft, 176 Smith St., Elora
Whitby HSM, Box 281, Whitby, L1N 5S1
Willoaghby HS, Mr. D.J. Thompson, R.R. 1, Niagara River
    Parkway
Women's Wentworth HS, c/o Mrs. S.A. Keeves, 3 Inglewood
    Drive, Hamilton
York Pioneer and HS, 40 Eglinton Ave. E., Toronto

MUNICIPAL GOVERNMENT

The smallest unit of Municipal Government in Ontario
is the Town and Township. These in turn are organized
together into Counties and Districts, although the basic
Municipal responsibilities (assessments, etc.) are retained by the smaller units. Recently the Government of
Ontario has been changing over from the County and
District system to one of Regional Municipalities, with
the latter assuming all the responsibilities of the
Towns and Townships. In the following list, each administrative area is indicated as being a Regional Municipality
(RM); County (C); or District (D) with the administrative
Town indicated in parentheses. (See map for administrative
boundaries.) Write to these offices to learn the addresses

of Town and Township offices.   Address all inquiries to
the Administrator.

A municipal directory is published annually and
distributed by the Government Bookstores. This publication lists all current Municipal Officers (city, town,
township, etc.) in the province.

Municipality of Metropolitan
   Toronto (City Hall, Toronto)
Durham (RM) (Whitby)
Haldimand-Norfolk (RM) (Cayuga)
Halton (RM) (Milton)
Hamilton-Wentworth (RM) (25
   Main W., Hamilton)
Niagara (RM) (St. Catherines)
Ottawa-Carleton (RM) (222
   Queen St., Ottawa)
Peel (RM) (Bramlea)
Sudbury (RM) (Box 370, Sudbury)
Waterloo (RM) (Marsland Centre,
   Waterloo)
York (RM) (Newmarket)
Muskoka (D) (Bracebridge)
Brant (C) (Brantford)
Bruce (C) (Walkerton)
Dufferin (C) (Orangeville)
Elgin (C) (St. Thomas)
Essex (C) (Essex)
Frontenac (C) (Kingston)
Grey (C) (Owen Sound)
Haliburton (C) (Minden)
Hastings (C) (Belleville)
Huron (C) (Goderich)
Kent (C) (Chatham)
Lambton (C) (Sarnia)
Lanark (C) (Perth)
Leeds & Grenville (C)
   (Brockville)

Lennox & Addington (C)
   (Napanee)
Middlesex (C) (367 Ridout N.,
   London)
Northumberland (C) (Cobourg)
Oxford (C) (Woodstock)
Perth (C) (Stratford)
Peterborough (C)
   (Peterborough)
Prescott & Russell (C)
   (L'Orignal)
Prince Edward (C) (Picton)
Renfrew (C) (Pembroke)
Simcoe (C) (Midhurst)
Stormont, Dundas & Glengarry
   (C) (Cornwall)
Victoria (C) (Lindsay)
Wellington (C) (Court House,
   Guelph)
Algoma (D) (Sault Ste. Marie)
Cochrane (D) (Timmins)
Kenora (D) (Kenora)
Manitoulin (D) (Gore Bay)
Nipissing (D) (North Bay)
Parry Sound (D) (Parry Sound)
Rainy River (D) (Fort Frances)
Sudbury (D) (Espanola)
Thunder Bay (D) (Thunder Bay)
Timiskaming (D) (Haileybury)

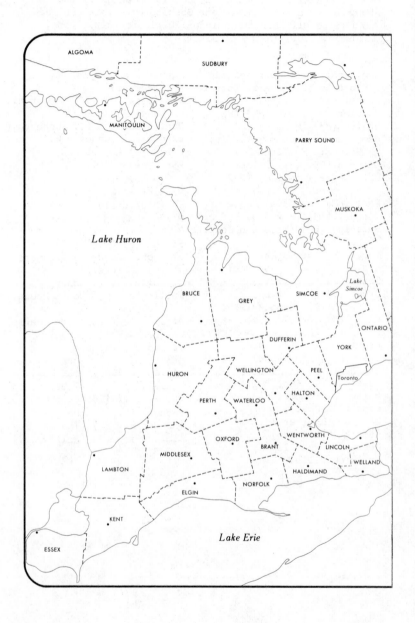

ALGOMA

SUDBURY

MANITOULIN

PARRY SOUND

MUSKOKA

Lake Huron

Lake
Simcoe

BRUCE

GREY

SIMCOE

ONTARIO

DUFFERIN

YORK

WELLINGTON

PEEL

HURON

Toronto

PERTH

WATERLOO

HALTON

OXFORD

WENTWORTH

BRANT

LINCOLN

MIDDLESEX

WELLAND

LAMBTON

HALDIMAND

ELGIN

NORFOLK

KENT

Lake Erie

ESSEX

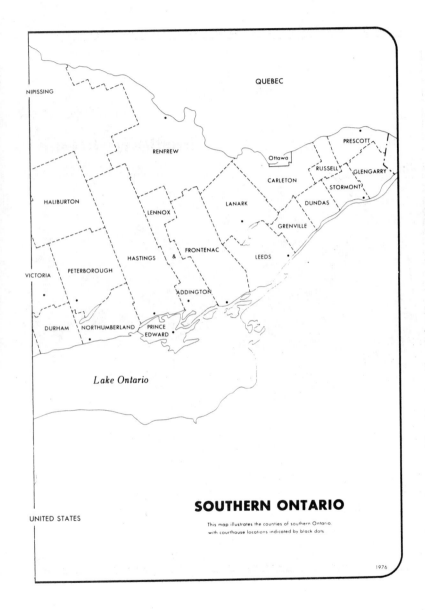

SOUTHERN ONTARIO

This map illustrates the counties of southern Ontario, with courthouse locations indicated by black dots.

1976

312

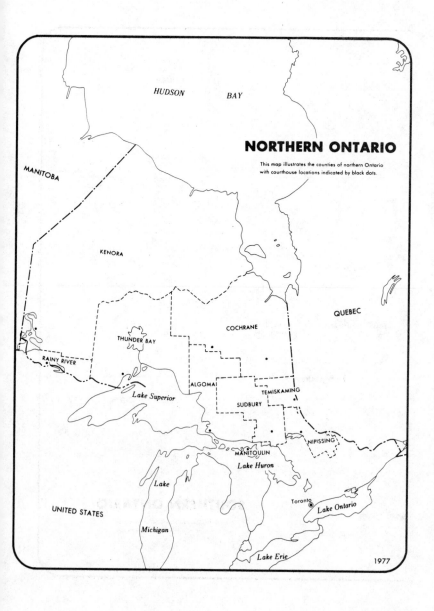

PRINCE EDWARD ISLAND

Prince Edward Island was first discovered by Jacques Cartier in 1534. Although the earliest colonists were French, their settlement was not extensive. In 1763, Prince Edward Island was acquired by the British who shortly after divided it into lots which were granted to persons in England who had the patronage of the Crown. Many of these landlords never saw their properties and were content to own them from afar, a policy which caused considerable trouble for the Island's settlers. In 1769, Prince Edward Island, which up until then formed a part of Nova Scotia, was created a separate colony. The first legislature met in 1773. In 1851, the Island was granted reponsible government and, in 1873 joined in Confederation with Canada. Capital and largest city is Charlottetown, and the province's population in 1970 was 110,000 (Major ethnic groups: 82% British Isles, 16% French).

MUNICIPAL GOVERNMENT

Although the province is divided into three counties, Prince, Queens and Kings, the municipal affairs are administered by the provincial legislature. The counties are subdivided into school districts and form some base for the court system, but play no active part in municipal government. There are several incorporated towns and villages. Information on available records can be obtained from Department of Municipal Affairs, Box 2000, Charlottetown, C1A 7N8.

PROVINCIAL ARCHIVES

ADDRESS: PUBLIC ARCHIVES OF PRINCE EDWARD ISLAND, P.O. Box 1000, Charlottetown, C1N 7M4.

CENSUS RECORDS: The Archives has the following incomplete censuses of the province: 1798, 1841, 1848, and 1861.

CHURCH RECORDS: An ongoing microfilming program for parish registers has been conducted by the Archives since 1974. Inquire of the Archives as to their specific holdings.

MAPS AND ATLASES SHOWING LANDOWNERS: The Archives has copies of Illustrated Atlas of the Province of Prince Edward Island (Meacham 1880) and Atlas of Prince Edward Island and the World (Cummins c. 1925). In addition to these, there is also a collection of 200 maps prepared by property owners for rent control of their properties. There are also other cadastral maps dating from 1810.

DIRECTORIES: All directories list the entire province. Those contained in the Archive's collection include 1864, 1871, 1889-90, 1900, 1904, 1909, 1914, 1929-30, 1937 and 1973.

LAND RECORDS: The Archives has the Land Registry Records, mortgage books, rent books and leases from 1767 to 1900. Material after this period is still with the local Registry Office.

MUNICIPAL RECORDS: Assessment Rolls, Collectors Rolls, Land Tax Ledgers, and Land Assessment Ledgers for the province covering the period 1832-1906 can be found in their holdings.

COURT RECORDS: The Archives hold the following court records: Admiralty Minute Books 1823-1918; Bankruptcy Court Minutes 1903-21; Chancery Court records 1794-1940; Charlottetown City Court depositions and convictions 1879-90; certain county court records 1873-1938; Small Debt Court records 1811-68; and Supreme Court records 1780-1940. As well, there are oaths of allegiance 1770 and 1901 and naturalization books 1865-93 from the Department of the Attorney General. Microfilmed records of the Probate Court are also found here and include the wills for 1805-1900.

SCHOOL RECORDS: The records of the Department of Education and the Board of Education 1853-1945 are deposited here. These include a variety of records of use to genealogists, except the class lists and school registers.

MILITARY RECORDS: Only a few scattered military returns are located at the Archives.

IMMIGRATION RECORDS: The Archives has a few passenger lists in its collections.

OTHER SOURCES: The Archives has a good collection of newspapers and photographs pertaining to the province. There are also some biographical files.

VITAL RECORDS: In the records of the Colonial Secretary and the Provincial Secretary are located the marriage bonds and licenses for the province covering the period 1784-1900.

CATALOGUES: The major holdings of the Archives are documented in the Union List of Manuscripts 1975.

VITAL RECORDS

Civil records of birth, marriage and death in Prince
Edward Island can be obtained from the Division of Vital
Statistics, Department of Health, P.O. Box 3000,
Charlottetown, C1A 7P1. Complete registration of all
events begins in 1906, although there are incomplete
marriage records from 1787 and a few birth records dating
back to 1850. The office does not have divorce records.
Birth certificates are only issued to the person registered
or the parents, and marriage records are only issued to
parties of the marriage. There is no restriction on the
issuance of death records.

All certificates issued by this office only contain
the name(s) of the registered person(s), the date and
place of the event, and the date of registration, with
the exception of the death certificate which also
indicates the age at time of death. Contact this office
for current information on their fees and services.

LAND RECORDS

Land grants, including Crown grants, are deposited
with the Office of the Registrar of Deeds, Charlottetown.
As well, the local court district should also be checked.
The provincial archives also house a large number of the
earlier land records.

JUDICIAL DISTRICTS

There are three county court districts in Prince
Edward Island. The districts are listed below along with
the appropriate address for each of the officials. The
officers and symbols referred to below include: C=Clerk,
S = Sheriff, and R = Registrar of Deeds. Address all
correspondence to the appropriate official at the Court
House in each locality.

     Queen's County (C, S, R: Charlottetown)
     Prince County   (C, S, R: Summerside)
     King's County   (C: Georgetown, S: Red Point,
                      R: Charlottetown)

Further information on Prince Edward Island's courts
can be obtained from Department of Justice, Box 2000,
Charlottetown, C1A 7N8.

For wills and probates, contact Registrar, Estates
Division, Supreme Court, Box 205, Charlottetown C1A 7K4.

EDUCATION

The Department of Education, Box 2000, Charlottetown has some information of interest to genealogists, including Annual Reports listing teacher information (names, etc.) from the late 1800's. Teachers' Superannuation records from 1931 which contain such information as names, birth dates, etc., and records of teachers' licences since the late 1800's. This department also maintains a list of schools and school board addresses.

MAP SOURCES

A road map of Prince Edward Island showing county boundaries is available on request from Department of the Tourism, Tourism Information Division, Box 2000, Charlottetown. Other map information can be obtained from the Canada Map Office, Ottawa.

SPECIAL COLLECTIONS

PRINCE EDWARD ISLAND HERITAGE FOUNDATION, 2 Kent Street, Box 922, Charlottetown, C1A 7L9. This Foundation has had a genealogical co-ordinator since 1974 and under her supervision has indexed a great deal of material relating to Prince Edward Island residents. Nominal indices exist for the Prince Edward Island Censuses (1798, 1841, 1861, 1871); Inquests for 1789-1850 (names of deceased, jurors, witnesses, etc.); Petitions for roads, bridges and land grants for 1770-1837; Marriage bonds and licenses for 1814-46 (by both bride and groom); and the Island's newspapers for 1787-1874 (birth, marriage, death primarily plus other notices in the early editions). As well, the Foundation has also collected a considerable number of family histories and cemetery transcripts. When contacting this organization, researchers are asked to indicate what other institutions they have also contacted on Prince Edward Island.

OTHER SOURCES OF INTEREST TO RESEARCHERS

Legislative Library, Box 7000, Charlottetown, C1A 7M4
Musée acadien de Miscouche, Box 28, Miscouche, C0B 1T0
Prince Edward Island Libraries, University Avenue,
    R.R. 7, Charlottetown, C1A 7N9
Queen's Printer, Department of the Provincial Secretary,
    Box 2000, Charlottetown, C1A 7N8 (for Prince Edward
    Island government publications)
Robertson Library, University of Prince Edward Island,
    Charlottetown, C1A 4P3

QUÉBEC

In 1534, Jacques Cartier landed in what is now Québec and claimed French sovereignty. However it wasn't until 1608 that a permanent settlement was established at Québec City by Samuel de Champlain. The first colonist family, that of Louis Hebert, arrived in 1617. The following period in the history of New France was rife with conflict between fur traders and colonists, and between New France and the British colonies to the south. In 1763, New France passed into British hands. At that time it was a well developed agricultural society with a population of about 65,000. In 1775 the Quebec Act created a British province in Canada composed of much of what is now Québec and Ontario and portions of the United States, and was one of the "Intolerable Acts" leading to the American Revolution. In 1784 large numbers of United Empire Loyalists settled in the Ontario portion of this old province of Canada and in the Eastern Townships of the present province of Québec. In 1791 the Constitutional Act divided the old province of Canada into Upper (Ontario) and Lower (Québec) Canada. This division continued until the Act of Union in 1841, which re-united the two provinces into the Province of Canada with Ontario known as Canada West and Québec known as Canada East. In 1867 Québec was a leader in bringing about Confederation, at which time it assumed its' present name. The Capital city is Québec City and the largest city in the province is Montréal. The population of Quebec in 1970 was 6,028,000 (major ethnic groups: 82% French; 12% British Isles).

PROVINCIAL ARCHIVES

ADDRESS: ARCHIVES NATIONALES DU QUÉBEC, Parc des Champs de Bataille, Québec City, G1S 1C8.

GENEALOGY: ARCHIVES NATIONALES DU QUÉBEC, Section de Généalogie, 1180 rue Berthelot, Québec City, G1R 3G3.
ARCHIVES NATIONALES DU QUÉBEC À MONTRÉAL, 85 rue Ste. Therese, Montréal, H2Y 1E4

CATALOGUES: The Archives Nationales du Québec has one major catalogue of its' holdings: État Général des Archives Publiques et Privées du Québec (Québec 1968). The Archives major holdings are also listed in the Union List of Manuscripts 1975.

*NOTE: Much of the material in the Archives Nationales du Québec has been discussed earlier in Chapter 3:13, and it will not be repeated here. Refer back to Chapter 3:13 for an indication of the Archive's holdings.

VITAL RECORDS

Vital statistics records have been registered with Ministere des Affaires Sociales, Régistre de la Population, 845 ave Joffre, Québec City, G1S OA6 since 1926, however, they actively discourage all genealogical inquiries and refer all correspondence to the offices of the judicial districts for copies of Birth, Marriage and Death certificates.

CROWN GRANTS

The Archives Nationales de Québec maintains a list of all the grants made by the Crown from 1763 - 1890. Inquiries should be directed there.

LAND REGISTRATION

A great many of the land transactions which have taken place in Quebec (subsequent to the Crown Grants) can be found in Notarial records. Inquiries of this nature should be made to either the Protonotaire de la Cour Supériere at the Court House in the appropriate Judicial District as listed below, or to the Archives Nationales de Québec.

JUDICIAL DISTRICTS

The Judicial Districts are perhaps the most important local repository of genealogical information in Quebec containing records of Birth, Marriage and Death, Land Records, Wills, and other papers. The most important official is the Protonotaire de la Cour Supérierre to whom the majority of the requests or information should be addressed. Other officials include: Greffier de la Couronne (Clerk of the Crown); Greffier de la Paix (Clerk of the Peace); and Sherriff. Send all correspondence to the Palais de Justice (Court House) of the appropriate District (see Map), at the locations indicated below in parentheses:

Abitibi (Amos; Chibougamau;
    La Sarre; Val d'Or)
Arthabaska (Arthabaska)
Beauce (St. Joseph de Beauce;
    Lac Mégantic)
Beauharnois (Valleyfield)
Bedford (Cowansville; Granby)
Bonaventure (New Carlisle)
Chicoutimi (Chicoutimi)
Drummond (Drummondville)
Gaspé (Percé; Havre-Aubert;
    Ste.-Anne-des-Monts)
Hauterive (Baie-Comeau)
Hull (Hull)
Iberville (St. Jean)
Joliette (Joliette)
Kamouraska (Rivière du Loup)
Labelle (Mont-Laurier;
    Maniwaki)
Mégantic (Thetford Mines)
Mingan (Sept-Îles)

Montmagny (Montmagny)
Montréal (Montréal)
Nicolet (Nicolet)
Pontiac (Cambell's Bay)
Québec (Québec City)
Richelieu (Sorel)
Rimouski (Rimouski;
    Amqui; Matane; Mont-
    Joli)
Roberval (Roberval;
    Alma)
Rouyn-Noranda (Rouyn)
Saguenay (La Malbaie)
St. François (Sherbrooke;
    Lac Mégantic)
St. Hyacinthe (St. Hya-
    cinthe)
St. Maurice (Shawinigan;
    La Tuque)
Témiscamingue (Ville-Marie)
Terrebonne (St. Jérôme)
Trois-Rivières (Trois-Riv-
    ières; Louiseville)

A short booklet entitled The Judicial System is available on request from Ministère de la Justice, Service de L'Information, 225 Grande Allée Est, Québec City, Qué. G1R 4C6. Complete addresses of the Court Houses are included in this publication as well as a description of Quebec's Judicial System.

EDUCATION

For additional information on School records and a list of the School Boards and their addresses, contact Department d'Éducation, 1035 de la Chevrotiere, Québec City, Qué. G1R 5A5.

MAP SOURCES

A provincial road map of Quebec is available on request from Tourist Branch, Department of Tourism, Fish and Game, 150 est, boul. St-Cyrille, Québec City, G1R 4Y3. A catalogue of Provincial Government produced maps is available for $1.00 from Ministère des Terres et Forêts, Service de la Cartographie, 1995 Ouest, Boulevard Charest, Québec City, G1N 4H9.

OTHER SOURCES OF INTEREST TO RESEARCHERS

GENERAL

*Bibliothèque Municipale de Montréal, Salle Gagnon, 1210
    Est, rue Sherbrooke, Montréal, H2L 1L9
*Bibliothèque Nationale du Québec, 1700 rue Saint-Denis,
    Montréal, H2X 3K6
Centre Canadien des Recherches Généalogiques, P.O. Box
    845, Upper Town, Québec City
Editeur Officiel du Québec, 675 est boul. St-Cyrille,
    G1R 4Y7 (for Québec government publications)
Fédération des Sociétés d' Histoire du Québec, Musée d'
    Outaouais, CP 7, Hull
Institut Généalogique Drouin, 4184 St. Denis, Montréal
Legislative Library, Parliament Building, Québec City,
    G1A 1A5
La Société Historique de Québec, Seminaire de Québec,
    C.P. 460, Québec City
Universities: Bishop's U. (Lennoxville); *Université
    Laval (Ste. Foy); Loyola College (Montréal); *McGill U.
    (Montréal); Le College Militaire Royal de Saint-Jean
    (Saint-Jean sur la Richelieu); *Université de Montréal
    (Montréal); Université de Sherbrooke (Sherbrooke); Sir
    George Williams U. (Montréal);*Université du Québec
    (Québec).

ARCHIVES

*Archives de la Ville de Québec, C.P. 37, Hôtel de ville,
    Québec, G1R 4S9
Archives de l' Hôtel-Dieu de Montréal, Religieuses
    hospitalières de St-Joseph, 251 ouest, ave des Pins,
    Montréal
*Archives de Sainte-Anne-de-la-Pocatière, La Pocatière,
    Québec, G0R 1Z0
*Archives du College Bourget, Rigaud, Québec, J0P 1P0
*Archives du College de Lévis, 9 Mgr Gosselin, Lévis,
    G6V 5K1
*Archives du Monastère de l' Hôtel-Dieu de Québec, 75
    rue des Remparts, Québec City, G1R 3R9
*Archives du Séminaire de Chicoutimi, 679 Chabanel,
    Chicoutimi, G7H 3S5
Archives du Séminaire de Joliette,455 boul. Base de Roc,
    Joliette, J6E 5P3
Archives du Séminaire de Nicolet, Grand Séminaire de
    Nicolet,700 boul Louis-Fréchette, Nicolet, J0G 1E0
*Archives du Séminaire de Québec, 2 rue de la Fabrique,
    Québec, G1R 4R7
Archives du Seminaire de Rimouski, 83 ouest, rue St-Jean-
    Bet, Rimouski
Archives du Séminaire de St-Hyacinthe, 450 rue Girourard,
    C.P. 370, St-Hyacinthe, V2S 7B8
*Archives du Séminaire de Trois-Rivières, Boul Laviolette,
    Trois-Rivières, G9A 5J1

Bibliothèque Municipale de Montréal, Salle Gagnon, 1210
     est rue Sherbrooke, Montréal, H2L 1L9
*Brome County HS, Box 690, Knowlton, JOE 1V0
Centre de Recherche en Histoire Économique du Canada
     Français, École des Hantes Études commerciales,
     Université de Montréal, 5255 rue Decelles, Montréal
*McCord Museum, 690 Sherbrooke St. W., Montréal, H3A 1E9
Monastère des Augustines de L' Hôpital-Général, 260 boul
     Langelier, Québec, G1K 5N1
Programme de Recherche en Démographie Historique, Depart-
     ment de démographie, Université de Montréal, Montréal,
     H3C 3V7
Séminaire de Saint-Sulpice de Montréal, 116 ouest rue
     Notre-Dame, Montréal, H2V 1T2
Service des Archives, Séminaire de Sherbrooke, 195 rue
     Marquette, Sherbrooke
Société d' histoire des Cantons de l' Est., Howardene,
     C.P. 1141, Sherbrooke, J1H 2T6
Sd'H régionale des Trois-Rivières, 190 rue Bonaventure,
     Trois-Rivières, G9A 2B1
SH de Jolitte, 2 nord rue St-Charles-Borromée, Jolitte,
     J6E 6H6
SH de la Côte-du Sud, La Pocatière, GOR 1Z0
*SH du Saguenay, C.P. 456, Chicoutimi, G7H 5C8
Société Saint-Jean-Baptiste de Montréal, 1182 boul St-
     Laurent, Montréal
Ville de Montréal, Division des Archives, 275 est rue
     Notre-Dame, Montréal, H2Y 1C6
Ville de Trois-Rivières, C.P. 368, Trois-Rivières

ASSOCIATIONS

Antiquarian and Nunismatic Society of Montréal, Chateau de
     Ramezay, 29 Notre-Dame St. E., Montréal
Canadian Railroad HA, P.O. Box 22, Station,B, Montréal
Compton County H and MS, Box 413, Cookshire, JOB 1M0
HS of Argenteuil County, P.O. Box 113, St Andrews East
HS of Bout-de- l'Île, 202 Senneville, Ste-Anne-de-
     Bellevue
*Institut d'histoire de l'Amérique française, 261
     Bloomfield, Montréal, H2V 3R6
Institut national Samuel de Champlain, C.P. 211, Québec
Mégantic County HS, Kinnear's Mills, Mégantic
Missiquoi HS, Box 186, Stanbridge East, JOJ 1A0
Richmond County HS, B.P. 329, Danville
Sd'H d' Arthabaska, 69 Beauchesne, Arthabaska
S d'H du Bas-St-Laurent, 300 rue des Ursulines, Rimouski
Sd'H des Cantons de l'Est, C.P. 1141, Sherbrooke
Sd'H du Cap-de-la-Madeleine, Box 212, Cap-de-la-Madeleine
SH de la Chaudiere, College du Dacre-Couir, Beauceville
SH de la Côte-du-Sud, C.P. 684, La Pocatière
SH de la Côte Nord, centre culturel, Baie Comeau
SH de Drummondville, c/o chambre de Commerce, rue St-Jean,
     Drummondville

SH de la Gaspésie, C.P. 380, Gaspé
Sd'H de L'Île Jesus, 1048 blvd Vanier, Duvernay
SH des Îles Percées, 111 rue Gilles-Boivin, Boucherville
SH du Lac-St-Louis, C.P. 1024, Pointe-Claire
SH de Lachine, 385 55eme Ave., Lachine
Sd'H de Longueuil, B.P. 175, Succursale A, Longueuil
SH de Matane, C.P. 308, Matane
SH de Montréal, Sec. 4420, rue Saint-Denis, Montréal
SH du Nord de l' Outaouais, 85 rue Emond, Hull
SH d' Odanak, Odanak
SH de l'Ouest du Québec, Musée de l' Outaouais, C.P. 7,
    Hull
SH de la Vallee du Chateauguay, Box 61, Howick
SH de la Vallee du Richelieu, 696 Martel, Chambly
SH de Vaudreuil-Soulanges, 431 boul. Roche, Vaudreuil
Sd'H et d'Archéologie de l'Abitibi, Centre Culturel de La
    Sarre, Abitibi-Ouest
Society of the Montreal Military and Maritime Museum, c/o
    The Old Fort, St. Helen's Island, P.O. Box 1024,
    Montréal
Stanstead HS, 100 Dufferin Road, Stanstead

MUNICIPAL GOVERNMENT

Following is a list of counties and territories in Quebec, with the county town listed in parenthases. For those counties which are without a parenthasized name, the county town is the same name as the county itself. Address all inquiries to the Secretary-Treasurer. A municipal directory is also available from the Editeur official Québec. Further information on the municipal system in Quebec can be obtained from the Department d'Affaires Municipales, 680 St-Amable, Quebec, P.Q. G1R 4Z3.

Argenteuil (Lachute)
Abitibi (Amos)
Arthabaska
Bagot (St-Liboire)
Beauce (Beauceville)
Beauharnois
Bellechasse (St-Raphael)
Berthier (Berthierville)
Bonaventure (New Carlisle)
Brome (Knowlton)
Chambly
Champlain (St-Geneviève-de-
    Batiscan)
Charlevoix Est (La Malbaie)
Charlevoix Ouest (Baie-St-
    Paul)
Chateauguay (Ste-Martine)

Chicoutimi
Compton (Cookshire)
Deux -Montagnes (Mirabel)
Dorchester (St-Hénédine)
Brummond (Drummondville)
Frontenac (Lac-Mégantic)
Gaspé-Est (Percé)
Gaspé-Ouest (Ste-Anne-des-
    Monts)
Gatineau (Maniwaki)
Hull
Huntingdon
Iberville
Iles-de-la-Madeleine (Ile-de-
    Havre-Aubert)
Joliette
Kamouraska (St-Pascal)

Labelle (Mont-Laurier)
Las-St-Jean Est (Alma)
Lac-St-Jean Ouest (Roberval)
Laprairie (La Prairie)
L'Assomption
Lévis (St-Romuald-d'Etchemin)
L'Islet (St-Jean-Port-Joli)
Lotbiniere (Ste-Croix)
Maskinongé (Louiseville)
Matane
Matapédia (Amqui)
Mégantic (Inverness)
Missisquoi (Bedford)
Mistissini (Quebec)
Montcalm (Ste-Julienne)
Montmagny
Montmorency (Château-Richer &
    Ste-Famille, I. d'O.)
Montreal
Napierville
New Québec (Québec)
Nicolet (Bécancour)
Papineau (Papineauville)
Pontiac (Campbell's Bay)

Portneuf (Cap-Santé)
Québec (Loretteville)
Richelieu (Sorel)
Richmond
Rimouski
Rivière-du-Loup
Rouville (Marieville)
Saguenay (Tadoussac)
St-Hyacinthe
St-Jean
St-Maurice (Yamachiche)
Shefford (Waterloo)
Sherbrooke
Soulanges (Coteau Landing)
Stanstead (Ayer's Cliff)
Témiscamingue (Ville-Marie)
Témiscouata (Notre-Dame-
    du-Lac)
Terrebonne (St-Jérôme)
Vaudreuil
Verchères
Wolfe (Ham-Sud)
Yamaska (St-François-du-Lac)

324

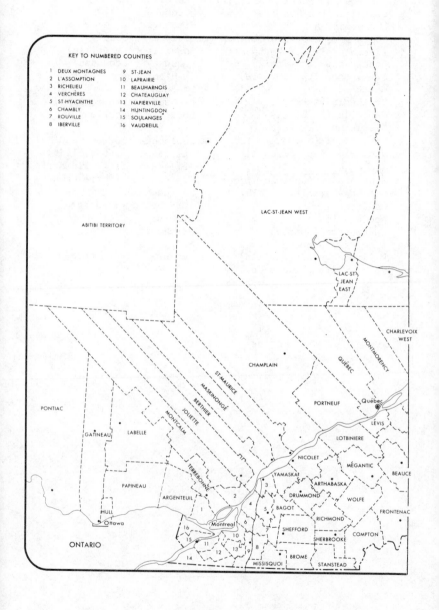

KEY TO NUMBERED COUNTIES

1 DEUX MONTAGNES
2 L'ASSOMPTION
3 RICHELIEU
4 VERCHÈRES
5 ST-HYACINTHE
6 CHAMBLY
7 ROUVILLE
8 IBERVILLE
9 ST-JEAN
10 LAPRAIRIE
11 BEAUHARNOIS
12 CHATEAUGUAY
13 NAPIERVILLE
14 HUNTINGDON
15 SOULANGES
16 VAUDREIUL

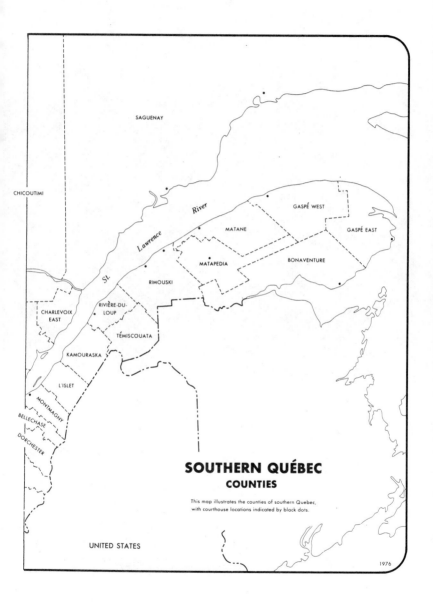

SAGUENAY

CHICOUTIMI

River

Lawrence

St.

GASPÉ WEST

MATANE

GASPÉ EAST

MATAPEDIA

BONAVENTURE

RIMOUSKI

CHARLEVOIX EAST

RIVIÈRE-DU-LOUP

TÉMISCOUATA

KAMOURASKA

L'ISLET

MONTMAGNY

BELLECHASE

DORCHESTER

SOUTHERN QUÉBEC
COUNTIES

This map illustrates the counties of southern Quebec,
with courthouse locations indicated by black dots.

UNITED STATES

1976

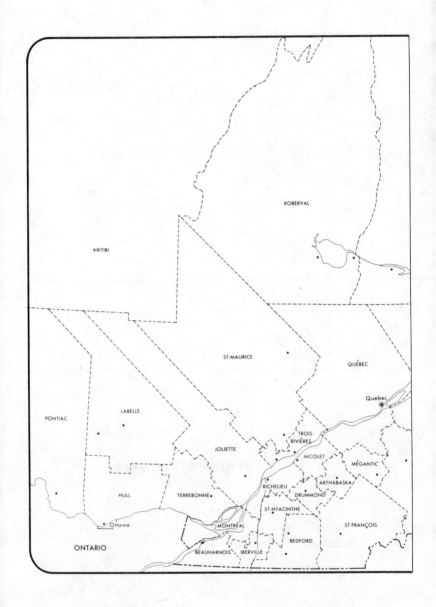

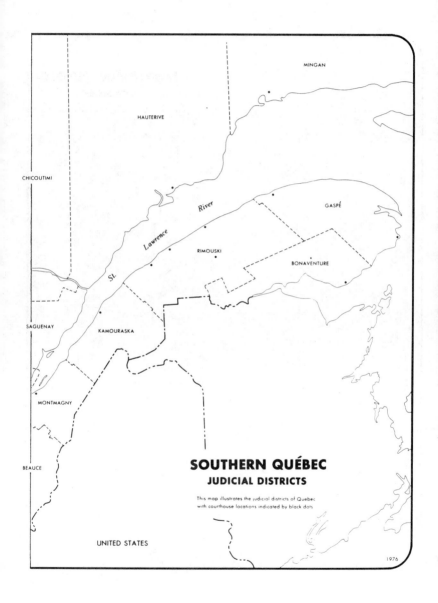

MINGAN

HAUTERIVE

CHICOUTIMI

River

Lawrence

St.

GASPÉ

RIMOUSKI

BONAVENTURE

SAGUENAY

KAMOURASKA

MONTMAGNY

BEAUCE

SOUTHERN QUÉBEC
JUDICIAL DISTRICTS

This map illustrates the judicial districts of Quebec
with courthouse locations indicated by black dots

UNITED STATES

1976

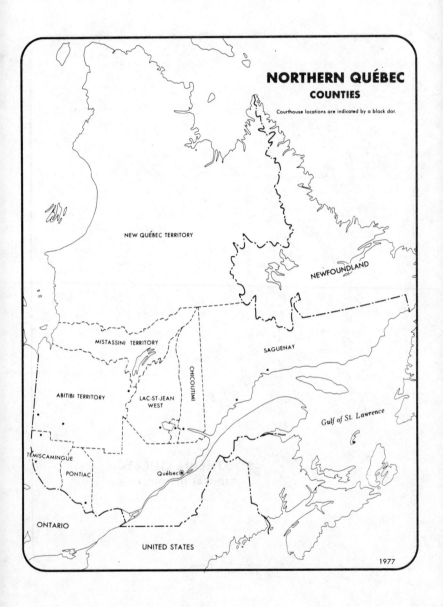

NORTHERN QUÉBEC

COUNTIES

Courthouse locations are indicated by a black dot.

NEW QUÉBEC TERRITORY

NEWFOUNDLAND

MISTASSINI TERRITORY

SAGUENAY

CHICOUTIMI

ABITIBI TERRITORY

LAC-ST-JEAN WEST

Gulf of St. Lawrence

TEMISCAMINGUE

PONTIAC

Québec

ONTARIO

UNITED STATES

1977

NORTHERN QUÉBEC
JUDICIAL DISTRICTS

Courthouse locations are indicated by a black dot.

MINGAN

NEWFOUNDLAND

CHICOUTIMI

HAUTERIVE

ABITIBI

ROBERVAL

Gulf of St. Lawrence

ROUYN-NORANDA

TÉMISCAMINGUE

PONTIAC

Québec

ONTARIO

UNITED STATES

1977

SASKATCHEWAN

The first white man to reach what is now Saskatchewan was Henry Kelsey, who made an exploratory trip there in 1690. Over the next 200 years, the principle industry of the province was fur trading, with virtually no settlement taking place until 1870. In 1869 an agreement was made between the Hudson's Bay Company and the government of Canada to transfer Rupert's Land (which included Saskatchewan) to the Dominion, The following year, Saskatchewan became part of the newly created North West Territories. In 1885, the North West Rebellion took place in what was later to become the Province of Saskatchewan. In 1905, Saskatchewan was separated from the North West Territories and created a province. The capital and largest city is Regina, and the second largest city is Saskatoon. The population of Saskatchewan in 1970 was 940,000 (major ethnic groups: 42% British Isles; 16% German; 9% Ukrainian; 7% Scandinavian; 6% French; 4% Netherlands; 3% Polish).

PROVINCIAL ARCHIVES

ADDRESSES: SASKATCHEWAN ARCHIVES BOARD, Library Building, University of Regina, Regina, S4S 0A2

SASKATCHEWAN ARCHIVES BOARD, Murray Memorial Building, University of Saskatchewan, Saskatoon, S7N 0W0

CENSUS RECORDS: The Archives has no nominal census returns, only statistical accounts.

CHURCH RECORDS: There are many original and microfilm copies of parish registers containing records of baptisms, confirmations, marriages and burials. Most of these are from Anglican churches in the province, but other denominations are represented as well. In most cases access to these records is subject to the permission of the donor.

MAPS AND ATLASES: The Archives has a set of Cummins Rural Directory of Saskatchewan from the 1920's showing rural landowners in the province.

DIRECTORIES: The following directories are available: McPhillips Directory of the Saskatchewan District (N.W.T.), 1888; Henderson's Directory of Manitoba and the N.W.T., 1900,1904; Henderson's Directory of Western Canada, 1905-

1908; Henderson's Western Canada Gazetteer and Directory,
1908; Wrigley's Saskatchewan Directory, 1921-1922; and
Overgard Directories for Saskatchewan, 1939, 1948, 1953.
There are also city directories for Regina from 1908,
Moose Jaw from 1909, Prince Albert from 1911, and Saskatoon
from 1908.

LAND RECORDS: Original files for homesteads and some
other Crown grants of land in the province from 1872 to
the present. There is a name index for homestead entries
on lands patented before 1930. In the case of land grants
since 1930, the legal land description is necessary in
order to locate the pertinent file. Presently the homestead records up to 1930 are being microfilmed by the
Genealogical Society of the Church of Jesus Christ of
Latter-Day Saints.

MUNICIPAL RECORDS: Records from a number of rural and
urban municipalities have been preserved in the original
or microfilm form. A few of these include assessment
rolls. Municipal corporation files from the Department
of Municipal Affairs sometimes include lists of petitioners, and occasionally an enumeration of residents at the
time the local government was established.

COURT RECORDS: There are court records from all judicial
centres in the province prior to 1931 but court records
are only available for searches through the appropriate
judicial center. Court records are indexed by court or
jurisdiction and by the name of the defendent and by the
name of the plaintiff.

SCHOOL RECORDS: There are only scattered records for
school districts in the Archives and very few of these
include attendance registers. However, there is a series
of files from the Department of Education which contain
reports and correspondence from each school district from
1899-to 1960.

MILITARY RECORDS: There is a list of volunteers and
reservists who resided in Saskatchewan 1914-1915, as well
as the nominal rolls of battalions of the Canadian
Expeditionary Force. There is also a list of soldiers
from Saskatchewan who died in World War II.

NEWSPAPERS: Wherever possible, back files of daily and
weekly newspapers from across the province have been microfilmed by the Archives. The earliest of these, the
Saskatchewan Herald from Battleford, dates from 1878.
There are complete holdings of all weeklies since 1943.

PRIVATE PAPERS: The papers of a great many individuals
in the province have been deposited in the Archives.

These are not exclusively those of prominent figures, but include diaries and reminiscences of many people who helped to build the province. In the 1950's the Archives prepared a series of questionnaires which were completed and returned by many pioneers. These questionnaires were about their lives and communities. Many tape-recorded interviews have been conducted with pioneers and noted personalities. Either the original recordings or transcripts of them are available for research use.

OTHER PUBLICATIONS AND MANUSCRIPTS: Clippings, pamphlets, genealogies and local histories containing biographical information can be found in the Archives. Some of these items are unpublished and so provide a unique and valuable source of information.

PHOTOGRAPHS: The Archives has a large collection of photographs of individuals, communities, farming activities and many other facets of life in the province. These are indexed and available to researchers.

CATALOGUES: There is no comprehensive publication listing all the holdings of the Archives of Saskatchewan. However, their major records are listed in the Union List of Manuscripts 1975.

VITAL RECORDS

All civil vital records in Saskatchewan are available from the Department of Health, Division of Vital Statistics, 3211 Albert Street, Regina, S4S OA6. Registration of Births, Marriages and Deaths became compulsory in 1889, but it is estimated that complete registration of all vital acts in the province did not result until about 1920-30. This office also has a very few records which date back to the 1870's. Some restrictions on the issuance of certificates are detailed on the application forms, which must be used when requesting copies of vital records. Contact this office for current information on their fees and services. The Vital Statistics Division also holds all Saskatchewan divorce records.

HOMESTEAD RECORDS

The Lands Branch, Department of Agriculture, Administration Building, Regina, Sask. S4S OB1, has some records relating to homesteads. These include the original Township Registers which indicate the type of disposition, date of sale or entry, name of person obtaining disposition, and the date when Letters Patent were issued; and

the Township Plans of Survey which, in some cases, have
the information as to the name of the person who obtained
a Grant indicated on a Township map. As well, they also
have "fiat" copies of Grants which are drafts from which
the Letters Patent were drawn up. All of this material
is indexed by land description only. For an alphabetical
list of patentees and other homestead records, contact
the Saskatchewan Archives in Saskatoon. Original copies
of the Letters Patent are deposited in the various Land
Titles Offices throughout the Province.

LAND REGISTRATION

There are eight (8) Land Registration Districts in
Saskatchewan (see map). All correspondence should be
addressed to the Registrar at the appropriate Land Titles
Office in the following locations:

Battleford	Prince Albert	Swift Current
Humboldt	Regina	Yorkton
Moose Jaw	Saskatoon	

JUDICIAL DISTRICTS

There are nineteen (19) Judicial Districts in the
province (see map). All correspondence should be addressed
to the specific official at the appropriate Court House
in the following locations. Court officials include:
Sheriff, Court Clerk, and Local Registrar at each location.

Arcola	Melfort	Saskatoon
Assiniboia	Melville	Shaunavon
Battleford	Moose Jaw	Swift Current
Estevan	Moosomin	Weyburn
Gravelbourg	Prince Albert	Wynyard
Humboldt	Regina	Yorkton
Kerrobert		

Further information on Saskatchewan's courts can be
obtained from the Department of the Attorney General,
Legislative Building, Regina, S4S 0B3

EDUCATION

Information regarding School Records and School Unit
addresses can be obtained from the Department of Education,
2220 College Avenue, Regina, S4P 2Y8.

MAP SOURCES

A road map of Saskatchewan can be obtained on request from the Saskatchewan Tourist Branch, Box 7105, Regina, S4P 0B5. A catalogue of maps of Saskatchewan can also be obtained on request from the Department of Tourism and Renewable Resources, Lands and Surveys Branch, 1840 Home Street, Regina, S4P 2L7.

OTHER SOURCES OF INTEREST TO RESEARCHERS

Fort Qu'Appelle and Lebret HS, Box 127, Fort Qu'Appelle
Legislative Library, Legislative Building, Regina, S4S 0B3
Mohyla Institute Archives, 1240 Temperence Street,
   Saskatoon, S7N 0P1
Moose Jaw Public Library, Archives Department, 461 Langdon
   Crescent, Moose Jaw, S6H 0X6
Plains HMS, Box 1363, Regina, S4P 3B8
Provincial Library, 1352 Winnipeg St., Regina, S4R 1V9
Queen's Printer, 1920 College Ave., Regina, S4P 1C4
Regina Public Library, 2311-12th Ave., Regina, S4P 0N3
*Royal Canadian Mounted Police, P.O. Box 6500, Regina,
   S4P 3V7
Saskatchewan History and Folklore Society, c/o 28-2240
   Robinson Street, Regina, S4H 2L2
Saskatoon Public Library, 311-23rd St. E., Saskatoon,
   S7K 0J6
Universities: U of Regina (Regina, S4S 0A2), *U. of
   Saskatchewan (Saskatoon, S7N 0W0)
Canadian Plains Research Centre, University of Regina,
   Regina, Saskatchewan

MUNICIPAL GOVERNMENT

Saskatchewan is divided into two hundred and ninety-two (292) Rural Municipalities in the southern part of the province. The northern part of the province is administered by the Northern Administration District. The Saskatchewan Municipal Directory published by the Department of Municipal Affairs, Box 7110, Regina, S4P 3R3, lists all city, town, village and Rural Municipality off-icials in a given year, available for a small fee. Address all correspondence to the Secretary-Treasurer of the Rural Municipality at the addresses given below:

Aberdeen (Aberdeen)
Abernethy (Abernethy)
Antelope Park (Marengo)
Antler (Redvers)
Arborfield (Arborfield)
Argyle (Gainsborough)
Arlington (Shaunavon)

Arm River (Davidson)
Auvergne (Ponteix)
Baildon (Box 52, Sub.#1,
   Moose Jaw)
Barrier Valley (McKague)
Battle River (Battleford)
Bayne (Bruno)

Bengough (Bengough)
Benson (Benson)
Big Arm (Stalwart)
Biggar (Biggar)
Big Quill (Wynyard)
Big Stick (Golden Prairie)
Birch Hills (Birch Hills)
Bjorkdale (Crooked River)
Blaine Lake (Blaine Lake)
Blucher (Bradwell)
Bone Creek (Shaunavon)
Bratt's Lake (Wilcox)
Britannia (Lloydminster)
Brock (Kisbey)
Brokenshell (Trosacho)
Browning (Lampman)
Buchanan (Buchanan)
Buckland (99 River, Prince
    Albert)
Buffalo (Wilkie)
Calder (Wroxton)
Caledonia (Milestone)
Cambria (Torquay)
Cana (Box 550, Melville)
Canaan (Lucky Lake)
Canwood (Canwood)
Carmichael (Gull Lake)
Caron (Caron)
Chaplin (Chaplin)
Chester (Glenavon)
Chesterfield (Eatonia)
Churchbridge (Churchbridge)
Clayton (Hyas)
Clinworth (Lemsford)
Coalfields (Bienfait)
Colonsay (Colonsay)
Connaught (Tisdale)
Corman Park (414 - 20 St.
    East, Saskatoon)
Cote (Kamsack)
Coteau (Birsay)
Coulee (1680 Chaplin St.
    East, Swift Current)
Craik (Craik)
Cupar (Markinch)
Cut Knife (Cut Knife)
Cymri (Midale)
Deer Forks (Burstall)
Douglas (Richard)
Duck Lake (Duck Lake)
Dufferin (Bethune)
Dundurn (Dundurn)

Eagle Creek (Arelea)
Edenwold (Balgonie)
Elcapo (Broadview)
Eldon (Maidstone)
Elfros (Elfros)
Elmsthorpe (Avonlea)
Emerald (Wishart)
Enfield (Central Butte)
Enniskillen (Oxbow)
Enterprise (Richmound)
Estevan (Estevan)
Excel (Viceroy)
Excelsior (Rush Lake)
Eyebrow (Eyebrow)
Eye Hill (Eye Hill)
Fertile Belt (Stockholm)
Fertile Valley (Conquest)
Fillmore (Fillmore)
Fish Creek (Wakaw)
Flett's Springs (Pathlow)
Foam Lake (Foam Lake)
Fox Valley (Fox Valley)
Francis (Francis)
Frenchman Butte (Paradise
    Hill)
Frontier (Frontier)
Garden River (Meath Park)
Garry (Jedburgh)
Glen Bain (Glen Bain)
Glen McPherson (Mankota)
Glenside (Biggar)
Golden West (Corning)
Good Lake (Canora)
Grandview (Kelfield)
Grant (Vonda)
Grass Lake (Reward)
Grassy Creek (Shaunavon)
Gravelbourg (Gravelbourg)
Grayson (Grayson)
Great Bend (Borden)
Greenfield (Turtleford)
Griffin (Griffin)
Gull Lake (Gull Lake)
Happyland (Leader)
Happy Valley (Big Beaver)
Harris (Harris)
Hart Butte (Coronach)
Hazel Dell (Okla)
Hazelwood (Kipling)
Heart's Hill (Luseland)
Hillsborough (48 High St.
    West, Moose Jaw)

Hillsdale (Neilburg)
Hoodoo (Cudworth)
Humboldt (Humboldt)
Huron (Tugaske)
Indian Head (Indian Head)
Insinger (Insinger)
Invergordon (Crystal
    Springs)
Invermay (Invermay)
Ituna Bon Accord (Ituna)
Kellross (Leross)
Kelvington (Kelvington)
Keys (Canora)
Key West (Ogema)
Kindersley (Kindersley)
King George (Dinsmore)
Kingsley (Kipling)
Kinistino (Kinistino)
Kutawa (Punnichy)
Lacedena (Lacedena)
Lac Pelletier (Neville)
Laird (Waldheim)
Lajord (Lajord)
Lake Alma (Lake Alma)
Lake Johnston (Mossbank)
Lake Lenore (Brieux)
Lake of the Rivers
    (Assiniboia)
Lakeside (Quill Lake)
Lakeview (Wadena)
Langenburg (Langenburg)
Last Mountain Valley
    (Govan)
Laurier (Radville)
Lawtonia (Hodgeville)
Leask (Leask)
Leroy (Leroy)
Lipton (Lipton)
Livingston (Arran)
Lomond (Goodwater)
Lone Tree (Climax)
Longlaketon (Earl Grey)
Loreburn (Loreburn)
Lost River (Allan)
Lumsden (Lumsden)
McCraney (Kenaston)
McKillop (Strasbourg)
McLeod (Neudorf)
Manitou Lake (Marsden)
Mankota (Mankota)
Maple Bush (Lawson)
Maple Creek (Maple Creek)
Mariposa (Broadacres)

Marquis (Marquis)
Marriott (Rosetown)
Martin (Wapella)
Maryfield (Maryfield)
Medstead (Medstead)
Mayfield (Maymont)
Meeting Lake (Mayfair)
Meota (Meota)
Mervin (Turtleford)
Milden (Milden)
Milton (Marengo)
Mirey Creek (Abbey)
Monet (Elrose)
Montmartre (Montmartre)
Montrose (Donavon)
Moose Creek (Alameda)
Moose Jaw (Moose Jaw)
Moose Mountain (Carlyle)
Moose Range (Carrot River)
Moosomin (Moosomin)
Morris (Young)
Morse (Morse)
Mountain View (Herschel)
Mount Hope (Semans)
Mount Pleasant (Carnduff)
Newcombe (Glidden)
Nipawin (Codette)
North Battleford (North
    Battleford)
North Qu'Appelle (Fort
    Qu'Appelle)
Norton (Pangman)
Oakdale (Coleville)
Old Post (Wood Mountain)
Orkney (Yorkton)
Parkdale (Glaslyn)
Paynton (Paynton)
Pense (Pense)
Perdue (Perdue)
Piapot (Piapot)
Pinto Creek (Kincaid)
Pittville (Hazlet)
Pleasantdale (Pleasantdale)
Pleasant Valley (McGee)
Ponass Lake (Rose Valley)
Poplar Valley (Rockglen)
Porcupine (Carragana)
Prairie (202 - 21st.,
    Battleford)
Prairiedale (Smiley)
Prairie Rose (Jansen)
Preeceville (Preeceville)
Prince Albert (Prince Albert)

Progress (Luseland)
Reciprocity (Alida)
Redberry (Hafford)
Redburn (Rouleau)
Reford (Wilkie)
Reno (Consul)
Riverside (Pennant)
Rocanville (Rocanville)
Rodgers (Courval)
Rosedale (Hanley)
Rosemount (Traynor)
Rosthern (Rosthern)
Round Hill (Rabbit Lake)
Round Valley (Unity)
Rudy (Broderick)
St. Andrews (Rosetown)
St. Louis (Hoey)
St. Peter (Annaheim)
St. Philips (Pelly)
Saltcoats (Saltcoats)
Sarnia (Holdfast)
Saskatchewan Landing
     (Stewart Valley)
Sasman (Kuroki)
Scott (Yellow Grass)
Senlac (Senlac)
Shamrock (Shamrock)
Shellbrook (Shellbrook)
Sherwood (1840 Cornwall,
     Regina)
Silverwood (Whitewood)
Sliding Hills (Mikado)
Snipe Lake (Eston)
Souris Valley (Oungre)
South Qu'Appelle
     (Qu'Appelle)
Spalding (Spalding)
Spiritwood (Spiritwood)
Spy Hill (Spy Hill)
Stanley (Fenwood)
Star City (Star City)
Stonehenge (Limerick)
Storthoaks (Storthoaks)

Surprise Valley (Minton)
Sutton (Gravelbourg)
Swift Current (Swift
     Current)
Tecumseh (Stoughton)

Terrell (Spring Valley)
The Gap (Ceylon)
Three Lakes (Middle Lake)
Tisdale (Tisdale)
Torch River (White Fox)
Touchwood (Punnichy)
Tramping Lake (Scott)
Tullymet (Balcarres)
Turtle River (Edam)
Usborne (Lanigan)
Val Marie (Val Marie)
Vanscoy (Vanscoy)
Victory (Beechy)
Viscount (Viscount)
Wallace (Yorkton)
Walpole (Wawota)
Waverley (Glentworth)
Wawken (Wawota)
Webb (Webb)
Wellington (Cedoux)
Weyburn (Weyburn)
Wheatlands (Mortlach)
Whiska Creek (Vanguard)
White Valley (Eastend)
Willner (Davidson)
Willow Bunch (Willow
     Bunch)
Willow Creek (Brooksby)
Willowdale (Whitewood)
Wilton (Marshall)
Winslow (Dodsland)
Wise Creek (Shaunavon)
Wolseley (Wolseley)
Wolverine (Burn)
Wood Creek (Simpson)
Wood River (Lafleche)
Wreford (Nokomis)

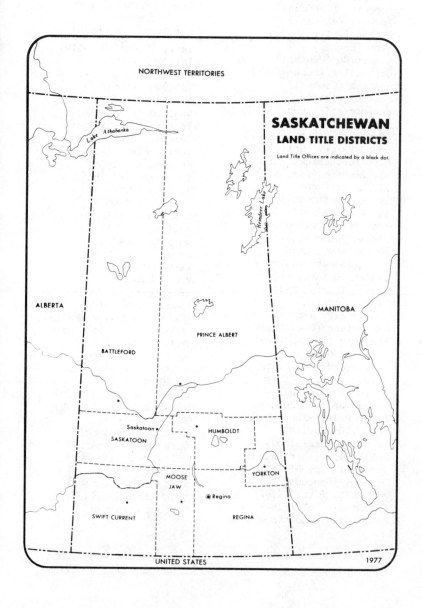

338

SASKATCHEWAN
LAND TITLE DISTRICTS

Land Title Offices are indicated by a black dot.

NORTHWEST TERRITORIES

Lake *Athabaska*

SASKATCHEWAN
JUDICIAL DISTRICTS

Courthouse locations are indicated by a black dot.

Reindeer Lake

ALBERTA

MANITOBA

PRINCE ALBERT

BATTLEFORD•

•MELFORT

SASKATOON•

HUMBOLDT•

KERROBERT•

WYNYARD•

YORKTON•

MELVILLE•

SWIFT CURRENT•   MOOSE JAW•   ⊙REGINA

MOOSOMIN•

GRAVELBOURG•

•WEYBURN   •ARCOLA

SHAUNAVON•   •ASSINIBOIA

•ESTEVAN

UNITED STATES

1977

NORTHWEST TERRITORIES

Established in 1870 when the government of Canada acquired Rupert's Land from the Hudson's Bay Company, the North West Territories originally included the areas that are now Saskatchewan, Alberta, most of Manitoba, northern Ontario, northern Quebec, the Yukon Territory and the present Northwest Territories. The Yukon was seperated in 1898 and Saskatchewan and Alberta in 1905. The present boundaries were established in 1912. Capital city is Yellowknife and the Territories' population in 1970 was estimated at 35,000, most of whom were Indian, Eskimo or Metis.

MUNICIPAL GOVERNMENT

The Northwest Territories has no formalized municipal organization of any historical extent. The administration of local areas is primarily controlled by the Territorial Council. For further information, contact the Director of Local Government, Yellowknife.

ARCHIVES

The Northwest Territories has no official territorial archives other than the Public Archives of Canada in Ottawa. The Saskatchewan and Alberta Archives also have material relating to the North West Territories, mainly prior to 1912.

One source of information is the Public Library Services of the Northwest Territories, Box 1100, Hay River, N.W.T. Researchers should also contact the Historical Program Co-ordinator, Government of the N.W.T., Natural and Cultural Affairs, Yellowknife, X1A 2L9.

VITAL RECORDS

All civil vital records for the Northwest Territories are available from the Registrar General of Vital Statistics, Yellowknife, N.W.T XOE 1H0. However, most records do not go back much further than the 1940's.

EDUCATION

Inquiries regarding school records and teachers' records should be directed to the Department of Education, Yellowknife XOE 1H0

LAND REGISTRATION

Inquiries regarding all land grants and transfers in the Northwest Territories should be directed to the Water, Forests and Land Division, Department of Indian Affairs and Northern Development, Centennial Tower Building, Ottawa, Ontario K1A 0H4; or to the Registrar of Titles, Northwest Territories Land Registration District, Yellowknife.

JUDICIAL DISTRICTS

Court records in the Northwest Territories are located in one registration district. Address all correspondence to the Clerk of the Territorial Council, Yellowknife. It should also be noted that the Alberta Court of Appeal is also the Court of Appeal for the Northwest Territories.

MAP SOURCES

A road map and general map of the Northwest Territories is available on request from Travelarctic, Yellowknife X1A 2L9. Further map information is available from the Canada Map Office, Ottawa, Ontario

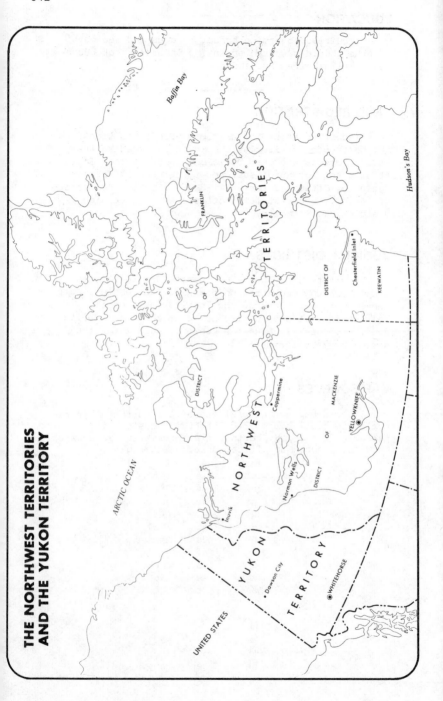

THE NORTHWEST TERRITORIES
AND THE YUKON TERRITORY

YUKON TERRITORY

In 1842 a Hudson's Bay Company fur trading post was established on Lake Francis, the first settlement in the Yukon. In 1870, it became part of the North West Territories, and in 1895 was created a special district within the N.W.T. In 1896, gold was discovered in the Klondike area which led to the Yukon's establishment as a seperate territory in 1898. Capital city is Whitehorse, and its population in 1970 was 17,000 (Major ethnic groups: 53% British Isles, 17% Indian, 7% French, 6% Scandinavian).

MUNICIPAL GOVERNMENT

Although there are several local improvement districts in the Yukon, these are of relatively recent origin and their administrative areas small in size. Generally, municipal functions are administered by the Territorial Council. For more information contact the Local Government, Box 2703, Whitehorse, Y1A 2C6.

ARCHIVES

ADDRESS: ARCHIVES OF THE YUKON TERRITORY, P.O. Box 2703, Whitehorse, Yukon Territory Y1A 2C6.

Although quite small, the archives has some records of value to genealogists. These include the records of the Territorial Government 1894 - 1951 (contains land, survey, immigration, etc. records; some indexes); Dawson Mining Recorder records 1895 - 1971 (contains applications, abstract indexes to claims, indexes of original locators, etc.) and the records of the Territorial Secretary and Registrar General 1898 - 1953 (contains lists of barristers, solicitors, doctors, engineers, dentists, and businessmen). The Public Archives of Canada also have records relating to the Yukon Territory.

LAND REGISTRATION

Land records in the Yukon Territory date from 1899. All inquiries should be directed to the Registrar of Land Titles, Box 2703, Whitehorse Y1A 2C6.

VITAL RECORDS

All civil vital records for the Yukon Territory are available from the Registrar General of Vital Statistics, Box 2703, Whitehorse, Y1A 2C6. Birth records begin in 1895, death and marriage records in 1899, and divorce records in 1944. Your "reason for requirement must be in order" for you to obtain copies of the birth, marriage and death records. Divorce records can only be obtained by the parties of the divorce. Contact this office for current information on their fees and services.

JUDICIAL DISTRICTS

There is one Supreme Court Judicial district for the Yukon. Address all correspondence to the Clerk of the Supreme Court, Federal Building, Whitehorse. Please note that, in addition to the Territorial Court, the British Columbia Court of Appeal is also the Court of Appeal for the Yukon Territory.

EDUCATION

For information on school records in the Yukon Territory, contact either the Territorial Archives in Whitehorse or the Department of Education, Box 2703, Whitehorse, Y1A 2C6.

MAP SOURCES

A road map of the Yukon is available on request from Yukon Department of Travel and Information, P.O. Box 2703, Whitehorse. Additional map information is available from the Canada Map Office, Ottawa, Ontario.

OTHER SOURCES OF INTEREST TO RESEARCHERS

Dawson Public Library, Box 198, Dawson City
Library Services Branch, 2071 2nd Ave., Whitehorse,
    Y1A 2C6
Whitehorse Public Library, Box 2703, Whitehorse, Y1A 2C6
Yukon HS, Box 4037, Whitehorse
Yukon Order of Pioneers, Dawson City

6
CONTINUING YOUR RESEARCH OVERSEAS

Canada is a nation of immigrants, most of whom can trace their origins to a European country or area. The point in time will come when you will have finished the research on your family in Canada, and will be ready to continue your research overseas.

Records which exist in other countries often vary enormously from those which you will have used in Canada, and it is important that you acquaint yourself with them in much the same manner as you did for Canadian records. In other words, it will be time to buy another genealogical reference book - this time, for the country of your ancestor's birth and origin.

There are a number of encyclopedic works on world-wide genealogy, each of which contains short summaries of basic genealogical sources in a number of countries around the world. Although these are handy guides, they do not contain enough information on any one of the countries included in them to enable researchers to conduct comprehensive research. However, they do provide an "overview" of the records which are available and can be valuable for those countries which do not have a published genealogical guide. Wherever possible, more comprehensive reference works should ALWAYS be used if you want to take full advantage of all the resources available to you in your overseas country. Three of these encyclopedic works are:

> Pine, Leslie: <u>American Origins</u> (Garden Hill, NY 1960;
> reprinted Baltimore 1977)
> Pine, Leslie: <u>The Genealogist's Encyclopedia</u> (NY 1969)
> Wellauer, Maralyn: <u>A Guide to Foreign Genealogical
> Research</u> (Milwaukee, Wisc. 1976)

The Genealogical Society of Utah has published a series of research reports discussing the major records of a large number of countries. They are inexpensive, and quite good. They can be obtained from the General Church Distribution Centre (see chapter 2.4 for address).

Records in many foreign countries are not organized on a national or provincial basis as they are in Canada (especially civil registration of births, etc), but are often located at local town offices. In order to conduct your research, it is ESSENTIAL that you know the name of the EXACT place (town, etc) of origin of your immigrant ancestor. Without it, your research will often prove frustrating and largely unsuccessful. To avoid disappointment, you must ensure that you have completely exhausted all avenues of research in Canada which could throw light onto his place of origin in Europe. Many of the records contained in preceeding chapters may contain this information.

Although this book is primarily meant to be a guide to CANADIAN records, this section has been included to provide a select list of organizations in other countries which will help researchers to acquaint themselves with the records available in their respective countries, or will direct them to appropriate publications.

The information contained in each listing (with their codes)
include NA National Archives, GS major genealogical societies, EC the address of the country's Embassy in Ottawa, and
SP select publications which deal with the genealogical records within the country. Because Civil Registration CR in
most countries is on a local town basis, no information other
than the year in which civil registration began in that country is given. Those countries marked with an asterisk have had
a research paper on their records published by the Genealogical Society of Utah.

*THE UNITED STATES

As most publications on genealogy available to Canadians are
published in the United States, it is likely that all Canadian researchers will have at least one book which will
provide general information on addresses in the U.S. In light
of this aspect, researchers are referred to the books already
in their possession for information on American sources. Of
the many available publications on genealogical records in
the United States, Val Greenwood's Researcher's Guide to
American Genealogy (Baltimore 1973) is perhaps the most comprehensive and should be acquired by anyone conducting extensive research in that country.

THE BRITISH ISLES

*ENGLAND AND WALES: NA Public Record Office, Chancery Lane,
London WC2A 1LR CR 1837, Registrar General, St Catherine's
House, 10 Kingsway, London WC2B 6JP GS Society of Genealo-
gists, 37 Harrington Gdns, London SW7 EC for Great Britain:
80 Elgin St, Ottawa K1P 5K7 SP Gardiner & Smith: Genealog-
Research in England and Wales (Salt Lake City 1966-70, 3 vols)
Hamilton-Edwards, Gerald: In Search of British Ancestry
(Baltimore 1974).

*SCOTLAND: NA Scottish Record Office, HM Register House,
Edinburgh EH1 3YX CR 1855, General Registry Office, New Reg-
ister House, Edinburgh EH1 3YT GS Scottish Genealogy Soc.,
21 Howard Pl, Edinburgh EH3 5JY SP Hamilton-Edwards, Gerald:
In Search of Scottish Ancestry (Baltimore 1972); Jonasson,
Eric: "Genealogical Sources in Scotland" in generations Vol 3
No 1 1978 (Manitoba Gen. Soc.)

*IRELAND, REPUBLIC OF: NA Public Record Office, Four Courts,
Dublin CR 1864, Registrar General's Office, Custom House,
Dublin GS Irish Gen. Research Soc., 7A Duke of York St, St.
James's Sq., London SW1Y 4LE, England EC 170 Metcalfe St.,
Ottawa K2P 1P3 SP Falley, Margaret: Irish and Scotch-Irish
Genealogical Research (Evanston, Ill. 1961-2, 2 vols);
Jonasson, Eric: "Genealogical Sources in Ireland" in genera-
tions Vol 1 No 2 1976 (Manitoba Gen. Soc.)

*IRELAND, NORTHERN: NA Public Record Office, Balmoral Ave,
Belfast CR 1921, General Registry Office, Oxford House,
Belfast BT1 4HL GS Ulster Genealogical & Historical Guild,
66 Balmoral Ave, Belfast BT9 6NY SP see Republic. NOTE:
pre-1921 records for Northern Ireland are in Dublin.

*FRANCE

NA Archives nationales de France, 60 rue des Francs-Bourg-
eous, 75141 Paris Cedex 03 CR 1792 GS Centre d'entr'aide
genealogique, "Les Frenes 52", 55 boul. de Charonne, 75011
Paris EC 42 Sussex Dr, Ottawa K1M 2C9 SP Meurgey de
Tupigny, Jacques: Guide des recherches genealogique aux
Archives Nationales (Paris 1956); Durye, Pierre: La genealogie (Paris 1963 - translated into English and published
as Genealogy: An Introduction to Continental Concepts, New
Orleans 1977)

OTHER COUNTRIES

ALBANIA: CR 1929. NOTE: Albania's government actively
discourages genealogical research.

*AUSTRIA: NA Osterreichisches staatsarchiv, Generaldirek-
tion, 1010 Wien, Minoritenplatz 1, Austria CR 1938 GS
Heraldisch-Genealogische Gesellschaft "Adler", A 1010 Wien,
Haarhof 41 EC 445 Wilbrod St, Ottawa K1N 6M7 SP see
Germany

BELGIUM: NA Archives Generales du Royaume, 2-6 rue de
Ruysbroeck, 1000 Bruxelles CR 1795 GS Service de
Centralisation des Etudes Genealogiques et Demographiques
de Belgique, 26 rue aux Laines, Bruxelles EC 85 Range Rd,
Ottawa K1N 8J6 SP Van Haegendoren, M.: Les Archives
Generales du Royaume (Bruxelles 1955 - inventory of NA)

BULGARIA: NA Centralen Darzaven Istoriceski Arhiv,
Sofija, ul. Zdanov 5 CR 1893 EC 325 Stewart St, Ottawa
K1N 6K5 SP Snezhind, Tosheva: Spravochnik na Bibliotek-
itev Bolgariya (Sofija 1963) (guide to Bulgarian libraries)

CZECHOSLOVAKIA: NA Bohemia: Archivni Sprava CSR, Obrancu
mira 133, Praha 6; and Slovakia: Slovenska Archivni Sprava,
Krizkova 5, Bratislava CR 1950 SP Miller, Olga:
Genealogical Research for Czech and Slovak Americans
(Detroit 1978). NOTE: send all genealogical inquiries to
the Consular Division, Embassy of Czechoslovak S.R., 171
Clemow Ave., Ottawa K1S 2B3.

*DENMARK: [NA] Rigsarkivet, Rigsdagsgarden 9, 1218 Koben-
havn K, Denmark; also see Det Danske Udvandrerarkiv (Danes'
Worldwide Archives),Konvalvej 2, 9000 Alborg 4 [CR] 1874
for parts of country, rest is church records only [GS]
Danske Genealogisk Institut, Nybrogade 30, 1203 Kobenhavn
[EC] 702-85 Range Rd, Ottawa K1N 8J6 [SP] Smith & Thomsen:
Genealogical Guidebook and Atlas of Denmark (Salt Lake City
1969); Stevenson, J. Grant: Danish Genealogical Research
(Provo Utah, 1965, 4 vols)

*FINLAND: [NA] Valtionarkisto/Riksarkivet, Rauhantu 17,
00170 Helsinki 17 [CR] still kept by churches [GS] Genealogiska Samfundet i Finland, Snellmansgaten 9-11, Helsinki
[EC] 222 Somerset St W, Ottawa K2P 2G3

GERMANY, EAST: [NA] Zentrales Staatsarchiv, Historische
Abteilung 11, 42 Merseburg, Weisse Mauer 48 [GS] Zentral-
stelle fur Genealogie in der Deutschen Demokratischen Repub-
lik,DDR-70 Leipzig, Georgi-Dimitroff-Platz 1, German Demo-
cratic Republic [CR] 1876 [SP] see West Germany

*GERMANY, WEST: [NA] none, state archives only [GS] Deutsche
Arbeitsgemeinschaft genealogischer Verbände e.V., D-33
Braunschweig, Steintorwall 15 (Stadarchiv), West Germany. [CR]
1876 [EC] 1 Waverley St, Ottawa K2P 0T8 [SP] Jensen &
Storrer: A Genealogical Handbook of German Research (Pleasant
Grove, Utah 1977); Smith, Clifford and Anna: Encyclopedia
of German-American Genealogical Research (NY 1976), also by
the same authors: American Genealogical Resources in German
Archives (AGRIGA) (NY 1977); Jonasson, Eric: "Genealogical
Sources in Germany" in generations Vol 2 No 1 1977 (Manitoba
Gen. Soc.)

GREECE: [NA] Genika Archeia Tou Kratous, Megaron Akadimias,
odos Eleftheriou Venizelou 28, Athenes [CR] 1856 [EC] Ste 110
Chateau Laurier Hotel, Ottawa K1N 8S7

*HUNGARY: [NA] Magyar Drszagos Leveltar, 1250 Budapest I,
Becsikapu ter 2-4 [CR] 1895, at NA [EC] 7 Delaware Ave,
Ottawa K2P 0Z2

*ICELAND: [NA] Thjodskjalasafn Islands, Hverfisgate 17,
Reykjavik [CR] primarily church records only, at NA [EC] c/o
Embassy of Iceland, 2022 Connecticut Ave NW, Washington D,C.
20008, USA or local consulates [SP] Jonasson, Eric: Tracing
Your Icelandic Family Tree (Winnipeg 1975)

*ITALY: [NA] Archivio Centrale Dello Stato, Piazzale Degli
Archivi, E.U.R., 00144 Roma [CR] 1870, for information cont
contact Instituto Centrale di Statistica, Via Cesare Balbo
16, Roma GS Genealogico Italiano, Castelli 19, Firenze
[EC] 170 Laurier Ave W, Ottawa K1P 5V5

LIECHTENSTEIN: Address all correspondence to the National Archives: Liechtensteinisches Landesarchiv, Fl., 9490 Vaduz.

LUXEMBOURG: [NA] Archives de l'Etat, Plateau du Saint-Esprit (BP 6), Luxembourg City 2 [GS] Conseil Heraldrique, c/o M. Robert Matagne, 25 rue Berthelot, Luxembourg City [CR] 1796 [EC] c/o Embassy of Luxembourg, 2210 Massachusetts Ave NW, Washington D.C. 20008, USA.

MONACO: Address all inquiries to the National Archives: Archives du Palais Princier de Monaco, Palais Princier, Monaco.R

*NETHERLANDS: [NA] Algemeen Riyksarchief, Bleijenburg 7, The Hague, The Netherlands [CR] 1811, some in 1796 [GS] Centraal Bureau voor Genealogie, Nassaulaan 18, The Hague; and Koninklijk Nederlandsch Genootschap voor Geslacht en Wapenkunde, 5 Bleijensburg, The Hague [EC] 275 Slater St, Ottawa K1P 5H9 [SP] "Searching for Your Ancestors in the Netherlands", available from Centraal Bureau above.

*NORWAY: [NA] Riksarkivet, Bankplassen 3, Oslo 1 [CR] 1870, at Demographic Section, Statistisk Sentralbyra, Dronningens Gate 16, Oslo [GS] Norsk Slektshistorisk Forening, Øvre Slottsgate 17, Oslo 1 [EC] 700-140 Wellington St, Ottawa K1P 5A2 [SP] Smith & Thomsen: <u>Genealogical Guidebook and Atlas of Norway</u> (Logan, Utah); also "How to Trace Your Ancestors in Norway" available from Embassy of Norway.

*POLAND: [NA] pre-1918 records: Archiwum Glowne Akt Dawnych, Dluga 7, Warszawa; and post-1918 records: Archiwum Akt Nowych, Al. Niepodleglosci 162, Warszawa [CR] various dates [EC] 443 Daly Ave, Ottawa K1N 6H3 [SP] best currently available is Konrad, J.: <u>Polish Family Research</u> (Munroe Falls, Ohio 1977) NOTE: all genealogical inquiries should be sent to Zespol Adwokacki, nr. 40, ul. Hibnera 13, Warszawa

PORTUGAL: [NA] Arquivo Nacional da Torre do Tombo, Palacio de S. Bento, Lisboa 2 CR 1832 [EC] 645 Island Park Dr., Ottawa K1Y 0C2

ROMANIA: [NA] Directia Generala a Archivelor Statului, Bulevardul Gh. Gheorghui-Dej. 29, Bucuresti, Romania [EC] 473 Wilbrod St, Ottawa K1N 6N1

SPAIN: [NA] Archivo Historico Nacional, Serrano 115, Madrid 6 [CR] 1870 [GS] Instituto Internacional di Genealogia y Heraldica, Spartado de Correas 7, Madrid [EC] 124 Springfield Rd, Stes 310-312, Ottawa K1M 2C8

*SWEDEN: [NA] Riksarkivet, Fack, 100 26, Stockholm 34, Sweden
[CR] church records only [GS] Genealogiska foreningen, Arkiv-
gatan 3, S-111 28 Stockholm; and Personhistoriska samfundet,
Riksarkivet, Fack, s-100 26 Stockholm [EC] 640-140 Welling-
ton St, Ottawa K1P 5A2 [SP] Johansson, Carl-Erik: <u>Cradled in
Sweden</u> (Logan, Utah 1972); also "Tracing Your Swedish
Ancestors" available from the Embassy of Sweden.

*SWITZERLAND: [NA] Schweizerisches Bundesarchiv, CH-3003 B
Bern, Archivstrasse 24 [CR] 1876 [GS] Genealogisch-Heraldisch
Gesellschaft, Leimgrubelstrasse 12, CH 8052 Zurich; and
Association Suisse Etude Genealogique, Blaukreuz Haus,
Psgraben 23, 4000 Basil [EC] 5 Marlborough Ave, Ottawa K1N
8E6

U.S.S.R. (RUSSIA):   Address all inquiries to the Consular
Division, Embassy of the U.S.S.R.,285 Charlotte St, Ottawa
K1N 8L5. They will check for birth, etc. records, but results
are quite slow (6 months to 1 year) and can be unsuccessful.
[GS] Russian Historical and Genealogical Society, 971 First
Ave., New York, NY, USA.

YUGOSLAVIA: [NA] Arhiv Jugoslavije, Vase Pelagica 33,
Beograde [CR] 1946 [EC] 17 Blackburn Ave, Ottawa K1N 8A2.

    Contact the following embassies for more information on
the genealogical sources in their respective countries:

<u>ARAB REPUBLIC OF EGYPT</u>: Embassy, 454 Laurier Ave E, Ottawa,
    K1N 6R3
<u>AUSTRALIA</u>: High Commn., 90 Sparks St, Ottawa K1P 5B8
<u>BAHAMAS</u>: High Commn., c/o Embassy of the Bahamas, 600 New
    Hampshire Ave NW, Washington DC 20037, USA
<u>BARBADOS</u>: High Commn., 200-151 Slater St, Ottawa K1P 5H3
<u>CHINA, PEOPLE'S REPUBLIC OF</u>: Embassy, 415 St Andrew St,
    Ottawa K1N 5H3
<u>CUBA</u>: Embassy, 700 Echo Dr, Ottawa K1S 1P3
<u>INDIA</u>: High Commn., 200 MacLaren St, Ottawa K2P 0L6
<u>INDONESIA</u>: Embassy, 255 Albert St, Ste 1010, Kent Sq, Bldg C,
    Ottawa K1P 6A9
<u>ISRAEL</u>: Embassy, 45 Powell Ave, Ottawa K1S 1Z9
<u>JAMAICA</u>: High Commn., 203-85 Range Rd, Ottawa K1N 8J6
<u>JAPAN</u>: Embassy, 75 Albert St, Room 1005, Ottawa K1P 5E7
<u>KOREA</u>: Embassy, 151 Slater St, Ottawa K1P 5H3
<u>LEBANON</u>: Embassy, 640 Lyon St, Ottawa K1S 3Z5
<u>MEXICO</u>: Embassy, 206-130 Albert St, Ottawa K1P 5G4
<u>NEW ZEALAND</u>: High Commn., 804-77 Metcalfe St, Ottawa K1P 5L6
<u>PAKISTAN</u>: Embassy, 170 Metcalfe St, Ottawa K2P 1P3
<u>PHILIPPINES</u>: Embassy, 130 Albert St, Ottawa K1P 5G4
<u>SOUTH AFRICA</u>: Embassy, 15 Sussex Dr, Ottawa K1M 1M8
<u>SRI LANKA</u>: High Commn., 85 Range Rd, Ottawa K1N 8J6
<u>SYRIAN ARAB REPUBLIC</u>: Embassy, 2215 Wyoming Ave NW, Washing-
    ton DC 20008, USA
<u>TURKEY</u>: Embassy, 197 Wurtemburg St, Ottawa K1N 8L9